THE
GEORGE W. BUSH
FOREIGN
POLICY
READER

Presidential Speeches with Commentary

Edited by
John W. Dietrich

M.E.Sharpe
Armonk, New York
London, England

Copyright © 2005 by M.E. Sharpe, Inc.

All rights reserved. No part of this book may be reproduced in any form
without written permission from the publisher, M.E. Sharpe, Inc.,
80 Business Park Drive, Armonk, New York 10504.

Library of Congress Cataloging-in-Publication Data

Bush, George W. (George Walker), 1946–
  The George W. Bush foreign policy reader : presidential speeches and commentary /
[edited by] John W. Dietrich.
    p. cm.
  Includes index.
  ISBN 0-7656-1556-8 (alk. paper) — ISBN 0-7656-1557-6 (pbk.: alk. paper)
  1. United States—Foreign relations—2001– 2. Bush, George W. (George Walker), 1946—
Political and social views. 3. Speeches, addresses, etc.,
American—History and criticism. I. Dietrich, John W., 1969- II. Title.

E902.B8695 2005
327.73'009'0511—dc22   2004030174

Printed in the United States of America

The paper used in this publication meets the minimum requirements of
American National Standard for Information Sciences
Permanence of Paper for Printed Library Materials,
ANSI Z 39.48-1984.

BM (c)   10   9   8   7   6   5   4   3   2   1
BM (p)   10   9   8   7   6   5   4   3   2   1

THE GEORGE W. BUSH FOREIGN POLICY READER

Ruth Willett,

For someone who watches the world with a sharp eye and open heart.

John W Dietrich

Table of Contents

Preface   ix

Chapter One
Bush and the World of 2000   3
1.1 A Period of Consequences   22
1.2 A Distinctly American Internationalism   26
1.3 Future Nuclear Arms Policy   32
1.4 Century of the Americas   34
Questions to Discuss   37

Chapter Two
The War on Terrorism   38
2.1 Declaring a War on Terrorism   50
2.2 President Bush Speaks to the UN   55
2.3 2002 State of the Union Address   59
2.4 Graduation Speech at West Point   63
Questions to Discuss   66

Chapter Three
Iraq   67
3.1 Remarks at the United Nations   85
3.2 Bush Outlines the Iraqi Threat   90
3.3 End of Major Combat Operations   95
3.4 Future of Iraq   98
3.5 Steps to Help Iraq Achieve Democracy   102
Questions to Discuss   107

Chapter Four
Security Issues — 108
4.1 Speaking to the Citadel Cadets — 126
4.2 Troop Redeployment — 131
4.3 National Missile Defense — 133
4.4 ABM Treaty — 136
4.5 Countering the Threat of WMD — 138
Questions to Discuss — 143

Chapter Five
Global Issues — 144
5.1 Global Climate Change — 161
5.2 Global Climate Initiatives — 165
5.3 The UN's Global Role — 169
5.4 Three Pillars of Peace and Security — 173
Questions to Discuss — 176

Chapter Six
Europe and Russia — 177
6.1 Future of Europe — 195
6.2 German Support Against Terror — 199
6.3 Historic NATO Summit — 203
6.4 Remarks to the People of Poland — 206
Questions to Discuss — 208

Chapter Seven
Relations with Asian Powers — 209
7.1 U.S., China Stand Against Terrorism — 222
7.2 Bush Speaks at Tsinghua University — 224
7.3 Welcoming Premier Wen of China — 227
7.4 Welcoming Koizumi of Japan — 229
7.5 Unity Between the U.S. and Japan — 231
Questions to Discuss — 234

Chapter Eight
Middle East Peace and Reform — 235
8.1 Sending Powell to the Middle East — 249
8.2 New Palestinian Leadership — 252
8.3 Bush Commends Sharon's Plan — 256
8.4 Freedom in Iraq and the Middle East — 258
Questions to Discuss — 264

Chapter Nine
Latin America and Africa 265
9.1 Summit of the Americas 281
9.2 U.S. Economic Ties with Africa 284
9.3 Millennium Challenge Account 287
9.4 A Vision of Africa 291
9.5 Fighting Global HIV/AIDS 294
9.6 Agenda for U.S.–African Relations 297
Questions to Discuss 302

Notes 303
Index 311

Preface

George W. Bush became president at a time of global peace, stability, and U.S. dominance. Since Bush was widely perceived to have little experience, or interest, in international issues, the relatively calm world and general lack of voters' interest in foreign policy issues worked to Bush's advantage in 2000. During the campaign, Bush did signal some differences with the outgoing Clinton administration. For example, he called for tougher policies toward Russia and China, warmer ties with Latin America, and enhancement of U.S. military strength. Many observers, though, expected his presidency would feature general continuity with the past and few bold policy initiatives.

When Bush ran for reelection in 2004, the world, the president, and the campaign focus were all radically different from 2000. The United States was engaged in a global war on terrorism and had major ongoing operations in Afghanistan and Iraq. At home, Americans felt a new sense of insecurity and vulnerability. The United States was still unquestionably the world's greatest power, but the country was more aware that power brings not only opportunities, but also leadership responsibilities and dangers from those who want to upset the existing international system. It also had become clearer that power does not always lead to unquestioning support from allies or easy defeat of enemies.

By 2004, Bush had changed personally. He focused great attention on foreign policy and elevated international priorities above certain domestic goals. In Bush's eyes, defeating international terrorism and spreading freedom were not only important for U.S. interests, but for the preservation of civilization. He, therefore, pursued these goals with an almost missionary zeal. In addition, he shifted his views and priorities to develop good relations with Russia and China, while focusing less attention than expected on Latin America.

When Bush campaigned for reelection he called himself a "war president." He frequently reminded voters of his actions against terrorism and other threats, and the need for strong leadership. Voters were also focused on foreign policy, with over one third choosing either Iraq or Terrorism as the one issue that mattered most in deciding their vote. Importantly, among voters selecting terrorism, Bush received over six votes to every one vote for the Democratic challenger, Senator John Kerry, but among those selecting Iraq as the most important issue, the numbers were nearly reversed. These results highlighted the way that some of Bush's policies had divided the country.

The differences between the conditions of 2000 and of 2004 stemmed, to a large degree, from the events of September 11, 2001. The terrorist attacks and Bush's response to them had an impact on U.S. relations with virtually every country, on global policy priorities, and on the strategic doctrines that guide U.S. policy. The differences also resulted from implementation of Bush's distinct underlying vision of international politics and America's world role. Whereas many expected four calm years focused on policy continuity, the world saw four traumatic years featuring revolutionary policies.

This volume introduces students and other readers to the key policy decisions of these momentous four years. Each chapter begins with an original essay providing background history and information, tracing Bush's policy choices, and highlighting key policy debates and outsider criticisms. The speeches in each chapter provide Bush's explanations of policy and visions for the future. They have been edited to exclude welcoming remarks, comments tied to specific, short-term circumstances, and reiterations of Bush's general views on terrorists, international goals, and America's world role. Each chapter concludes with a series of discussion questions that point readers to important passages or ideas included in Bush's speeches. The aim is to present a balanced portrait of Bush's actions and motivations, so that readers can reach their own judgments on Bush's policies and their implications for future U.S. policy.

This work owes much to Alvin Z. Rubinstein, who co-edited a similar volume on President Clinton's foreign policy, but more importantly introduced me to both the field of political science and this project. Many colleagues and friends were helpful in the course of this project, but I would especially like to thank Gayle Meyers for her insight on two key chapters, Ronald Bobroff for his diplomatic history expertise, and Linda Asselin and several student assistants for their secretarial and research assistance. Special recognition goes to my wife Dinusha for her support and sharp editing skills and my daughter Lia for her patience. Thanks also to Niels Aaboe, Amanda Allensworth, Amy Odum, Irina Burns, and others at M.E. Sharpe who patiently led me through the publishing process.

THE
GEORGE W. BUSH
FOREIGN
POLICY
READER

Chapter 1

Bush and the World of 2000

For many generations of Americans, there has been one major event that has served as a defining moment in national or world affairs. The attack on Pearl Harbor turned December 7 into a date that would "live in infamy." The assassination of President John F. Kennedy riveted the country. The terrorist attacks of September 11, 2001 (9/11) are this generation's defining event. The images and emotions of that day are seared into the memories of hundreds of millions of people around the world. Since then, Americans have seen dramatic changes in their daily lives, political views, and perceptions of personal and national security.

The events of 9/11 had a particularly powerful effect on the foreign policy of President George W. Bush and his administration. September 11 forced Bush to turn more attention to foreign policy, reinforced his conviction that the country needed strong presidential leadership, and gave him a sense of mission. The attacks also changed Bush's policy priorities. New challenges, such as building an antiterrorism coalition and overthrowing regimes in Afghanistan and Iraq came to the fore, while other issues were lowered on the agenda. In addition, the war on terrorism has redefined who is a U.S. ally and who is an enemy. On a deeper level, 9/11 challenged the continued relevance of the long-standing strategic doctrines of containment and deterrence. Domestically, influence shifted away from Congress toward the executive branch. And among the President's advisers, power shifted toward those favoring strong responses.

Bush's foreign policy, therefore, can be divided into two periods. The first period began when presidential candidate Bush laid out his vision of the world and it continued through his first eight months in office. The second period began with the events of 9/11 and continued through the rest of the first Bush administration. Although useful, this division should not be over-read as implying that Bush was completely reborn on 9/11, with no preexisting policy challenges or personal views. Focusing only on the second period would leave the observer with little sense of what Bush's policies might have been in the absence of 9/11. Bush's specific actions in response to the attacks would also be harder to understand. Most important, ignoring the first period would make it impossible to judge whether Bush's longer-term bold, and by some accounts revolutionary, post–9/11 policies are entirely a function of 9/11, or whether those events simply reinforced and refocused his preexisting views on America's national security and world role. Some background knowledge about Bush's personal foreign policy experience, his decision-making style, the major policies he planned for his administration, his overall foreign policy vision, and the people he appointed as key advisers is, therefore, crucial to understanding Bush's foreign policy both before and after 9/11.

Campaign 2000 and the Education of George W. Bush

During the long presidential campaign, foreign policy received little attention in comparison to issues such as taxes, education, and personal character. Traditionally, bold foreign policy debates are rare during campaigns for two key reasons. First, few voters focus great attention on foreign policy except at times of crisis. In 2000, the world seemed relatively safe and calm, and the United States enjoyed vastly superior military, economic, and political power over any potential rising foe. Some policy challenges remained, but the United States mostly enjoyed the rare luxury of choosing when and where it wanted to be engaged. Unsurprisingly, polls during the 2000 campaign showed that only four percent of voters chose an international issue as the most important problem facing the country. Second, candidates prefer to maintain policy flexibility should they be elected, so they rarely go on record with policy specifics.

Some observers speculated, though, that Bush's lack of foreign policy focus resulted not from a quiet world or campaign strategy, but rather from his inexperience and disinterest in the area. Since his previous top political post had been Governor of Texas, Bush could not match the foreign policy credentials of his Democratic rival Al Gore, who had served in Vietnam before becoming a U.S. Senator and then a Vice President, known for his role in crafting administration foreign policy. For Bush, the problem was exacerbated by the fact that, for much of his life, he had adopted what one observer called "a principled provincialism," an active avoidance of foreign policy.[1]

Although he went to school during the Vietnam War, Bush was not an activist in favor or against the war. Rather than serving in Vietnam, he joined the Texas Air National Guard. His father had held several key governmental positions. Despite that influence and opportunity, Bush rarely had traveled internationally or met with foreign leaders. Furthermore, Bush showed little interest in academic or think tank-sponsored discussions of foreign policy. Most of his political career centered on

Texas state politics and a limited number of domestic issues. Bush supporters tried to downplay the importance of past experience and stress Bush's intellectual curiosity about foreign policy. Still, critics questioned whether he had the necessary background to lead the world's only superpower.

Bush's poor showing on specific foreign policy facts reinforced these questions. An incident in November 1999 highlighted the problem. During a general interview, a Boston TV reporter challenged Bush to name the leaders of four global hotspots: Chechnya, Taiwan, Pakistan, and India. Of the four, Bush correctly identified only the surname of Taiwan's leader, Lee Teng-hui. Many commentators noted that the test had been unfair, since Bush had no advance warning and the questions were considered extremely difficult. For weeks, though, press reports of Bush's campaign referred back to the encounter.

Some also questioned Bush's overall intelligence because of his poor grades in school and lack of focus in his early adult life. He also was hurt by his tendency to misspeak and mispronounce words. He referred to Greeks as "Grecians," confused the countries of Slovakia and Slovenia, and made bold pronouncements such as, "If the terriers and bariffs are torn down, this economy will grow."[2] Under pressure and constant scrutiny, all speakers make errors, but "Bushspeak" and "Bushisms" became the butt of jokes on late night TV and Internet sites.

The combination of Bush's lack of experience and perceived lack of intelligence took a major toll. In one poll, only 10 percent of respondents chose Bush when asked whether Bush or Gore would be the better foreign policy leader. The impact low foreign policy numbers would have on election results was unclear, but most observers agreed it was a major political weakness. Therefore, making specific foreign policy pronouncements became less important than Bush making clear and cogent statements demonstrating his overall mastery of the issues. He also needed to build a strong team of advisers that would help offset his weaknesses.

In early 1999, Bush consulted with many foreign policy specialists. He then assembled a group of eight to be his tutors on world affairs. The group was co-chaired by Condoleezza Rice, a former provost at Stanford, who had served for two years as an expert on Russia in Bush's father's National Security Council (NSC). Bush described Rice as the person who "can explain to me foreign policy matters in a way I can understand."[3] She became Bush's alter ego on foreign policy, to the point that her writings and comments on policy were considered a direct reflection of Bush's views. The other co-chair was Paul Wolfowitz, Dean at Johns Hopkins University, who had served in several previous administrations and was known for his strong vision of how to use American power.

The group came to be known as the Vulcans, named after the ancient god of the forge. One notable characteristic of the group was that none of them had held a major position in Bush senior's administration. In fact, many of the advisers were more in tune with the views of President Ronald Reagan than the elder Bush. Second, as Rice acknowledged, "If there is a weakness in the team, it's that it's heavy on security issues."[4] Only one of the eight had extensive experience in international economics. These characteristics likely reflected, but also reinforced Bush's underlying policy preferences.

The Vulcans met repeatedly with Bush, often engaging in three-hour long sessions at his Crawford, Texas Ranch. They also prepared regular briefings for Bush on recent world events. It was, perhaps, the most intense tutorial in which a candidate has ever engaged. Some critics questioned whether Bush would become a puppet of his advisers. However, members of the group always stressed that Bush was not just a blank slate waiting to be filled with information, but rather had underlying views and asked probing questions.

The Vulcans' tutorial never completely dispelled concerns about Bush's foreign policy qualifications. Overall, though, the Vulcans succeeded in two major goals: worry about Bush's credentials lessened once he surrounded himself with a team of topflight advisers and Bush show a marked improvement in his knowledge base and confidence on foreign policy issues as the campaign went on. After Bush's debates with Gore, most commentary stressed that, while Gore still had the upper hand factually, Bush had proven that he could hold his own on foreign policy.

Bush's Decision-Making Style

Bush's experiences in business and Texas politics, his interactions with the Vulcans, and his comments during the 2000 campaign give some preliminary insight into his decision-making style. Overall, Bush believed that a leader should establish a broad vision for policy, solicit information from a strong and loyal team of advisers, and then make decisive and firm decisions. This style would affect how he interacted with his advisers, Congress, and the broader policy-making system.

One root of Bush's decision-making style has been his underlying personality. Bush is known for his ability to use humor to put people at ease, but he can be serious on issues about which he cares deeply and take them on as missions. He has charisma and can convince an audience that they should support his vision. He believes strongly in balancing work time with recreation, which leads him to favor efficient meetings, short policy memos, and quick decisions. He becomes impatient if the decision process does not match his timetable. He prefers facts and real life experience to deep philosophies.[5]

Bush's style was also affected by his experiences. Three aspects of his life stand out. First, Bush's management background, since he is the first U.S. president to have an MBA. At Harvard business school, executives are trained to be team leaders. The executive should take advantage of his team to delegate work and get expertise in particular areas, but should guide the team through the decision process and make final decisions. Second, Bush had a ringside seat to watch the workings of Reagan's and his father's White House. Both of those administrations were known for conflicts among advisers that often spilled out in leaked information and tell-all books. The Bush administration was also known for poor coordination of information flow under chief of staff John Sununu, in whose firing George W. played a part. Finally, while in his forties, Bush turned to an evangelical faith to help him quit alcohol and reprioritize his life. Bush's new faith allowed little ambiguity, reinforced his tendency to see issues in terms of good and evil, and reinforced the idea that he should not question previously reached conclusions.[6]

Bush's preferred style was evident with the Vulcans. Bush came to discussions with some preliminary vision on the given topic. This vision was not the deeply thought out, intellectual framework of some politicians. Instead, it was what Bush often describes as a "gut" feeling.[7] Bush then gathered his advisers, much as a CEO might gather his company vice presidents, so that they could report on their particular areas of expertise. He liked to learn through a process of specific questions and answers. He accepted disagreement among his advisers, but expected them to not carry grudges against each other, to never go outside the circle to complain, and to fall in line behind his final decision. Once Bush reached a conclusion, it rarely varied subsequently.

Bush believed that the president should be the dominant player not only within the executive branch, but in the overall policy-making system. During the 2000 campaign, he spoke strongly of the need to grant presidents "fast-track" trade negotiation authority, which limits congressional amendments or reservations to presidentially negotiated trade agreements. Bush also supported presidential control of military missions. In May 2000, the Senate considered an amendment that would have cut off funds for U.S. forces in Kosovo unless Congress authorized an extension. The idea had support from many Republicans who saw it as a way of limiting President Bill Clinton's flexibility. In an unusual move for a presidential candidate, Bush termed the proposal "legislative overreach"[8] and lobbied against it. The proposal was defeated by a coalition of Democrats and a few Republicans who supported Bush's view.

Cast in a positive light, Bush's style has seemed to enjoy many of the virtues of recent presidents without suffering from some of their weaknesses. Reagan was known for his big policy visions, but also for his lack of interest in policy details and implementation. Richard Perle, a Vulcan who served under Reagan commented about Bush: "Like Reagan, he's got a predisposition for certain broad ideas," but "I think he's intellectually more curious than Reagan was."[9] On the other hand, Bush's father was known for his policy expertise, but had trouble with "the vision thing." Clinton was extremely interested in policy detail and had some broader vision, but was also determined to hear all sides and consider all angles that he was often vacillating and inconsistent. Bush arguably had vision, took some interest in detail, and made firm decisions.

Cast in a more negative light, Bush's style has had its own weaknesses. First, he tended to base his vision on gut feeling rather than extensive knowledge. Critics have questioned the origins of those gut feelings and worried that Bush subsequently interpreted facts to match his intuition. In this regard, Bush's response when asked in April 1999 if Clinton was doing enough to stop Iraq from developing weapons of mass destruction is very revealing: "My gut tells me no, but I do not have enough facts to be able to back that up with a statement."[10] Second, Bush's leadership style encouraged conformity, leading him to gather together a group of homogenous advisers. He thus risked becoming a victim of "groupthink," where group members repress conflicting opinions in the interest of social cohesion and tailor their advice to reinforce the leader's views. Third, Bush tended to put people and issues into neat black and white categories and to reach conclusions that were not easily altered by later realities. In a complicated world with shades of gray, he risked being trapped by his own rigid categories and decision making. Finally, his desire to center so much policy control in the hands of the president and a small group of advisers risked minimizing congressional input and reestablishing the "imperial" presidencies of the Cold War era with little outside control of executive power.

Bush's Foreign Policy Priorities

In the course of the 2000 campaign, Bush gave four main foreign policy speeches that laid out his views and priorities. In a September 23, 1999 speech, he addressed a number of defense and security issues (Speech 1.1). He noted that America now had unrivaled power and had benefited from the recent spread of freedom throughout the world. These conditions presented the challenge of turning American influence into peace. Bush also cautioned that important threats remained, so the country had to be ready to defend itself and its allies. He summarized his plans by saying, "I will renew the bond of trust between the American president and the American military. I will defend the American people against missiles and terror. And I will begin creating the military of the next century." To restore trust, he suggested increasing defense spending, refocusing military missions on winning wars not peacekeeping, and bringing "clarity and focus" to the position of commander-in-chief. These statements were clear attacks on Clinton's priorities, decision-making style, and interactions with military officials. The main focus of Bush's second point was strong support for a national missile defense system. On terrorism, he stated, "Every group or nation must know, if they sponsor such attacks, our response will be devastating" and "the best defense can be a strong and swift offense." These statements were not the main focus of the speech, but gave important clues to Bush's post–9/11 policies. Bush's final goal was to promote military transformation by employing new tactics and high technology weaponry.

On November 19, 1999, Bush gave a broader speech on foreign policy at the Ronald Reagan Presidential Library (Speech 1.2). He began by referring approvingly to Reagan's international legacy and sought to tie his own policies to the Reagan tradition. Bush argued a president must mix clear-eyed realism with American ideals of spreading freedom and dignity. The ideal policy approach was "a distinctly American internationalism. Idealism, without illusions. Confidence, without conceit. Realism, in the service of American ideals." Bush also expressed extreme confidence in America's world role saying, "We firmly believe our nation is on the right side of history—the side of man's dignity and God's justice." To assure adoption of the correct approach and live up to its world responsibilities, the United States had to act confidently and guard against the dual temptations of isolationism and policy drift.

In this wide-ranging speech, Bush mentioned a host of important issues, but the main focus was on U.S. relations with China and Russia. In Bush's view, both were powerful countries that were still in economic and political transition, therefore, their long-term intentions remained unknown. Over time, Clinton had developed warmer relations with China and had come to describe it as a strategic partner. Bush pointedly said, "China is a competitor, not a strategic partner" and called some of its policies "alarming." On the other hand, Bush defended enhancing trade ties with China, so he did not take the true hard-line stance favored by some. On Russia, Bush spoke of the need to focus relations more on security concerns and less on American efforts to encourage Russian reform. Focusing on Russia was good politics, because Gore had been a major player in Clinton's Russia policy, which Bush argued had been too optimistic about the chance of reforms, too tied to particular leaders, too accepting that funds were stolen by corrupt officials, and too lenient on Russia's actions in Chechnya.

In the following months, Gore suggested that Bush's tough stances on China and Russia showed that he still operated with a Cold War era mentality. Bush sought to address that charge and further explain his security goals in a May 23, 2000 speech at the National Press Club (Speech 1.3). Bush suggested, "It is time to leave the Cold War behind and defend against the new threats of the twenty-first century." He warned of emerging dangers that "come from rogue states, terrorist groups and other adversaries seeking weapons of mass destruction and the means to deliver them." He then shifted to policy toward Russia, the primary focus of the speech. Bush argued that Russia was no longer an enemy, so the United States needed to move beyond Cold War era doctrines of deterrence. He expressed support for nuclear weapons cuts to levels significantly below the existing negotiated level and for removing as many weapons as possible from high-alert status. Importantly, he suggested that the United States should consider unilateral reductions. Gore countered that Bush's ideas would undermine years of arms control agreements and that Russia was unlikely to quietly accept a U.S. missile defense.

Bush's final major foreign policy speech of the 2000 campaign was given in the electorally crucial state of Florida on August 25, 2000 (Speech 1.4). Coming from Texas, Bush had long been interested in Latin America, particularly Mexico. Bush declared that, if he became president, he would look "South, not as an afterthought, but as a fundamental commitment" and that the twenty-first century could be "the century of the Americas." He pledged to help democracy spread throughout Latin America and to promote economic growth. He also noted that the United States must treat its neighbors with dignity and respect. Bush made quick references to two of the region's troubled areas, Cuba and Colombia, but the overall tone of the speech was upbeat.

Bush's World View in Comparison to Others

During campaigns and the early stages of administrations, the press, academics, and others often try to explain a politician's viewpoint in relation to those of previous leaders or existing schools of thought. These comparisons can serve as a quick way for observers to decide whether they generally support the person's opinions. The comparisons also can provide some guidance as to how a leader might react to crises that emerge during his time in office. Various observers tried to describe Bush's initial world vision as falling into one of four existing schools of thought. These efforts proved problematic. Although Bush's vision overlapped each of the existing groups on certain points, his views taken as a whole formed a distinct new world vision that has aptly been termed "assertive nationalism."[11]

To better understand assertive nationalism, the four existing world visions will be reviewed and compared to Bush's views (Table 1). Then, the key aspects of assertive nationalism will be highlighted. In this process, it is important to remember that these world visions are ideal types, so particular individuals may not fit perfectly into any one framework.

From the earliest days of the country, "isolationists" have argued that the United States could best preserve its security and distinctive character by keeping itself as removed as possible from international power politics. Modern isolationists have had to adapt to global interconnections and America's world power, so they advocate restraint rather than total retreat from world affairs. They often oppose free trade agreements and support protective tariffs for American industry. They favor a strong defense, which would focus on protecting U.S. soil and core interests. They are sharply opposed to many multilateral institutions and agreements, which they feel pull the United States into global problem areas, limit policy flexibility, and interfere with America's sovereign right to decide its own policies. In the 2000 presidential campaign, these views were represented by Patrick Buchanan. Isolationist views also were widespread among Republicans in Congress, particularly those who had come to office in the 1990s.

During the campaign, Gore suggested that Bush's lack of foreign policy experience would lead him to be shaped "by the ideologies and inveterate antipathies of his party—the right wing, partisan isolationism of the Republican Congressional leadership."[12] This suggestion never stuck, because Bush directly rejected isolationism in his speeches and comments. Bush strongly supported free trade and a global military role. Bush, though, did agree with isolationists' opposition to purely humanitarian military interventions. Also, he shared some of their distrust of multilateral institutions and certain multilateral agreements, such as the Kyoto Protocol on global warming and the Comprehensive Test Ban Treaty.

In opposition to isolationism, there are three main versions of internationalist thought. "Liberal internationalists" favor expanding trade ties, military agreements, and participation in multilateral institutions as a way of enmeshing the United States and other world powers in a global community, so that international society will more closely parallel stable domestic societies. They recognize the need to defend the United States, but also support some military actions, preferably in conjunction with allies, to enforce international norms and to end massive human rights

Table 1. Comparison of Foreign Policy

	U.S. should engage in free trade and military alliances	U.S. should act unilaterally despite allied objections	U.S. should promote nation-building to establish democracy	U.S. should focus on non-security issues
Isolationism	No	Yes	No	No
Liberal Internationalism	Yes	No	Yes	Yes
Traditional Internationalism	Yes	No	No	Sometimes
Neoconservativism	Yes	Yes	Yes	No
Assertive Nationalism	Yes	Yes	No	No

abuses or humanitarian crises. In addition, they feel that the modern world powers must move beyond security calculations to address global economic downturns, poverty, environmental destruction, and other emerging global issues. In the 2000 campaign, liberal internationalist views were represented by Al Gore

In the presidential debates and elsewhere, Bush and Gore agreed on many core foreign policy issues. However, Bush criticized Clinton and Gore for cutting defense spending and being too soft on potential challengers, such as China. Bush also repeatedly argued that U.S. forces should be used to win wars and advance American interests, not to lead humanitarian efforts. Bush and Rice strongly argued that liberal internationalists felt "that the United States is exercising power legitimately only when it is doing so on behalf of someone or something else" when in fact helping humanity should be "a second-order effect [because] America's pursuit of the national interest will create conditions that promote freedom, markets, and peace."[13] Bush and Rice also criticized Clinton's commitment to multilateralism, saying that the administration's "attachment to largely symbolic agreements and its pursuit of, at best, illusory 'norms' of international behavior have become an epidemic."[14]

"Traditional internationalists" emerged within Republican Party after World War II when key leaders decided to reject isolationism and support internationalist efforts such as the UN and global anticommunism. This decision led to a large degree of consensus with the more liberal internationalist democrats, since both groups favored trade, strong military alliances, and international institutions. The two groups diverged, however, on two key points. First, traditional internationalists preferred greater focus on security and national defense issues in opposition to the broader economic and environmental goals of the liberals. Second, although they agreed that power gave the United States some moral obligation and practical incentive to help weaker countries and stop humanitarian crises, they were wary of purely humanitarian intervention in the absence of American interests. They were even more wary of nation building, helping to re-establish a country's political, economic, and legal systems. During the 2000 campaign, there was no candidate clearly espousing these views, so the last notable exemplar was George H.W. Bush.

As a loyal and proud son, Bush did not directly attack his father's policies, but he held quite different views than traditional internationalists. Rice stressed, "The world is a different place than it was in 1990 or 1991 or 1992."[15] Therefore, Bush and his advisers rejected the cautious, gradual policies of the elder Bush in favor of bold actions to address new challenges. Whereas the elder Bush worked closely with U.S. allies and led a UN coalition in the Persian Gulf War, the younger Bush was more willing to act alone if necessary. Bush was also less supportive of humanitarian intervention than his father, who saw it as a moral obligation. During the debates, he was careful to blame problems that emerged in Somalia not on his father's initial 1992 intervention but on the subsequent nation-building efforts of the Clinton administration. On separate occasions, though, he noted that military action anywhere in Africa was unlikely under his administration.

A final recognized internationalist school of thought is the neoconservative, or "neocon" movement. The movement began in the late 1960s, and reached its first peak of policy influence during the Reagan administration. Neocons pushed Reagan's ideas of pursuing U.S. interests through both military strength and the promotion of American values. Under the elder Bush and Clinton, the neocons fell from power and receded as an intellectual force. In the late 1990s, neocons reemerged with a new generation of supporters joining older players. They argued that since rising powers, rogue states, and terrorists present ongoing threats to U.S. power and interests, the United States must be ever-vigilant and willing to use force early to defend the country. While other issues can impact U.S. interests, they are never as central as security threats. The neocons also believed that spreading democracy is crucial, not only for philosophical reasons, but because it promotes global trade, prevents the rise of abusive authoritarianism, and brings the United States new allies. Furthermore, neocons argued that the United States must work to maintain predominance in the world in order to defend itself and promote its values, but also because its hegemony has been good for the overall international system. During the primaries, many neocons supported Senator John McCain against Bush and repeatedly wrote opinion pieces arguing that Bush was too much like Gore. Others, such as Wolfowitz and Perle, became advisers for Bush.

Bush's worldview had much in common with the neocons. He relied more on advice from that group of Republicans than from the isolationists or traditional internationalists. He agreed with their warnings that the world remained full of threats and their calls for a strong military. He also agreed that both American power and American values were good for the world. He was not prepared, however, to accept the neocon's missionary campaign to actively spread democracy. For example, although he broke with many isolationist and traditional internationalist Republicans in supporting Clinton's intervention in Kosovo, he did so not to challenge authoritarian rule and spread democracy but because he saw the Balkans as strategically important. In addition, while he supported the neocons' desire for a tougher policy on China, he would not push democracy promotion to the point of jeopardizing American commercial interests.

The Key Ideas of Bush's Assertive Nationalism

Bush's assertive nationalism rested on four core precepts about foreign policy and America's role in the world.

Guarantee the Tools of American Power

Bush felt strongly that the United States should be the world's leader, which entailed ensuring that it had the military tools to defend itself, support its allies, and challenge its enemies. A strong economy was also important, but Bush generally treated economic growth and strength as a domestic, not foreign, policy issue. For Bush, rebuilding the military, showing the will to use American force, and reinforcing ties with allies were the priorities. He pointed out that U.S. military spending as a percentage of GNP was at its lowest since before World War II; yet, there had been an average of one deployment every nine weeks during the last years under Clinton. He felt this mismatch of funds and commitments had left the military with poorly paid soldiers, a lack of spare parts, and not enough commitment to weapons research. Some of the military decrease under Clinton resulted from a widespread desire to get a "peace dividend" of reduced spending after the Cold War, but Bush felt Clinton had gone too far and had left the U.S. dangerously weak.

Bush also felt that Clinton had left the U.S. without world respect because he had not shown enough will to use force to defend American interests. Bush argued, "There are limits to the smiles and scowls of diplomacy. Armies and missiles are not stopped by stiff notes of condemnation. They are held in check by strength and purpose and the promise of swift punishment" (Speech 1.2). Bush did not give specifics on where he would employ force, but put the world on notice that he would not hesitate to use force when necessary to preserve U.S. interests.

Finally, Bush sought to enhance ties with American allies. For example, he criticized Clinton for visiting China for a week without stopping off in Japan, South Korea, or the Philippines to reinforce the support of the United States. He argued that traditional U.S. allies in Latin America should no longer be ignored. He voiced strong support for Israel and for commitments to NATO allies. To some degree, Bush's focus on strengthening alliances may seem to contradict his support for unilateral actions, but this discrepancy can be reconciled by understanding two points. First, Bush and his advisers assumed that allied countries, namely democracies and those favoring free markets, generally would have common goals and common enemies. Therefore, building alliances would not entail compromise among competing positions, but rather alliances would represent coalitions of like-minded countries. Second, Bush assumed that other countries would acknowledge that the power of the United States gave it a special role in the world and a leadership position in any alliance. Bush's views on allies were very similar to his views on advisers. Both should be guided by a broad vision laid out by their leader. They could then voice their often similar opinions. The ultimate decision, though, would be made by the leader and the others would be expected to follow that decision and present a united front.

Harbor Resources

Bush felt that enhanced U.S. power should not be squandered on unnecessary missions or policy priorities. During the whole campaign, Bush, in sharp contrast to Gore, made only passing references to problems of global poverty, the spread of such diseases as AIDS, and environmental issues. His main stance on the international environment was to oppose the 1997

Kyoto Protocol on greenhouse gases as being too costly for American businesses and unfairly exempting developing countries. Similarly, Bush sought to limit U.S. military missions in strategically less important areas. For example, Bush repeatedly excluded the entire continent of Africa from lists of U.S. priorities.

Most dramatically, in sharp contrast to both liberal internationalist and neocon views, Bush argued that the United States should not use its military for purely humanitarian missions and nation building. He repeatedly argued that the purpose of the military was to win wars. Therefore, he argued, "[The United States] should not send our troops to stop ethnic cleansing and genocide in nations outside our strategic interest."[16] Bush and Rice often spoke disparagingly of the idea that the United States could be the world's policeman. Furthermore, Bush made "nation building" sound close to a dirty word during the debates. Interestingly, when pressed for specifics, Bush supported almost every U.S. intervention of the last several decades. He singled out only action to restore democracy in Haiti as a clear misuse of American force, but in each of the other cases, he argued that the action was justified for security, not moral, reasons and should not involve long-term commitment.

Challenge Enemies

Bush argued that U.S. power was good for the country and good for the world, but acknowledged that it made the United States the target of any rising power. Therefore, the United States had to remain vigilant and ready to defend its leadership position. Bush singled out three threats requiring particular attention: Russia, China, and rogue countries, such as Iraq and North Korea. At times, terrorists were included in the category of rogues, but Bush rarely spoke directly about terrorist threats before 9/11.

In 2000, Russia and China were the two most powerful countries outside of the U.S. alliance structure. Bush argued in his speech at the Reagan Library that both countries were still in transition to capitalism and democracy. Both had unsettled regional issues, particularly Chechnya for Russia and Taiwan for China. Each maintained strong military forces that could complicate U.S. goals and directly threaten the U.S. homeland. Bush spoke sharply against future international economic aid for Russia and made no calls to enhance trade or to encourage Russian entry into international economic institutions. On security issues, he did call for a mutual reduction in nuclear forces to reflect reduced bilateral tensions, but seemed prepared to ignore Russian concerns about the eastward expansion of NATO and about a U.S. missile defense system. On China, Bush favored the continued expansion of the commercial ties that his father's policies had helped ensure, but described China as a competitor and focused attention on China's recent military build-up. Bush also hinted that he was prepared to use force to protect Taiwan and stated he would go forward with missile defense despite Chinese objections.

Finally, Bush warned of the growing danger posed by rogue states that sought weapons of mass destruction. During the primaries, Bush was asked what he would do if Iraq's president, Saddam Hussein, was found to be developing weapons of mass destruction (WMD). Bush answered, "I'd take 'em out."[17] He later scaled his rhetoric back, saying that there would be a "consequence" for Saddam Hussein.[18] These comments show that Bush was thinking of these threats well before 9/11 and was prepared to adopt new policies to meet these new enemies. In 2000, though, his comments on these threats were generally shorter and less specific than those on threats from America's traditional enemies.

Act Unilaterally When Needed

The final, and arguably most revolutionary, piece of Bush's world vision was his willingness to act unilaterally. This willingness reflected Bush's view that the United States had achieved such power that it no longer needed to compromise its goals in pursuit of allied support. Second, Bush had supreme faith that the United States as a democratic, free market, peace-loving country would always be following the proper course. If others objected to the American policies, either they were U.S. enemies or they were allies who simply had not yet seen the wisdom of U.S. actions. He felt that there was no logic in delaying action to build a multilateral coalition, since the coalition would logically form once the United States committed to action.

Bush's willingness to act unilaterally also reflected his distrust of the UN and other multilateral institutions. Bush was not as hostile to these institutions as others in his party. He did, though, feel that the UN's role should be circumscribed until it was reformed. Bush saw the UN as inefficient—spending an increasingly large budget, without attaining clear successes. AdditionallyIn addition, Bush felt that the UN frequently debated issues without taking firm actions. These realities went against Bush's strong belief in accountability of programs and efficient discussion followed by bold action. Bush would act multilaterally if institutions and coalitions supported his positions, but would act unilaterally, if needed.

Assembling the Team

After years of campaigning and a month's delay in being declared the official winner, Bush was ready to formally build his foreign policy team. The Bush transition was comparatively smooth because Bush already had an existing team, namely the Vulcans and other campaign advisers. Still, his appointments were carefully watched. Analysts believed that he needed a strong team around him to balance his inexperience on foreign policy. Some observers assumed Bush would often be dominated by his advisers, so they speculated about who would really control policy decisions. In addition, conflicting views among isolationists, traditional internationalists, neocons, and assertive nationalists within the Republican Party made the make-up of the team crucial.

Richard "Dick" Cheney

The first person formally brought into the foreign policy team was Dick Cheney, selected by Bush as his vice presidential running mate in July 2000. Cheney had had a long record of service in both executive branch posts and Congress, so he was seen as adding important experience and intellectual weight to the Bush team. He had served in the Nixon and Ford White Houses. During the 1980s, he was one of the most consistent supporters of President Reagan and he built a very conservative voting record in the House of Representatives. In 1989, George H.W. Bush appointed him secretary of defense. He was a key player during the Cold War's end and in the Persian Gulf War. After Bush senior's defeat, Cheney became CEO of the Halliburton Company.

The selection of his father's adviser as vice president reinforced the view that Bush was closely tied to his father's views. Notably, though, Cheney's voting record was far more conservative than the views of the elder Bush. Also, he was seen as a real hawk often pressing for more aggressive military action. He was also known as a pessimist, who often based his advice on worst-case scenarios.

Cheney quickly signaled that he intended the vice president's post to be more than symbolic saying, "I'm not just going to go to funerals and fund-raisers."[19] Given his strong foreign and defense policy credentials, he was assumed to have considerable influence over Bush. He also exerted influence by leading the Bush transition team. Once in office, Cheney assembled an unusually large and expert staff that, at times, functioned independently of the NSC staff and the intelligence agencies.

Colin Powell

Bush's first cabinet level appointment was Colin Powell as secretary of state. Powell had not been part of the Vulcans, but had advised Bush independently and stood with Bush at the National Press Club speech on security issues. He was also well known to the Bush family and the Washington community. Powell entered the army in 1958 as a commissioned officer, and rose to be a four-star general and chairman of the Joint Chiefs of Staff under the elder Bush and Clinton. He retired from the military in 1993. During his service, he spent some time in the field, but also spent considerable time in Washington as a policy adviser. After his retirement, there was much speculation that Powell would run for office; instead, he spent his time as a motivational speaker and advocate for volunteerism, but he had remained well informed on key foreign policy and defense issues.

Early in his career, Powell was deeply affected by his experiences in Vietnam. As a consequence, he later developed the "Powell Doctrine," namely that U.S. military power should only be used in overwhelming strength and to achieve well-defined strategic interests. After Iraq's invasion of Kuwait, Powell urged caution and supported allowing time for economic sanctions to force a change in Iraq's policies. Once the decision was made to fight the Persian Gulf War, he fell in line with the administration's views and his planning was seen as a key factor in the U.S. victory. Still, many Republicans were disappointed by his caution. Similarly, many Democrats were frustrated when he repeatedly advised the Clinton administration not to use force in the Balkans. He was often referred to as a "reluctant warrior."

Within Bush's team, Powell was the real outsider. His advocacy for working with allies and not unnecessarily challenging enemies put him closer to the traditional internationalism of Bush's father. Few of Powell's supporters were given key posts in the administration. Even on a personal level, Powell seemed out of place. On the day Bush announced the appointment at his Texas ranch, Powell jokingly commented, "I'm from the South Bronx, and I don't care what you say, those cows look dangerous."[20] Even before Bush took office, Powell's relations with key officials in the Department of Defense, and possibly with Bush himself seemed destined for tension. Powell, though, was seen as a team player who would fall in line with Bush's decisions. He had the advantage of domestic and international respect. Many U.S. allies hoped Powell would become the dominant policy figure.

Condoleezza "Condi" Rice

To no one's surprise, Bush chose Condoleezza "Condi" Rice, his top foreign policy adviser from the campaign, as his National Security Adviser. She became the first woman to hold this position. From her childhood, Rice had demonstrated determination, self-confidence, and the ability to pick up information and skills quickly. She received a doctoral degree from the University of Denver, where she has focused on Russian politics, then became a professor at Stanford, where she impressed a number of Republican leaders who had ties to Stanford's Hoover Institute. In 1989, she joined the elder Bush's administration as a Russian and East European expert at the NSC, and she played a role in negotiating the unification of Germany. She then returned to Stanford as provost, the chief academic and budget officer of the university.

Rice began her adult life as a Democrat, but switched parties to support Reagan because she felt Carter had not taken a forceful position against the 1979 Soviet invasion of Afghanistan. Her professional career was always focused on Russia. In her role as campaign adviser, she admitted, "I've been pressed to understand parts of the world that have not been part of my scope. I'm really a Europeanist."[21] This focus led some to question her general experience, and whether she would apply her views on the Cold War and subsequent Russian collapse to other rising powers. Some also questioned whether she would be able to stand up to the heavyweights in the administration. No one doubted, however, that her close personal ties to Bush would keep her in the policy-making loop.

Donald Rumsfeld

The one major foreign policy appointment surprise was Bush's choice of Donald Rumsfeld as secretary of defense. Rumsfeld had been out of government service for a number of years. He began his Washington career in the 1960s as a Congressman from Illinois. He served the Nixon administration as ambassador to NATO and the Ford White House as Chief of Staff from 1974–75. At that point, he brought Cheney in as his deputy. In 1975, Rumsfeld was appointed secretary of defense. Some considered him a rising star in the party; others noted his prickly personality and clashes with other rising Republicans, such as George H.W. Bush. After 1977, Rumsfeld spent most of his time in the private sector.

During his time out of government, Rumsfeld stayed active on two defense issues central to Bush's views. First, he advocated modernizing U.S. armed forces, so that they could be deployed more quickly, fight coordinated battles, and employ the latest military technology. Second, he was a strong supporter of a national missile defense. In 1998, he chaired a panel, the Rumsfeld Commission, which concluded that countries such as North Korea and Iran could be able to threaten the United States with long-range missiles within five years of a decision to develop such capability. These conclusions played a role in encouraging the Clinton administration to go forward with research on a defense system. Thus, although Rumsfeld's selection was a surprise, he seemed a natural part of the Bush team.

Paul Wolfowitz

Paul Wolfowitz, co-chair of the Vulcans, was appointed deputy secretary of defense, the number two position at the Pentagon, after having been passed over as secretary of defense. He was a leading neocon intellectual and often considered the most ideological member of Bush's team. Early in his career, he came to believe that the United States needed a strong military to defeat the Soviet threat. Under President Ford, Wolfowitz worked with the then CIA director Bush on a planning exercise called "Team B." The group challenged existing intelligence estimates and argued for a tougher response to the Soviets. In subsequent administrations, he served in a number of Departments of State and Defense posts. In 1992, his ongoing support for aggressive security policies was demonstrated by a memo in which he argued that the United States should work to keep its military predominance, even if that meant acting unilaterally or preemptively. His views were outside the mainstream of the elder Bush's administration, so the memo's conclusions were disavowed by top officials when it was leaked to the press. He spent the Clinton years out of government service as an active intellectual and writer.

Wolfowitz's beliefs epitomizes neocon thinking that a strong United States ready to address threats and provide leadership is good and necessary for the world. During the 1990s, he concluded that leaving Saddam Hussein in power after the Gulf War had been a major error and repeatedly advocated U.S. support for Iraqi opposition groups. Wolfowitz's thinking, though, also included a strong moral component. He wrote, "Nothing could be less realistic than the version of the 'realist' view of foreign policy that dismisses human rights as an important tool of American foreign policy," since "promoting democracy has actually advanced American interests."[22] Because of his strong views and long history of written statements, few Washington insiders were neutral on Wolfowitz—to some he was a visionary and hero, to others a dangerous force that would try to push Bush into the neocon school of thought.

1.1 A Period of Consequences

The Citadel
Charleston, South Carolina
September 23, 1999

Our world, shaped by American courage, power and wisdom, now echoes with American ideals. We won a victory, not just for a nation, but for a vision. A vision of freedom and individual dignity—defended by democracy, nurtured by free markets, spread by information technology, carried to the world by free trade. The advance of freedom—from Asia to Latin America to East and Central Europe—is creating the conditions for peace. For America, this is a time of unrivaled military power, economic promise, and cultural influence. It is, in Franklin Roosevelt's phrase, "the peace of overwhelming victory."

Now a new generation of American leaders will determine how that power and influence are used—a generation after the hard but clear struggle against an evil empire. Our challenge is not as obvious, but just as noble: To turn these years of influence into decades of peace.

But peace is not ordained, it is earned. It is not a harbor where we rest, it is a voyage we must chart. Even in this time of hope and confidence, we can see the signs of uncertainty. We see the contagious spread of missile technology and weapons of mass destruction. We know that this era of American preeminence is also an era of car bombers and plutonium merchants and cyber terrorists and drug cartels and unbalanced dictators—all the unconventional and invisible threats of new technologies and old hatreds. These challenges can be overcome, but they can not be ignored.

Building a durable peace will require strong alliances, expanding trade and confident diplomacy. It will require tough realism in our dealings with China and Russia. It will require firmness with regimes like North Korea and Iraq—regimes that hate our values and resent our success. I will address all these priorities in the future. But I want to begin with the foundation of our peace—a strong, capable and modern military.

The American armed forces have an irreplaceable role in the world. They give confidence to our allies; deter the aggression of our enemies; and allow our nation to shape a stable peace. The common defense is the sworn duty and chief responsibility of a president. And, if elected, I will set three goals: I will renew the bond of trust between the American president and the American military. I will defend the American people against missiles and terror. And I will begin creating the military of the next century.

Our military is without peer, but it is not without problems. . . . I have great faith in those who serve our nation—in the temper of their will and the quality of their spirit. . . . But even the highest morale is eventually undermined by back-to-back deployments, poor pay, shortages of spare parts and equipment, and rapidly declining readiness.

Not since the years before Pearl Harbor has our investment in national defense been so low as a percentage of GNP. Yet rarely has our military been so freely used—an average of one deployment every nine weeks in the last few years. Since the end of the Cold War, our ground forces have been deployed more frequently, while our defense budget has fallen by nearly 40 percent. . . .

This Administration wants things both ways: To command great forces, without supporting them. To launch today's new causes, with little thought of tomorrow's consequences. . . ..

Recently, after years of neglect, a significant pay raise was finally passed. My first budget will go further—adding a billion dollars in salary increases. . . . And we must improve the quality of training at our bases and national training centers. Shortfalls on the proving ground become disasters on the battlefield.

But our military requires more than good treatment. It needs the rallying point of a defining mission. And that mission is to deter wars—and win wars when deterrence fails. Sending our military on vague, aimless and endless deployments is the swift solvent of morale. As president, I will order an immediate review of our overseas deployments—in dozens of countries. The long standing commitments we have made to our allies are the strong foundation of our current peace. I will keep these pledges to defend friends from aggression. The problem comes with open-ended deployments and unclear military missions. In these cases we will ask, "What is our goal, can it be met, and when do we leave?" As I've said before, I will work hard to find political solutions that allow an orderly and timely withdrawal from places like Kosovo and Bosnia. We will encourage our allies to take a broader role. We will not be hasty. But we will not be permanent peacekeepers, dividing warring parties. This is not our strength or our calling.

America will not retreat from the world. On the contrary, I will replace diffuse commitments with focused ones. I will replace uncertain missions with well-defined objectives. This will preserve the resources of American power and public will. The presence of American forces overseas is one of the most profound symbols of our commitment to allies and friends. And our allies know that if America is committed everywhere, our commitments are everywhere suspect. We must be selective in the use of our military, precisely because America has other great responsibilities that cannot be slighted or compromised. And this review of our deployments will also reduce the tension on an overstretched military. Nothing would be better for morale than clarity and focus from the commander-in-chief.

My second goal is to build America's defenses on the troubled frontiers of technology and terror. The protection of America itself will assume a high priority in a new century. Once a strategic afterthought, homeland defense has become an urgent duty.

For most of our history, America felt safe behind two great oceans. But with the spread of technology, distance no longer means security. North Korea is proving that even a poor and backward country, in the hands of a tyrant, can reach across oceans to threaten us. It has developed missiles capable of hitting Hawaii and Alaska. Iran has made rapid strides in its missile program, and Iraq persists in a race to do the same. . . .

Add to this the threat of biological, chemical and nuclear terrorism—barbarism emboldened by technology. These weapons can be delivered, not just by ballistic missiles, but by everything from airplanes to cruise missiles, from shipping containers to suitcases. And consider the prospect of information warfare, in which hacker terrorists may try to disrupt finance, communication, transportation and public health.

Let me be clear. Our first line of defense is a simple message: Every group or nation must know, if they sponsor such attacks, our response will be devastating. But we must do more. At the earliest possible date, my administration will deploy anti-ballistic missile systems, both theater and national, to guard against attack and blackmail. To make this possible, we will offer Russia the necessary amendments to the anti-ballistic missile treaty—an artifact of Cold War confrontation. Both sides know that we live in a different world from 1972, when that treaty was signed. If Russia refuses the changes we propose, we will give prompt notice, under the provisions of the treaty, that we can no longer be a party to it. I will have a solemn obligation to protect the American people and our allies, not to protect arms control agreements signed almost thirty years ago.

We will defend the American homeland by strengthening our intelligence community—focusing on human intelligence and the early detection of terrorist operations both here and abroad. And when direct threats to America are discovered, I know that the best defense can be a strong and swift offense—including the use of Special Operations Forces and long-range strike capabilities. And there is more to be done preparing here at home. I will put a high priority on detecting and responding to terrorism on our soil. The federal government must take this threat seriously—working closely with researchers and industry to increase surveillance and develop treatments for chemical and biological agents.

But defending our nation is just the beginning of our challenge. My third goal is to take advantage of a tremendous opportunity—given few nations in history—to extend the current peace into the far realm of the future. A chance to project America's peaceful influence, not just across the world, but across the years.

This opportunity is created by a revolution in the technology of war. Power is increasingly defined, not by mass or size, but by mobility and swiftness. Influence is measured in information, safety is gained in stealth, and force is projected on the long arc of precision-guided weapons. This revolution perfectly matches the strengths of our country—the skill of our people and the superiority of our technology. The best way to keep the peace is to redefine war on our terms. Yet today our military is still organized more for Cold War threats than for the challenges of a new century—for industrial age operations, rather than for information age battles. . . .

As president, I will begin an immediate, comprehensive review of our military—the structure of its forces, the state of its strategy, the priorities of its procurement—conducted by a leadership team under the Secretary of Defense. I will give the Secretary a broad mandate—to challenge the status quo and envision a new architecture of American defense for decades to come. We will modernize some existing weapons and equipment. . . . The real goal is to move beyond marginal improvements—to replace existing programs with new technologies and strategies. To use this window of opportunity to skip a generation of technology. This will require spending more—and spending more wisely. . . .

When our comprehensive review is complete, I will expect the military's budget priorities to match our strategic vision—not the particular visions of the services, but a joint vision for change. . . . I intend to force new thinking and hard choices. . . .

Even if I am elected, I will not command the new military we create. That will be left to a president who comes after me. The results of our effort will not be seen for many years. The outcome of great battles is often determined by decisions on funding and technology made decades before, in the quiet days of peace. But these choices on spending and strategy either support the young men and women who must fight the future's wars—or betray their lives and squander their valor. . . .

Moments of national opportunity are either seized or lost, and the consequences reach across decades. Our opportunity is here—to show that anew generation can renew America's purpose.

1.2   A Distinctly American Internationalism

Ronald Reagan Presidential Library
Simi Valley, California
November 19, 1999

It is an honor to be with you at the Reagan Library.... We live in the nation President Reagan restored, and the world he helped to save. A world of nations reunited and tyrants humbled. A world of prisoners released and exiles come home. And today there is a prayer shared by free people everywhere: God bless you, Ronald Reagan.

Two months ago, at the Citadel in South Carolina, I talked about American defense. This must be the first focus of a president, because it is his first duty to the Constitution. Even in this time of pride and promise, America has determined enemies, who hate our values and resent our success—terrorists and crime syndicates and drug cartels and unbalanced dictators. The Empire has passed, but evil remains....

In the defense of our nation, a president must be a clear-eyed realist. There are limits to the smiles and scowls of diplomacy. Armies and missiles are not stopped by stiff notes of condemnation. They are held in check by strength and purpose and the promise of swift punishment.

But there is more to say, because military power is not the final measure of might. Our realism must make a place for the human spirit. This spirit, in our time, has caused dictators to fear and empires to fall. And it has left an honor roll of courage and idealism: Scharansky, Havel, Walesa, Mandela. The most powerful force in the world is not a weapon or a nation but a truth: that we are spiritual beings, and that freedom is "the soul's right to breathe." ...

America cherishes that freedom, but we do not own it. We value the elegant structures of our own democracy—but realize that, in other societies, the architecture will vary. We propose our principles, we must not impose our culture.

Yet the basic principles of human freedom and dignity are universal. People should be able to say what they think. Worship as they wish. Elect those who govern them. These ideals have proven their power on every continent....

Some have tried to pose a choice between American ideals and American interests—between who we are and how we act. But the choice is false. America, by decision and destiny, promotes political freedom—and gains the most when democracy advances. America believes in free markets and free trade—and benefits most when markets are opened. America is a peaceful power—and gains the greatest dividend from democratic stability. Precisely because we have no territorial objectives, our gains are not measured in the losses of others. They are counted in the conflicts we avert, the prosperity we share and the peace we extend.

Sometimes this balance takes time to achieve—and requires us to deal with nations that do not share our values. Sometimes the defenders of freedom must show patience as well as resolution. But that patience comes of confidence, not compromise. We believe, with Alexander Hamilton, that the "spirit of commerce" has a tendency to "soften the manners of men." We believe, with George Washington, that "Liberty, when it begins to take root, is a plant of rapid growth." And we firmly believe our nation is on the right side of history—the side of man's dignity and God's justice.

Few nations have been given the advantages and opportunities of our own. Few have been more powerful as a country, or more successful as a cause. But there are risks, even for the powerful....

America's first temptation is withdrawal—to build a proud tower of protectionism and isolation. In a world that depends on America to reconcile old rivals and balance ancient ambitions, this is the shortcut to chaos. It is an approach that abandons our allies, and our ideals. The vacuum left by America's retreat would invite challenges to our power. And the result, in the long run, would be a stagnant America and a savage world.

American foreign policy cannot be founded on fear. Fear that American workers can't compete. Fear that America will corrupt the world—or be corrupted by it. This fear has no place in the party of Reagan, or in the party of Truman. In times of peril, our nation did not shrink from leadership. At this moment of opportunity, I have no intention of betraying American interests, American obligations and American honor.

America's second temptation is drift—for our nation to move from crisis to crisis like a cork in a current. Unless a president sets his own priorities, his priorities will be set by others—by adversaries, or the crisis of the moment, live on CNN. American policy can become random and reactive—untethered to the interests of our country.

America must be involved in the world. But that does not mean our military is the answer to every difficult foreign policy situation—a substitute for strategy. American internationalism should not mean action without vision, activity without priority, and missions without end—an approach that squanders American will and drains American energy. American foreign policy must be more than the management of crisis. It must have a great and guiding goal: to turn this time of American influence into generations of democratic peace.

This is accomplished by concentrating on enduring national interests. And these are my priorities. An American president should work with our strong democratic allies in Europe and Asia to extend the peace. He should promote a fully democratic Western Hemisphere, bound together by free trade. He should defend America's interests in the Persian Gulf and advance peace in the Middle East, based upon a secure Israel. He must check the contagious spread of weapons of mass destruction, and the means to deliver them. He must lead toward a world that trades in freedom. And he must pursue all these goals with focus, patience and strength.

I will address these responsibilities as this campaign continues. To each, I bring the same approach: A distinctly American internationalism. Idealism, without illusions. Confidence, without conceit. Realism, in the service of American ideals.

Today I want to talk about Europe and Asia—the world's strategic heartland—our greatest priority. Home of long-time allies, and looming rivals. . . . The challenge comes because two of Eurasia's greatest powers—China and Russia—are powers in transition. And it is difficult to know their intentions when they do not know their own futures. If they become America's friends, that friendship will steady the world. But if not, the peace we seek may not be found.

China, in particular, has taken different shapes in different eyes at different times. An empire to be divided. A door to be opened. A model of collective conformity. A diplomatic card to be played. One year, it is said to be run by "the butchers of Beijing." A few years later, the same administration pronounces it a "strategic partner."

We must see China clearly—not through the filters of posturing and partisanship. China is rising, and that is inevitable. Here, our interests are plain: We welcome a free and prosperous China. We predict no conflict. We intend no threat. And there are areas where we must try to cooperate: preventing the spread of weapons of mass destruction, attaining peace on the Korean peninsula.

Yet the conduct of China's government can be alarming abroad, and appalling at home. Beijing has been investing its growing wealth in strategic nuclear weapons, new ballistic missiles, a blue-water navy and a long-range airforce. It is an espionage threat to our country. Meanwhile, the State Department has reported that "all public dissent against the party and government [has been] effectively silenced"—a tragic achievement in a nation of 1.2 billion people. China's government is an enemy of religious freedom and a sponsor of forced abortion—policies without reason and without mercy.

All of these facts must be squarely faced. China is a competitor, not a strategic partner. We must deal with China without ill-will—but without illusions. . . .

We must show American power and purpose in strong support for our Asian friends and allies—for democratic South Korea across the Yellow Sea, for democratic Japan and the Philippines across the China seas, for democratic Australia and Thailand. This means keeping our pledge to deter aggression against the Republic of Korea, and strengthening security ties with Japan. This means expanding theater missile defenses among our allies. And this means honoring our promises to the people of Taiwan. We do not deny there is one China. But we deny the right of Beijing to impose their rule on a free people. As I've said before, we will help Taiwan to defend itself. . . .

If I am president, China will find itself respected as a great power, but in a region of strong democratic alliances. It will be unthreatened, but not unchecked. China will find in America a confident and willing trade partner. And with trade comes our standing invitation into the world of economic freedom. China's entry into the World Trade Organization is welcome, and this should open the door for Taiwan as well. But given China's poor record in honoring agreements, it will take a strong administration to hold them to their word. If I am president, China will know that America's values are always part of America's agenda. Our advocacy of human freedom is not a formality of diplomacy, it is a fundamental commitment of our country. It is the source of our confidence that communism, in every form, has seen its day.

And I view free trade as an important ally in what Ronald Reagan called "a forward strategy for freedom." The case for trade is not just monetary, but moral. Economic freedom creates habits of liberty. And habits of liberty create expectations of democracy. There are no guarantees, but there are good examples, from Chile to Taiwan. Trade freely with China, and time is on our side.

Russia stands as another reminder that a world increasingly at peace is also a world in transition. Here, too, patience is needed—patience, consistency, and a principled reliance on democratic forces. In the breadth of its land, the talent and courage of its people, the wealth of its resources, and the reach of its weapons, Russia is a great power, and must always be treated as such. Few people have suffered more in this century. And though we trust the worst is behind them, their troubles are not over. This past decade, for Russia, has been an epic of deliverance and disappointment.

Our first order of business is the national security of our nation—and here both Russia and the United States face a changed world. Instead of confronting each other, we confront the legacy of a dead ideological rivalry—thousands of nuclear weapons, which, in the case of Russia, may not be secure. And together we also face an emerging threat—from rogue nations, nuclear theft and accidental launch. All this requires nothing short of a new strategic relationship to protect the peace of the world.

We can hope that the new Russian Duma will ratify START II, as we have done. But this is not our most pressing challenge. The greater problem was first addressed in 1991 by Senator Lugar and Senator Sam Nunn. In an act of foresight and statesmanship, they realized that existing Russian nuclear facilities were in danger of being compromised. Under the Nunn-Lugar program, security at many Russian nuclear facilities has been improved and warheads have been destroyed. . . .

We will still, however, need missile defense systems—both theater and national. If I am commander-in-chief, we will develop and deploy them. Under the mutual threat of rogue nations, there is a real possibility the Russians could join with us and our friends and allies to cooperate on missile defense systems. But there is a condition. Russia must break its dangerous habit of proliferation.

In the hard work of halting proliferation, the Comprehensive Test Ban Treaty is not the answer. . . . It does not stop proliferation, especially to renegade regimes. It is not verifiable. It is not enforceable. And it would stop us from ensuring the safety and reliability of our nation's deterrent, should the need arise. On these crucial matters, it offers only words and false hopes and high intentions—with no guarantees whatever. We can fight the spread of nuclear weapons, but we cannot wish them away with unwise treaties.

Dealing with Russia on essential issues will be far easier if we are dealing with a democratic and free Russia. Our goal is to promote, not only the appearance of democracy in Russia, but the structures, spirit, and reality of democracy. This is clearly not done by focusing our aid and attention on a corrupt and favored elite. Real change in Russia—as in China—will come not from above, but from below. From a rising class of entrepreneurs and business people. From new leaders in Russia's regions who will build a new Russian state, where power is shared, not controlled. Our assistance, investments and loans should go directly to the Russian people, not to enrich the bank accounts of corrupt officials. . . .

Even as we support Russian reform, we cannot excuse Russian brutality. When the Russian government attacks civilians—killing women and children, leaving orphans and refugees—it can no longer expect aid from international lending institutions. The Russian government will discover that it cannot build a stable and unified nation on the ruins of human rights. That it cannot learn the lessons of democracy from the textbook of tyranny. We want to cooperate with Russia on its concern with terrorism, but that is impossible unless Moscow operates with civilized self-restraint.... All our goals in Eurasia will depend on America strengthening the alliances that sustain our influence in Europe and East Asia and the Middle East. Alliances are not just for crises summoned into action when the fire bell sounds. They are sustained by contact and trust. The Gulf War coalition, for example, was raised on the foundation of a president's vision and effort and integrity. Never again should an American president spend nine days in China, and not even bother to stop in Tokyo or Seoul or Manila. Never again should an American president fall silent when China criticizes our security ties with Japan.

For NATO to be strong, cohesive and active, the President must give it consistent direction: on the alliance's purpose; on Europe's need to invest more in defense capabilities; and, when necessary, in military conflict. To be relied upon when they are needed, our allies must be respected when they are not....

Likewise, international organizations can serve the cause of peace. I will never place U.S. troops under UN command—but the UN can help in weapons inspections, peacekeeping and humanitarian efforts. If I am president, America will pay its dues—but only if the UN's bureaucracy is reformed, and our disproportionate share of its costs is reduced. There must also be reform of international financial institutions—the World Bank and the IMF. They can be a source of stability in economic crisis. But they should not impose austerity, bailing out bankers while impoverishing a middle class. They should not prop up failed and corrupt financial systems. These organizations should encourage the basics of economic growth and free markets. Spreading the rule of law and wise budget practices. Promoting sound banking laws and accounting rules. Most of all, these institutions themselves must be more transparent and accountable.

All the aims I've described today are important. But they are not imperial. America has never been an empire. We may be the only great power in history that had the chance, and refused—preferring greatness to power and justice to glory....

The duties of our day are different. But the values of our nation do not change. Let us reject the blinders of isolationism, just as we refuse the crown of empire. Let us not dominate others with our power—or betray them with our indifference. And let us have an American foreign policy that reflects American character. The modesty of true strength. The humility of real greatness.

1.3   Future Nuclear Arms Policy

National Press Club
Washington, DC
May 23, 2000

Today, I am here with some of our nation's leading statesmen and defense experts. And there is broad agreement that our nation needs a new approach to nuclear security that matches a new era.

When it comes to nuclear weapons, the world has changed faster than U.S. policy. The emerging security threats to the United States, its friends and allies and even to Russia now come from rogue states, terrorist groups and other adversaries seeking weapons of mass destruction and the means to deliver them. Threats also come from insecure nuclear stockpiles and the proliferation of dangerous technologies.

Russia itself is no longer our enemy. The cold-war logic that led to creation of massive stockpiles on both sides is now outdated. Our mutual security need no longer depend on a nuclear balance of terror. While deterrence remains the first line of defense against nuclear attack, the standoff of the cold war was born of a different time. . . .

Yet almost a decade after the end of the cold war, our nuclear policy still resides in that already distant past. The Clinton-Gore administration has . . . remained locked in a cold-war mentality. It is time to leave the cold war behind and defend against the new threats of the twenty-first century.

America must build effective missile defenses based on the best available options at the earliest possible date. . . . The Clinton administration at first denied the need for a national missile defense system. Then it delayed. Now the approach it proposes is flawed, a system initially based on a single site, when experts say that more is needed. A missile defense system should not only defend our country; it should defend our allies, with whom I will consult as we develop our plans. And any change in the ABM Treaty must allow the technologies and experiments required to deploy adequate missile defenses. The administration is driving toward a hasty decision on a political timetable. No decision would be better than a flawed agreement that ties the hands of the next president and prevents America from defending itself.

Yet there are positive, practical ways to demonstrate to Russia that we are no longer enemies. Russia, our allies in the world need to understand our intentions. America's development of missile defenses is a search for security, not a search for advantage.

America should rethink the requirements for nuclear deterrence in a new security environment. The premises of cold-war nuclear targeting should no longer dictate the size of our arsenal. As president, I will ask the secretary of defense to conduct an assessment of our nuclear force posture and determine how best to meet our security needs. While the exact number of weapons can come only from such an assessment, I will pursue the lowest possible number consistent with our national security.

It should be possible to reduce the number of American nuclear weapons significantly further than what has been already agreed to under Start II without compromising our security in any way. We should not keep weapons that our military planners do not need. These unneeded weapons are the expensive relics of dead conflicts, and they do nothing to make us more secure.

In addition, the United States should remove as many weapons as possible from high-alert, hair-trigger status. Another unnecessary vestige of cold-war confrontation, preparation for quick launch within minutes after warning of an attack was the rule during the era of superpower rivalry. But today for two nations at peace, keeping so many weapons on high alert may create unacceptable risks of accidental or unauthorized launch.

So as president I will ask for an assessment of what we can safely do to lower the alert status of our forces. These changes to our forces should not require years and years of detailed arms control negotiations. There is a precedent that proves the power of leadership. In 1991, the United States invited the Soviet Union to join it in removing tactical nuclear weapons from the arsenal. Huge reductions were achieved in a matter of months, making the world much safer more quickly. Similarly, in the area of strategic nuclear weapons, we should invite the Russian government to accept the new vision that I have outlined and act on it.

But the United States should be prepared to lead by example because it is in our best interests and the best interests of the world. This would be an act of principled leadership, a chance to seize the moment and begin a new era of nuclear security, a new era of cooperation on proliferation and nuclear safety.

The cold-war era is history. Our nation must recognize new threats, not fixate on old ones. On the issue of nuclear weapons, the United States has an opportunity to lead to a safer world, both to defend against nuclear threats and reduce nuclear tensions. It is possible to build a missile defense and defuse confrontation with Russia. America should do both.

1.4 Century of the Americas

Florida International University
Miami, Florida
August 25, 2000

Those who ignore Latin America do not fully understand America itself. And those who ignore our hemisphere do not fully understand American interests. . . .

This hemisphere, united by geography, has often been divided by history. In the nineteenth century, many strong nations wanted weak neighbors they could dominate. But those days have passed. In the twenty-first century, strong nations will benefit from healthy, confident, democratic neighbors. . . . We seek, not just good neighbors, but strong partners. We seek, not just progress, but shared prosperity. With persistence and courage, we shaped the last century into an American century. With leadership and commitment, this can be the century of the Americas. . . .

The Clinton/Gore administration has had no strategy. We have seen summits without substance, and reaction instead of action. We were promised fast-track trade authority—as every American president has had for twenty-five years. And yet this administration failed to get it. We were promised a Free Trade Area of the Americas. Yet it never happened. Chile was promised partnership in NAFTA. And it was "delayed." . . .

Should I become president, I will look South, not as an afterthought, but as a fundamental commitment of my presidency. Just as we ended the great divide between East and West, so today we can overcome the North-South divide. This begins with a renewed commitment to democracy and freedom in this hemisphere because human freedom, in the long run, is our best weapon against poverty, disease and tyranny. . . .

The United States is destined to have a "special relationship" with Mexico, as clear and strong as we have had with Canada and Great Britain. Historically, we have had no closer friends and allies. And with Canada, our partner in NATO and NAFTA, we share, not just a border, but a bond of good will. Our ties of history and heritage with Mexico are just as deep. Differences are inevitable between us. But they will be differences among family, not between rivals. . . .

We must talk about the availability and cleanliness of water on both sides of the border, about opening the promise of NAFTA to small businesses and entrepreneurs about economic development in areas of Mexico that send illegal immigrants to this country, about improving health and criminal justice in both nations.

Mexico is an emerging success story. Yet elsewhere in this hemisphere, democracy is still on trial—threatened by the false prophets of populism. I look forward to working closely with the nations of this hemisphere but recognize that they cannot be bullied into progress. We will treat all Americans—North, Central and South—with dignity. I will improve our bilateral relations and work with the Organization of American States to confront the problems of our hemisphere.

My administration will strengthen the architecture of democracy in Latin America—the institutions that make democracy real and successful. The basics of democracy should be refreshed with programs that train responsible police and judges. We will encourage professional and civilian-controlled militaries, through contact with our own. The principles of free speech should be advanced through American media exchanges. We will create a new "American Fellows" program, inviting young men and women throughout the Americas to work for a year in various agencies of our government. We will encourage party-building and help monitor elections. These are ways to treat the symptoms of corruption and discord before they turn into violence and abuse of human rights.

To all the nations of Latin America I say: As long as you are on the road toward liberty, you will not be alone. As long as you are moving toward freedom, you will have a steady friend in the United States of America.... Our country is sometimes impatient with the progress of democracy in Latin America. We forget that democracy is a long march. In our country, democracy grew to maturity over time, and only with great work and sacrifice. It is no different today throughout the Americas. America must recognize that not only can our neighbors learn from us, but we can learn from them....

Listening to our neighbors—treating them with dignity—is what I mean by respect. But respect is not unconditional. It must be earned. We will respect those who respect the rights of their citizens. In our hemisphere, there is one clear example where this does not happen. The leadership of Cuba has not even begun the journey to that goal. So I challenge the Castro regime to surprise the world and adopt the ways of democracy. Until it frees political prisoners, and holds free elections and allows free speech, I will keep the sanctions in place....

The first goal in our hemisphere is democracy. Our second goal is free trade in the all the Americas, which will be a step toward free trade in all the world.... If the United States cannot offer new trade with the nations of Latin America, they will find it elsewhere—as they are doing already in new agreements with the European Union.... I don't fault our European friends for making these deals. We dropped the ball, and they're running with it. But we must get back into the game, and here is how I propose to do it.

First, I will secure fast-track authority—the ability to pass or reject trade agreements without amendment....

Our goal will be free trade agreements with all the nations of Latin America. We can do so in cooperation with our NAFTA partners. We should do so with Chile, and Brazil and Argentina, the anchor states of Mercosur. Brazil is the largest economy in Latin America, with such vast economic potential, and our relations must reflect this. We will also work toward free trade with the smaller nations of Central America and the Caribbean. We must be flexible because one-size-fits-all negotiations are not always the answer. But the ultimate goal will remain constant—free trade from northernmost Canada to the tip of Cape Horn.

My administration will foster democracy and level barriers to trade. But we have a third great goal. We must defend the security and stability of our hemisphere against the grave threats of organized crime, narcotics traffickers, and terrorist groups. Forces that work together to subvert economies, corrupt governments and destroy lives.

America cannot blame others for the narcotics trade. After all, we are the market that sustains it. And we have a responsibility to confront this problem, with a balanced policy of education, and treatment and law enforcement....On the supply side, we can help countries like Bolivia and Peru in promoting crop substitutes....

One country particularly ravaged by narco-trafficking is Colombia... Colombia's President, Andres Pastrana, has begun the fight against drugs, corruption and poverty. But the Colombian government must operate from a position of strength. That is why I support the $1.3 billion in aid the Congress has passed and the President has signed. This money should help build up the capabilities of Colombia's armed forces. Even though I do not advocate the use of American troops in battle, our forces can help train the Colombian military. Our aid will help the Colombian government protect its people, fight the drug trade, halt the momentum of the guerillas and bring about a sensible and peaceful resolution to this conflict....

By trading freely we will share with one another and learn from one another. By diplomacy and common enterprise, we will gain a deeper understanding and respect for one another. By defending each other against present dangers, we will secure for ourselves a peaceful future.

Questions to Discuss

1. How do Bush's comments about terrorists, rogue states, and the spread of weapons of mass destruction in Speeches 1.1, 1.2, and 1.3 provide insight into his later actions in the war on terrorism and Iraq?

2. In all of his campaign speeches, Bush focuses on the idea that there is a new era in U.S. foreign policy. What changes occurred in the last decades to create this new era and how did Bush's policies respond to the new conditions?

3. In Speech 1.2, Bush describes a "distinctly American internationalism." Is American foreign policy significantly different from the policies of other countries?

4. In Speeches 1.2 and 1.3, Bush focuses on policies toward America's Cold War enemies, Russia and China. Does his tough rhetoric reflect the tensions of the past or the realities of the uncertain present?

5. In Speech 1.4, Bush argues for a new focus on Latin America. What international conditions are necessary for the United States to shift attention away from its post–World War II focus on Europe and Asia?

Chapter 2

The War on Terrorism

On September 11, 2001 President Bush was in Florida at an event promoting education reform. Upon learning that a plane had flown into the World Trade Center in New York, his first thought was that the pilot had suffered a heart attack. Upon hearing that a second plane had crashed into the other trade tower, his views sharply changed and he recalled thinking, "They had declared war on us . . . we were going to war."[1] After a chaotic day of further attacks and rapid planning, Bush spoke to the country on the evening of 9/11. In his short speech, Bush declared what would become a guiding principle of his presidency: "We will make no distinction between the terrorists who committed these acts and those who harbor them."[2] During the presidential campaign, Bush's lack of foreign policy experience and possible dependence on advisers were major issues. Strikingly, Bush made this momentous declaration without significant consultation with Vice President Dick Cheney, Secretary of State Colin Powell, or Secretary of Defense Donald Rumsfeld.

The attacks of 9/11 and Bush's response to them radically altered his presidency, U.S. foreign policy, and the lives of millions of people around the world. In the coming months, Bush and his advisers began to plan out the war, rally the American public, build an international coalition, and fight the first phase of a global war on terrorism.

Why War?

Terrorism—defined as premeditated, politically motivated violence typically perpetrated against civilians—is not a new phenomenon. Historically, it has been used primarily by weaker groups that would otherwise lose conventional battles. In the past, Americans had been victims of sabotage, hijackings, hostage takings, assassinations, and other terrorist acts. In world and U.S. history, terrorist acts have generally been handled as crimes, prompting police investigations and legal cases. Prior to Bush's presidency, no U.S. president had declared a "war" on terrorism. Bush's use of this term was an important signal of a new, more aggressive policy and reflected four key ideas: 1) 9/11 was viewed as part of a trend in terrorist actions, not an isolated incident, 2) key observers agreed that the al Qaeda terrorist network led by Osama bin Laden represented a new, more dangerous kind of threat, 3) Bush believed that 9/11 highlighted the ineffectiveness of past antiterrorist actions, and 4) Bush felt a personal, visceral hatred of the terrorists.

Although the coordination and destruction of the 9/11 attacks shocked the country, the idea of a terrorist attack on U.S. soil was not a great surprise to knowledgeable observers. During the previous decade, terrorists had detonated a truck bomb at the World Trade Center in 1993, bombed the U.S. military barracks in Saudi Arabia in 1996, heavily damaged U.S. embassies in Kenya and Tanzania in 1998, and attacked the *USS Cole* while it was docked in Yemen in 2000. A number of failed efforts to bomb major sites in New York, hijack airplanes, and so on had also occurred. Total U.S. casualties from these attacks were less than a hundred, but the threat appeared to be ongoing and mounting.

The string of attacks showed that the al Qaeda network presented a new type of threat. Traditionally, terrorist groups had been small, poorly funded, limited in training and equipment, and focused on narrow political aims. Osama bin Laden's network defied each of these stereotypes. Beginning in the late 1980s, bin Laden organized al Qaeda as an international coalition of terrorist groups. By 2001, the network had operatives in over 60 countries. Conservative estimates were that 50,000 people had passed though al Qaeda terrorist training camps. The group was funded in part by bin Laden, the son of a billionaire construction manager. Funds also came from many wealthy supporters in Saudi Arabia and elsewhere. In addition, money was funneled from several charities and less legitimate sources, including drug smuggling. Al Qaeda used money to buy equipment, set up camps, fund specific operations, and help support the Islamic fundamentalist Taliban group as it rose to power in Afghanistan. In turn, the Taliban allowed al Qaeda to set up training camps and other facilities in Afghanistan.

Al Qaeda had more material resources than any previous terrorist organization, but also a broader political agenda. Bin Laden outlined that agenda and its justifications in several speeches and documents, including the 1998 "Declaration of the World Islamic Front for Jihad against the Jews and the Crusaders." In that document, he first discussed three particular problems. First, the United States, since the Gulf War, had based troops in Saudi Arabia, the home of Islam's holiest sites. He argued that the presence of these foreign bases went directly against the prophet Mohammed's deathbed words that followers of no other religion should be allowed in the holy lands. Second, the United States had maintained tough economic sanctions on Iraq that, in bin Laden's eyes, hurt and humiliated average Muslim citizens. Finally, the United States and other Western countries continued to support Israel and its actions against Palestinians. Bin Laden argued that these three problems were not isolated incidents. Rather, these and other actions showed that the West was still engaged in a long-term crusade to dominate and oppress Muslims. According to bin Laden, Westerners sought political influence, control of economic resources such as oil, and the spread of Western culture with its individualism, materialism, and moral laxity. Islamic law held that it was the personal duty of all Muslims to engage in *jihad*, or holy war, against repressors. Thus, bin Laden concluded, "To kill Americans and their allies, both civil and military, is an individual duty of every Muslim who is able, in any country where this is possible."[3] Importantly, the enemies to be attacked included U.S. allies, such as Israel and West European countries, but also governments in the Middle East that had established ties with the West and been corrupted away from Islamic purity. Thus, many terrorist attacks targeted fellow Muslims in Saudi Arabia, Turkey, and so on. Some analysts have suggested that the United States has really been drawn into a long-term civil war between Muslim moderates and fundamentalists such as bin Laden, who hope to bring back what they consider a purer form of Islam.

In a pre-inauguration briefing of Bush and top advisers, CIA director George Tenet listed al Qaeda as one of the top three security threats facing the United States. Furthermore, during the summer of 2001, intercepted communication from known al Qaeda supporters included increased "chatter" that a major strike was coming. Before 9/11, the administration had begun to study ways to increase pressure against al Qaeda, but no major plans had reached the president's desk. These facts led to ongoing questions about intelligence failures in predicting the attacks and whether Bush did all he could to prevent 9/11. Based on the early congressional committee's findings and a general desire to understand the attacks, many victims' families, Democrats, and some Republicans pushed for establishment of an independent commission to investigate 9/11. The administration at first opposed such a commission, citing possible distraction from fighting the war and the top secret nature of intelligence. In November 2002, Bush bowed to ongoing pressure and agreed to a commission, but only after careful negotiations with Congress over its membership and when the commission could subpoena people to testify. Some critics perceived the administration's actions as efforts to either prevent investigation or guarantee that the commission would not place blame on Bush's officials. The commission's 2004 report became a best seller. It gave new insight into the attacks and into systemic failures of U.S. intelligence agencies and policymakers, but did not point a clear finger of blame at any specific person or event before 9/11.

The terrorist attacks of the 1990s did not go uninvestigated or unpunished. For example, four men were convicted for their roles in the first Trade Center attack and sentenced to 240 years in prison each and four others were convicted for their roles in planning the African embassy bombings. Legal actions, though, were often complicated by lack of reliable information and political considerations when attacks occurred abroad. There also was mounting frustration that terrorism was continuing despite convictions. These factors contributed to President Clinton's 1998 authorization of missile attacks against a suspected chemical weapons factory in Sudan and al Qaeda training camps in Afghanistan following the embassy bombings. These missile attacks were onetime warnings, not sustained efforts. Many in the Bush administration later derided them as "pounding sand," because they hit largely empty training camps. Bush concluded further legal actions or limited strikes would have little impact.

Bush also had strong personal feelings against the terrorists. In a telling call from Air Force One the morning of 9/11, Bush told Cheney, "We're going to find out who did this and we're going to kick their asses."[4] On September 16, Bush commented to reporters, "This crusade, this war on terrorism, is going to take awhile."[5] His use of the word crusade drew instant international attention because of its historic and religious connotations. Bush may not have chosen the word intentionally and did not use it subsequently, but he did continue to refer to the terrorists as evil or evildoers. Many politicians would shy away from such terminology, feeling that it would paint the world in black and white terms, or sound as if the United States was on a religious mission. For Bush, his personal and religious views made use of such terms natural. In an interview Bush noted, "Some find it not diplomatic to speak of 'good and evil'. . . . I feel like I represent how the American people feel."[6]

Evidence that 9/11 was part of an emerging pattern of terrorism and that al Qaeda was strong and possibly gaining power, combined with Bush's views that past antiterrorist actions had been too weak and terrorists were evil, left Bush believing the only recourse was war.

Rallying the Country

Once Bush decided to wage a global war on terrorism, he knew that he had to find the right balance of expressing grief over the losses of 9/11 and garnering support to avenge them. He needed to educate the American people about the new world threat of terrorism and about what a war on terrorism would actually involve. Furthermore, he had to focus attention on the actions of al Qaeda, but avoid the appearance of launching a war against Muslims in general, or accepting terrorism by other groups.

Bush tried to address these various goals and rally the American public in a speech to Congress on September 20, 2001 (Speech 2.1). Tellingly, Bush's speech was very similar to one given over fifty years earlier by President Truman as he sought to rally the country for a global war against communism. Truman argued in 1947 that communism posed a growing challenge not only to specific countries, but to peace and freedom worldwide. Second, he contended that countries faced a black and white choice between two alternative ways of life and two different sets of allies. Finally, Truman stated that the postwar United States was in a unique position, and, therefore, had a responsibility to lead global efforts to support all free peoples resisting subjugation and communism.

In Bush's September 20, 2001 speech, he argued that the September 11 attacks demonstrated that international terrorists and their supporters had emerged as the new, global "enemies of freedom." That night and later, Bush compared the terrorists directly to the previous era's totalitarians, arguing that they seek to control every aspect of life and impose their views through violence. Like Truman, Bush argued that no country could be neutral in this conflict: all had to choose between radicalism and freedom, between support for terrorism and support for civilization, between evil and good. Most crucially, Bush echoed Truman in arguing that the United States had a unique global responsibility to defend freedom through direct action or support of others. Bush announced a multifaceted, long term, global war on terrorism "until every terrorist group of global reach has been found, stopped and defeated." He closed with strong comments about the righteousness of the American action.

Declaring the Bush Doctrine of global antiterrorism similar to the Truman Doctrine of global anticommunism had two major benefits. It helped rally public support not for one action, but for a long-term commitment, and it provided the guiding strategic outline many felt to be lacking from U.S. foreign policy since the end of the Cold War. Doctrines, however, come with some dangers to consider: 1) sweeping rhetoric that defines the world in black and white terms can limit tactical options; 2) linking efforts into a grand cause can lead to public disillusionment in the overall cause when specific setbacks occur; 3) an activist United States may be perceived by other countries as an international bully; 4) declaring terrorism to be the number one problem could shift attention away from other issues or skew debates on other important policy goals; and 5) the policy-making system may become too driven by the executive branch, which tends to assert power in times of national crises.

Rallying an International Coalition

To win a global war on terrorism, the United States needed international support. Bush was, therefore, careful to argue that the attacks of 9/11 threatened all civilized countries. He also repeatedly pointed out that people from many countries and faiths had died in the attacks. Initially, international support and solidarity were impressive, but that did not guarantee support for specific U.S. actions. Bush, Powell, and others began making phone calls and meeting with dozens of foreign leaders to rally support.

Bush formalized his requests for assistance in a speech given at the UN General Assembly on November 10, 2001 (Speech 2.2). He argued, "Every nation has a stake in this cause." He stressed that all countries had to work against terrorists or join the Taliban in facing consequences, but could play different roles in the antiterrorist coalition depending on their capabilities. Importantly, he used the word "coalition" rather than "alliance" to show that the group might involve different countries at different times and required no long-term acceptance of U.S. leadership. Again here, Bush closed the speech with words that put the war in grand terms.

Building a global coalition radically reshuffled U.S. alliance patterns. The United States needed its traditional allies, but recruited nontraditional allies as well. Before 9/11, American–Russian relations were tense, but they improved significantly when President Vladimir Putin was one of the first foreign leaders to call Bush and offer aid. China, previously portrayed by Bush as repressive and a rising threat to U.S. power, was welcomed into the coalition. Yemen, previously criticized for human rights violations and for its lack of cooperation in investigating the *USS Cole* bombing, soon was negotiating the arrival of U.S. military trainers and equipment. Heading the list of leaders rehabilitated in U.S. eyes by cooperation on terrorism was Pervez Musharraf of Pakistan. Pakistan was crucial because it borders Afghanistan and its intelligence service had supported the rise of the Taliban. To reward Pakistan for Musharraf's decision to support U.S. actions, Bush waived sanctions imposed as a result of Pakistan's 1998 testing of a nuclear weapon, supported new legislation which would allow him to waive sanctions imposed after Musharraf's 1999 coup, and began planning major aid packages.

Although recognizing the necessity of a coalition, Bush and his advisers did not abandon their unilateralist leanings. Building the coalition would not be allowed to shape the mission. Countries, individually or collectively, that objected to U.S. actions would not be given veto power over those actions. In a key September 15 meeting, Bush told his top advisers, "At some point, we may be the only ones left. That's okay with me. We are America."[7] Bush also maintained his view that the best way to build a coalition was through active leadership that would convince doubters. Bush recounted at an NSC meeting that, when a European leader had suggested the need for increased consultation and discussions, he had responded "My belief is the best way that we hold this coalition together is to be clear on our objectives and to be clear that we are determined to achieve them. You hold a coalition together by strong leadership and that's what we intend to provide."[8] Clearly, the global war on terrorism would be directed from Washington, not Europe, the UN, or elsewhere.

Phase One in the War on Terrorism: Challenging al Qaeda

In the first months of the war on terrorism, the United States concentrated on four areas: building intelligence networks, limiting the financial resources of terrorists, taking direct action against al Qaeda globally, and fighting in Afghanistan. Many felt the 9/11 attacks indicated the inadequacy and poor coordination of U.S. intelligence operations. Domestically, the administration tried to correct these problems by supporting the Patriot Act, which granted law enforcement new powers of investigation, and by establishing a director of Homeland Security, who would coordinate a diverse array of intelligence and law enforcement programs. Internationally, the administration sought new sources and increased coordination with other intelligence services, including those of formerly unfriendly countries, such as Syria and Sudan.

The attacks of September 11 were not expensive operations, but past evidence showed that limiting terrorists' financial capabilities often limited the frequency and scale of attacks. On September 24, 2001, Bush signed Executive Order 13224 blocking the U.S. funds of terrorists and anyone associated with them. The United States then led efforts to pass UN Security Council Resolution 1373, which froze assets on a global basis. Bush highlighted the efforts' importance by insisting that he, not Secretary of the Treasury Paul O'Neill, announce the measures. The financial efforts were complicated by a number of factors: terrorists naturally did not declare their intentions when opening bank accounts, some of the money raised by terrorists came through charities and other organizations, and crackdowns were politically sensitive in the Middle East because quite prominent people were believed to have financial ties to al Qaeda. Still, assets of 210 entities and individuals in the United States were blocked within six months. Internationally, 161 countries and jurisdictions took financial actions to freeze over $116 million in assets. These numbers spoke to both the administration's success in building a coalition and the previous financial strength of al Qaeda.

Most dramatic were direct actions taken against specific suspects. Hundreds were arrested throughout the United States, Western Europe, Asia, and the Middle East. Some were later released for lack of evidence, but many terrorist cells were broken. True war, though, required attacking the trainers and leaders of the movement. In the first days after 9/11, officials debated where to focus military strikes. Afghanistan was a clear target, but Rumsfeld suggested that the idea of a global war would be furthered by taking simultaneous global action. Deputy Secretary of Defense Paul Wolfowitz suggested that Iraq was the ideal second front. The president and his top advisers discussed the Iraq option in depth, but no top official supported immediate action. Bush, therefore, decided to focus on Afghanistan. He then chose to include U.S. ground troops, the most aggressive of three options presented to him. Bush also chose to keep control of military operations in American, rather than NATO or UN, hands.

Fighting a war in Afghanistan presented a number of problems. First, the United States had to answer "who was the enemy?" Al Qaeda had attacked the United States, but Bush also held the Taliban responsible. The groups had connections, but were distinct and based in different areas. Also, many Afghanis supported neither al Qaeda nor the Taliban, so could become innocent victims. Second, the political situation in Afghanistan was extremely complex. The Taliban controlled the majority of the territory, but they were just one faction in a decades-long civil war and still faced a major foe in the Northern Alliance. Taliban and Northern Alliance loyalties were based not only on ethnic divisions, but also on personal grudges and political expediency. Any U.S. action would be seen as favoring one group or faction in the civil war and could lead to long-term instability if foreign troops were removed quickly after victory. Finally, Afghanistan presented serious military challenges. The United States had no major military bases in the region, so introducing ground troops was difficult. Even bombing had to wait until the military could establish bases for search and recovery missions. The United States had limited ground intelligence and no history of ties to key factions. Afghanistan is a mountainous country, with little transportation infrastructure and brutal winters. The problems these factors could cause were highlighted in the 1980s when the Soviet Union's military had invaded Afghanistan and been unable to defeat local fighters. Many years of civil war and general poverty also meant that Afghanistan had few clear targets to attack. One last consideration was that Bush wanted to begin a massive humanitarian assistance campaign as soon as the military started attacking.

Bush pressed for quick military action and the U.S. attacks began on October 7. During the first weeks, the military attacked primarily with planes and missiles, while a small group of CIA operatives helped coordinate Northern Alliance troops and tried to win over local leaders with promises of arms and cash. There was no immediate surrender and soon it was unclear what was left to bomb from the air. Many in the press, and even some in the administration, began to question the military's tactics and whether the United States was headed for a Vietnam-like quagmire in both Afghanistan and the broader war on terrorism. In November, with more U.S. troops on the ground and key victories by the Northern Alliance, the momentum of the war changed in a matter of days and the Taliban were completely defeated. An estimated 10,000 Taliban and 1,000 civilians were killed. The training bases were destroyed and al Qaeda's leadership fled. Only a handful of U.S. soldiers were killed in battle. United States forces then turned their attention to the Tora Bora region in eastern Afghanistan, where bin Laden and others were believed to be living in caves. The United States pounded the region, but relied on local troops and Pakistani soldiers to guard the border to Pakistan. It is believed top al Qaeda officials were able to slip across the border. Thus, the first phase of the war on terrorism had no dramatic finale because bin Laden and other leaders remained at large.

Phase Two in the War on Terrorism: "The Axis of Evil"

On January 29, 2002, Bush went before Congress to present his first State of the Union Address (Speech 2.3). The speech was radically different from what anyone might have anticipated a year earlier. Bush, a man elected despite his lack of foreign policy credentials, now drew ovation after ovation for his leadership in the war on terrorism. More than half of the speech was devoted to the war. Even some domestic priorities were expressed in the context of the war. Bush outlined how the country had responded to 9/11 and what he saw as the successes of the first phase of operations. He then symbolically opened the second phase of the war by stating that countries that sponsor terrorism and pursue WMD, notably North Korea, Iran, and Iraq, "and their terrorist allies, constitute an axis of evil, arming to threaten the peace of the world."

"Axis of Evil" was a phrase coined by Bush's top speechwriter Michael Gerson as a modification of another speechwriter's idea of an "axis of hatred" between Iraq and terrorists. Gerson intentionally employed the word "evil" to reinforce that the war was not simply a political or military dispute, but a clash of deepest values. The word "axis" conjured up Hitler's Axis powers of World War II. North Korea, Iran, and Iraq were singled out, but before the speech administration officials debated dropping Iran and adding others, such as Syria, to the list.

Bush suggested that the axis countries could provide terrorists with weapons "giving them the means to match their hatred." Bin Laden was known to be interested in obtaining nuclear arms and few doubted that he would use them. In addition, the axis could directly use its weapons to attack, blackmail, and terrorize the United States and its allies. Many administration officials had been worried about WMD for years. Even before his election, Bush had spoken about addressing new threats, but 9/11 extended these fears and policy possibilities to a different set of scenarios and a different set of enemies.

Reaction to the axis of evil phrase was mixed. Some observers supported the president's contentions and argued that it was better to err on the side of action given the tremendous stakes. Others questioned the existence of a cooperative axis. North Korea had no known ideological ties to either Iran or Iraq. Iran and Iraq were long-time enemies that had fought an extremely brutal, eight-year war in the 1980s. The real focus of the phrase, though, was the possible connection between axis states and terrorists. All three countries were on the U.S. government's list of states sponsoring terrorism. North Korea was on the list mainly because of kidnappings in the 1970s. Iraq was believed to support some terrorists, but was not a major supplier. In addition, Saddam was a secular leader who had repressed religious groups, so any ties to al Qaeda would be strained. Iran was a major supporter of Islamic terrorists, but the Iranians mostly followed the Shi'a branch of Islam, while the Taliban and most of al Qaeda followed the Sunni branch. Also, reformers had recently gained some power, so future ties to terrorists were less certain. The one idea shared by all axis members and al Qaeda was anti-Americanism. The question was whether a common enemy could unite such a diverse group.

Other critics argued that by putting such different countries into a single group, the United States could trap itself into a one size fits all policy. North Korea was believed to have more advanced technology than the other two countries, but also was operating under a 1994 agreement with the United States to end nuclear weapons development. Iraq's weapons programs were hurt significantly during the Persian Gulf War and remained subject to UN inspection. Iran was thought to be pursuing weapons, but many Europeans and others hoped that Iran's goals could be altered. Given their different levels of technology and different political realities, designing a single successful policy might prove impossible. Tough rhetoric and policies could also backfire, if they pushed anti-American nationalists back to prominence. Furthermore, critics suggested that focusing on the axis countries threatened to distract time and resources from the ongoing war against al Qaeda.

New Strategy for a New War

The axis of evil idea also showed an important switch in Bush's thinking: given the potential destructiveness of a well-armed terrorist, the United States could not risk further attacks, so it had to go on the offensive and challenge enemies before they could obtain weapons or attack. This idea was further delineated in a June 1, 2002 Bush speech at West Point (Speech 2.4) and was formalized in the *National Security Strategy* issued in September 2002. Bush argued that the possibility of terrorists acquiring WMD meant existing strategies of containment and deterrence could no longer be relied upon to preserve U.S. security. Containment was the concept at the center of U.S. policy during the Cold War. The United States would contain the spread of communism, much as one might contain and isolate an infectious disease. Deterrence was the central principle of the nuclear age. Deterrence focused on preventing actions by threatening retaliation so great that no rational person would strike first. Bush argued that terrorism could not be contained in the same way as previous threats since it was stateless and that deterrence was ineffective against terrorists since there was no base or citizens to retaliate against and because one could not guarantee rationality among terrorists.

In this new, threatening world, Bush argued, "We must take the battle to the enemy, disrupt his plans, and confront the worst threats before they emerge." In other words, the United States needed a strategy of "preemption." The idea of preemption is well established within international law and practice. For example, in 1967, when Arab countries massed forces on Israel's border and threatened to invade, most of the world agreed that Israel could preemptively bomb those forces and still claim to be fighting a defensive war. This scenario parallels the idea that if you are followed into a dark alley and threatened with a gun, you have a legal right to defend yourself without waiting for your assailant to actually shoot you. What Bush was really suggesting, though, was not wars of "preemption"—responding to a clear, imminent threat, but rather wars of "prevention"—responding to the possibility of danger in the future. The latter is more analogous to Israel's controversial 1981 bombing of a nuclear facility at Osiraq to inhibit Iraq's nuclear development. To use the previous personal example, it is comparable to using force before you reach the alley, because the person following you seems threatening and the bulge in his pocket appears to be a weapon. Hesitancy to act in the alley might cost you your wallet; whereas hesitancy with a nuclear-armed enemy might cost millions of lives. Bush felt the possible loss of millions justified a low threshold for perceiving suspicious intent and capabilities.

The strategy of prevention has been questioned on three main grounds. First, some feel that it makes the United States judge, jury, and executioner for the world. If a state appears dangerous, the strategy allows the United States to attack across lines of state sovereignty, even without UN approval, and claim legally justifiable, defensive action. The line between such an action and imperialism is not well defined. Second, the basis for defining a threat that justifies action is unclear. Would it rest on presumed intentions, so that only countries perceived to be aggressive would be stopped from attaining WMD? Would it rest solely on weapons capability? If so, how early in the weapons development process could the United States act and how could it ensure that its intelligence on capabilities was correct? A third widely discussed problem is one of precedent. If the United States is justified in acting preventively, other countries could argue similar justification. For example, India could attack Pakistan, arguing it was preventing a future attack from a known enemy. Russia could crackdown harshly on Chechnya citing the need for security. Terrorists or axis states themselves could argue that they had to strike the United States before the United States could strike them. Many of these questions remain theoretical, but some were soon tested in the war in Iraq.

2.1 Declaring a War on Terrorism

United States Capitol
Washington, DC
September 20, 2001

In the normal course of events, Presidents come to this chamber to report on the state of the Union. Tonight, no such report is needed. It has already been delivered by the American people.

We have seen it in the courage of passengers, who rushed terrorists to save others on the ground.... We have seen the state of our Union in the endurance of rescuers, working past exhaustion. We have seen the unfurling of flags, the lighting of candles, the giving of blood, the saying of prayers—in English, Hebrew, and Arabic. We have seen the decency of a loving and giving people who have made the grief of strangers their own.

My fellow citizens, for the last nine days, the entire world has seen for itself the state of our Union—and it is strong.

Tonight we are a country awakened to danger and called to defend freedom. Our grief has turned to anger, and anger to resolution. Whether we bring our enemies to justice, or bring justice to our enemies, justice will be done....

And on behalf of the American people, I thank the world for its outpouring of support. America will never forget the sounds of our National Anthem playing at Buckingham Palace, on the streets of Paris, and at Berlin's Brandenburg Gate....

Nor will we forget the citizens of 80 other nations who died with our own: dozens of Pakistanis; more than 130 Israelis; more than 250 citizens of India; men and women from El Salvador, Iran, Mexico and Japan; and hundreds of British citizens. America has no truer friend than Great Britain. Once again, we are joined together in a great cause—so honored the British Prime Minister has crossed an ocean to show his unity of purpose with America. Thank you for coming, friend.

On September the 11th, enemies of freedom committed an act of war against our country. Americans have known wars—but for the past 136 years, they have been wars on foreign soil, except for one Sunday in 1941. Americans have known the casualties of war—but not at the center of a great city on a peaceful morning. Americans have known surprise attacks—but never before on thousands of civilians. All of this was brought upon us in a single day—and night fell on a different world, a world where freedom itself is under attack.

Americans have many questions tonight. Americans are asking, "Who attacked our country?" The evidence we have gathered all points to a collection of loosely affiliated terrorist organizations known as al Qaeda. They are the same murderers indicted for bombing American embassies in Tanzania and Kenya, and responsible for bombing the USS Cole.

Al Qaeda is to terror what the Mafia is to crime. But its goal is not making money; its goal is remaking the world—and imposing its radical beliefs on people everywhere.

The terrorists practice a fringe form of Islamic extremism that has been rejected by Muslim scholars and the vast majority of Muslim clerics—a fringe movement that perverts the peaceful teachings of Islam. The terrorists' directive commands them to kill Christians and Jews, to kill all Americans, and make no distinction among military and civilians, including women and children.

This group and its leader—a person named Osama bin Laden—are linked to many other organizations in different countries, including the Egyptian Islamic Jihad and the Islamic Movement of Uzbekistan. There are thousands of these terrorists in more than 60 countries. They are recruited from their own nations and neighborhoods and brought to camps in places like Afghanistan, where they are trained in the tactics of terror. They are sent back to their homes or sent to hide in countries around the world to plot evil and destruction.

The leadership of al Qaeda has great influence in Afghanistan and supports the Taliban regime in controlling most of that country. In Afghanistan, we see al Qaeda's vision for the world.

Afghanistan's people have been brutalized—many are starving and many have fled. Women are not allowed to attend school. You can be jailed for owning a television. Religion can be practiced only as their leaders dictate. A man can be jailed in Afghanistan if his beard is not long enough.

The United States respects the people of Afghanistan—after all, we are currently its largest source of humanitarian aid—but we condemn the Taliban regime.... And tonight, the United States of America makes the following demands on the Taliban: Deliver to United States authorities all the leaders of al Qaeda who hide in your land. Release all foreign nationals, including American citizens, you have unjustly imprisoned. Protect foreign journalists, diplomats and aid workers in your country. Close immediately and permanently every terrorist training camp in Afghanistan, and hand over every terrorist, and every person in their support structure, to appropriate authorities. Give the United States full access to terrorist training camps, so we can make sure they are no longer operating.

These demands are not open to negotiation or discussion. The Taliban must act, and act immediately. They will hand over the terrorists, or they will share in their fate.

I also want to speak tonight directly to Muslims throughout the world. We respect your faith. It's practiced freely by many millions of Americans, and by millions more in countries that America counts as friends. Its teachings are good and peaceful, and those who commit evil in the name of Allah blaspheme the name of Allah. The terrorists are traitors to their own faith, trying, in effect, to hijack Islam itself. The enemy of America is not our many Muslim friends; it is not our many Arab friends. Our enemy is a radical network of terrorists, and every government that supports them.

Our war on terror begins with al Qaeda, but it does not end there. It will not end until every terrorist group of global reach has been found, stopped and defeated.

Americans are asking, why do they hate us? They hate what we see right here in this chamber—a democratically elected government. Their leaders are self-appointed. They hate our freedoms—our freedom of religion, our freedom of speech, our freedom to vote and assemble and disagree with each other.

They want to overthrow existing governments in many Muslim countries, such as Egypt, Saudi Arabia, and Jordan. They want to drive Israel out of the Middle East. They want to drive Christians and Jews out of vast regions of Asia and Africa.

These terrorists kill not merely to end lives, but to disrupt and end a way of life. With every atrocity, they hope that America grows fearful, retreating from the world and forsaking our friends. They stand against us, because we stand in their way.

We are not deceived by their pretenses to piety. We have seen their kind before. They are the heirs of all the murderous ideologies of the twentieth century. By sacrificing human life to serve their radical visions—by abandoning every value except the will to power—they follow in the path of fascism, and Nazism, and totalitarianism. And they will follow that path all the way, to where it ends: in history's unmarked grave of discarded lies.

Americans are asking: How will we fight and win this war? We will direct every resource at our command—every means of diplomacy, every tool of intelligence, every instrument of law enforcement, every financial influence, and every necessary weapon of war—to the disruption and to the defeat of the global terror network. . . .

Our response involves far more than instant retaliation and isolated strikes. Americans should not expect one battle, but a lengthy campaign, unlike any other we have ever seen. It may include dramatic strikes, visible on TV, and covert operations, secret even in success. We will starve terrorists of funding, turn them one against another, drive them from place to place, until there is no refuge or no rest. And we will pursue nations that provide aid or safe haven to terrorism. Every nation, in every region, now has a decision to make. Either you are with us, or you are with the terrorists. From this day forward, any nation that continues to harbor or support terrorism will be regarded by the United States as a hostile regime.

Our nation has been put on notice: We are not immune from attack. We will take defensive measures against terrorism to protect Americans. Today, dozens of federal departments and agencies, as well as state and local governments, have responsibilities affecting homeland security. These efforts must be coordinated at the highest level. So tonight I announce the creation of a Cabinet-level position reporting directly to me— the Office of Homeland Security. . . .

These measures are essential. But the only way to defeat terrorism as a threat to our way of life is to stop it, eliminate it, and destroy it where it grows.

Many will be involved in this effort, from FBI agents to intelligence operatives to the reservists we have called to active duty. All deserve our thanks, and all have our prayers. And tonight, a few miles from the damaged Pentagon, I have a message for our military: Be ready. I've called the Armed Forces to alert, and there is a reason. The hour is coming when America will act, and you will make us proud.

This is not, however, just America's fight. And what is at stake is not just America's freedom. This is the world's fight. This is civilization's fight. This is the fight of all who believe in progress and pluralism, tolerance and freedom.

We ask every nation to join us. We will ask, and we will need, the help of police forces, intelligence services, and banking systems around the world. The United States is grateful that many nations and many international organizations have already responded—with sympathy and with support. Nations from Latin America, to Asia, to Africa, to Europe, to the Islamic world. Perhaps the NATO Charter reflects best the attitude of the world: An attack on one is an attack on all. . . .

Americans are asking: What is expected of us? I ask you to live your lives, and hug your children. I know many citizens have fears tonight, and I ask you to be calm and resolute, even in the face of a continuing threat. . . . Tonight I thank my fellow Americans for what you have already done and for what you will do. And ladies and gentlemen of the

Congress, I thank you, their representatives, for what you have already done and for what we will do together.

Tonight, we face new and sudden national challenges. We will come together to improve air safety, to dramatically expand the number of air marshals on domestic flights, and take new measures to prevent hijacking. We will come together to promote stability and keep our airlines flying, with direct assistance during this emergency. We will come together to give law enforcement the additional tools it needs to track down terror here at home. We will come together to strengthen our intelligence capabilities to know the plans of terrorists before they act, and find them before they strike. We will come together to take active steps that strengthen America's economy, and put our people back to work. . . .

After all that has just passed—all the lives taken, and all the possibilities and hopes that died with them—it is natural to wonder if America's future is one of fear. Some speak of an age of terror. I know there are struggles ahead, and dangers to face. But this country will define our times, not be defined by them. As long as the United States of America is determined and strong, this will not be an age of terror; this will be an age of liberty, here and across the world.

Great harm has been done to us. We have suffered great loss. And in our grief and anger we have found our mission and our moment. Freedom and fear are at war. The advance of human freedom—the great achievement of our time, and the great hope of every time—now depends on us. Our nation—this generation—will lift a dark threat of violence from our people and our future. We will rally the world to this cause by our efforts, by our courage. We will not tire, we will not falter, and we will not fail. . . .

I will not forget this wound to our country or those who inflicted it. I will not yield; I will not rest; I will not relent in waging this struggle for freedom and security for the American people.

The course of this conflict is not known, yet its outcome is certain. Freedom and fear, justice and cruelty, have always been at war, and we know that God is not neutral between them. Fellow citizens, we'll meet violence with patient justice—assured of the rightness of our cause, and confident of the victories to come.

2.2 President Bush Speaks to the UN

United Nations General Assembly
New York, New York
November 10, 2001

We meet in a hall devoted to peace, in a city scarred by violence, in a nation awakened to danger, in a world uniting for a long struggle. Every civilized nation here today is resolved to keep the most basic commitment of civilization: We will defend ourselves and our future against terror and lawless violence.

The United Nations was founded in this cause. In a second world war, we learned there is no isolation from evil. We affirmed that some crimes are so terrible they offend humanity, itself. And we resolved that the aggressions and ambitions of the wicked must be opposed early, decisively, and collectively, before they threaten us all. That evil has returned, and that cause is renewed. . . .

The suffering of September the 11th was inflicted on people of many faiths and many nations. All of the victims, including Muslims, were killed with equal indifference and equal satisfaction by the terrorist leaders. The terrorists are violating the tenets of every religion, including the one they invoke. . . .

Time is passing. Yet, for the United States of America, there will be no forgetting September the 11th. We will remember every rescuer who died in honor. We will remember every family that lives in grief. We will remember the fire and ash, the last phone calls, the funerals of the children. And the people of my country will remember those who have plotted against us. We are learning their names. We are coming to know their faces. There is no corner of the Earth distant or dark enough to protect them. However long it takes, their hour of justice will come.

Every nation has a stake in this cause. As we meet, the terrorists are planning more murder—perhaps in my country, or perhaps in yours. They kill because they aspire to dominate. They seek to overthrow governments and destabilize entire regions. . . .

Few countries meet their exacting standards of brutality and oppression. Every other country is a potential target. And all the world faces the most horrifying prospect of all: These same terrorists are searching for weapons of mass destruction, the tools to turn their hatred into holocaust.

They can be expected to use chemical, biological and nuclear weapons the moment they are capable of doing so. No hint of conscience would prevent it.

This threat cannot be ignored. This threat cannot be appeased. Civilization, itself, the civilization we share, is threatened. History will record our response, and judge or justify every nation in this hall.

The civilized world is now responding. We act to defend ourselves and deliver our children from a future of fear. We choose the dignity of life over a culture of death. We choose lawful change and civil disagreement over coercion, subversion, and chaos. . . .

The conspiracies of terror are being answered by an expanding global coalition. Not every nation will be a part of every action against the enemy. But every nation in our coalition has duties. . . .

Some nations want to play their part in the fight against terror, but tell us they lack the means to enforce their laws and control their borders. We stand ready to help. Some governments still turn a blind eye to the terrorists, hoping the threat will pass them by. They are mistaken. And some governments, while pledging to uphold the principles of the UN, have cast their lot with the terrorists. They support them and harbor them, and they will find that their welcome guests are parasites that will weaken them, and eventually consume them.

For every regime that sponsors terror, there is a price to be paid. And it will be paid. The allies of terror are equally guilty of murder and equally accountable to justice.

The Taliban are now learning this lesson—that regime and the terrorists who support it are now virtually indistinguishable. Together they promote terror abroad and impose a reign of terror on the Afghan people. . . . .The United States, supported by many nations, is bringing justice to the terrorists in Afghanistan. We're making progress against military targets, and that is our objective. Unlike the enemy, we seek to minimize, not maximize, the loss of innocent life. . . .

I make this promise to all the victims of that regime: The Taliban's days of harboring terrorists and dealing in heroin and brutalizing women are drawing to a close. And when that regime is gone, the people of Afghanistan will say with the rest of the world: good riddance.

I can promise, too, that America will join the world in helping the people of Afghanistan rebuild their country. Many nations, including mine, are sending food and medicine to help Afghans through the winter. America has air-dropped over 1.3 million packages of rations into Afghanistan. Just this week, we air-lifted 20,000 blankets and over 200 tons of provisions into the region. We continue to provide humanitarian aid, even while the Taliban tried to steal the food we send.

More help eventually will be needed. The United States will work closely with the United Nations and development banks to reconstruct Afghanistan after hostilities there have ceased and the Taliban are no longer in control. And the United States will work with the UN to support a post-Taliban government that represents all of the Afghan people.

In this war of terror, each of us must answer for what we have done or what we have left undone. After tragedy, there is a time for sympathy and condolence. And my country has been very grateful for both. The memorials and vigils around the world will not be forgotten. But the time for sympathy has now passed; the time for action has now arrived.

The most basic obligations in this new conflict have already been defined by the United Nations. On September the 28th, the Security Council adopted Resolution 1373. Its requirements are clear: Every United Nations member has a responsibility to crack down on terrorist financing. We must pass all necessary laws in our own countries to allow the confiscation of terrorist assets. We must apply those laws to every financial institution in every nation.

We have a responsibility to share intelligence and coordinate the efforts of law enforcement. If you know something, tell us. If we know something, we'll tell you. And when we find the terrorists, we must work together to bring them to justice. We have a responsibility to deny any sanctuary, safe haven or transit to terrorists. Every known terrorist camp must be shut down, its operators apprehended, and evidence of their arrest presented to the United Nations. We have a responsibility to deny weapons to terrorists and to actively prevent private citizens from providing them.

These obligations are urgent and they are binding on every nation with a place in this chamber. Many governments are taking these obligations seriously, and my country appreciates it. Yet, even beyond Resolution 1373, more is required, and more is expected of our coalition against terror.

We're asking for a comprehensive commitment to this fight. We must unite in opposing all terrorists, not just some of them. In this world there are good causes and bad causes, and we may disagree on where the line is drawn. Yet, there is no such thing as a good terrorist. No national aspiration, no remembered wrong can ever justify the deliberate murder of the innocent. Any government that rejects this principle, trying to pick and choose its terrorist friends, will know the consequences. . . .

The war against terror must not serve as an excuse to persecute ethnic and religious minorities in any country. Innocent people must be allowed to live their own lives, by their own customs, under their own religion. And every nation must have avenues for the peaceful expression of opinion and dissent. When these avenues are closed, the temptation to speak through violence grows.

We must press on with our agenda for peace and prosperity in every land.... The American government also stands by its commitment to a just peace in the Middle East. We are working toward a day when two states, Israel and Palestine, live peacefully together within secure and recognize borders as called for by the Security Council resolutions. We will do all in our power to bring both parties back into negotiations. But peace will only come when all have sworn off, forever, incitement, violence and terror.

The steps I described will not be easy. For all nations, they will require effort. For some nations, they will require great courage. Yet, the cost of inaction is far greater. The only alternative to victory is a nightmare world where every city is a potential killing field.

As I've told the American people, freedom and fear are at war. We face enemies that hate not our policies, but our existence; the tolerance of openness and creative culture that defines us. But the outcome of this conflict is certain: There is a current in history and it runs toward freedom. Our enemies resent it and dismiss it, but the dreams of mankind are defined by liberty—the natural right to create and build and worship and live in dignity....

We did not ask for this mission, yet there is honor in history's call. We have a chance to write the story of our times, a story of courage defeating cruelty and light overcoming darkness. This calling is worthy of any life, and worthy of every nation. So let us go forward, confident, determined, and unafraid.

2.3 2002 State of the Union Address

United States Capitol
Washington, DC
January 29, 2002

As we gather tonight, our nation is at war, our economy is in recession, and the civilized world faces unprecedented dangers. Yet the state of our Union has never been stronger.

We last met in an hour of shock and suffering. In four short months, our nation has comforted the victims, begun to rebuild New York and the Pentagon, rallied a great coalition, captured, arrested, and rid the world of thousands of terrorists, destroyed Afghanistan's terrorist training camps, saved a people from starvation, and freed a country from brutal oppression.

The American flag flies again over our embassy in Kabul. Terrorists who once occupied Afghanistan now occupy cells at Guantanamo Bay. And terrorist leaders who urged followers to sacrifice their lives are running for their own. America and Afghanistan are now allies against terror. We'll be partners in rebuilding that country. . . .

Our progress is a tribute to the spirit of the Afghan people, to the resolve of our coalition, and to the might of the United States military. When I called our troops into action, I did so with complete confidence in their courage and skill. And tonight, thanks to them, we are winning the war on terror. The men and women of our Armed Forces have delivered a message now clear to every enemy of the United States: Even 7,000 miles away, across oceans and continents, on mountaintops and in caves—you will not escape the justice of this nation. . . .

Our cause is just, and it continues. Our discoveries in Afghanistan confirmed our worst fears, and showed us the true scope of the task ahead. We have seen the depth of our enemies' hatred in videos, where they laugh about the loss of innocent life. And the depth of their hatred is equaled by the madness of the destruction they design. We have found diagrams of American nuclear power plants and public water facilities, detailed in-structions for making chemical weapons, surveillance maps of American cities, and thorough descriptions of landmarks in America and throughout the world.

What we have found in Afghanistan confirms that, far from ending there, our war against terror is only beginning.... Thanks to the work of our law enforcement officials and coalition partners, hundreds of terrorists have been arrested. Yet, tens of thousands of trained terrorists are still at large. These enemies view the entire world as a battlefield, and we must pursue them wherever they are....

Our nation will continue to be steadfast and patient and persistent in the pursuit of two great objectives. First, we will shut down terrorist camps, disrupt terrorist plans, and bring terrorists to justice. And, second, we must prevent the terrorists and regimes who seek chemical, biological or nuclear weapons from threatening the United States and the world.

Our military has put the terror training camps of Afghanistan out of business, yet camps still exist in at least a dozen countries. A terrorist underworld—including groups like Hamas, Hezbollah, Islamic Jihad, Jaish-i-Mohammed—operates in remote jungles and deserts, and hides in the centers of large cities.

While the most visible military action is in Afghanistan, America is acting elsewhere. We now have troops in the Philippines, helping to train that country's armed forces to go after terrorist cells that have executed an American, and still hold hostages. Our soldiers, working with the Bosnian government, seized terrorists who were plotting to bomb our embassy. Our Navy is patrolling the coast of Africa to block the shipment of weapons and the establishment of terrorist camps in Somalia.

My hope is that all nations will heed our call, and eliminate the terrorist parasites who threaten their countries and our own. Many nations are acting forcefully. Pakistan is now cracking down on terror, and I admire the strong leadership of President Musharraf.

But some governments will be timid in the face of terror. And make no mistake about it: If they do not act, America will.

Our second goal is to prevent regimes that sponsor terror from threatening America or our friends and allies with weapons of mass destruction. Some of these regimes have been pretty quiet since September the 11th. But we know their true nature. North Korea is a regime arming with missiles and weapons of mass destruction, while starving its citizens.

Iran aggressively pursues these weapons and exports terror, while an unelected few repress the Iranian people's hope for freedom.

Iraq continues to flaunt its hostility toward America and to support terror. The Iraqi regime has plotted to develop anthrax, and nerve gas, and nuclear weapons for over a decade. This is a regime that has already used poison gas to murder thousands of its own citizens—leaving the bodies of mothers huddled over their dead children. This is a regime that agreed to international inspections—then kicked out the inspectors. This is a regime that has something to hide from the civilized world.

States like these, and their terrorist allies, constitute an axis of evil, arming to threaten the peace of the world. By seeking weapons of mass destruction, these regimes pose a grave and growing danger. They could provide these arms to terrorists, giving them the means to match their hatred. They could attack our allies or attempt to blackmail the United States. In any of these cases, the price of indifference would be catastrophic.

We will work closely with our coalition to deny terrorists and their state sponsors the materials, technology, and expertise to make and deliver weapons of mass destruction. We will develop and deploy effective missile defenses to protect America and our allies from sudden attack. And all nations should know: America will do what is necessary to ensure our nation's security.

We'll be deliberate, yet time is not on our side. I will not wait on events, while dangers gather. I will not stand by, as peril draws closer and closer. The United States of America will not permit the world's most dangerous regimes to threaten us with the world's most destructive weapons. Our war on terror is well begun, but it is only begun. This campaign may not be finished on our watch—yet it must be and it will be waged on our watch. . . .

September the 11th brought out the best in America, and the best in this Congress. And I join the American people in applauding your unity and resolve. Now Americans deserve to have this same spirit directed toward addressing problems here at home. I'm a proud member of my party—yet as we act to win the war, protect our people, and create jobs in America, we must act, first and foremost, not as Republicans, not as Democrats, but as Americans.

It costs a lot to fight this war. We have spent more than a billion dollars a month—over $30 million a day—and we must be prepared for future operations. . . . Our men and women in uniform deserve the best weapons, the best equipment, the best training—and they also deserve another pay raise. My budget includes the largest increase in defense spending in two decades—because while the price of freedom and security is high, it is never too high. Whatever it costs to defend our country, we will pay.

The next priority of my budget is to do everything possible to protect our citizens and strengthen our nation against the ongoing threat of another attack. Time and distance from the events of September the 11th will not make us safer unless we act on its lessons. America is no longer protected by vast oceans. We are protected from attack only by vigorous action abroad, and increased vigilance at home. My budget nearly doubles funding for a sustained strategy of homeland security, focused on four key areas: bioterrorism, emergency response, airport and border security, and improved intelligence....

Once we have funded our national security and our homeland security, the final great priority of my budget is economic security for the American people. To achieve these great national objectives—to win the war, protect the homeland, and revitalize our economy—our budget will run a deficit that will be small and short-term, so long as Congress restrains spending and acts in a fiscally responsible manner....

During these last few months, I've been humbled and privileged to see the true character of this country in a time of testing. Our enemies believed America was weak and materialistic, that we would splinter in fear and selfishness. They were as wrong as they are evil.... None of us would ever wish the evil that was done on September the 11th. Yet after America was attacked, it was as if our entire country looked into a mirror and saw our better selves. We were reminded that we are citizens, with obligations to each other, to our country, and to history. We began to think less of the goods we can accumulate, and more about the good we can do....

All fathers and mothers, in all societies, want their children to be educated, and live free from poverty and violence. No people on Earth yearn to be oppressed, or aspire to servitude, or eagerly await the midnight knock of the secret police.... No nation owns these aspirations, and no nation is exempt from them. We have no intention of imposing our culture. But America will always stand firm for the non-negotiable demands of human dignity: the rule of law; limits on the power of the state; respect for women; private property; free speech; equal justice; and religious tolerance.... We seek a just and peaceful world beyond the war on terror.

In this moment of opportunity, a common danger is erasing old rivalries. America is working with Russia and China and India, in ways we have never before, to achieve peace and prosperity. In every region, free markets and free trade and free societies are proving their power to lift lives. Together with friends and allies from Europe to Asia, and Africa to Latin America, we will demonstrate that the forces of terror cannot stop the momentum of freedom....

In a single instant, we realized that this will be a decisive decade in the history of liberty, that we've been called to a unique role in human events. Rarely has the world faced a choice more clear or consequential. Steadfast in our purpose, we now press on. We have known freedom's price. We have shown freedom's power. And in this great conflict, my fellow Americans, we will see freedom's victory.

2.4 Graduation Speech at West Point

United States Military Academy
West Point, New York
June 1, 2002

Every West Point class is commissioned to the Armed Forces. Some West Point classes are also commissioned by history, to take part in a great new calling for their country. . . .

Officers graduating [in 1942] helped . . . defeating Japan and Germany, and then reconstructing those nations as allies. West Point graduates of the 1940s saw the rise of a deadly new challenge—the challenge of imperial communism—and opposed it from Korea to Berlin, to Vietnam, and in the Cold War. . . .

History has also issued its call to your generation. In your last year, America was attacked by a ruthless and resourceful enemy. You graduate from this Academy in a time of war, taking your place in an American military that is powerful and is honorable. Our war on terror is only begun, but in Afghanistan it was begun well. . . .

This war will take many turns we cannot predict. Yet I am certain of this: Wherever we carry it, the American flag will stand not only for our power, but for freedom. Our nation's cause has always been larger than our nation's defense. We fight, as we always fight, for a just peace—a peace that favors human liberty. We will defend the peace against threats from terrorists and tyrants. We will preserve the peace by building good relations among the great powers. And we will extend the peace by encouraging free and open societies on every continent.

Building this just peace is America's opportunity, and America's duty. From this day forward, it is your challenge, as well, and we will meet this challenge together. You will wear the uniform of a great and unique country. America has no empire to extend or utopia to establish. We wish for others only what we wish for ourselves—safety from violence, the rewards of liberty, and the hope for a better life.

In defending the peace, we face a threat with no precedent. Enemies in the past needed great armies and great industrial capabilities to endanger the American people and our nation. The attacks of September the 11th required a few hundred thousand dollars in the hands of a few dozen evil and deluded men. All of the chaos and suffering they caused came at much less than the cost of a single tank. The dangers have not passed. This government and the American people are on watch, we are ready, because we know the terrorists have more money and more men and more plans.

The gravest danger to freedom lies at the perilous crossroads of radicalism and technology. When the spread of chemical and biological and nuclear weapons, along with ballistic missile technology—when that occurs, even weak states and small groups could attain a catastrophic power to strike great nations. Our enemies have declared this very intention, and have been caught seeking these terrible weapons. They want the capability to blackmail us, or to harm us, or to harm our friends—and we will oppose them with all our power.

For much of the last century, America's defense relied on the Cold War doctrines of deterrence and containment. In some cases, those strategies still apply. But new threats also require new thinking. Deterrence—the promise of massive retaliation against nations—means nothing against shadowy terrorist networks with no nation or citizens to defend. Containment is not possible when unbalanced dictators with weapons of mass destruction can deliver those weapons on missiles or secretly provide them to terrorist allies.

We cannot defend America and our friends by hoping for the best. We cannot put our faith in the word of tyrants, who solemnly sign nonproliferation treaties, and then systemically break them. If we wait for threats to fully materialize, we will have waited too long.

Homeland defense and missile defense are part of stronger security, and they're essential priorities for America. Yet the war on terror will not be won on the defensive. We must take the battle to the enemy, disrupt his plans, and confront the worst threats before they emerge. In the world we have entered, the only path to safety is the path of action. And this nation will act.

Our security will require the best intelligence, to reveal threats hidden in caves and growing in laboratories. Our security will require modernizing domestic agencies such as the FBI, so they're prepared to act, and act quickly, against danger. Our security will require transforming the military you will lead—a military that must be ready to strike at a moment's notice in any dark corner of the world. And our security will require all Americans to be forward-looking and resolute, to be ready for preemptive action when necessary to defend our liberty and to defend our lives. . . .

All nations that decide for aggression and terror will pay a price. We will not leave the safety of America and the peace of the planet at the mercy of a few mad terrorists and tyrants. We will lift this dark threat from our country and from the world. . . .

As we defend the peace, we also have an historic opportunity to preserve the peace. We have our best chance since the rise of the nation state in the seventeenth century to build a world where the great powers compete in peace instead of prepare for war. . . .

Competition between great nations is inevitable, but armed conflict in our world is not. More and more, civilized nations find ourselves on the same side—united by common dangers of terrorist violence and chaos. America has, and intends to keep, military strengths beyond challenge—thereby, making the destabilizing arms races of other eras pointless, and limiting rivalries to trade and other pursuits of peace.

Today the great powers are also increasingly united by common values, instead of divided by conflicting ideologies. The United States, Japan and our Pacific friends, and now all of Europe, share a deep commitment to human freedom, embodied in strong alliances such as NATO. And the tide of liberty is rising in many other nations. . . .

When the great powers share common values, we are better able to confront serious regional conflicts together, better able to cooperate in preventing the spread of violence or economic chaos. In the past, great power rivals took sides in difficult regional problems, making divisions deeper and more complicated. Today, from the Middle East to South Asia, we are gathering broad international coalitions to increase the pressure for peace. We must build strong and great power relations when times are good; to help manage crisis when times are bad. America needs partners to preserve the peace, and we will work with every nation that shares this noble goal.

And finally, America stands for more than the absence of war. We have a great opportunity to extend a just peace, by replacing poverty, repression, and resentment around the world with hope of a better day. Through most of history, poverty was persistent, inescapable, and almost universal. In the last few decades, we've seen nations from Chile to South Korea build modern economies and freer societies, lifting millions of people out of despair and want. And there's no mystery to this achievement. . . .

A truly strong nation will permit legal avenues of dissent for all groups that pursue their aspirations without violence. An advancing nation will pursue economic reform, to unleash the great entrepreneurial energy of its people. A thriving nation will respect the rights of women, because no society can prosper while denying opportunity to half its citizens. . . .America has a greater objective than controlling threats and containing resentment. We will work for a just and peaceful world beyond the war on terror.

Questions to Discuss

1. In Speech 2.1, Bush declares a "war" on terrorism. Should terrorist acts be handled as a crime or an act of war?

2. In Speech 2.1, Bush says that terrorists hate the United States because of its freedoms. Does this explain their motivation? Why did Bush choose not to focus on ways that past or present American policies were perceived by bin Laden and others?

3. In Speeches 2.1 and 2.2, Bush portrays the war on terrorism as a battle for all civilization, supported by God and the march of history. What do these comments show about Bush's view of America's role in the world?

4. In Speech 2.3, Bush identifies an "Axis of Evil." Does this phrase overstate either the unifying factors among the countries, or the link between countries pursuing WMD and terrorists?

5. In Speech 2.4, Bush argues that modern threats make past policies of deterrence and containment outdated and require the United States to follow a doctrine of preemptive wars. Are the modern threats significantly different from past threats?

Chapter 3

Iraq

The United States' relations with Iraq first became tense in 1958, when the country's pro-Western monarchy was overthrown by a pro-Soviet government. Tensions escalated after 1968 when the Baath Party seized power and rallied Arab nationalists against alleged American imperialism. Saddam Hussein was the security chief of the Baath regime. In 1979, he assumed the presidency. In both positions, he built a core group of supporters through rewards for loyalty, but used arrests, torture, and mass killings—including attacks with chemical weapons—to destroy opposition and maintain control of Iraq's people. In 1980, Saddam led Iraq to war with its neighbor Iran. The year previously, a fundamentalist Islamic regime had overthrown the pro-American Shah of Iran. Following the classic idea that the "the enemy of my enemy is my friend," U.S.–Iraqi relations warmed. The United States provided Iraq with both military and intelligence aid. In the brutal war, Iraq employed every tactic available to fight to a stalemate after eight years.

The warmer U.S.–Iraqi ties were short-lived. In August 1990, Iraq invaded its small neighbor Kuwait. Kuwait was a U.S. ally and oil supplier. Furthermore, its territory could serve as a launching ground for an invasion of oil rich Saudi Arabia. President George H.W. Bush announced that Iraq's invasion was unacceptable. He built a wide-ranging international coalition backed by UN resolutions, demanding that Iraq withdraw from Kuwait. Bush hoped that international pressure and a credible threat of force would lead Iraq to withdraw, but Saddam refused. Therefore, the coalition, led by the U.S. military, used five weeks of aerial bombardment and four days of ground fighting to drive Iraq's army from Kuwait in the spring of 1991.

The ease of victory in Kuwait raised the possibility of sending coalition forces into Iraq to overthrow Saddam. This option was firmly rejected by President Bush, then Secretary of Defense Dick Cheney, and then Chairman of the Joint Chiefs of Staff Colin Powell. George W. Bush later praised their decision based on the arguments that an American invasion would have exceeded the UN-approved goal of liberating Kuwait, would likely have destroyed Arab support for the coalition, and would have left the United States in charge of a potentially unstable post-Saddam Iraq. At the time, many officials also felt an invasion was unnecessary because Saddam was now weakened and could fall to domestic opposition. In fact, Bush senior encouraged rebellions by Kurds in northern Iraq and Shiites in the south, but provided minimal support when the groups rose up. Saddam was able to brutally crush the opposition and tighten his grip on power. This outcome tarnished the coalition victory, but the Gulf War was still generally popular and felt to be a success.

The war left several lasting impressions on policy makers about Saddam's aggressiveness, unwillingness to bow to diplomatic pressure, and ability to maintain control over Iraq. The war also had several important practical legacies. The first was the declaration of no fly-zones for the Iraqi air force over large parts of Iraq's territory in order to lessen further attacks against the Kurds and Shiites. In the following decade, U.S. and British aircraft flew roughly 150,000 missions over Iraq to enforce these zones. The aircraft were often fired on by Iraqi air defense systems and the coalition retaliated against targets within and beyond the no-fly zones. The second legacy was the continuation of UN economic sanctions, initially imposed when Iraq invaded Kuwait, to encourage Iraqi compliance with UN weapons inspections. The sanctions cost Iraq billions in lost revenue from oil exports and limited the import of many necessities. Beginning in 1996, the UN tried to avert a humanitarian crisis by establishing an "oil-for-food" program, which allowed Iraq to export some oil to pay for food and other supplies. Still, an estimated 500,000 Iraqis died from malnutrition and preventable diseases as a result of the sanctions. Saddam used these results to rally domestic opposition to the UN and international opposition to the sanctions. U.S. officials countered that Saddam was responsible because the sanctions would have been lifted if he had cooperated. Furthermore, he was allegedly spending Iraq's limited revenue on new buildings and luxury items rather than necessities for the people. The war's third legacy was UN Resolution 687, under which Iraq agreed to inspections to document and then destroy its WMD capabilities. The inspectors found that previous intelligence reports had underestimated Iraq's chemical and biological weapons stockpiles and progress toward nuclear weapons. The inspectors oversaw the destruction of thousands of weapons, but feared that Iraq was concealing weapons and research. Over time, Iraq increasingly interfered with the inspectors' access to information and blocked admittance to certain sites. The UN repeatedly urged compliance with the inspections, but took only limited action to punish Iraq's lack of cooperation. In 1998, Saddam prohibited all inspections of new sites and the UN inspectors were withdrawn.

Thus, Bush inherited a relationship that had been tense for decades and a series of policies that had achieved mixed results. Iraq's ambitions and power had been significantly contained, but Saddam remained in power with unclear ambitions and unknown weapons capabilities. Iraq remained subject to several UN resolutions, but international support for tough sanctions had eroded due to their humanitarian impact. The UN appeared to have little will to aggressively enforce inspection or disarmament pledges. Bush, therefore, felt new efforts were needed.

Some of Bush's advisers, especially Secretary of Defense Rumsfeld and Deputy Secretary of Defense Wolfowitz, argued that the time had come for bold action. They suggested that the United States actively seek regime change by increasing aid to opposition groups, particularly the Iraqi National Congress headed in exile by Pentagon favorite Ahmed Chalabi. They even considered using U.S. forces to seize Iraq's southern oil wells in order to establish an enclave for opposition forces. Others, though, felt that the Iraqi opposition groups were weak and corrupt and a mass uprising in the south was unlikely after the Shiites' experience following the Gulf War. Therefore, the administration's main early tactical goal became to increase economic pressure by encouraging the UN to adopt "smart sanctions," preventing Iraq's importation of military goods, but relaxing restrictions on more general trade. Despite significant efforts by Powell and others, the administration was unable to win support from Russia, France, and others who favored even weaker sanctions. The setback left administration officials in general agreement that new actions were needed, but without clear plans or consensus on what that action should be. Importantly, no top Bush advisers were yet advocating a major U.S. military campaign against Iraq.

The Impact of 9/11

The terrorist attacks of September 11 quickly altered the administration's discussions on Iraq. The sophistication of the attacks and Iraq's known hostility to the United States suggested the possibility of Iraq's direct involvement. The day after the attack Bush reportedly told his top counterterrorism adviser, Richard A. Clarke, to look carefully for evidence of Saddam's involvement. On September 17, Bush told his national security team, "I believe Iraq was involved."[1] At the time, there was no direct evidence of Iraqi involvement; Bush's comment reveals his preexisting suspicion of Saddam and suggests a predisposition by the president and others to view subsequent intelligence information through a particular lens. Interestingly, Wolfowitz rated the chance of Iraqi involvement at only 10 to 50 percent. Still, he argued that the attack gave the United

States an opportunity to broaden the war on terrorism to include Iraq. Such action, he suggested, would quickly and decisively resolve a long-standing problem and demonstrate that supporters of terrorism would also face punishment.[2] The Iraq option was considered the weekend after 9/11; however, none of the president's top advisers expressed support for attacking Iraq at that point. Bush concluded that Afghanistan would be the focus during phase one of the war.

The most crucial impact of the 9/11 attacks on Iraq policy was to convince Bush and several key advisers, such as Vice President Cheney, that America was vulnerable to attack by enemies driven by deep hatred and willing to use any means available. The deaths and destruction of 9/11 were horrible, but as Cheney commented, "As unfathomable as this was, it could have been so much worse if they had weapons of mass destruction."[3] That fear was heightened in subsequent months as envelopes containing anthrax were mailed to several news offices and politicians; documents were found in Afghanistan detailing al Qaeda's interest in WMD, and U.S. intelligence agencies reported talk that a "dirty bomb," which uses conventional explosives to spread radiological material, was going to be employed in an attack on Washington. When Bush and his advisers considered who might have the capability and motivation to help terrorists obtain WMD, Iraq was at the top of the list.

Bush began to publicly mention the possibility of future terrorist attacks with WMD in October 2001. These warnings culminated in his January 2002 State of the Union address, during which he famously described states pursuing WMD and terrorists as forming an "axis of evil, arming to threaten the peace of the world" (Speech 2.3). The speech included single sentences on North Korea and Iran, followed by a full paragraph on Iraq. Bush suggested, "Iraq continues to flaunt its hostility toward America and to support terror." He asserted that Iraq had ended weapons inspections because it had "something to hide from the civilized world." The argument that Iraq's failure to comply with inspectors should be interpreted as proof of hostile intentions was a centerpiece of the administration's logic. Other observers suggested Iraq's policies might reflect a desire to stand up to outside pressure or to maintain strategic ambiguity.

Despite Bush's tough words, there were few public signs of action on Iraq in the spring of 2002. In actuality, major military planning had begun months earlier. Bush had asked Rumsfeld to review and update the Pentagon's existing war plan for Iraq in November 2001. On December 28, General Tommy Franks, the regional commander, held the first of many briefings for Bush and his top advisers on possible combat operations.[4] Over the next months, the plans were refined, forces and supplies were gradually moved into the area, and over $100 million was given to the CIA to enhance covert operations and intelligence gathering in Iraq.

Bush gave the first extensive justification for using these forces in a June 2002 speech at West Point (Speech 2.4). Bush argued that the threat posed by terrorists and their allies required preemptive action to deny hostile states the ability to acquire WMD. The speech did not mention Iraq at all, but it was widely accepted that Iraq was the test case.

Making the Case for War

By August 2002, details of military planning were dominating discussions on Iraq. It appeared, the issue had become when to attack, not whether such an attack was justified or prudent. Secretary of State Powell felt that Bush needed to consider all of the ramifications of his decision before acting, so he requested a rare personal meeting with Bush. At the meeting on August 5, Powell made many of the arguments that critics of the war would later advance. He suggested that the war could prove economically costly, with a possible sharp rise in oil prices adding to the direct costs of fighting the war and rebuilding Iraq. He argued that war could be militarily costly as well, particularly if Saddam chose to use chemical or other unconventional weapons in a final effort to save his regime. He worried that war could increase anti-American sentiment and thereby destabilize the region. Powell noted that war in Iraq most certainly would divert attention and resources away from all other goals, including the ongoing effort to capture Osama bin Laden and his supporters in Afghanistan. He also raised the issue that defeating Iraq would put the United States in charge of rebuilding a country that had been ravaged by decades of abusive rule and that lacked both national unity and popular opposition leaders. As Powell vividly expressed it, "You are going to be the proud owner of 25 million people."[5] Powell did not at that point, or any other, directly recommend against war, because he felt that would intrude on presidential authority.

The second half of Powell's message to Bush was that, if the United States was going to proceed, building an international coalition was important. He suggested that a coalition could help provide basing and logistical assistance, would internationalize the issue to avoid changes of U.S. unilateralism, and might intimidate Saddam enough to generate concessions and avoid war. Powell argued that allies could not be expected to jump when Bush called unless they had been part of the process leading to war and that working through the UN was one good way to include others in the process.

Others in the administration, such as Cheney and many defense department officials, were much less interested in returning to the UN. They felt that the U.S. military did not need significant assistance from others, that UN involvement risked slowing down the decision-making process, and that past evidence showed Saddam would not yield to international pressure. Bush saw merit in going to the UN not from a great commitment to multilateralism or great faith in inspections, but because it was a practical way of rallying a coalition. Therefore, in mid-August, Bush decided to use an upcoming speech at the UN to make the case against Iraq. At Cheney's suggestion, though, the speech also would include a challenge to the UN to prove its relevance by enforcing its own resolutions.

The degree of division within the administration over tactics and Cheney's increasingly hard line on Iraq were made evident by Cheney's August 26 speech at a Veterans of Foreign Wars (VFW) convention. Of note, the speech's concept, but not content, had been approved by Bush. Cheney argued that a return of inspectors "would provide no assurance whatsoever of [Saddam's] compliance with UN resolutions" and could even "provide false comfort that Saddam was somehow 'back in his box'."[6] He then asserted without any qualifiers that "Saddam Hussein now has weapons of mass destruction." This statement went further than Bush or any major intelligence agencies' documents had gone before. Cheney concluded, "The risks of inaction are far greater than the risk of action." In an administration known for unified messages and not airing disputes in public, Cheney's speech was a major departure from regular practice. It shifted the burden of proof onto Powell and those who argued that UN or nonmilitary options could succeed.

Bush remained committed to making a September 12 speech at the UN, so debate between the Cheney and Powell camps shifted to how tough the speech should be and whether it should call for a new UN resolution. Powell felt that, if the speech made a case to the UN, it had to ask for something at the end. Also, several key U.S. allies, including England's Tony Blair, saw a new resolution as an important reaffirmation of international views. Those on the other side felt that there were already enough resolutions on Iraq to justify action and that pursuing a new resolution would only reinforce the UN's tendency to debate, rather than take, action. The night before the speech, Bush personally wrote into speech draft number 24, "We will work with the UN Security Council for the necessary resolutions" (Speech 3.1).

At the UN, Bush went considerably over his allotted time, as he commented on the UN's future and made the case against Iraq. He warned of the dangers posed by outlaw regimes. Like a prosecutor, he listed evidence of Iraqi noncompliance with UN resolutions to try to prove that Iraq was indeed an outlaw with dangerous capabilities. On weapons, he did not repeat Cheney's firm assertion, but suggested that Iraq had a history of deceit, known weapons that were unaccounted for by the UN inspectors, and ongoing programs. Dramatically, he claimed that, if Iraq acquired fissile material, "it would be able to build a nuclear weapon within a year." Near the end of the speech, Bush spoke of the need to bring "liberty" to the Iraqi people. Bush had to be careful, since many diplomats felt that Saddam would never negotiate if Bush announced a goal of regime change. Many also felt that direct action to overthrow Saddam before he attacked others would be a violation of state sovereignty, which was enshrined in international law and the UN Charter. Bush concluded his case with a call for the UN to act "decisively," but made it clear that the United States was willing to act alone. Bush was again treading a thin line. The credible threat of force was important, and U.S. determination might rally others to action, but Bush did not want to offend other countries or UN officials by suggesting that the United States had already determined its course of action and was now just seeking international political cover.

Bush's UN speech was generally well received and appeared to create momentum for action. Bush, therefore, turned his attention to winning congressional support for a broad resolution authorizing the use of force. To rally support, on October 7, 2002 in Cincinnati, Bush gave a second major speech outlining the case for war (Speech 3.2). The basic outlines of the case were similar to the UN speech, but Bush lessened the emphasis on enforcing UN resolutions, and put more focus on Iraq's direct threat to U.S. interests, and on the need for regime change. Bush also increased the strength of some claims against Iraq. He declared unequivocally, "[Iraq] possesses and produces chemical and biological weapons." This conclusion mirrored Cheney's statements and an October 2002 National Intelligence Estimate (NIE), but the NIE included many qualifiers about the quality of existing intelligence and surety of conclusions. Bush also stressed Iraq's link to terrorism. He did not claim that Iraq was directly involved in the 9/11 attacks, but many listeners may well have drawn that conclusion. Bush then firmly and vividly linked the threats posed by Iraq's weapons of mass destruction and terrorism saying, "Facing clear evidence of peril, we cannot wait for the final proof—the smoking gun—that could come in the form of a mushroom cloud." Bush argued that past policies had not succeeded in ending the threat, so new pressure was needed. To address congressional worries he said, "Approving this resolution does not mean that military action is imminent or unavoidable" and commented, "If we have to act, we will take every precaution that is possible. We will plan carefully; we will act with the full power of the United States military; we will act with allies at our side, and we will prevail." Later, Democratic presidential candidate John Kerry cited these words in explaining how his vote in favor of the resolution was not the same as blanket support for the war, or for when and how it was fought.

Bush's arguments and other evidence were enough to convince solid majorities in both Houses of Congress and large percentages of American citizens polled during this period. Others, though, continued to question parts of the case for war. Some observers objected to the whole idea of preemption. They argued that preemptive strikes would violate international law, make the United States the aggressor, and set a dangerous precedent that other countries might follow. These critics, and others who did support preemption in some cases, also argued that Bush had not proven that Iraq posed an imminent threat. They suggested that past inspections and sanctions had greatly lessened Iraq's capabilities. Also, even if Iraq did acquire certain weapons, Saddam might be deterred from using them, as he apparently had been during the Gulf War. Critics also suggested that Bush had merged two distinct problems by linking Iraq and al Qaeda. They pointed out that there was no evidence of extensive collaboration between the two. Furthermore, the critics questioned whether Saddam would ever relinquish control of weapons he had worked so hard to acquire, or risk international retaliation if a terrorist weapon was traced back to Iraq.

Beyond security issues, many observers were sympathetic with the idea of ending Saddam's rule, but they pointed out that there had been no recent increase in brutality and that Saddam was just one of many abusive leaders in the world. Action in Iraq would either start a trend of invasions or set a double standard if action was taken only in strategic areas. There were also questions of whether the United States, or even the UN, had any legal authority to intervene in a sovereign state's domestic politics, no matter how brutal the regime.

Because some critics discounted Bush's interest in establishing an effective UN or ending all dictatorships, and questioned the evidence supporting an imminent threat, other motives for war were also forwarded. Two often suggested ideas were that Bush was finishing his father's war or fighting for oil. The former theory rested on the premises that Bush senior's decision not to invade Iraq in 1991 was now being portrayed by some as a job half done, that some Bush advisers felt frustration with Iraq because of earlier experiences, and that Bush had personal enmity towards Saddam because he targeted Bush senior for assassination in 1993. In Bush's words, "[He] tried to kill my Dad."[7]

The theory of oil as a motive for U.S. focus on Iraq had been raised extensively since the Persian Gulf War. Supporters of this idea pointed out that Iraq controlled significant oil reserves. If the United States could ensure access to or control over that oil, it could garner huge new profits for U.S. companies, ensure lower oil prices, and potentially gain leverage over other countries that depended on Middle East oil.[8] Supporters of this view also noted that Bush, Cheney, and others in the administration had close connections to the oil industry. They pointed to Cheney's statement in his VFW speech: "Armed with an arsenal of these weapons of terror, and seated atop 10 percent of the world's oil reserves, Saddam Hussein could then be expected to seek domination of the entire Middle East, [and] take control of a great portion of the world's energy supplies."[9]

The Final Steps to War

The main burden of crafting and winning international support for the proposed new UN resolution fell to Powell, although other officials contributed ideas and draft proposals. The task was fraught with difficulties. First, Saddam made just enough concessions about possible new inspections to blunt the momentum for action engendered by Bush's September UN speech. Also, a resolution needed to be crafted that was strong enough to actually limit Saddam's power, but not so strong that it would be rejected out of hand by Saddam, or be perceived by others as demanding unattainable concessions as an excuse to trigger war. In addition, many countries saw the resolution as part of deeper debates about the future of the international system. France and other countries hoped to prove that negotiations could attain the goals that Americans argued could only be attained through force. They also hoped to show that international institutions served an important purpose and should not be subverted by U.S. unilateralism.

On November 8, 2002, the UN Security Council unanimously passed Resolution 1441, which gave Iraq "a final opportunity to comply with its disarmament obligations." The resolution required Iraq to provide a complete declaration of its WMD programs and to give inspectors "immediate, unimpeded, unconditional and unrestricted access" to all sites. The U.S. officials hoped that the declaration requirement would trap Saddam either way. If he declared the existence of programs, he would prove that he lied in the past; if he denied the existence of programs, any evidence found of current programs would put him in material breach of his obligations. Originally, the French hoped for wording saying that if Iraq failed to comply, a second resolution to authorize force would be necessary, but the resolution's final wording required only that the Security Council meet again to "consider the situation" and warned of "serious consequences," UN-speak for war.

At the time, winning unanimous support for the resolution was considered a major achievement for Powell. The resolution was hailed for showing a united international position, putting the burden on Iraq to prevent war, and strengthening legal justifications for war. In time, some of the resolution's wording would be portrayed as too vague and as just papering over disputes that would later divide the United States from some allies and from the UN process.

In December, Iraq submitted over 12,000 pages of documents claiming that it had no existing weapons programs. U.S. officials quickly dismissed the claims, but other countries insisted that they be carefully considered. The UN inspectors reentered Iraq. The U.S. officials soon became frustrated at the slow pace of inspections and perceived weak statements by inspectors about Iraq's lack of cooperation and possible weapons programs. Bush was frustrated that international attention was shifting to disputes over the timing and process of inspections, rather than the possible threat that Iraq posed. That shift made it possible for key countries, such as France and Russia, to declare their opposition to an immediate war, even though they had supported resolution 1441.

Bush, therefore, made two major final attempts to justify the war and rally domestic and international support. He spoke extensively about Iraq in his 2003 State of the Union Address and sent Powell to the UN on February 5 to present the U.S. evidence on Iraq's weapons programs and ties to terrorism. In the State of the Union Address, Bush once again suggested that regimes seeking WMD posed a grave danger and that, learning from the September 11 attacks, the United States now had to act decisively before threats became imminent. As in other speeches, Bush detailed what was believed to be in Iraq's arsenal, but here mentioned a British report that Saddam "recently sought significant quantities of uranium from Africa."[10] Bush also put great focus on recent Iraqi actions to impede the full inspections called for under Resolution 1441. The next week, Powell went to the UN with a multimedia presentation based on U.S. intelligence. Powell was chosen because, among Bush's top advisers, he had the best relationship with foreign governments and was seen as the least likely to support war. His statements supporting action thus might carry more weight. Powell used much of the same evidence that Bush had cited, but discarded some claims that he felt were not supported by good intelligence.

Neither Bush's speech nor Powell's evidence convinced undecided countries. Much of the U.S. evidence was circumstantial, required interpreting intercepted communications and other evidence in certain ways, and came from unverifiable sources. Also, much of the case rested on interpreting Saddam's future intentions from his past behavior and anti-

American views. As Rumsfeld explained in later congressional testimony, the administration "did not act in Iraq because we had discovered dramatic new evidence of Iraq's pursuit of weapons of mass murder. We acted because we saw the existing evidence in a new light, through the prism of our experience on September 11th."[11] Some countries not using that prism reached different conclusions on the need for war.

With encouragement from England and others, the United States did make one last effort to rally international opinion by floating a new UN resolution authorizing action. The resolution was withdrawn, though, when France threatened to veto and the resolution appeared unlikely to get support from an overall majority of countries on the Security Council. Nevertheless, the United States and a "coalition of the willing" went ahead to prepare for war, while both U.S. alliances with Europe and the UN appeared severely weakened.

The War and Its Immediate Aftermath

On March 20, 2003, a coalition of roughly 100,000 American, 25,000 British, 2,000 Australian and 200 Polish soldiers began a ground offensive in Iraq. These troops numbered far fewer than the over 600,000 troops assembled for the Gulf War. Rumsfeld led the decision to rely on a smaller, faster, higher technology force, in line with his views on defense transformation. The decision initially appeared sound, as the battles were even more one-sided than expected. Less than 150 U.S. soldiers were killed as coalition forces rapidly gained control of most territory. Some military leaders on the ground, though, complained that the tactics overstretched supply lines and left troops vulnerable to rearguard attacks. Later, other critics suggested that the small number of troops made it impossible to prevent looting and establish order.

There was no formal surrender by the Iraqi government to signal an end to the war. On May 1, 2003, Bush flew to the *USS Abraham Lincoln* and spoke on its flight deck. Under a giant banner reading "Mission Accomplished," Bush declared, "Major combat operations in Iraq have ended" (Speech 3.3). Bush noted the new military strategies employed and focused most of his speech on the security motives behind the war. No weapons of mass destruction had yet been found, but Bush suggested that there were already hundreds of sites being searched. He also directly linked Iraq to terrorism saying, "The battle of Iraq is one victory in a war on terror that began on September the 11, 2001." He also indicated that more actions might occur in the future against regimes with ties to terrorism or weapons of mass destruction. This comment led to speculation about future policy plans for North Korea, Iran, Syria, and others.

In his May 1 speech, Bush also signaled the move from a period of war planning and fighting to one of rebuilding Iraq. Planning for a postwar Iraq had been going on for months under the umbrella of the State Department's "Future of Iraq Project." However, as war neared, officials in the Defense Department argued that they should take the lead. In January, Bush agreed to give most authority to the Defense Department's Office of Reconstruction and Humanitarian Assistance led by Army Lieutenant General Jay M. Garner. Garner's team did not have good relations with some State Department officials who had been planning for months. The defense team had only weeks to prepare plans. Garner himself said, "This is an ad hoc operation" and his team "didn't really have enough time to plan."[12] Also, many of the plans were based on what proved to be false assumptions: 1) that the Iraqi people would welcome the troops as liberators and be patiently supportive as the United States asserted control, 2) that exile politicians would be welcomed back as natural leaders, 3) that the biggest short-term problem would be a humanitarian crisis rather than basic lawlessness and looting, 4) that most members of Iraq's army would be either killed or captured, not just slip away, and 5) that Iraq's physical and political infrastructure would still be in place to help U.S. reconstruction efforts. The idea was to free Iraq and then quickly turn its governance over to Iraqis; unfortunately, this form of rapid nation building proved impractical almost as soon as it was implemented.

The administration quickly acknowledged the flaws of its strategy. In May, Garner was replaced by L. Paul Bremer. Bremer quickly asserted U.S. control by disbanding the Iraqi army and banning 30,000 senior Baath Party officials from government service. He also postponed efforts to establish an Iraqi interim government until July. In Bremer's words, "Occupation is an ugly word, not one Americans feel comfortable with, but it is a fact."[13] American dominance was further confirmed with a May 22 Security Council resolution that gave the United States and England almost total control over Iraq's political and economic institutions.

The various May moves changed the tone from short-term liberation to long-term occupation. This new reality angered many Iraqi leaders. Administration critics also suggested that disbanding the army and banning Baath leaders complicated reconstruction prospects since new institutions would need to be created without help from many qualified Iraqis. Citizens on the ground appeared less concerned with these issues and more concerned with the lack of basic necessities and utilities. Iraq's infrastructure was damaged in both the 1991 and 2003 wars, poorly maintained under Saddam, looted for anything valuable in the war's first days, and was being sabotaged by opposition forces. Those forces also continued to attack coalition troops and workers. Bush and other administration officials portrayed the violence as the work of a few foreign extremists and the last remnants of Saddam's loyalists. In July 2003, Bush even challenged the fighters saying, "Bring them on. We've got the force necessary to deal with the security situation."[14] At this point, Bush appeared confident that Iraq's weapons would be found, the insurgency would be easily suppressed, and stability and democracy would be established, forcing prewar doubters to change their views.

Difficult Challenges and Shifting Plans

As the summer of 2003 wore on and efforts were made to establish an Iraqi Council of Governance and other governing institutions, the difficulties of bringing stability, let alone democracy, to Iraq became clearer. The region that became Iraq was ruled by the Ottoman Empire for several centuries before England gained control during World War I. The English hoped to maintain influence in the strategically important and oil-rich area, but wanted to expend minimal resources to control its politically restive population. Therefore, they merged three former Ottoman provinces under the rule of a new king who was loyal to and dependent on the English. Today, Iraq's population remains divided into three main ethnic groups: Sunni Arabs, Sunni Kurds, and Shiite Arabs. About 60 percent of the population is Shiite, but they, along with the Kurds, historically have been repressed by Sunni leaders. There are multiple competing factions within each of the three groups. With Saddam's regime gone, dozens of groups began vying for power and distrusting any policy that was seen as aiding another group. Efforts to attain stability and democracy were further hindered by the legacy of years of oppression and misrule by Saddam's government, a weakened economy, limited freedom of speech and press, killed or exiled opposition leaders and intellectuals, and a political system based on self-interest and sheer survival. In addition, some scholars and other people questioned whether Arab culture or Islam is compatible with democracy. To counter these arguments, the administration suggested that freedom is a universal desire and that Iraqis have the skills to govern effectively.

By late summer, three other important factors came into play. First, insurgent violence continued. There now appeared to be multiple groups involved: Saddam loyalists, foreign terrorists, domestic Islamic fundamentalists, Sunni and Shiite factions, common criminals, and more. The groups shared little except a goal of disrupting the occupation by attacking coalition soldiers, foreign workers, and Iraqis who worked with the coalition. Second, the costs of establishing security and rebuilding Iraq were mounting; however, few countries were interested in contributing troops or money as long as violence continued and the mission was seen as a U.S. operation. Third, while a majority of Iraqis in Baghdad continued to support the intervention and remained optimistic about the country's long-term prospects, worries about security and lack of services led only one-third to feel that life was better than it had been before the invasion.[15]

On September 7, 2003, Bush spoke about the two-year battle against terrorism, the ongoing problems in Iraq, and plans for Iraq's future in light of the new realities (Speech 3.4). Bush argued that progress had been made against al Qaeda worldwide. Interestingly, although he mentioned that Iraq had "sponsored terror [and] possessed and used weapons of mass destruction," he did not directly restate the idea that those weapons could have been given to terrorists and made no mention of the ongoing failure to find the weapons. Bush argued that the violence in Iraq made it "the central front" in the war on terror. Critics of the administration were quick to suggest that only the U.S. invasion and ensuing instability had given Iraq this role. Bush made a point of portraying the attacks as "localized" and carried out only by former members of Saddam's regime and foreign terrorists, so not reflective of general Iraqi opposition to U.S. goals.

To move forward, he identified a strategy with three components: "Destroying the terrorists, enlisting the support of other nations for a free Iraq and helping the Iraqis assume responsibility for their own defense and their own future." The second component represented an important change. The plan was to encourage existing coalition members to contribute new troops, but also to ask the UN to create a multilateral force in Iraq. This concept was a significant shift away from the early days of near total U.S. control and from the administration's previously cool response to UN security operations.

Over the subsequent months, the insurgency in Iraq not only continued, but escalated. There was an increase in the number of attacks per day, the sophistication of weapons used, the number of deaths caused, and the number of regions in which attacks occurred. The administration chose to continue its three component strategy, but with some further shifts in emphasis. Over time, each component had its successes, as well as its failures. Efforts continued to end the terrorism by killing or capturing insurgents and seizing weapons. The high point came with Saddam's capture in December 2003. Unfortunately, putting an end to his calls for rebellion did not end the violence. The U.S. forces were militarily far superior to any of the insurgent groups, but the violence proved anew that defeating an army in open battle is far easier than stopping guerilla fighters and terrorists. The U.S. military could have been sent into insurgent strongholds, but at a heavy political price. Many of the groups operated in cities. Some based operations near mosques and religious shrines. Attacks were likely to cause significant civilian casualties and damage to religious sites, thereby creating even more anti-American sentiment.

The United States continued to encourage military and economic contributions from both individual states and the UN. The number of countries contributing troops reached over two dozen, but many of the troop contributions were small. U.S. and British forces continued to do the bulk of the tough work. This situation was exacerbated in spring 2004 when Spain, following a terrorist attack in Madrid, became the first of several countries to withdraw troops from Iraq. The lack of troop and financial contributions in part reflected the international sentiments that the United States had created the problem, so it should not expect others to pay the costs and that the United States wanted to share the burdens, but still not share the decision making. It also reflected fear of the ongoing violence. This fear increased when terrorist groups began kidnapping and, in some cases, beheading foreigners in Iraq. Fear also played a role in limiting UN operations. UN Secretary General Kofi Annan became very focused on the dangers after an August 2003 attack on the UN compound in Baghdad. The UN did increase its role in Iraq over time, but became less interested in establishing a major presence just at the time Bush was more willing to accept such a UN role.

The idea of shifting governmental and security responsibility to Iraqis led Bush to a November 2003 decision to establish an interim Iraqi government by June 2004. Transferring authority would eventually allow the United States to follow Bush's pledge to withdraw. It also was hoped that violence would decline and the remaining insurgents would lose popular support once they could no longer claim to be fighting for the nation against outsiders. The plan faced many obstacles. The first obstacle was how to organize a government so quickly. Major problems emerged in spring 2004 when Shiite leader Grand Ayatollah Ali al-Sistani demanded elections be held. The United States argued that elections were impractical given time constraints and local conditions. Ultimately, UN officials played a key role in pacifying al-Sistani, developing the structure of Iraq's interim government, and selecting its members. The second obstacle was whether any leader chosen by the United States or UN would be seen as a puppet under foreign influence. The third obstacle was how to quickly train a new Iraqi army and police force and ensure they would be strong enough to control the violence. To help build the government and army, the United States relaxed some of Bremer's earlier restrictions on involvement of former officials. Efforts, though, were complicated by the insurgents' repeated attacks on the new security forces.

Despite continued violence and political disputes among Iraqi groups, which hoped to maximize their power in the new system, the plan to transfer authority went forward. On May 24, 2004, Bush spoke again about Iraq's future (Speech 3.5). In the speech, Bush acknowledged recent violence, but remained upbeat about Iraq's future and the role it could play as a test case and catalyst for his goal of spreading democracy in the Middle East. He noted that the transfer of authority was important since "Iraqis are proud people who resent foreign control of their affairs, just as we would." This was a subtle acknowledgment that not all opposition to U.S. rule came from extremists. To preserve stability after the transfer of authority, the United States would maintain close to 140,000 troops in Iraq under a U.S. commander, but the Iraqi government technically could ask them to leave. Bush also announced a future timetable: national elections in January 2005 to elect a transitional assembly that would govern Iraq and write a new constitution by fall 2005, and establishment of a permanent government by the end of 2005. Bush concluded the speech by restating the reasons for war. He again explained the war as part of the overall war on terror, but the goal of a free Iraq was given more prominence than it was in speeches before the war.

The transfer of authority occurred a few days ahead of schedule for security reasons. Iyad Allawi became prime minister. Allawi was a secular Shiite, a former Baathist who later opposed Saddam for years from exile, a former CIA employee, and a man with a reputation for tough action. Under Allawi, violence decreased briefly, but then flared anew. In September 2003, U.S. deaths in Iraq crossed the 1,000 mark. More than 85 percent of the deaths occurred after Bush declared major combat operations over. Bush and Allawi remained optimistic about Iraq's long-term future, but many administration critics suggested that Bush was not facing reality, that conditions would remain difficult or worsen in the future, and that U.S. troops could remain in Iraq for over a decade.

Questioning Justifications of the War

The ongoing violence in Iraq and the Bush administration's inability, or unwillingness, to make the operation a true multilateral effort led to some criticism of the war; however, questions about Bush's justifications for the war have proved to be the most significant in shaping attitudes towards the war, towards the strategy of preemption, and towards Bush himself. These questions arose quickly after the U.S. forces failed to find WMD. The lack of WMD was important for two main reasons. Bush had argued that the weapons and their possible transfer to terrorists presented a security threat that justified preemptive action. Also, Iraq's noncompliance with UN resolutions demanding the reporting and disarmament of weapons was cited as part of the legal basis for war.

In the first weeks after the war, Bush and other officials stressed that Iraq was a large country and that Saddam had become a master at hiding weapons programs, so it might take time to discover the weapons. They also were quick to highlight any evidence of programs. For example, in late May, 2003, CIA officials and Bush both touted the discovery of two mobile laboratories, even though there was still much dispute over whether they were actually biological weapons factories or were used to produce hydrogen-filled balloons for target practice. As time passed and weapons were still not found, Bush shifted talk away from the existence of actual weapons to statements that, "Iraq had a weapons program,"[16] which could have posed a future threat. With doubts about Iraq's capabilities continuing to build, Bush reluctantly agreed in February 2004 to an independent investigation of the evidence. Notably, that investigation would not be completed until after the 2004 presidential elections.

In the meantime, investigations by journalists, congressional committees, and others questioned claims made by Bush and his advisers about specific weapons programs. For example, Bush raised the idea, in his 2003 State of the Union Address, that Iraq had pursued uranium from Africa. This statement became a major issue when it was learned that the United States earlier had sent a special investigator to examine the claim and had concluded it had no merit. In fact, the CIA recommended deleting the claim from Bush's October speech in Cincinnati because of its questionable legitimacy. Also, in several speeches, Bush referred to Iraq's purchase of high-strength aluminum tubes that could be used in centrifuges as evidence of an ongoing nuclear weapons program. In fact, Department of Energy experts and other intelligence agencies disputed this CIA interpretation of the tubes as early as the summer of 2002. Whether Bush was aware of these various disputes is unclear. At a minimum, CIA Director George Tenet and National Security Adviser Rice were aware of some of the disputes. Bush himself was reportedly initially unimpressed by a December 21, 2003 CIA presentation on the intelligence regarding Iraq's weapons, but was reassured when Tenet declared it "a slam dunk case."[17]

Bush's claims on the extent of Iraq's ties to al Qaeda also have come under scrutiny. In June 2004, the independent commission established by Bush and Congress to investigate the September 11 attacks reported its conclusion, stating that Iraq and al Qaeda did not appear to have a "collaborative relationship."[18] The commission noted talks between Iraqi officials and Osama bin Laden in 1994, but reported that Iraq had never subsequently responded to al Qaeda requests for aid. Responding to the commission findings, Bush said, "The reason I keep insisting that there was a relationship between Iraq and Saddam and al Qaeda" is "because there was a relationship between Iraq and al Qaeda."[19] He cited the 1994 discussions and other meetings as proof and suggested that the commission had only really dismissed a specific connection to the 9/11 attacks, which the administration had never directly claimed.

A few critics have suggested that Bush was simply lying about the evidence before the war. More observers, though, have suggested that Bush and his top advisers' interpretations of evidence were affected by their preexisting view that Saddam was an irrational leader with a history of WMD use and their new belief that it was essential to prevent a 9/11-type attack with WMD. Rice tellingly commented, "A policymaker cannot afford to be on the wrong side, underestimating the ability of a tyrant like Saddam Hussein."[20]

Throughout the disputes, Bush firmly held to his position that the threat was real and the war justified. For Bush, as long as Saddam remained in power and retained the intent to acquire weapons, he was a threat. Therefore, even in the face of significant criticism and doubts, Bush stayed with his reelection campaign message: "Knowing what I know today, I would have made the same decision. The world is safer with Saddam in a prison cell."[21]

Bush has called the war and its effects "the story of the twenty-first century."[22] The full implications of that story will not become clear for years. Unquestionably, though, both the lead up to the war and its aftermath have joined the attacks of 9/11 as the most crucial foreign policy events of the Bush administration.

3.1 Remarks at the United Nations

United Nations General Assembly
New York, New York
September 12, 2002

We meet one year and one day after a terrorist attack brought grief to my country, and brought grief to many citizens of our world.... We've accomplished much in the last year—in Afghanistan and beyond. We have much yet to do—in Afghanistan and beyond. Many nations represented here have joined in the fight against global terror, and the people of the United States are grateful.

The United Nations was born in the hope that survived a world war—the hope of a world moving toward justice, escaping old patterns of conflict and fear. The founding members resolved that the peace of the world must never again be destroyed by the will and wickedness of any man. We created the United Nations Security Council, so that, unlike the League of Nations, our deliberations would be more than talk, our resolutions would be more than wishes. After generations of deceitful dictators and broken treaties and squandered lives, we dedicated ourselves to standards of human dignity shared by all, and to a system of security defended by all.

Today, these standards, and this security, are challenged. Our commitment to human dignity is challenged by persistent poverty and raging disease. The suffering is great, and our responsibilities are clear. The United States is joining with the world to supply aid where it reaches people and lifts up lives, to extend trade and the prosperity it brings, and to bring medical care where it is desperately needed....

Our common security is challenged by regional conflicts—ethnic and religious strife that is ancient, but not inevitable....

Above all, our principles and our security are challenged today by outlaw groups and regimes that accept no law of morality and have no limit to their violent ambitions. In the attacks on America a year ago, we saw the destructive intentions of our enemies. This threat hides within many nations, including my own. In cells and camps, terrorists are plotting further destruction, and building new bases for their war against civilization. And our greatest fear is that terrorists will find a shortcut to their mad ambitions when an outlaw regime supplies them with the technologies to kill on a massive scale.

In one place—in one regime—we find all these dangers, in their most lethal and aggressive forms, exactly the kind of aggressive threat the United Nations was born to confront.

Twelve years ago, Iraq invaded Kuwait without provocation. And the regime's forces were poised to continue their march to seize other countries and their resources. Had Saddam Hussein been appeased instead of stopped, he would have endangered the peace and stability of the world. Yet this aggression was stopped—by the might of coalition forces and the will of the United Nations.

To suspend hostilities, to spare himself, Iraq's dictator accepted a series of commitments. The terms were clear, to him and to all. And he agreed to prove he is complying with every one of those obligations.

He has proven instead only his contempt for the United Nations, and for all his pledges. By breaking every pledge—by his deceptions, and by his cruelties—Saddam Hussein has made the case against himself.

In 1991, Security Council Resolution 688 demanded that the Iraqi regime cease at once the repression of its own people, including the systematic repression of minorities. . . . This demand goes ignored.

Last year, the UN Commission on Human Rights found that Iraq continues to commit extremely grave violations of human rights, and that the regime's repression is all pervasive. Tens of thousands of political opponents and ordinary citizens have been subjected to arbitrary arrest and imprisonment, summary execution, and torture by beating and burning, electric shock, starvation, mutilation, and rape. . . .

In 1991, the UN Security Council, through Resolutions 686 and 687, demanded that Iraq return all prisoners from Kuwait and other lands. Iraq's regime agreed. It broke its promise. Last year the Secretary General's high-level coordinator for this issue reported that Kuwait, Saudi, Indian, Syrian, Lebanese, Iranian, Egyptian, Bahraini, and Omani nationals remain unaccounted for—more than 600 people. One American pilot is among them.

In 1991, the UN Security Council, through Resolution 687, demanded that Iraq renounce all involvement with terrorism, and permit no terrorist organizations to operate in Iraq. Iraq's regime agreed. It broke this promise. In violation of Security Council Resolution 1373, Iraq continues to shelter and support terrorist organizations that direct violence against Iran, Israel, and Western governments. Iraqi dissidents abroad are targeted for murder. In 1993, Iraq attempted to assassinate the Emir of Kuwait and a former American President. Iraq's government openly praised the attacks of September the 11th. And al Qaeda terrorists escaped from Afghanistan and are known to be in Iraq.

In 1991, the Iraqi regime agreed to destroy and stop developing all weapons of mass destruction and long-range missiles, and to prove to the world it has done so by complying with rigorous inspections. Iraq has broken every aspect of this fundamental pledge.

From 1991 to 1995, the Iraqi regime said it had no biological weapons. After a senior official in its weapons program defected and exposed this lie, the regime admitted to producing tens of thousands of liters of anthrax and other deadly biological agents for use with Scud warheads, aerial bombs, and aircraft spray tanks. UN inspectors believe Iraq has produced two to four times the amount of biological agents it declared. . . Right now, Iraq is expanding and improving facilities that were used for the production of biological weapons.

United Nations' inspections also revealed that Iraq likely maintains stockpiles of VX, mustard and other chemical agents, and that the regime is rebuilding and expanding facilities capable of producing chemical weapons. And in 1995, after four years of deception, Iraq finally admitted it had a crash nuclear weapons program prior to the Gulf War. We know now, were it not for that war, the regime in Iraq would likely have possessed a nuclear weapon no later than 1993.

Today, Iraq continues to withhold important information about its nuclear program—weapons design, procurement logs, experiment data, an accounting of nuclear materials and documentation of foreign assistance. Iraq employs capable nuclear scientists and technicians. It retains physical infrastructure needed to build a nuclear weapon. Iraq has made several attempts to buy high-strength aluminum tubes used to enrich uranium for a nuclear weapon. Should Iraq acquire fissile material, it would be able to build a nuclear weapon within a year. . . .

In 1990, after Iraq's invasion of Kuwait, the world imposed economic sanctions on Iraq. Those sanctions were maintained after the war to compel the regime's compliance with Security Council resolutions. . . . Saddam Hussein has subverted this program, working around the sanctions to buy missile technology and military materials. He blames the suffering of Iraq's people on the United Nations, even as he uses his oil wealth to build lavish palaces for himself, and to buy arms for his country. By refusing to comply with his own agreements, he bears full guilt for the hunger and misery of innocent Iraqi citizens.

In 1991, Iraq promised UN inspectors immediate and unrestricted access to verify Iraq's commitment to rid itself of weapons of mass destruction and long-range missiles. Iraq broke this promise, spending seven years deceiving, evading, and harassing UN inspectors before ceasing cooperation entirely. . . . As we meet today, it's been almost four years since the last UN inspectors set foot in Iraq, four years for the Iraqi regime to plan, and to build, and to test behind the cloak of secrecy.

We know that Saddam Hussein pursued weapons of mass murder even when inspectors were in his country. Are we to assume that he stopped when they left? The history, the logic, and the facts lead to one conclusion: Saddam Hussein's regime is a grave and gathering danger. To suggest otherwise is to hope against the evidence. To assume this regime's good faith is to bet the lives of millions and the peace of the world in a reckless gamble. And this is a risk we must not take.

Delegates to the General Assembly, we have been more than patient. We've tried sanctions. We've tried the carrot of oil for food, and the stick of coalition military strikes. But Saddam Hussein has defied all these efforts and continues to develop weapons of mass destruction. . . .

The conduct of the Iraqi regime is a threat to the authority of the United Nations, and a threat to peace. Iraq has answered a decade of UN demands with a decade of defiance. All the world now faces a test, and the United Nations a difficult and defining moment. Are Security Council resolutions to be honored and enforced, or cast aside without consequence? Will the United Nations serve the purpose of its founding, or will it be irrelevant?

The United States helped found the United Nations. We want the United Nations to be effective, and respectful, and successful. We want the resolutions of the world's most important multilateral body to be enforced. And right now those resolutions are being unilaterally subverted by the Iraqi regime. Our partnership of nations can meet the test before us, by making clear what we now expect of the Iraqi regime.

If the Iraqi regime wishes peace, it will immediately and unconditionally forswear, disclose, and remove or destroy all weapons of mass destruction, long-range missiles, and all related material . . . end all support for terrorism and act to suppress it . . . cease persecution of its civilian population . . . release or account for all Gulf War personnel whose fate is still unknown . . . immediately end all illicit trade outside the oil-for-food program. . . .

If all these steps are taken, it will signal a new openness and accountability in Iraq. And it could open the prospect of the United Nations helping to build a government that represents all Iraqis—a government based on respect for human rights, economic liberty, and internationally supervised elections.

The United States has no quarrel with the Iraqi people; they've suffered too long in silent captivity. Liberty for the Iraqi people is a great moral cause, and a great strategic goal. The people of Iraq deserve it; the security of all nations requires it. Free societies do not intimidate through cruelty and conquest, and open societies do not threaten the world with mass murder. The United States supports political and economic liberty in a unified Iraq. . . .

My nation will work with the UN Security Council to meet our common challenge. If Iraq's regime defies us again, the world must move deliberately, decisively to hold Iraq to account. We will work with the UN Security Council for the necessary resolutions. But the purposes of the United States should not be doubted. The Security Council resolutions will be enforced—the just demands of peace and security will be met—or action will be unavoidable. And a regime that has lost its legitimacy will also lose its power.

Events can turn in one of two ways: If we fail to act in the face of danger, the people of Iraq will continue to live in brutal submission. The regime will have new power to bully and dominate and conquer its neighbors, condemning the Middle East to more years of bloodshed and fear. The regime will remain unstable—the region will remain unstable, with little hope of freedom, and isolated from the progress of our times. With every step the Iraqi regime takes toward gaining and deploying the most terrible weapons, our own options to confront that regime will narrow. And if an emboldened regime were to supply these weapons to terrorist allies, then the attacks of September the 11th would be a prelude to far greater horrors.

If we meet our responsibilities, if we overcome this danger, we can arrive at a very different future. The people of Iraq can shake off their captivity. They can one day join a democratic Afghanistan and a democratic Palestine, inspiring reforms throughout the Muslim world. These nations can show by their example that honest government, and respect for women, and the great Islamic tradition of learning can triumph in the Middle East and beyond. And we will show that the promise of the United Nations can be fulfilled in our time.

Neither of these outcomes is certain. Both have been set before us. We must choose between a world of fear and a world of progress. We cannot stand by and do nothing while dangers gather. We must stand up for our security, and for the permanent rights and the hopes of mankind. By heritage and by choice, the United States of America will make that stand. And, delegates to the United Nations, you have the power to make that stand, as well.

3.2 Bush Outlines the Iraqi Threat

Cincinnati Museum Center
Cincinnati, Ohio
October 7, 2002

Tonight I want to take a few minutes to discuss a grave threat to peace, and America's determination to lead the world in confronting that threat.

The threat comes from Iraq. It arises directly from the Iraqi regime's own actions—its history of aggression, and its drive toward an arsenal of terror. Eleven years ago, as a condition for ending the Persian Gulf War, the Iraqi regime was required to destroy its weapons of mass destruction, to cease all development of such weapons, and to stop all support for terrorist groups. The Iraqi regime has violated all of those obligations. It possesses and produces chemical and biological weapons. It is seeking nuclear weapons. It has given shelter and support to terrorism, and practices terror against its own people. The entire world has witnessed Iraq's eleven-year history of defiance, deception and bad faith.

We also must never forget the most vivid events of recent history. On September the 11th, 2001, America felt its vulnerability—even to threats that gather on the other side of the earth. We resolved then, and we are resolved today, to confront every threat, from any source, that could bring sudden terror and suffering to America.

Members of the Congress of both political parties, and members of the United Nations Security Council, agree that Saddam Hussein is a threat to peace and must disarm. We agree that the Iraqi dictator must not be permitted to threaten America and the world with horrible poisons and diseases and gases and atomic weapons. Since we all agree on this goal, the issue is: how can we best achieve it?

Many Americans have raised legitimate questions: about the nature of the threat; about the urgency of action—why be concerned now; about the link between Iraq developing weapons of terror, and the wider war on terror. These are all issues we've discussed broadly and fully within my administration. And tonight, I want to share those discussions with you.

First, some ask why Iraq is different from other countries or regimes that also have terrible weapons. While there are many dangers in the world, the threat from Iraq stands alone—because it gathers the most serious dangers of our age in one place. Iraq's weapons of mass destruction are controlled by a murderous tyrant who has already used chemical weapons to kill thousands of people. This same tyrant has tried to dominate the Middle East, has invaded and brutally occupied a small neighbor, has struck other nations without warning, and holds an unrelenting hostility toward the United States. By its past and present actions, by its technological capabilities, by the merciless nature of its regime, Iraq is unique...

Some ask how urgent this danger is to America and the world. The danger is already significant, and it only grows worse with time. If we know Saddam Hussein has dangerous weapons today—and we do—does it make any sense for the world to wait to confront him as he grows even stronger and develops even more dangerous weapons?

In 1995... the regime was forced to admit that it had produced more than 30,000 liters of anthrax and other deadly biological agents.... We know that the regime has produced thousands of tons of chemical agents, including mustard gas, sarin nerve gas, VX nerve gas.... And surveillance photos reveal that the regime is rebuilding facilities that it had used to produce chemical and biological weapons....

Iraq possesses ballistic missiles with a likely range of hundreds of miles.... We've also discovered through intelligence that Iraq has a growing fleet of manned and unmanned aerial vehicles that could be used to disperse chemical or biological weapons across broad areas. We're concerned that Iraq is exploring ways of using these UAVS for missions targeting the United States. And, of course, sophisticated delivery systems aren't required for a chemical or biological attack; all that might be required are a small container and one terrorist or Iraqi intelligence operative to deliver it.

And that is the source of our urgent concern about Saddam Hussein's links to international terrorist groups. Over the years, Iraq has provided safe haven to terrorists such as Abu Nidal [and] Abu Abbas, who was responsible for seizing the Achille Lauro and killing an American passenger. And we know that Iraq is continuing to finance terror and gives assistance to groups that use terrorism to undermine Middle East peace.

We know that Iraq and the al Qaeda terrorist network share a common enemy—the United States of America. We know that Iraq and al Qaeda have had high-level contacts that go back a decade. Some al Qaeda leaders who fled Afghanistan went to Iraq. These include one very senior al Qaeda leader who received medical treatment in Baghdad this year, and who has been associated with planning for chemical and biological attacks. We've learned that Iraq has trained al Qaeda members in bomb-making and poisons and deadly gases. And we know that after September the 11th, Saddam Hussein's regime gleefully celebrated the terrorist attacks on America. Iraq could decide on any given day to provide a biological or chemical weapon to a terrorist group or individual terrorists. Alliance with terrorists could allow the Iraqi regime to attack America without leaving any fingerprints.

Some have argued that confronting the threat from Iraq could detract from the war against terror. To the contrary; confronting the threat posed by Iraq is crucial to winning the war on terror.... Saddam Hussein is harboring terrorists and the instruments of terror, the instruments of mass death and destruction. And he cannot be trusted. The risk is simply too great that he will use them, or provide them to a terror network.

Terror cells and outlaw regimes building weapons of mass destruction are different faces of the same evil. Our security requires that we confront both. And the United States military is capable of confronting both.

Many people have asked how close Saddam Hussein is to developing a nuclear weapon. Well, we don't know exactly, and that's the problem.... The evidence indicates that Iraq is reconstituting its nuclear weapons program. Saddam Hussein has held numerous meetings with Iraqi nuclear scientists, a group he calls his "nuclear mujahideen," his nuclear holy warriors. Satellite photographs reveal that Iraq is rebuilding facilities at sites that have been part of its nuclear program in the past. Iraq has attempted to purchase high-strength aluminum tubes and other equipment needed for gas centrifuges, which are used to enrich uranium for nuclear weapons.

If the Iraqi regime is able to produce, buy, or steal an amount of highly enriched uranium a little larger than a single softball, it could have a nuclear weapon in less than a year. And if we allow that to happen, a terrible line would be crossed. Saddam Hussein would be in a position to blackmail anyone who opposes his aggression. He would be in a position to dominate the Middle East. He would be in a position to threaten America. And Saddam Hussein would be in a position to pass nuclear technology to terrorists.

Some citizens wonder, after eleven years of living with this problem, why do we need to confront it now? And there's a reason. We've experienced the horror of September the 11th. We have seen that those who hate America are willing to crash airplanes into buildings full of innocent people. Our enemies would be no less willing, in fact, they would be eager, to use biological or chemical, or a nuclear weapon.

Knowing these realities, America must not ignore the threat gathering against us. Facing clear evidence of peril, we cannot wait for the final proof—the smoking gun—that could come in the form of a mushroom cloud....

Some believe we can address this danger by simply resuming the old approach to inspections, and applying diplomatic and economic pressure.

Yet this is precisely what the world has tried to do since 1991. The UN inspections program was met with systematic deception.... The world has also tried economic sanctions—and watched Iraq use billions of dollars in illegal oil revenues to fund more weapons purchases, rather than providing for the needs of the Iraqi people.

The world has tried limited military strikes to destroy Iraq's weapons of mass destruction capabilities—only to see them openly rebuilt, while the regime again denies they even exist. The world has tried no-fly zones to keep Saddam from terrorizing his own people—and in the last year alone, the Iraqi military has fired upon American and British pilots more than 750 times.

After eleven years during which we have tried containment, sanctions, inspections, even selected military action, the end result is that Saddam Hussein still has chemical and biological weapons and is increasing his capabilities to make more. And he is moving ever closer to developing a nuclear weapon.

Clearly, to actually work, any new inspections, sanctions or enforcement mechanisms will have to be very different. America wants the UN to be an effective organization that helps keep the peace. And that is why we are urging the Security Council to adopt a new resolution setting out tough, immediate requirements.... The time for denying, deceiving, and delaying has come to an end. Saddam Hussein must disarm himself—or, for the sake of peace, we will lead a coalition to disarm him.

Many nations are joining us in insisting that Saddam Hussein's regime be held accountable. They are committed to defending the international security that protects the lives of both our citizens and theirs. And that's why America is challenging all nations to take the resolutions of the UN Security Council seriously. And these resolutions are clear.... By taking these steps, and by only taking these steps, the Iraqi regime has an opportunity to avoid conflict. Taking these steps would also change the nature of the Iraqi regime itself. America hopes the regime will make that choice. Unfortunately, at least so far, we have little reason to expect it. And that's why two administrations—mine and President Clinton's—have stated that regime change in Iraq is the only certain means of removing a great danger to our nation.

I hope this will not require military action, but it may.... If we have to act, we will take every precaution that is possible. We will plan carefully; we will act with the full power of the United States military; we will act with allies at our side, and we will prevail.

There is no easy or risk-free course of action. Some have argued we should wait—and that's an option. In my view, it's the riskiest of all options, because the longer we wait, the stronger and bolder Saddam

Hussein will become. . . . there can be no peace if our security depends on the will and whims of a ruthless and aggressive dictator. I'm not willing to stake one American life on trusting Saddam Hussein.

Failure to act would embolden other tyrants, allow terrorists access to new weapons and new resources, and make blackmail a permanent feature of world events. The United Nations would betray the purpose of its founding, and prove irrelevant to the problems of our time. And through its inaction, the United States would resign itself to a future of fear. That is not the America I know. That is not the America I serve. We refuse to live in fear. . . .

Some worry that a change of leadership in Iraq could create instability and make the situation worse. The situation could hardly get worse, for world security and for the people of Iraq. The lives of Iraqi citizens would improve dramatically if Saddam Hussein were no longer in power, just as the lives of Afghanistan's citizens improved after the Taliban. . . .

America believes that all people are entitled to hope and human rights, to the non-negotiable demands of human dignity. People everywhere prefer freedom to slavery; prosperity to squalor; self-government to the rule of terror and torture. America is a friend to the people of Iraq. Our demands are directed only at the regime that enslaves them and threatens us. When these demands are met . . . the long captivity of Iraq will end, and an era of new hope will begin. . . .

Later this week, the United States Congress will vote on this matter. I have asked Congress to authorize the use of America's military, if it proves necessary, to enforce UN Security Council demands. Approving this resolution does not mean that military action is imminent or unavoidable. The resolution will tell the United Nations, and all nations, that America speaks with one voice and is determined to make the demands of the civilized world mean something. Congress will also be sending a message to the dictator in Iraq: that his only chance—his only choice is full compliance, and the time remaining for that choice is limited. . . .

The attacks of September the 11th showed our country that vast oceans no longer protect us from danger. Before that tragic date, we had only hints of al Qaeda's plans and designs. Today in Iraq, we see a threat whose outlines are far more clearly defined, and whose consequences could be far more deadly. . . . We did not ask for this present challenge, but we accept it. Like other generations of Americans, we will meet the responsibility of defending human liberty against violence and aggression.

3.3 End of Major Combat Operations

USS Abraham Lincoln
San Diego, California
October 29, 2001

My fellow Americans: Major combat operations in Iraq have ended. In the battle of Iraq, the United States and our allies have prevailed. And now our coalition is engaged in securing and reconstructing that country.

In this battle, we have fought for the cause of liberty, and for the peace of the world. Our nation and our coalition are proud of this accomplishment—yet, it is you, the members of the United States military, who achieved it. Your courage, your willingness to face danger for your country and for each other, made this day possible. Because of you, our nation is more secure. Because of you, the tyrant has fallen, and Iraq is free. . . .

This nation thanks all the members of our coalition who joined in a noble cause. We thank the Armed Forces of the United Kingdom, Australia, and Poland, who shared in the hardships of war. We thank all the citizens of Iraq who welcomed our troops and joined in the liberation of their own country. And tonight, I have a special word for Secretary Rumsfeld, for General Franks, and for all the men and women who wear the uniform of the United States: America is grateful for a job well done. . . .

In the images of falling statues, we have witnessed the arrival of a new era. For a hundred of years of war, culminating in the nuclear age, military technology was designed and deployed to inflict casualties on an ever-growing scale. In defeating Nazi Germany and Imperial Japan, Allied forces destroyed entire cities, while enemy leaders who started the conflict were safe until the final days. Military power was used to end a regime by breaking a nation.

Today, we have the greater power to free a nation by breaking a dangerous and aggressive regime. With new tactics and precision weapons, we can achieve military objectives without directing violence against civilians. No device of man can remove the tragedy from war; yet it is a great moral advance when the guilty have far more to fear from war than the innocent.

In the images of celebrating Iraqis, we have also seen the ageless appeal of human freedom. Decades of lies and intimidation could not make the Iraqi people love their oppressors or desire their own enslavement.

Men and women in every culture need liberty like they need food and water and air. Everywhere that freedom arrives, humanity rejoices; and everywhere that freedom stirs, let tyrants fear.

We have difficult work to do in Iraq. We're bringing order to parts of that country that remain dangerous. We're pursuing and finding leaders of the old regime, who will be held to account for their crimes. We've begun the search for hidden chemical and biological weapons and already know of hundreds of sites that will be investigated. We're helping to rebuild Iraq, where the dictator built palaces for himself, instead of hospitals and schools. And we will stand with the new leaders of Iraq as they establish a government of, by, and for the Iraqi people.

The transition from dictatorship to democracy will take time, but it is worth every effort. Our coalition will stay until our work is done. Then we will leave, and we will leave behind a free Iraq.

The battle of Iraq is one victory in a war on terror that began on September the 11, 2001—and still goes on. That terrible morning, 19 evil men—the shock troops of a hateful ideology—gave America and the civilized world a glimpse of their ambitions. They imagined, in the words of one terrorist, that September the 11th would be the "beginning of the end of America." By seeking to turn our cities into killing fields, terrorists and their allies believed that they could destroy this nation's resolve, and force our retreat from the world. They have failed.

In the battle of Afghanistan, we destroyed the Taliban, many terrorists, and the camps where they trained. We continue to help the Afghan people lay roads, restore hospitals, and educate all of their children. Yet we also have dangerous work to complete. . . .

From Pakistan to the Philippines to the Horn of Africa, we are hunting down al Qaeda killers. Nineteen months ago, I pledged that the terrorists would not escape the patient justice of the United States. And as of tonight, nearly one-half of al Qaeda's senior operatives have been captured or killed.

The liberation of Iraq is a crucial advance in the campaign against terror. We've removed an ally of al Qaeda, and cut off a source of terrorist funding. And this much is certain: No terrorist network will gain weapons of mass destruction from the Iraqi regime, because the regime is no more.

In these 19 months that changed the world, our actions have been focused and deliberate and proportionate to the offense. We have not forgotten the victims of September the 11th—the last phone calls, the cold murder of children, the searches in the rubble. With those attacks, the terrorists and their supporters declared war on the United States. And war is what they got.

Our war against terror is proceeding according to principles that I have made clear to all: Any person involved in committing or planning terrorist attacks against the American people becomes an enemy of this country, and a target of American justice.

Any person, organization, or government that supports, protects, or harbors terrorists is complicit in the murder of the innocent, and equally guilty of terrorist crimes.

Any outlaw regime that has ties to terrorist groups and seeks or possesses weapons of mass destruction is a grave danger to the civilized world—and will be confronted.

And anyone in the world, including the Arab world, who works and sacrifices for freedom has a loyal friend in the United States of America. . . . .The use of force has been—and remains—our last resort. Yet all can know, friend and foe alike, that our nation has a mission: We will answer threats to our security, and we will defend the peace.

Our mission continues. Al Qaeda is wounded, not destroyed. The scattered cells of the terrorist network still operate in many nations, and we know from daily intelligence that they continue to plot against free people. The proliferation of deadly weapons remains a serious danger. The enemies of freedom are not idle, and neither are we. Our government has taken unprecedented measures to defend the homeland. And we will continue to hunt down the enemy before he can strike.

The war on terror is not over; yet it is not endless. We do not know the day of final victory, but we have seen the turning of the tide. No act of the terrorists will change our purpose, or weaken our resolve, or alter their fate. Their cause is lost. Free nations will press on to victory.

Other nations in history have fought in foreign lands and remained to occupy and exploit. Americans, following a battle, want nothing more than to return home. . . .

Those we lost were last seen on duty. Their final act on this Earth was to fight a great evil and bring liberty to others. All of you—all in this generation of our military—have taken up the highest calling of history. You're defending your country, and protecting the innocent from harm. And wherever you go, you carry a message of hope—a message that is ancient and ever new. In the words of the prophet Isaiah, "To the captives, 'come out,'—and to those in darkness, 'be free'."

3.4 Future of Iraq

White House
Washington, DC
September 7, 2003

Nearly two years ago, following deadly attacks on our country, we began a systematic campaign against terrorism. These months have been a time of new responsibilities, and sacrifice, and national resolve and great progress.

America and a broad coalition acted first in Afghanistan, by destroying the training camps of terror, and removing the regime that harbored al Qaeda.... And we acted in Iraq, where the former regime sponsored terror, possessed and used weapons of mass destruction, and for twelve years defied the clear demands of the United Nations Security Council. Our coalition enforced these international demands in one of the swiftest and most humane military campaigns in history.

For a generation leading up to September the 11th, 2001, terrorists and their radical allies attacked innocent people in the Middle East and beyond, without facing a sustained and serious response. The terrorists became convinced that free nations were decadent and weak. And they grew bolder, believing that history was on their side. Since America put out the fires of September the 11th, and mourned our dead, and went to war, history has taken a different turn. We have carried the fight to the enemy. We are rolling back the terrorist threat to civilization, not on the fringes of its influence, but at the heart of its power.

This work continues. In Iraq, we are helping the long suffering people of that country to build a decent and democratic society at the center of the Middle East. Together we are transforming a place of torture chambers and mass graves into a nation of laws and free institutions. This undertaking is difficult and costly—yet worthy of our country, and critical to our security.

The Middle East will either become a place of progress and peace, or it will be an exporter of violence and terror that takes more lives in America and in other free nations. The triumph of democracy and tolerance in Iraq, in Afghanistan and beyond would be a grave setback for international terrorism. The terrorists thrive on the support of tyrants and the resentments of oppressed peoples. When tyrants fall, and resentment gives way to hope, men and women in every culture reject the ideologies of terror, and turn to the pursuits of peace. Everywhere that freedom takes hold, terror will retreat.

Our enemies understand this. They know that a free Iraq will be free of them—free of assassins, and torturers, and secret police. They know that as democracy rises in Iraq, all of their hateful ambitions will fall like the statues of the former dictator. And that is why, five months after we liberated Iraq, a collection of killers is desperately trying to undermine Iraq's progress and throw the country into chaos.

Some of the attackers are members of the old Saddam regime, who fled the battlefield and now fight in the shadows. Some of the attackers are foreign terrorists, who have come to Iraq to pursue their war on America and other free nations. We cannot be certain to what extent these groups work together. We do know they have a common goal—reclaiming Iraq for tyranny.

Most, but not all, of these killers operate in one area of the country. The attacks you have heard and read about in the last few weeks have occurred predominantly in the central region of Iraq, between Baghdad and Tikrit—Saddam Hussein's former stronghold. The north of Iraq is generally stable and is moving forward with reconstruction and self-government. The same trends are evident in the south, despite recent attacks by terrorist groups.

Though their attacks are localized, the terrorists and Saddam loyalists have done great harm. They have ambushed American and British service members—who stand for freedom and order. They have killed civilian aid workers of the United Nations—who represent the compassion and generosity of the world. They have bombed the Jordanian embassy—the symbol of a peaceful Arab country. And last week they murdered a respected cleric and over a hundred Muslims at prayer—bombing a holy shrine and a symbol of Islam's peaceful teachings. This violence is directed not only against our coalition, but against anyone in Iraq who stands for decency, and freedom and progress.

There is more at work in these attacks than blind rage. The terrorists have a strategic goal. They want us to leave Iraq before our work is done. They want to shake the will of the civilized world. In the past, the terrorists have cited the examples of Beirut and Somalia, claiming that if you inflict harm on Americans, we will run from a challenge. In this, they are mistaken.

Two years ago, I told the Congress and the country that the war on terror would be a lengthy war, a different kind of war, fought on many fronts in many places. Iraq is now the central front. Enemies of freedom are making a desperate stand there—and there they must be defeated. This will take time and require sacrifice. Yet we will do what is necessary, we will spend what is necessary, to achieve this essential victory in the war on terror, to promote freedom and to make our own nation more secure. . . .

Our strategy in Iraq has three objectives: destroying the terrorists, enlisting the support of other nations for a free Iraq and helping Iraqis assume responsibility for their own defense and their own future.

First, we are taking direct action against the terrorists in the Iraqi theater, which is the surest way to prevent future attacks on coalition forces and the Iraqi people. We are staying on the offensive, with a series of precise strikes against enemy targets increasingly guided by intelligence given to us by Iraqi citizens.

Since the end of major combat operations, we have conducted raids seizing many caches of enemy weapons and massive amounts of ammunition, and we have captured or killed hundreds of Saddam loyalists and terrorists. So far, of the fifty-five most wanted former Iraqi leaders, forty-two are dead or in custody. We are sending a clear message: anyone who seeks to harm our soldiers can know that our soldiers are hunting for them.

Second, we are committed to expanding international cooperation in the reconstruction and security of Iraq, just as we are in Afghanistan. Our military commanders in Iraq advise me that the current number of American troops—nearly 130,000—is appropriate to their mission. They are joined by over 20,000 service members from twenty-nine other countries. Two multinational divisions, led by the British and the Poles, are serving alongside our forces—and in order to share the burden more broadly, our commanders have requested a third multinational division to serve in Iraq.

Some countries have requested an explicit authorization of the United Nations Security Council before committing troops to Iraq. I have directed Secretary of State Colin Powell to introduce a new Security Council resolution, which would authorize the creation of a multinational force in Iraq, to be led by America.

I recognize that not all of our friends agreed with our decision to enforce the Security Council resolutions and remove Saddam Hussein from power. Yet we cannot let past differences interfere with present duties. Terrorists in Iraq have attacked representatives of the civilized world, and opposing them must be the cause of the civilized world. Members of the United Nations now have an opportunity—and the responsibility—to assume a broader role in assuring that Iraq becomes a free and democratic nation.

Third, we are encouraging the orderly transfer of sovereignty and authority to the Iraqi people. Our coalition came to Iraq as liberators and we will depart as liberators. Right now Iraq has its own Governing Council, comprised of twenty-five leaders representing Iraq's diverse people. The Governing Council recently appointed cabinet ministers to run government departments. Already more than 90 percent of towns and cities have functioning local governments, which are restoring basic services. We're helping to train civil defense forces to keep order, and an Iraqi police service to enforce the law, a facilities protection service, Iraqi border guards to help secure the borders, and a new Iraqi army. In all these roles, there are now some 60,000 Iraqi citizens under arms, defending the security of their own country, and we are accelerating the training of more.

Iraq is ready to take the next steps toward self-government. The Security Council resolution we introduce will encourage Iraq's Governing Council to submit a plan and a timetable for the drafting of a constitution and for free elections. From the outset, I have expressed confidence in the ability of the Iraqi people to govern themselves. Now they must rise to the responsibilities of a free people and secure the blessings of their own liberty.

Our strategy in Iraq will require new resources. We have conducted a thorough assessment of our military and reconstruction needs in Iraq, and also in Afghanistan. I will soon submit to Congress a request for $87 billion.... Secretary Powell will meet with representatives of many nations to discuss their financial contributions to the reconstruction of Afghanistan. Next month, he will hold a similar funding conference for the reconstruction of Iraq. Europe, Japan and states in the Middle East all will benefit from the success of freedom in these two countries, and they should contribute to that success.

The people of Iraq are emerging from a long trial. For them, there will be no going back to the days of the dictator, to the miseries and humiliation he inflicted on that good country. For the Middle East and the world, there will be no going back to the days of fear, when a brutal and aggressive tyrant possessed terrible weapons. And for America, there will be no going back to the era before September the 11th, 2001—to false comfort in a dangerous world. We have learned that terrorist attacks are not caused by the use of strength; they are invited by the perception of weakness. And the surest way to avoid attacks on our own people is to engage the enemy where he lives and plans. We are fighting that enemy in Iraq and Afghanistan today so that we do not meet him again on our own streets, in our own cities.... We accept the duties of our generation. We are active and resolute in our own defense. We are serving in freedom's cause—and that is the cause of all mankind.

3.5 Steps to Help Iraq Achieve Democracy

United States Army War College
Carlisle, Pennsylvania
May 24, 2004

I've come here tonight to report to all Americans, and to the Iraqi people, on the strategy our nation is pursuing in Iraq, and the specific steps we're taking to achieve our goals.

The actions of our enemies over the last few weeks have been brutal, calculating, and instructive. We've seen a car bombing take the life of a 61-year-old Iraqi named Izzedin Saleem, who was serving as President of the Governing Council. This crime shows our enemy's intention to prevent Iraqi self-government, even if that means killing a lifelong Iraqi patriot and a faithful Muslim. . . . We've also seen images of a young American facing decapitation. This vile display shows a contempt for all the rules of warfare, and all the bounds of civilized behavior. It reveals a fanaticism that was not caused by any action of ours, and would not be appeased by any concession.

We suspect that the man with the knife was an al Qaeda associate named Zarqawi. He and other terrorists know that Iraq is now the central front in the war on terror. And we must understand that, as well. The return of tyranny to Iraq would be an unprecedented terrorist victory, and a cause for killers to rejoice. It would also embolden the terrorists, leading to more bombings, more beheadings, and more murders of the innocent around the world.

The rise of a free and self-governing Iraq will deny terrorists a base of operation, discredit their narrow ideology, and give momentum to reformers across the region. This will be a decisive blow to terrorism at the heart of its power, and a victory for the security of America and the civilized world.

Our work in Iraq has been hard. Our coalition has faced changing conditions of war, and that has required perseverance, sacrifice, and an ability to adapt. The swift removal of Saddam Hussein's regime last spring had an unintended effect: Instead of being killed or captured on the battlefield, some of Saddam's elite guards shed their uniforms and melted into the civilian population. These elements of Saddam's repressive regime and secret police have reorganized, rearmed, and adopted sophisticated terrorist tactics. They've linked up with foreign fighters and terrorists. . . . These groups and individuals have conflicting ambitions, but they share a goal: They hope to wear out the patience of Americans, our coalition, and Iraqis before the arrival of effective self-government, and before Iraqis have the capability to defend their freedom. . . .

Helping construct a stable democracy after decades of dictatorship is a massive undertaking. Yet we have a great advantage. Whenever people are given a choice in the matter, they prefer lives of freedom to lives of fear. . . . The terrorists' only influence is violence, and their only agenda is death. Our agenda, in contrast, is freedom and independence, security and prosperity for the Iraqi people. And by removing a source of terrorist violence and instability in the Middle East, we also make our own country more secure.

Our coalition has a clear goal, understood by all—to see the Iraqi people in charge of Iraq for the first time in generations. America's task in Iraq is not only to defeat an enemy, it is to give strength to a friend—a free, representative government that serves its people and fights on their behalf. And the sooner this goal is achieved, the sooner our job will be done.

There are five steps in our plan to help Iraq achieve democracy and freedom. We will hand over authority to a sovereign Iraqi government, help establish security, continue rebuilding Iraq's infrastructure, encourage more international support, and move toward a national election that will bring forward new leaders empowered by the Iraqi people.

The first of these steps will occur next month, when our coalition will transfer full sovereignty to a government of Iraqi citizens who will prepare the way for national elections. On June 30th, the Coalition Provisional Authority will cease to exist, and will not be replaced. The occupation will end, and Iraqis will govern their own affairs. . . . America and other countries will continue to provide technical experts to help Iraq's ministries of government, but these ministries will report to Iraq's new prime minister.

The United Nations Special Envoy, Lakhdar Brahimi, is now consulting with a broad spectrum of Iraqis to determine the composition of this interim government. . . . In addition to a president, two vice presidents, and a prime minister, twenty-six Iraqi ministers will oversee government departments, from health to justice to defense. This new government will be advised by a national council, which will be chosen in July by Iraqis representing their country's diversity. This interim government will exercise full sovereignty until national elections are held. . . .

All along, some have questioned whether the Iraqi people are ready for self-government, or even want it. And all along, the Iraqi people have given their answer. In settings where Iraqis have met to discuss their country's future, they have endorsed representative government. . . .

The June 30th transfer of sovereignty is an essential commitment of our strategy. Iraqis are proud people who resent foreign control of their affairs, just as we would. After decades under the tyrant, they are also reluctant to trust authority. By keeping our promise on June 30th, the coalition will demonstrate that we have no interest in occupation. And full sovereignty will give Iraqis a direct interest in the success of their own government. . . .

The second step in the plan for Iraqi democracy is to help establish the stability and security that democracy requires. Coalition forces and the Iraqi people have the same enemies—the terrorists, illegal militia, and Saddam loyalists who stand between the Iraqi people and their future as a free nation. Working as allies, we will defend Iraq and defeat these enemies. America will provide forces and support necessary for achieving these goals. . . . Given the recent increase in violence, we'll maintain our troop level at the current 138,000 as long as necessary. . . . If they need more troops, I will send them. . . .

In the city of Fallujah, there's been considerable violence by Saddam loyalists and foreign fighters, including the murder of four American contractors. American soldiers and Marines could have used overwhelming force. Our commanders, however, consulted with Iraq's Governing Council and local officials, and determined that massive strikes against the enemy would alienate the local population, and increase support for the insurgency. So we have pursued a different approach. We're making security a shared responsibility in Fallujah. Coalition commanders have worked with local leaders to create an all-Iraqi security force, which is now patrolling the city. Our soldiers and Marines will continue to disrupt enemy attacks on our supply routes, conduct joint patrols with Iraqis to destroy bomb factories and safe houses, and kill or capture any enemy.

We want Iraqi forces to gain experience and confidence in dealing with their country's enemies. We want the Iraqi people to know that we trust their growing capabilities, even as we help build them. . . . Successful fighting units need a sense of cohesion, so we've lengthened and intensified their training. Successful units need to know they are fighting for the future of their own country, not for any occupying power, so we are ensuring that Iraqi forces serve under an Iraqi chain of command. Successful fighting units need the best possible leadership, so we improved the vetting and training of Iraqi officers and senior enlisted men. . . .

A new team of senior military officers is now assessing every unit in Iraq's security forces. I've asked this team to oversee the training of a force of 260,000 Iraqi soldiers, police, and other security personnel. . . .

The eventual goal is an Iraqi army of 35,000 soldiers in 27 battalions, fully prepared to defend their country.

After June 30th, American and other forces will still have important duties. American military forces in Iraq will operate under American command as a part of a multinational force authorized by the United Nations. Iraq's new sovereign government will still face enormous security challenges, and our forces will be there to help.

The third step in the plan for Iraqi democracy is to continue rebuilding that nation's infrastructure, so that a free Iraq can quickly gain economic independence and a better quality of life. Our coalition has already helped Iraqis to rebuild schools and refurbish hospitals and health clinics, repair bridges, upgrade the electrical grid, and modernize the communications system. And now a growing private economy is taking shape. A new currency has been introduced. Iraq's Governing Council approved a new law that opens the country to foreign investment for the first time in decades. Iraq has liberalized its trade policy, and today an Iraqi observer attends meetings of the World Trade Organization. Iraqi oil production has reached more than two million barrels per day, bringing revenues of nearly $6 billion so far this year, which is being used to help the people of Iraq. And thanks in part to the efforts of former Secretary of State James Baker, many of Iraq's largest creditors have pledged to forgive or substantially reduce Iraqi debt incurred by the former regime. . . .

We're urging other nations to contribute to Iraqi reconstruction—and thirty-seven countries and the IMF and the World Bank have so far pledged $13.5 billion in aid. . . .

A new Iraq will also need a humane, well-supervised prison system. Under the dictator, prisons like Abu Ghraib were symbols of death and torture. That same prison became a symbol of disgraceful conduct by a few American troops who dishonored our country and disregarded our values. America will fund the construction of a modern, maximum security prison. . . . We will demolish the Abu Ghraib prison, as a fitting symbol of Iraq's new beginning.

The fourth step in our plan is to enlist additional international support for Iraq's transition. At every stage, the United States has gone to the United Nations—to confront Saddam Hussein, to promise serious consequences for his actions, and to begin Iraqi reconstruction. Today, the United States and Great Britain presented a new resolution in the Security Council to help move Iraq toward self-government. . . . Despite past disagreements, most nations have indicated strong support for the success of a free Iraq. And I'm confident they will share in the responsibility of assuring that success. . . .

The fifth and most important step is free, national elections, to be held no later than next January. . . . In that election, the Iraqi people will choose a transitional national assembly, the first freely-elected, truly representative national governing body in Iraq's history. This assembly will serve as Iraq's legislature, and it will choose a transitional government with executive powers. The transitional national assembly will also draft a new constitution, which will be presented to the Iraqi people in a referendum scheduled for the fall of 2005. Under this new constitution, Iraq will elect a permanent government by the end of next year. . . .

Completing the five steps to Iraqi elected self-government will not be easy. There's likely to be more violence before the transfer of sovereignty, and after the transfer of sovereignty. The terrorists and Saddam loyalists would rather see many Iraqis die than have any live in freedom. But terrorists will not determine the future of Iraq. . . .

I sent American troops to Iraq to defend our security, not to stay as an occupying power. I sent American troops to Iraq to make its people free, not to make them American. Iraqis will write their own history, and find their own way. As they do, Iraqis can be certain, a free Iraq will always have a friend in the United States of America. . . .

We did not seek this war on terror, but this is the world as we find it. We must keep our focus. We must do our duty. History is moving, and it will tend toward hope, or tend toward tragedy. Our terrorist enemies have a vision that guides and explains all their varied acts of murder. . . . It is a totalitarian political ideology, pursued with consuming zeal, and without conscience.

Our actions, too, are guided by a vision. We believe that freedom can advance and change lives in the greater Middle East, as it has advanced and changed lives in Asia, and Latin America, and Eastern Europe, and Africa. . . . America and all the world will be safer when hope has returned to the Middle East.

These two visions—one of tyranny and murder, the other of liberty and life—clashed in Afghanistan. . . .These two visions have now met in Iraq, and are contending for the future of that country. The failure of freedom would only mark the beginning of peril and violence. But, my fellow Americans, we will not fail. We will persevere, and defeat this enemy, and hold this hard-won ground for the realm of liberty.

Questions to Discuss

1. In Speeches 3.1 and 3.2, Bush argues that Iraq's past history of aggression and deception prove current and future hostile intent. Is Bush overstating the threat or showing a predisposition to view Iraq's actions from a particular perspective?

2. In Speech 3.2, Bush argues that Iraq poses a "unique" threat. Is Iraq different from North Korea, Iran, Pakistan, Israel, or other countries that have pursued WMD?

3. In Speech 3.2, Bush said that if the United State went to war in Iraq, it would "take every precaution that is possible . . . plan carefully . . . act with the full power of the United States military [and] act with allies at our side." Did Bush adequately follow through on each of these points?

4. In several speeches, Bush connects the war in Iraq to the overall war on terrorism. Is this connection justified?

5. In Speeches 3.3, 3.4 and 3.5, Bush expresses optimism about Iraq's future stability and development of democracy. Is this optimism justified? Did Bush put greater focus on these goals because Iraq's presumed weapons of mass destruction arsenal had not been found?

Chapter 4

Security Issues

During the 2000 presidential campaign, George W. Bush repeatedly stressed that, despite recent positive developments such as the end of the Cold War and growth of U.S. power, the United States continued to face significant security threats (Speech 1.1). Bush argued that the United States needed to build the military of the twenty-first century, pursue new technologies for defense, and address the rising danger of weapons proliferation. He kept focus on these themes in the first months of his administration and each was recast and reinvigorated by the 9/11 attacks, so they proved to be some of the major policies of his administration.

Shaping the Military of the Twenty-First Century

Bush asked Secretary of Defense Rumsfeld to conduct a comprehensive review of the U.S. military strategy, force structure and budget priorities. Most military experts agreed with Bush that a review and "military transformation" was long overdue. During the Cold War, U.S. defense planning was based around a "two war strategy," in which the United States would simultaneously fight the Soviet Union and a regional power. Weapons purchases, training priorities, and strategic planning were driven by the strategy's dual goals. At the Cold War's end, the strategy was redefined to mean the ability to simultaneously fight two regional wars, for example in the Middle East and the Korean peninsula. Then, the need for noncombat missions increased and new threats emerged. Therefore, efforts to address a wide range of specific policy problems—from humanitarian crises to peacekeeping to drugs to proliferation—were grafted onto the two war strategy. At the same time, many people hoped to reap a "peace dividend" by shifting money from defense to domestic programs. By the late 1990s, the military's responsibilities had increased, but its budget had decreased by about one-quarter from 1990 levels. Also, many weapons had been purchased to fight an old enemy and were less useful in modern contingencies. A full-scale review was necessary to get military goals and capabilities back in balance, to consider appropriate responses to emerging threats and to address the many ways that technology had changed the battlefield in recent years.

Rumsfeld quickly created more than twenty panels to review particular planning questions. The panels included many civilians and outside experts. Criticism soon emerged from uniformed military and congressional officials who felt that their views were being excluded from the process. There was also frustration with Rumsfeld's insistence on closed panels that released little information until their reviews were complete. Finally, some strong defense supporters in Congress were disappointed that increases in defense spending were being delayed until completion of the review and that Bush's first budget request largely mirrored President Clinton's plans. Many held Rumsfeld personally responsible for the slow and controversial review process, and he was widely criticized.

The closer the review got to completion, the more worries were expressed about its likely implications. These worries highlighted the existence of divergent views on key policy questions: How large should the U.S. military be in a world largely at peace? Should money be spent on increasing salaries and benefits for personnel or on new weapons acquisitions? Does a focus on future generations of weapons leave the country without necessary tools in the short run? How would base closings and spending cuts affect local economies? These and other questions seemed likely to trigger sharp battles between the political parties, between the executive and legislative branches, between civilian and military officials, and within the military itself.

During the summer of 2001, some panels' findings were released and other details leaked out, but the full review was not yet complete on September 11. When the administration finally released its ideas on September 30 in the Congressionally mandated Quadrennial Defense Review (QDR), the political atmosphere was very different than had been anticipated. The attacks of September 11 seemed to confirm the ideas that America now faced very different threats and would need very different tools. The attacks also lessened partisan and other disputes over defense issues as most people rallied around the need for a strong, national response. Increased budgetary support allowed the military to invest in new technologies, even as it continued older programs. Rumsfeld's personal reputation and influence also rose as he handled briefings and made tough statements. Some quipped, "[He] may not have been a very good secretary of defense, but he is a remarkable secretary of war."[1] Finally, by triggering military action in Afghanistan, 9/11 had an indirect effect on military transformation by providing a theater in which to demonstrate some of the country's newest weapons and military strategies.

A major Bush speech on military policy in December 2001 stressed how 9/11 had ushered in a new era that "required [America] once again to change the way our military thinks and fights" (Speech 4.1). It was now not a matter of choice, but of necessity. Bush's speech also included a long discussion of how new communications technology, precision-guided munitions, and unmanned Predator drones had led to quick victory in Afghanistan.

In the QDR and other policy statements, the Bush administration introduced several ideas. The two war strategy was modified: the United States should still be able two fight wars, but it would only plan enough forces to occupy one country. The idea of planning around country threats was replaced by a process of identifying vulnerable areas, for example information networks and space assets. The QDR also advanced six transformational goals, including projecting global power, protecting information networks and space capabilities, and coordinating different U.S. forces. Bush also formalized his goal of maintaining the world's top military force in *The National Security Strategy of the United States of America* (NSS) issued in September 2002. The NSS declared:

> The United States must and will maintain the capability to defeat any attempt by an enemy—whether a state or nonstate actor—to impose its will on the United States, our allies, or our friends. . . . Our forces will be strong enough to dissuade potential adversaries from pursuing a military build-up in hopes of surpassing, or equaling, the power of the United States.[2]

The administration's goals for transformation were applauded by many analysts, but some felt that the QDR and other plans lacked real detail. As Rumsfeld and Bush attempted to add those details through the budget process in 2002 and 2003, they were helped by the post–9/11 political environment, but they still faced difficulties tied to some of the unsettled questions of summer 2001. Increasing defense spending by more than 25 percent in three years, made for easy acceptance of administration requests for programs such as a new class of Army combat vehicles, a new type of Navy destroyer, and new Predators. On the other hand, when the administration tried to cut existing programs, it often met resistance. The Army's Crusader artillery program was cut, but only after several failed attempts and Rumsfeld took the unusual step of writing an editorial in the *Washington Post* explaining the decision. A new round of base closings was agreed to, but congressional pressure forced it to be postponed until 2005. Congress also continued to fund programs for M-1 tanks and B-1 bombers at levels higher than administration requests. Similarly, when Rumsfeld sought to bring transformation to personnel and procurement issues in 2003, he achieved mixed results. He did succeed in changing many civil-service rules for the Pentagon, but he lost on efforts to reorganize the Defense Department's assistant secretaries and to get new authority to shift money from one defense program to another.

The war in Iraq provided another test of the administration's strategies and military transformation. The extensive use of special operations troops, advanced communications and munitions technology, along with the decision to use fewer, faster-moving ground troops was seen as a reflection of the new Pentagon. When the initial fighting went well, the administration, and Rumsfeld specifically, earned new political capital. When commanders in the field began to complain about vulnerable supply lines and violence continued, that capital waned.

By 2004, continued violence in Iraq had greatly lessened bipartisan support for Bush's military policies. In addition, mounting budget deficits made many in Congress question Bush's proposed 7 percent increase in defense spending for fiscal year 2005. Long-term commitments to many expensive weapons programs also made further innovation difficult.

During the 2000 campaign and early stages of Rumsfeld's review, Bush suggested the need to reevaluate America's alignment of foreign-based troops. These plans were delayed by events, but during the 2004 campaign Bush returned to the idea. He noted that U.S. troops "remained where the wars of the last century ended, in Europe and in Asia" (Speech 4.2). He suggested bringing home 60,000 to 70,000 uniformed personnel, and about 100,000 family members and civilian employees over the next decade. Other troops would move to new locations "to deal with unexpected threats." Bush did not give details in the speech, but the plan was to remove troops from large bases in Germany and South Korea and to establish new bases in the United States and in Eastern Europe.

Bush argued these changes would allow the United States to better employ its modernized military, reduce stress on military families, and save money. Critics suggested that money savings would be minimal, since new facilities would have to be built in the United States. They also suggested the move was politically motivated since it would please military families and alter expected tough debates on base closings. More importantly, they questioned why basing troops in the United States would make it easier to respond to global challenges and why troops were being removed from Germany and South Korea just as Bush was trying to reestablish good ties with U.S. allies and to confront North Korea.

National Missile Defense

The desire for some form of missile defense emerged almost as soon as missiles were first used as weapons during WWII. When changes in technology brought intercontinental missiles and increasingly powerful nuclear weapons, many Americans' sense of isolation and security was punctured and interest in a defense grew. Early desires for a defense were, however, thwarted by a lack of suitable technology.

Later, missile defenses were also held back by acceptance of the major nuclear strategies of deterrence and Mutual Assured Destruction (MAD). Deterrence involves using the threat of massive retaliation to prevent enemy attacks. For example, during the Cold War, no rational Soviet leader would attack the United States, since U.S. basing strategy and missile numbers assured that some U.S. missiles would survive any attack and be used to destroy Russian cities. Mutual Assured Destruction is achieved when both sides in a conflict have assured massive retaliatory capability. It leads to a tense, but stable, standoff between the adversaries. Belief in the stability of MAD was so strong that the United States and Soviet Union signed the Anti-Ballistic Missile Systems (ABM) Treaty in 1972. The treaty prohibited development of any nationwide missile defense system. It also banned the development of sea-based, air-based, mobile, or space-based missile defense systems. The treaty had no set end date, but allowed either country to withdraw with six-months notice.

In 1983, Ronald Reagan announced a desire to move beyond the inherent risks and moral questions raised by MAD to develop a space-based system. Reagan's Strategic Defense Initiative, dubbed "Star Wars" by critics, triggered great global debate. Technical difficulties and the end of the Cold War soon changed the debate. George H.W. Bush supported continuing research on new defense technologies, but came to focus the program on protection from an accidental nuclear launch rather than an intentional, massive attack. Public focus on the issue increased during the Persian Gulf War when U.S. forces used the Patriot defense system against short-range Scud missiles launched by Iraq. In his first term, Bill Clinton renounced the goal of a space-based shield and shifted much of the research focus to theater missile defense systems, such as the Patriot. In contrast, Republicans in Congress remained strong advocates of a broader national missile defense (NMD) that would protect the continental United States. Under domestic political pressure, Clinton agreed in 1996 to begin developing a nationwide system that could be deployed by 2003. In 1998, pressure for a defense increased when a group of private experts headed by Donald Rumsfeld reported their conclusions that intelligence agencies had underestimated the speed of proliferation and that North Korea and

Iran could have missiles capable of reaching the United States within five years. These developments shifted focus away from accidental Russian launches toward defense against rogue states. In 1999, Clinton signed the National Missile Defense Act, which stated that U.S. policy is "to deploy as soon as is technologically possible an effective national defense system." International pressure and two failed tests of defense technology led Clinton to announce in August 2000 that he would leave the main decisions on NMD development to the next president.

Bush was a strong supporter of broad missile defenses. His first budget request increased funding for NMD by 57 percent. In May 2001, he detailed his plans. Bush acknowledged that deterrence and the ABM treaty had served a purpose, but argued, "Today, the sun comes up on a vastly different world" where missiles are pursued by "some of the world's least-responsible states" (Speech 4.3). The United States should, therefore, move beyond the outdated ABM treaty and pursue a variety of defense options. Bush specifically mentioned sea-based capabilities and efforts to stop missiles in their boost phase, both of which represented important expansions beyond previous research plans. He also mentioned a desire to protect U.S. allies. Support for such a broad shield was designed, in part, to lessen allies' concerns that they would be left unprotected, but again expanded the program beyond previous goals. Bush acknowledged that the initial systems would provide only limited defense, but suggested that the country could build on its research successes in time.

Bush's plans met mixed reactions both domestically and abroad. The idea of a protective defense was inherently appealing, but critics disagreed with Bush on four key areas: level of threat, defense capabilities, financial costs, and international implications. Bush explicitly said the defense was not meant to meet a massive Russian attack, and he put little focus on accidental launches. The debate centered on the threat posed by rogue states. More countries were attaining WMD capability, but there was dispute over the speed and extent of their progress. The bigger dispute was over these countries' intentions. Countries might pursue weapons for a number of reasons, for example possible offensive action, deterrence, or international prestige. Only the first motive would justify a defense. Also, critics suggested that, even if countries had aggressive intentions, principles of deterrence would still prevent an attack on the United States. The administration countered these points by suggesting that many new countries sought offensive capabilities and that the United States should not gamble on the rationality of rising leaders.

If a threat warranted a defense, there was still the major question of whether a defense was technologically feasible. Reagan's space-based plans largely had been abandoned. Land-based systems of interceptor missiles armed with kill vehicles that would home in on the offensive warhead and smash into it at 15,000 miles per hour now garnered the most attention. This defense strategy required advances in radar and rocket technology and risked being countered by the enemy deploying multiple armed missiles or decoys that would complicate targeting the warhead. This system suffered two major failed tests under Clinton. Another option was to focus on the offensive missile's boost phase—a period when it is traveling slower and cannot deploy decoys. This strategy required basing advanced radar and defense systems close to launch sites and required acting very quickly after launch. Critics of NMD argued that these technical challenges made a perfect defense impossible. They also suggested that the closer the defense got to perfection the more it would encourage enemies to find other methods of delivering bombs, such as boats or simple suitcases. Bush and administration officials argued that complex technological programs always had setbacks early on, that one should never underestimate U.S. ingenuity and that the limits of technology would remain unknown unless research was conducted. Most crucially, they suggested that an imperfect defense was better than no defense.

By 2000, the United States had spent over $50 billion on defense projects. The ultimate cost of NMD was unknown since research was still in the early stages. The Congressional Budget Office estimated Bush's plans might ultimately cost $238 billion; some private estimates were significantly higher.[3] Critics felt that these were high figures to spend on unproven technology. They also suggested that the money could be better spent on programs to address domestic priorities, homeland defense, or foreign aid programs that might lessen anti-American feelings abroad. Bush countered that one could not put a price on security.

The final criticisms of NMD stemmed from its international implications. Russian and Chinese officials repeatedly expressed concern about proposed defenses. In 2000, they issued a joint statement warning of "the most grave adverse consequences"[4] if the United States proceeded. Russian officials argued that a defense would destabilize MAD and lead to a new arms race as countries would pursue new weapons and technologies to overwhelm the system. They also argued that the ABM treaty was the "cornerstone" of arms control and international security, so the U.S. withdrawal would bring all arms control agreements into question. China was even more concerned that a defense might limit its deterrent capabilities, because it had only about two dozen missiles. Chinese officials also worried that NMD might allow the United States to be more aggressive internationally and, specifically, to protect Taiwan. Criticism also came from some U.S. allies in Europe. They stressed the importance of the

ABM treaty and worried about antagonizing Russia just as it was reaching out to the West. Allies also recognized that a defense could affect their security. If U.S. enemies could not attack the United States, they might instead attack allies. Also, some radar stations would need to be based abroad. Bush stressed that the defense would not be sophisticated enough to call into question Russian or Chinese deterrent capabilities and that all countries would be safer from rogue attacks if a global defense was built.

In his May 2001 speech and elsewhere, Bush promised consultations with allies and Russia; however, he continued to make firm statements leading to doubts that anything he might hear would alter his plans. Missile defense was a major focus of Bush's first trip to Europe in June 2001. At a NATO summit, he faced sharp allied questioning. In meetings with Russian President Vladimir Putin, disagreement continued. Bush, though, was pleased that some European allies expressed support. More importantly, Putin expressed some flexibility on the issue. In a July meeting with Bush, Putin agreed to link discussions on defense systems with possible significant mutual reductions in offensive nuclear arsenals. Bush kept pressure on Russia. In August, he stated that the United States would withdraw from the ABM treaty "at a time convenient to America."[5] In Congress, worries over costs and international implications continued. On September 7, a congressional committee voted to cut $1.3 billion from Bush's proposed NMD budget and to require congressional approval of any test that would violate the ABM treaty.

As on plans for defense transformation, 9/11 reshaped the NMD debate. Some critics suggested the attacks proved that a missile defense would provide no protection against determined enemies. Supporters contended it showed the threat of an attack against the United States was real. More dramatically, 9/11 increased bipartisanship and lowered opposition to the administration's security policies. Coordinated action in the war on terrorism also reinforced a warming of U.S.–Russian relations.

Through the fall of 2001, U.S. and Russian officials met repeatedly. For a time, it appeared the two sides might agree to rework the ABM treaty to allow enhanced U.S. testing and research. The administration even postponed three missile tracking tests to allow more time for negotiation. Ultimately, though, no agreement could be reached. The United States refused a Russian request that they be briefed on every future test. More crucially, there really was no way to pursue the type of research program Bush supported while abiding by a treaty designed expressly to limit such testing.

On December 13, 2001, Bush announced that he had given formal notice to Russia that the United States would withdraw from the ABM treaty in six months. He again stressed that the ABM treaty was signed "in a vastly different world" (Speech 4.4). He argued that 9/11 showed the greatest threats to the United States and Russia now came from rogue states and terrorists with WMD. The inclusion of terrorism as a justification for NMD was new since his May speech and Bush's linking of terrorists and rogue states was an important reflection of his views. The speech included a discussion of how Russia was no longer a threat and was building ties with the United States. After the announcement, Putin expressed disappointment with Bush's action, but Putin's decision to work with the United States on other issues and his recognition that Russia had little leverage on the issue led him to state that the action would not lead to the long-feared break in U.S.–Russian relations. There was no mention of China in the speech, although Bush did call Chinese officials ahead of time to set up new security discussions.

With Russia's quiet reaction and the post–9/11 political environment, debates on NMD shifted from whether the United States would pursue a system, to what system would be developed. Bush favored simultaneous work on multiple defense projects using different technologies. He announced that the United States would begin by basing interceptors in Alaska and California in 2004. A failed test in December 2002 and production delays halted further testing and reignited debates over the system's reliability. Members of Congress and others continued to question funding increases for such unproven technology. Meanwhile, fears remain about possible international responses, such as a renewed arms race or suspicion of U.S. intentions, should the system become more effective in the future.

Global Efforts to Deal with Proliferation

Bush agreed with the conventional wisdom that the proliferation of WMD, particularly nuclear weapons, would hurt U.S. interests. These weapons would put the United States and its allies directly at risk, threaten stability in key regions, and potentially limit the U.S. ability to project global power. Bush, though, was more pessimistic than many observers. He doubted the effectiveness of existing treaties and inspection requirements; he also believed that if certain states achieved WMD capability, they would use the weapons.

The September 11 attacks demonstrated the vulnerability of the United States and its enemies' determination. Bush feared the next terrorist attack could involve WMD. Therefore, his December 2001 speech on military policy, his announcement of U.S. intentions to withdraw from the ABM treaty, and other statements all contained references to dangers posed both by terrorists and rogue states. In his 2002 State of the Union message, Bush gave this new threat a name, calling Iraq, Iran, North Korea, and their terrorist allies the "Axis of Evil" (Speech 2.3).

Bush's December 2001 speech stressed the emergence of the new threat, but laid out policy plans that followed past practices. He said, "We will strengthen nonproliferation treaties and toughen export controls" (Speech 4.1). He also announced plans to "expand efforts to provide peaceful employment for scientists who formerly worked in Soviet weapons facilities."

The key existing treaty was the Nuclear Non-Proliferation Treaty (NPT) signed in 1968. This treaty allowed the five nuclear weapons powers of the time—the United States, Soviet Union, England, France, and China—to retain their weapons. All other countries pledged to refrain from procuring or developing nuclear weapons, and to allow inspections by the International Atomic Energy Association (IAEA) to verify compliance. In response to complaints that the treaty would permanently establish a two-tiered world, the existing powers pledged to work toward nuclear disarmament, although no timetable was given, and to develop export policies that would help other countries develop peaceful nuclear power. Over time, close to 190 countries signed the agreement. Israel, India, and Pakistan all refused to sign and later joined the nuclear club. Iraq, Iran, North Korea, and Libya all signed the NPT, but apparently still continued to pursue weapons. Therefore, many observers felt that the treaty reinforced good behavior of states that had no interest in weapons, but did little to stop those who actively sought weapons. Views were divided on whether tighter export controls and more intrusive inspections would alter behavior.

The programs in Russia cited by Bush were part of the Cooperative Threat Reduction (CTR) program, often called Nunn-Lugar after its original legislative sponsors. The program was designed to help former Soviet states eliminate WMD and establish safeguards against weapons material or technical knowledge leaking out of the region. Programs secured nuclear storage cites, enhanced security for nuclear missiles, dismantled chemical weapons facilities, and helped scientists transition to new research fields. There were frequent complaints of slow progress, mismanaged funds, and lack of Russian cooperation. In early 2001, Bush suggested a 12 percent cutback in CTR funding, but after 9/11 he reversed his position and announced an expansion of the program. In June 2002, the United States and other G-8 countries announced plans to raise $20 billion—half of which would be provided by the United States—over a ten-year period to secure and eliminate weapons materials from Russia and other former Soviet states.

During 2002, the administration completed a comprehensive review on proliferation. Bush concluded that evidence of ongoing state programs and al Qaeda's interest in WMD showed that the United States faced a growing threat and needed new policies. Those new policies were enshrined in the NSS and in the *National Strategy to Combat Weapons of Mass Destruction* released in December 2002. In these documents, the administration argued a number of points: 1) the United States could no longer be sure that its enemies would lack WMD; 2) the United States needed to put more focus on defense of its territory, through NMD and enhanced homeland security; 3) the government should make plans to manage the consequences of attacks at home and abroad; and 4) the United States should continue nonproliferation programs, but needed to enhance them with a more proactive counterproliferation strategy.

Many of Bush's initiatives were not new. Following the Gulf War, which had highlighted the dangers posed by rising regional powers, the Clinton administration began the Defense Counterproliferation Initiative in 1993. Programs were established to defend against attacks and to limit their impact on military forces or domestic populations. The attacks of 9/11 and Bush's strong views, though, gave new impetus to these programs and put new focus on missile defense.

The most significant change between Clinton and Bush's counterproliferation strategies was Bush's public call for preemptive attacks "to forestall or prevent such hostile acts by our adversaries."[6] Bush first publicly discussed the idea of preemption in a June 2002 (Speech 2.4). The central idea was to destroy the weapons capabilities and, if necessary, the regimes of countries deemed unlikely to act responsibly or respond rationally to deterrence. Preemption was a driving force behind the 2003 war in Iraq. Critics suggested the concept went against international law and set a dangerous precedent. They also argued that the Iraq case showed the problem of what evidence could be used to justify an attack. Preemption also was a policy applicable to only a narrow window of opportunity. A country would have to make significant progress toward weapons capability to justify an attack, but had to be attacked before they acquired a weapon or the attack might trigger a devastating response.

Another new part of the Bush's counterproliferation strategy was increased focus on the interdiction of exported weapons and materials. In December 2002, U.S. satellites detected 15 missiles being loaded onto a ship in North Korea. The ship was believed to be heading to Yemen. After days of debate over international law, the administration asked a nearby Spanish naval vessel to stop and board the ship. The United States hoped that public discovery of the missiles would embarrass Yemen into refusing to claim them. Instead, Yemen demanded the ship be allowed to continue, so Spain and the United States had to back down. In a May 2003 speech in Poland, Bush announced a new Proliferation Security Initiative (PSI) (Speech 6.4). In line with international law, PSI participant countries agreed to search any vessel flying their flag or in their internal waters that is "reasonably suspected of transporting such cargoes to or from states or nonstate actors of proliferation concern."[7] Importantly, Bush did not organize PSI under NATO or UN authority.

Bush's focus on proliferation was welcomed by many U.S. and foreign specialists who had warned of this danger for years; however, his programs were criticized on four main grounds. First, previous proliferation efforts had focused on universal norms against any state acquiring WMD, but Bush's plans clearly divided the world into U.S. allies that were allowed to develop weapons and U.S. enemies that posed dangers. Second, some argued that Bush had put too much focus on limiting weapons capabilities and not enough on addressing motivations for proliferation. They suggested that efforts to bring peace in the Middle East, or dialogue on the Korean peninsula might have a more lasting impact. Third, they suggested that Bush's tough policies made compromise difficult and actually reinforced North Korean and Iranian views that the United States was a threat to their security. Fourth, they felt that Bush's broader nuclear policies made the United States appear hypocritical. Bush had refused to support the Comprehensive Test Ban Treaty, withdrawn from the ABM treaty, pressed for study of low yield bunker-buster nuclear weapons, and refused to move the United States to complete disarmament as called for in the NPT treaty. Bush thus appeared to demand significant change from others, but little from the United States.

The war in Iraq and new evidence of North Korean and Iranian activities kept global focus on Bush's policies. In December 2003, sharp attention was drawn to proliferation when it was revealed that Libya had purchased nuclear plans and material from a black-market network led by A.Q. Khan, the father of Pakistan's nuclear bomb. Further investigation discovered that the network was extensive and had found several willing buyers. Bush detailed the network's activities in a February 2004 speech (Speech 4.5). He laid out a seven point U.S. response that called for significant changes in international policies. Bush proposed expansion of PSI, renewed a call for a UN resolution criminalizing proliferation, and supported expansion of Nunn-Lugar programs to countries besides Russia. He then described the NPT's allowance of civilian nuclear programs as a "loophole" that allowed proliferators to develop weapons technology under the guise of civilian programs. He called for nuclear exporters to "refuse to sell enrichment and reprocessing equipment and technologies to any state that does not already possess full-scale, functioning enrichment and reprocessing plants" and to refuse to sell any nuclear equipment to countries that did not sign the IAEA's Additional Protocol that permits more intrusive inspections. Thus, Bush called into question a central idea of the NPT that countries should have access to peaceful nuclear technology.

Bush's ideas were hailed by some as a bold new direction. Others suggested that he had been too easy on Pakistan's leadership, which claimed ignorance of Khan's activities and pardoned him after a public confession. Bush was still criticized for saying little about changing U.S. policies. The speech also heightened existing tension between the administration and the IAEA. Bush did not consult with IAEA officials before the speech and he opposed IAEA suggestions that the production of all nuclear fuel be placed under international control.

Over the next few months, over sixty countries, including a hesitant Russia, joined PSI. The UN Security Council adopted resolution 1540, which called on states to refrain from aiding efforts by nonstate actors to acquire WMD and to take cooperative action to prevent illegal trafficking in WMD materials. The proposed new limits on exports were controversial and opposed both by some importing and some exporting states.

Specific Policies on the Axis of Evil, Plus One

In addition to Iraq, the three countries that received the most attention under Bush's proliferation policies were North Korea, Iran, and Libya. The administration's handling of these cases revealed policies that were generally tough, but were adapted case-by-case to meet to local conditions and allies' views.

North Korea

American and North Korean tensions date back to the 1945 division of the Korean peninsula to create a pro-Soviet north and pro-American south. In 1950, North Korea, led by Kim Il Sung, invaded the south. A U.S.-led UN force helped defend the south. Three years of fighting ended with a suspension of hostilities, but no formal peace treaty, and left the countries divided by one of the world's most militarized borders. In subsequent years, South Korea became a close U.S. ally, home of 30,000 U.S. troops, a thriving capitalist economy and, eventually, a democracy. North Korea remained a Soviet and Chinese ally, with a communist economy that performed increasingly poorly, and a Stalinist, authoritarian state.

North Korea first acquired a Soviet built nuclear power plant in the 1960s. In 1985, it finally signed the NPT, but then delayed IAEA inspections. This action led to fears that North Korea was engaged in clandestine efforts to produce nuclear weapons. In March 1993, North Korea announced it was withdrawing from the NPT. President Clinton responded by threatening military action against North Korea's nuclear facilities. After eighteen tense months, U.S. and North Korean officials signed the Agreed Framework in October 1994. Under the agreement, North Korea pledged to remain party to the NPT, to freeze construction and operation of nuclear reactors capable of producing weapons-grade material, and to allow IAEA inspections. The United States agreed to provide two safer nuclear reactors and heavy oil for energy needs, and to remove barriers to full economic and diplomatic relations. At the time, there was worry that the deal might be perceived as successful nuclear blackmail, but steps to move away from a war no one wanted were applauded. During the next few years, relations again grew tense. Both sides accused the other of reneging on the Agreed Framework. However, tensions eased in 2000 when South Korea's President Kim Dae Jung began a "sunshine policy" of bilateral contacts with the North and U.S. Secretary of State Madeleine Albright visited North Korea.

The first clear view into Bush's Korea policy came in March 2001 when Kim Dae Jung visited Washington. Before the visit, Secretary of State Powell suggested that the administration would continue Clinton's diplomatic initiatives, but he was rebuked publicly by other officials and soon announced a hard line. Bush told Kim that he did not support the sunshine policy and would take a tough position on North Korea's actions. Bush's response stemmed from his view that the Agreed Framework had given North Korea too many rewards while not ensuring disarmament and that North Korea could not be trusted to abide by agreements. In addition, he felt personal animosity toward North Korea's leader. In an unusually candid interview, Bush told a *Washington Post* reporter, "I loathe Kim Jong Il! I've got a visceral reaction to this guy because he is starving his people.... Maybe it's my religion, ... but I feel passionate about this."[8]

In October 2002, a new crisis emerged. A U.S. delegation confronted North Korea with intelligence evidence of a new uranium-enrichment program. The program was separate from the plutonium-based program frozen under the Agreed Framework. North Korean officials first claimed the enrichment program was for civilian use, then subsequently denied its existence. The Bush administration did not release news of the confrontational meeting for two weeks, during which time the Senate voted to support the war in Iraq. When they did discuss the meeting, U.S. officials demanded an unconditional end to the program. The United States did not immediately renounce the Agreed Framework, but fuel shipments were suspended by November. North Korea reacted angrily to U.S. pressure.

Over the next months, it withdrew from the NPT, expelled IAEA monitors, reopened its plutonium reprocessing facility, and reactivated a reactor capable of producing enough plutonium for six nuclear weapons per year.

In response to the North Korean moves, the United States talked tough, but took little firm action. Officially, a military option was not taken off the table; however, as the country prepared for war with Iraq, Bush made distinctions between the two countries. Also, there was little international support for the use of force against a well-armed North Korea since any military operation would entail high destruction and casualties. Economic levers were limited since North Korea had little foreign trade. North Korea's economy was already so weak that a move to temporarily stop U.S. food aid shipments was roundly criticized by allies. The administration pressed for UN action, but Russian and Chinese objections stopped even a mildly-worded proposed resolution. North Korea suggested addressing the tensions at bilateral talks, but Bush did not want a repeat of the Agreed Framework's concessions and he favored multilateral talks so the region's countries could help pressure North Korea.

In April 2003, the logjam was broken when North Korea—perhaps influenced by the U.S. determination shown in the Iraq war—agreed to multilateral talks, first including China and later Russia, Japan, and South Korea. All of these countries had a vested interest in a nuclear-free North Korea, but they did not always agree on the mix of incentives and punishments to achieve that goal. Publicly, Bush welcomed the series of talks as a chance for a diplomatic solution. It was clear, though, that sharp disagreement existed within the administration. For example, Under Secretary of State for Arms Control John R. Bolton called North Korea a "hellish nightmare" in a July 2003 speech.[9] Others, including Jack Pritchard, special envoy for negotiations with North Korea until he resigned in August 2003, favored a policy mixing incentives and punishments. In the talks, North Korean officials stated that they had already developed weapons, but there has been no independent confirmation of the claim. During the course of the series of meetings, the U.S. position evolved on several issues. The United States refused to sign a nonaggression treaty, but did suggest a less formal agreement of nonaggression. The United States first said incentives would come only after full North Korean disarmament, but later proposed a step-by-step process of North Korean action and reward. The two sides remained far apart, however, on the basic question of whether North Korea would freeze or completely dismantle its weapons program. Many feared North Korea would never agree to U.S. terms and that it was stalling in hopes of a better deal or to gain time to build up its arsenal.

Iran

Tensions between the United States and Iran also were long-standing and had become intense. Under the leadership of Reza Shah Pahlevi, Iran had been a close U.S. ally and increasingly Westernized. The 1979 revolution led by Ayatollah Khomeini completely reversed conditions. The Shah was deposed and replaced by a government based on fundamentalist Islamic ideology. The United States was declared the "great Satan," American diplomats were held hostage for over a year, and anything considered Western was criticized. American officials sharply criticized Iran on human rights issues, for seeking to export its revolution and for supporting terrorism. Over time, the rhetorical vehemence of the two sides lessened, but the countries maintained no formal diplomatic or trade ties. In the 1990s, reformers led by Prime Minister Mohammad Khatami gained some power. The Clinton administration expressed hope for further reform despite the continued power of religious conservatives. Many European officials were even more optimistic about reform prospects and increased diplomatic and trade ties to support Khatami.

In the first years of his administration, Bush did not focus great attention on Iran or its nuclear programs. Bush criticized Iranian steps away from reform—such as conservative vetoes of women's rights, press freedom and electoral reform legislation—and praised anti-government student protestors, but did not call directly for regime change. After 9/11, the administration expressed appreciation for Iran's support of the Northern Alliance in Afghanistan and encouragement of an Iraqi group it influenced to join a coalition of groups opposing Saddam Hussein. He repeatedly expressed concern that Russian commercial nuclear deals with Iran could lead to weapons advances, but Bush backed off when Putin vehemently insisted on Russia's right to continue the deals.

In August 2002, focus on Iran's nuclear program increased greatly, when an Iranian exile group released information on a huge centrifuge complex that could create weapons grade uranium. In time, Iranian officials acknowledged the facilities and the existence of a broader nuclear program. They were adamant, though, that all their facilities were for peaceful use and were intended to provide the country with cheap electricity to stimulate economic growth. This rationale was questioned by many, since Iran is a major oil producer. After the facilities were publicly revealed, the Bush administration said it had been aware of them and was concerned; however, with much of its attention focused on Iraq and North Korea, the United States left the further investigations of Iran's programs up to the IAEA.

International Atomic Energy Association inspectors soon grew frustrated. Iranian officials made efforts to delay inspections and repeatedly changed their claims. For example, Iranian officials first insisted that the centrifuges were made domestically. When samples of highly enriched uranium were found on the centrifuges, the officials said they must have been contaminated abroad. When asked about the suppliers, the officials claimed the centrifuges had been purchased through middlemen from an unknown source. In June 2003, Bush, supported by the IAEA's findings and frustrations, announced that the international community "will not tolerate construction of a nuclear weapon. Iran would be dangerous if they had a nuclear weapon."[10] U.S. options were limited, however, since European and Russian ties to Iran largely ruled out military or tough economic action unless a clearer threat could be demonstrated.

Focus, therefore, shifted to a planned November IAEA board meeting in which evidence would be reviewed. The 35 country panel then would decide whether to refer the matter to the UN Security Council for consideration of punitive sanctions. The United States planned to press for a tough stance, but foreign ministers from England, France, and Germany announced on October 20 that Iran had agreed to temporarily suspend enrichment efforts and allow aggressive inspections in return for pledges of future dialogue and European efforts to stop referral to the UN. American plans also were complicated by an IAEA report that harshly criticized Iran, but stopped short of declaring that it had violated the NPT. The November meeting was extremely tense and provided further indication of a rift between the United States and its European allies. Eventually, a compromise resolution was passed that "strongly deplore[d] Iran's past failures and breaches" and stated that any further evidence of a weapons program would immediately trigger a new meeting to consider referral to the UN.[11]

Hope that the compromise had resolved the situation soon vanished. In 2004, Iranian conservatives continued to limit moderates' electoral power, new evidence emerged that Iran had concealed information, and Iran suggested that international criticism was driven by U.S. bias. European governments, which were frustrated that their efforts at engagement had yielded poor results, became increasingly supportive of a tougher position. Still, although Iran was criticized again at a June 2004 IAEA meeting, referral to the UN was again deferred.

Libya

The one major nonproliferation success of the period was the December 2003 renunciation of WMD programs by Libya, a country on which few experts had focused great attention. Moves toward Libyan disarmament began in March 2003 when the son and heir-apparent of Libyan leader Moammar Gaddafi contacted British intelligence officers. During the following months, Libya turned over troves of documents and allowed British and U.S. officials to inspect previously secret chemical and nuclear facilities. Libyan officials were not entirely forthcoming and did not reveal an order they had made for centrifuge parts. U.S. intelligence learned of the deal and, in the first major use of PSI, the ship carrying the parts was seized. Libya then revealed new details, which showed its program was considerably more sophisticated than expected and which played a major part in revealing Khan's black-market network.

Bush took evident pleasure in his surprise December 19 announcement that Gaddafi had committed to dismantle all WMD programs. He took the occasion to review U.S. efforts in Iraq, Iran, and North Korea and suggested that these countries and others should emulate Libya's actions. Bush also pledged better relations as a reward for Libya's decision, which resulted in the April 2004 lifting of most U.S. economic sanctions, new trade talks, and the reestablishment of diplomatic ties.

Administration officials claimed Libya's actions showed the merits of their tough approach on proliferation. They noted that talks first began just as the United States was preparing to invade Iraq and that the interdiction of parts had been the final piece in convincing Libya to fully renounce its efforts. A former National Security Council official familiar with the process, though, suggested that Libya's disarmament was better seen as the final step in ending Libya's international isolation through a series of explicit quid pro quos.[12] In 1999, after Libya turned over for trial two intelligence officers involved in the 1988 bombing of Pan Am flight 103 over Lockerbie, Scotland which killed 270, the UN suspended sanctions against Libya. In 2003, Libya accepted responsibility for the bombing and agreed to compensate the victims' families, so UN sanctions were fully removed. Libya was told U.S. sanctions would not be lifted until they addressed concerns over WMD. Critics of Bush were more than happy to point out that the "Libyan model" of talks and incentives more closely mirrored past U.S. and European actions than it did Bush's counterproliferation tactics. Still, the carrots used to entice Libya may not have been as effective if the administration had not first threatened it with a big stick.

4.1 Speaking to the Citadel Cadets

The Citadel
Charleston, South Carolina
December 11, 2001

I have come to talk about the future security of our country, in a place where I took up this subject two years ago when I was candidate for President. In September 1999, I said here at the Citadel that America was entering a period of consequences that would be defined by the threat of terror, and that we faced a challenge of military transformation. That threat has now revealed itself, and that challenge is now the military and moral necessity of our time. So, today, I will set forth the commitments essential to victory in our war against terror. . . .

Four days ago, I joined the men and women of the USS Enterprise to mark the sixtieth anniversary of Pearl Harbor. December 7th, 1941 was a decisive day that changed our nation forever. In a single moment, America's "splendid isolation" was ended. And the four years that followed transformed the American way of war. . . .

Even more importantly, an American President and his successors shaped a world beyond a war. They rebuilt Europe with the Marshall Plan, formed a great alliance for freedom in NATO, and expressed the hope of collective security in the United Nations. America took the lead, becoming freedom's defender and assuming responsibilities that only we could bear.

September 11th, 2001—three months and a long time ago—set another dividing line in our lives and in the life of our nation. An illusion of immunity was shattered. A faraway evil became a present danger. And a great cause became clear: We will fight terror and those who sponsor it, to save our children from a future of fear.

To win this war, we have to think differently. The enemy who appeared on September 11th seeks to evade our strength and constantly searches for our weaknesses. So America is required once again to change the way our military thinks and fights. And starting on October 7th, the enemy in Afghanistan got the first glimpses of a new American military that cannot, and will not, be evaded. . . .

We are also beginning to see the possibilities of a world beyond the war on terror. We have a chance, if we take it, to write a hopeful chapter in human history. All at once, a new threat to civilization is erasing old lines of rivalry and resentment between nations. Russia and America are building a new cooperative relationship. India and the United States are increasingly aligned across a range of issues, even as we work closely with Pakistan. Germany and Japan are assuming new military roles, appropriate to their status as great democracies.

The vast majority of countries are now on the same side of a moral and ideological divide. We're making common cause with every nation that chooses lawful change over chaotic violence—every nation that values peace and safety and innocent life. . . .

Our lives, our way of life, and our every hope for the world depend on a single commitment: The authors of mass murder must be defeated, and never allowed to gain or use the weapons of mass destruction.

America and our friends will meet this threat with every method at our disposal. We will discover and destroy sleeper cells. We will track terrorist movements, trace their communications, disrupt their funding, and take their network apart, piece by piece.

Above all, we're acting to end the state sponsorship of terror. Rogue states are clearly the most likely sources of chemical and biological and nuclear weapons for terrorists. Every nation now knows that we cannot accept—and we will not accept—states that harbor, finance, train, or equip the agents of terror. Those nations that violate this principle will be regarded as hostile regimes. They have been warned, they are being watched, and they will be held to account.

Preventing mass terror will be the responsibilities of Presidents far into the future. And this obligation sets three urgent and enduring priorities for America. The first priority is to speed the transformation of our military.

When the Cold War ended, some predicted that the era of direct threats to our nation was over. Some thought our military would be used overseas—not to win wars, but mainly to police and pacify, to control crowds and contain ethnic conflict. They were wrong.

While the threats to America have changed, the need for victory has not. We are fighting shadowy, entrenched enemies—enemies using the tools of terror and guerrilla war—yet we are finding new tactics and new weapons to attack and defeat them. This revolution in our military is only beginning, and it promises to change the face of battle.

Afghanistan has been a proving ground for this new approach. These past two months have shown that an innovative doctrine and high-tech weaponry can shape and then dominate an unconventional conflict. . . .

Our commanders are gaining a real-time picture of the entire battlefield, and are able to get targeting information from sensor to shooter almost instantly. Our intelligence professionals and special forces have cooperated with battle-friendly Afghan forces—fighters who know the terrain, who know the Taliban, and who understand the local culture. And our special forces have the technology to call in precision air strikes—along with the flexibility to direct those strikes from horseback, in the first cavalry charge of the twenty-first century.

This combination—real-time intelligence, local allied forces, special forces, and precision air power—has really never been used before. The conflict in Afghanistan has taught us more about the future of our military than a decade of blue ribbon panels and think-tank symposiums.

The Predator is a good example. This unmanned aerial vehicle is able to circle over enemy forces, gather intelligence, transmit information instantly back to commanders, then fire on targets with extreme accuracy. Before the war, the Predator had skeptics, because it did not fit the old ways. Now it is clear the military does not have enough unmanned vehicles. We're entering an era in which unmanned vehicles of all kinds will take on greater importance—in space, on land, in the air, and at sea.

Precision-guided munitions also offer great promise. In the Gulf War, these weapons were the exception—while in Afghanistan, they have been the majority of the munitions we have used. We're striking with greater effectiveness, at greater range, with fewer civilian casualties. More and more, our weapons can hit moving targets. When all of our military can continuously locate and track moving targets—with surveillance from air and space—warfare will be truly revolutionized.

The need for military transformation was clear before the conflict in Afghanistan, and before September the 11th. Here at the Citadel in 1999, I spoke of keeping the peace by redefining war on our terms. The same recommendation was made in the strategic review that Secretary Rumsfeld briefed me on last August—a review that I fully endorse. What's different today is our sense of urgency—the need to build this future force while fighting a present war. It's like overhauling an engine while you're going at eighty miles an hour. Yet we have no other choice.

Our military has a new and essential mission. For states that support terror, it's not enough that the consequences be costly—they must be devastating. The more credible this reality, the more likely that regimes will change their behavior—making it less likely that America and our friends will need to use overwhelming force against them....

Our country is united in supporting a great cause—and in supporting those who fight for it. We will give our men and women in uniform every resource, every weapon, every tool they need to win the long battle that lies ahead.

America's next priority to prevent mass terror is to protect against the proliferation of weapons of mass destruction and the means to deliver them. I wish I could report to the American people that this threat does not exist—that our enemy is content with car bombs and box cutters—but I cannot.

One former al Qaeda member has testified in court that he was involved in an effort ten years ago to obtain nuclear materials. And the leader of al Qaeda calls that effort "a religious duty." Abandoned al Qaeda houses in Kabul contained diagrams for crude weapons of mass destruction. And as we all know, terrorists have put anthrax into the U.S. mail, and used sarin gas in a Tokyo subway.

And almost every state that actively sponsors terror is known to be seeking weapons of mass destruction and the missiles to deliver them at longer and longer ranges. Their hope is to blackmail the United States into abandoning our war on terror, and forsaking our friends and allies and security commitments around the world. Our enemies are bound for disappointment. America will never be blackmailed, and we will never forsake our commitment to liberty.

To meet our new threats, I have directed my National Security Advisor and my Homeland Security Director to develop a comprehensive strategy on proliferation. Working with other countries, we will strengthen nonproliferation treaties and toughen export controls. Together, we must keep the world's most dangerous technologies out of the hands of the world's most dangerous people.

A crucial partner in this effort is Russia—a nation we are helping to dismantle strategic weapons, reduce nuclear material, and increase security at nuclear sites. Our two countries will expand efforts to provide peaceful employment for scientists who formerly worked in Soviet weapons facilities. The United States will also work with Russia to build a facility to destroy tons of nerve agent. I'll request an over-all increase in funding to support this vital mission.

Even as we fight to prevent proliferation, we must prepare for every possibility. At home, we must be better prepared to detect, protect against, and respond to the potential use of weapons of mass destruction. Abroad, our military forces must have the ability to fight and win against enemies who would use such weapons against us. . . .

The attacks on our nation made it even more clear that we need to build limited and effective defenses against a missile attack. Our enemies seek every chance and every means to do harm to our country, our forces, and our friends. And we will not permit it.

Suppose the Taliban and the terrorists had been able to strike America or important allies with a ballistic missile. Our coalition would have become fragile, the stakes in our war much, much higher. We must protect Americans and our friends against all forms of terror, including the terror that could arrive on a missile. . . .

In order to do so, we must move beyond the 1972 Anti-Ballistic Missile Treaty, a treaty that was written in a different era, for a different enemy. America and our allies must not be bound to the past. We must be able to build the defenses we need against the enemies of the twenty-first century.

Our third and final priority in the fight against mass terror is to strengthen the advantage that good intelligence gives our country. Every day I make decisions influenced by the intelligence briefing of that morning. To reach decisions, a President needs more than data and information. A President needs real and current knowledge and analysis of the plans, intentions, and capabilities of our enemies.

The last several months have shown that there is no substitute for good intelligence officers, people on the ground. These are the people who find the targets, follow our enemies, and help us disrupt their evil plans.

The United States must rebuild our network of human intelligence. And we will apply the best new technology to gather intelligence on the new threats. Sophisticated systems like Global Hawk, an unmanned surveillance plane, are transforming our intelligence capabilities. Our technological strengths produce great advantages, and we will build on them.

Our intelligence services and federal law enforcement agencies must work more closely together, and share timely information with our state and local authorities. The more we know, the more terrorist plans we can prevent and disrupt, and the better we'll be able to protect the American people.

And in all they do, our intelligence agencies must attract the best people—the best collectors, the best analysts, the best linguists. We will give them the training they need and the compensation they deserve. . . .

The course we follow is a matter of profound consequence to many nations. If America wavers, the world will lose heart. If America leads, the world will show its courage. America will never waver. America will lead the world to peace.

Our cause is necessary. Our cause is just. And no matter how long it takes, we will defeat the enemies of freedom.

4.2 Troop Redeployment

Veterans of Foreign Wars Convention
Cincinnati, Ohio
August 16, 2004

These are crucial times. We have an historic opportunity to win the war on terror by spreading freedom and peace. Our commitments are being kept by the men and women of our military. I've had the privilege of traveling to bases around our country and around the world. I've seen their great decency and their unselfish courage. I assure you, ladies and gentlemen, the cause of freedom is in really good hands.

Those who wear our uniform deserve the full support of our government. For almost four years, my administration has strengthened our military. We have enacted the largest increases in defense spending since Ronald Reagan served as the Commander-in-Chief. We've increased military pay by 21 percent. We have provided better housing and better training and better maintenance. . . .

We have more work to do to defend freedom and protect our country. We will ensure that our forces are well-prepared, and well-positioned to meet the threats of the future. Our Armed Forces have changed a lot. They're more agile and more lethal, they're better able to strike anywhere in the world over great distances on short notice. Yet for decades, America's Armed Forces abroad have essentially remained where the wars of the last century ended, in Europe and in Asia. America's current force posture was designed, for example, to protect us and our allies from Soviet aggression—the threat no longer exists.

More than three years ago, we launched a comprehensive review of America's global force posture—the numbers, types, locations, and capabilities of U.S. forces around the world. We've consulted closely with our allies and with Congress; we've examined the challenges posed by today's threats and emerging threats. And so, today I announce a new plan for deploying America's Armed Forces.

Over the coming decade, we'll deploy a more agile and more flexible force, which means that more of our troops will be stationed and deployed from here at home. We'll move some of our troops and capabilities to new locations, so they can surge quickly to deal with unexpected threats. We'll take advantage of twenty-first century military technologies to rapidly deploy increased combat power.

The new plan will help us fight and win these wars of the twenty-first century. It will strengthen our alliances around the world, while we build new partnerships to better preserve the peace. It will reduce the stress on our troops and our military families. Although we'll still have a significant presence overseas, under the plan I'm announcing today, over the next ten years, we will bring home about 60,000 to 70,000 uniformed personnel, and about 100,000 family members and civilian employees.

See, our service members will have more time on the home front, and more predictability and fewer moves over a career. Our military spouses will have fewer job changes, greater stability, more time for their kids and to spend with their families at home. The taxpayers will save money, as we configure our military to meet the threats of the twenty-first century. There will be savings as we consolidate and close bases and facilities overseas no longer needed to face the threats of our time and defend the peace.

The world has changed a great deal, and our posture must change with it, for the sake of our military families, for the sake of our taxpayers, and so we can be more effective at projecting our strength and spreading freedom and peace.

4.3 National Missile Defense

National Defense University
Washington, DC
May 1, 2001

This afternoon, I want us to think back some thirty years to a far different time in a far different world. The United States and the Soviet Union were locked in a hostile rivalry. The Soviet Union was our unquestioned enemy; a highly-armed threat to freedom and democracy. Far more than that wall in Berlin divided us. Our highest ideal was—and remains—individual liberty. Theirs was the construction of a vast communist empire. Their totalitarian regime held much of Europe captive behind an iron curtain.

We didn't trust them, and for good reason. Our deep differences were expressed in a dangerous military confrontation that resulted in thousands of nuclear weapons pointed at each other on hair-trigger alert. Security of both the United States and the Soviet Union was based on a grim premise: that neither side would fire nuclear weapons at each other, because doing so would mean the end of both nations.

We even went so far as to codify this relationship in a 1972 ABM Treaty, based on the doctrine that our very survival would best be insured by leaving both sides completely open and vulnerable to nuclear attack. The threat was real and vivid. . . .

Today, the sun comes up on a vastly different world. The Wall is gone, and so is the Soviet Union. Today's Russia is not yesterday's Soviet Union. . . . Today's Russia is not our enemy, but a country in transition with an opportunity to emerge as a great nation, democratic, at peace with itself and its neighbors. . . .

Yet, this is still a dangerous world, a less certain, a less predictable one. More nations have nuclear weapons and still more have nuclear aspirations. Many have chemical and biological weapons. Some already have developed the ballistic missile technology that would allow them to deliver weapons of mass destruction at long distances and at incredible speeds. And a number of these countries are spreading these technologies around the world.

Most troubling of all, the list of these countries includes some of the world's least-responsible states. Unlike the Cold War, today's most urgent threat stems not from thousands of ballistic missiles in the Soviet hands, but from a small number of missiles in the hands of these states, states for whom terror and blackmail are a way of life. They seek weapons of mass destruction to intimidate their neighbors, and to keep the United States and other responsible nations from helping allies and friends in strategic parts of the world.

When Saddam Hussein invaded Kuwait in 1990 . . . the international community would have faced a very different situation had Hussein been able to blackmail with nuclear weapons. Like Saddam Hussein, some of today's tyrants are gripped by an implacable hatred of the United States of America. They hate our friends, they hate our values, they hate democracy and freedom and individual liberty. Many care little for the lives of their own people. In such a world, Cold War deterrence is no longer enough. . . .

Today's world requires a new policy, a broad strategy of active nonproliferation, counterproliferation and defenses. We must work together with other like-minded nations to deny weapons of terror from those seeking to acquire them. We must work with allies and friends who wish to join with us to defend against the harm they can inflict. And together we must deter anyone who would contemplate their use.

We need new concepts of deterrence that rely on both offensive and defensive forces. Deterrence can no longer be based solely on the threat of nuclear retaliation. Defenses can strengthen deterrence by reducing the incentive for proliferation.

We need a new framework that allows us to build missile defenses to counter the different threats of today's world. To do so, we must move beyond the constraints of the thirty-year-old ABM Treaty. This treaty does not recognize the present, or point us to the future. It enshrines the past. No treaty that prevents us from addressing today's threats, that prohibits us from pursuing promising technology to defend ourselves, our friends and our allies is in our interests or in the interests of world peace.

This new framework must encourage still further cuts in nuclear weapons. Nuclear weapons still have a vital role to play in our security and that of our allies. We can, and will, change the size, the composition, the character of our nuclear forces in a way that reflects the reality that the Cold War is over. I am committed to achieving a credible deterrent with the lowest-possible number of nuclear weapons consistent with our national security needs. . . .

Several months ago, I asked Secretary of Defense Rumsfeld to examine all available technologies and basing modes for effective missile defenses that could protect the United States, our deployed forces, our friends and our allies. . . .

The Secretary has identified near-term options that could allow us to deploy an initial capability against limited threats. In some cases, we can draw on already established technologies that might involve land-based and sea-based capabilities to intercept missiles in mid-course or after they re-enter the atmosphere. We also recognize the substantial advantages of intercepting missiles early in their flight, especially in the boost phase. The preliminary work has produced some promising options for advanced sensors and interceptors that may provide this capability. If based at sea or on aircraft, such approaches could provide limited, but effective, defenses.

We have more work to do to determine the final form the defenses might take. We will explore all these options further. We recognize the technological difficulties we face and we look forward to the challenge. Our nation will assign the best people to this critical task.... We know that some approaches will not work. We also know that we will be able to build on our successes. When ready, and working with Congress, we will deploy missile defenses to strengthen global security and stability.

I've made it clear from the very beginning that I would consult closely on the important subject with our friends and allies who are also threatened by missiles and weapons of mass destruction.... These will be real consultations. We are not presenting our friends and allies with unilateral decisions already made. We look forward to hearing their views, the views of our friends, and to take them into account....

We'll also need to reach out to other interested states, including China and Russia. Russia and the United States should work together to develop a new foundation for world peace and security in the twenty-first century. We should leave behind the constraints of an ABM Treaty that perpetuates a relationship based on distrust and mutual vulnerability. This Treaty ignores the fundamental breakthroughs in technology during the last thirty years. It prohibits us from exploring all options for defending against the threats that face us, our allies and other countries. That's why we should work together to replace this Treaty with a new framework that reflects a clear and clean break from the past, and especially from the adversarial legacy of the Cold War. This new cooperative relationship should look to the future, not to the past. It should be reassuring, rather than threatening. It should be premised on openness, mutual confidence and real opportunities for cooperation, including the area of missile defense. It should allow us to share information so that each nation can improve its early warning capability, and its capability to defend its people and territory. And perhaps one day, we can even cooperate in a joint defense....

This is a time for vision; a time for a new way of thinking; a time for bold leadership.... We must all look at the world in a new, realistic way, to preserve peace for generations to come.

4.4 ABM Treaty

The White House
Washington, DC
December 13, 2001

I've just concluded a meeting of my National Security Council. We reviewed what I discussed with my friend, President Vladimir Putin, over the course of many meetings, many months. And that is the need for America to move beyond the 1972 Anti Ballistic Missile treaty.

Today, I have given formal notice to Russia, in accordance with the treaty, that the United States of America is withdrawing from this almost thirty-year-old treaty. I have concluded the ABM treaty hinders our government's ability to develop ways to protect our people from future terrorist or rogue state missile attacks.

The 1972 ABM treaty was signed by the United States and the Soviet Union at a much different time, in a vastly different world. One of the signatories, the Soviet Union, no longer exists. And neither does the hostility that once led both our countries to keep thousands of nuclear weapons on hair-trigger alert, pointed at each other. The grim theory was that neither side would launch a nuclear attack because it knew the other would respond, thereby destroying both.

Today, as the events of September the 11th made all too clear, the greatest threats to both our countries come not from each other, or other big powers in the world, but from terrorists who strike without warning, or rogue states who seek weapons of mass destruction.

We know that the terrorists, and some of those who support them, seek the ability to deliver death and destruction to our doorstep via missile. And we must have the freedom and the flexibility to develop effective defenses against those attacks. Defending the American people is my highest priority as Commander in Chief, and I cannot and will not allow the United States to remain in a treaty that prevents us from developing effective defenses.

At the same time, the United States and Russia have developed a new, much more hopeful and constructive relationship. We are moving to replace mutually assured destruction with mutual cooperation. . . .

We're already working closely together as the world rallies in the war against terrorism. I appreciate so much President Putin's important advice and cooperation as we fight to dismantle the al Qaeda network in Afghanistan. I appreciate his commitment to reduce Russia's offensive nuclear weapons. I reiterate our pledge to reduce our own nuclear arsenal between 1,700 and 2,200 operationally deployed strategic nuclear weapons. President Putin and I have also agreed that my decision to withdraw from the treaty will not, in any way, undermine our new relationship or Russian security. . . .

This is a day for looking forward with hope, and anticipation of greater prosperity and peace for Russians, for Americans and for the entire world.

4.5 Countering the Threat of WMD

National Defense University
Washington, DC
February 11, 2004

On September the 11th, 2001, America and the world witnessed a new kind of war. We saw the great harm that a stateless network could inflict upon our country, killers armed with box cutters, mace, and nineteen airline tickets. Those attacks also raised the prospect of even worse dangers—of other weapons in the hands of other men. The greatest threat before humanity today is the possibility of secret and sudden attack with chemical or biological or radiological or nuclear weapons. . . .

In the Cold War, Americans lived under the threat of weapons of mass destruction, but believed that deterrents made those weapons a last resort. What has changed in the twenty-first century is that, in the hands of terrorists, weapons of mass destruction would be a first resort—the preferred means to further their ideology of suicide and random murder. These terrible weapons are becoming easier to acquire, build, hide, and transport. . . .

America, and the entire civilized world, will face this threat for decades to come. We must confront the danger with open eyes, and unbending purpose. I have made clear to all the policy of this nation: America will not permit terrorists and dangerous regimes to threaten us with the world's most deadly weapons. . . . We're determined to confront those threats at the source. We will stop these weapons from being acquired or built. We'll block them from being transferred. We'll prevent them from ever being used.

One source of these weapons is dangerous and secretive regimes that build weapons of mass destruction to intimidate their neighbors and force their influence upon the world. These nations pose different challenges; they require different strategies.

The former dictator of Iraq possessed and used weapons of mass destruction against his own people. For twelve years, he defied the will of the international community. He refused to disarm or account for his illegal weapons and programs. He doubted our resolve to enforce our word and now he sits in a prison cell, while his country moves toward a democratic future.

To Iraq's east, the government of Iran is unwilling to abandon a uranium enrichment program capable of producing material for nuclear weapons. The United States is working with our allies and the International Atomic Energy Agency to ensure that Iran meets its commitments and does not develop nuclear weapons.

In the Pacific, North Korea has defied the world, has tested long-range ballistic missiles, admitted its possession of nuclear weapons, and now threatens to build more. Together with our partners in Asia, America is insisting that North Korea completely, verifiably, and irreversibly dismantle its nuclear programs.

America has consistently brought these threats to the attention of international organizations. We're using every means of diplomacy to answer them. . . .

In recent years, another path of proliferation has become clear, as well. America and other nations are learning more about black-market operatives who deal in equipment and expertise related to weapons of mass destruction. These dealers are motivated by greed, or fanaticism, or both. They find eager customers in outlaw regimes, which pay millions for the parts and plans they need to speed up their weapons programs. And with deadly technology and expertise going on the market, there's the terrible possibility that terrorists groups could obtain the ultimate weapons they desire most.

The extent and sophistication of such networks can be seen in the case of a man named Abdul Qadeer Khan. . . . A.Q. Khan is known throughout the world as the father of Pakistan's nuclear weapons program. What was not publicly known, until recently, is that he also led an extensive international network for the proliferation of nuclear technology and know-how.

For decades, Mr. Khan remained on the Pakistani government payroll, earning a modest salary. Yet, he and his associates financed lavish lifestyles through the sale of nuclear technologies and equipment to outlaw regimes stretching from North Africa to the Korean Peninsula. . . .He and his associates sold the blueprints for centrifuges to enrich uranium, as well as a nuclear design stolen from the Pakistani government. The network sold uranium hexafluoride, the gas that the centrifuge process can transform into enriched uranium for nuclear bombs. Khan and his associates provided Iran and Libya and North Korea with designs for Pakistan's older centrifuges, as well as designs for more advanced and efficient models. The network also provided these countries with components, and in some cases, with complete centrifuges. . . .

This picture of the Khan network was pieced together over several years by American and British intelligence officers. Our intelligence services gradually uncovered this network's reach, and identified its key experts and agents and money men.... A.Q. Khan has confessed his crimes, and his top associates are out of business. The government of Pakistan is interrogating the network's members, learning critical details that will help them prevent it from ever operating again. President Musharraf has promised to share all the information he learns about the Khan network, and has assured us that his country will never again be a source of proliferation....

As a result of our penetration of the network, American and the British intelligence identified a shipment of advanced centrifuge parts.... We followed the shipment of these parts to Dubai, and watched as they were transferred to the *BBC China* . . . bound for Libya, it was stopped by German and Italian authorities....

The interception of the *BBC China* came as Libyan and British and American officials were discussing the possibility of Libya ending its WMD programs. The United States and Britain confronted Libyan officials with this evidence of an active and illegal nuclear program. About two months ago, Libya's leader voluntarily agreed to end his nuclear and chemical weapons programs, not to pursue biological weapons, and to permit thorough inspections by the International Atomic Energy Agency and the Organization for the Prohibition of Chemical Weapons. We're now working in partnership with these organizations and with the United Kingdom to help the government of Libya dismantle those programs and eliminate all dangerous materials. Colonel Ghadafi made the right decision, and the world will be safer once his commitment is fulfilled. We expect other regimes to follow his example. Abandoning the pursuit of illegal weapons can lead to better relations with the United States, and other free nations. Continuing to seek those weapons will not bring security or international prestige, but only political isolation, economic hardship, and other unwelcome consequences....

Breaking this network is one major success in a broad-based effort to stop the spread of terrible weapons. We're adjusting our strategies to the threats of a new era. America and the nations of Australia, France and Germany, Italy and Japan, the Netherlands, Poland, Portugal, Spain and the United Kingdom have launched the Proliferation Security Initiative to interdict lethal materials in transit. Our nations are sharing intelligence information, tracking suspect international cargo, conducting joint military exercises. We're prepared to search planes and ships, to seize weapons and missiles and equipment that raise proliferation concerns....

There is a consensus among nations that proliferation cannot be tolerated. Yet this consensus means little unless it is translated into action. Every civilized nation has a stake in preventing the spread of weapons of mass destruction. These materials and technologies, and the people who traffic in them, cross many borders. To stop this trade, the nations of the world must be strong and determined. We must work together, we must act effectively. Today, I announce seven proposals to strengthen the world's efforts to stop the spread of deadly weapons.

First, I propose that the work of the Proliferation Security Initiative be expanded to address more than shipments and transfers. Building on the tools we've developed to fight terrorists, we can take direct action against proliferation networks. We need greater cooperation not just among intelligence and military services, but in law enforcement, as well. . . .

Second, I call on all nations to strengthen the laws and international controls that govern proliferation. At the UN last fall, I proposed a new Security Council resolution requiring all states to criminalize proliferation, enact strict export controls, and secure all sensitive materials within their borders. The Security Council should pass this proposal quickly. And when they do, America stands ready to help other governments to draft and enforce the new laws that will help us deal with proliferation.

Third, I propose to expand our efforts to keep weapons from the Cold War and other dangerous materials out of the wrong hands. In 1991, Congress passed the Nunn-Lugar legislation. . . . Under this program, we're helping former Soviet states find productive employment for former weapons scientists. We're dismantling, destroying and securing weapons and materials left over from the Soviet WMD arsenal. . . . We should expand this cooperation elsewhere in the world. We will retain [sic] WMD scientists and technicians in countries like Iraq and Libya. We will help nations end the use of weapons-grade uranium in research reactors. I urge more nations to contribute to these efforts. . . .

As we track and destroy these networks, we must also prevent governments from developing nuclear weapons under false pretenses. The Nuclear Non-Proliferation Treaty was designed more than thirty years ago to prevent the spread of nuclear weapons beyond those states which already possessed them. Under this treaty, nuclear states agreed to help non-nuclear states develop peaceful atomic energy if they renounced the pursuit of nuclear weapons. But the treaty has a loophole which has been exploited by nations such as North Korea and Iran. These regimes are allowed to produce nuclear material that can be used to build bombs under the cover of civilian nuclear programs.

So today, as a fourth step, I propose a way to close the loophole. The world must create a safe, orderly system to field civilian nuclear plants without adding to the danger of weapons proliferation. The world's leading nuclear exporters should ensure that states have reliable access at reasonable cost to fuel for civilian reactors, so long as those states renounce enrichment and reprocessing. Enrichment and reprocessing are not necessary for nations seeking to harness nuclear energy for peaceful purposes. The forty nations of the Nuclear Suppliers Group should refuse to sell enrichment and reprocessing equipment and technologies to any state that does not already possess full-scale, functioning enrichment and reprocessing plants. . . .

For international norms to be effective, they must be enforced. It is the charge of the International Atomic Energy Agency to uncover banned nuclear activity around the world and report those violations to the UN Security Council. We must ensure that the IAEA has all the tools it needs to fulfill its essential mandate. America and other nations support what is called the Additional Protocol, which requires states to declare a broad range of nuclear activities and facilities, and allow the IAEA to inspect those facilities.

As a fifth step, I propose that by next year, only states that have signed the Additional Protocol be allowed to import equipment for their civilian nuclear programs. Nations that are serious about fighting proliferation will approve and implement the Additional Protocol. . . .

We must also ensure that IAEA is organized to take action when action is required. So, a sixth step, I propose the creation of a special committee of the IAEA Board which will focus intensively on safeguards and verification. This committee, made up of governments in good standing with the IAEA, will strengthen the capability of the IAEA to ensure that nations comply with their international obligations.

And, finally, countries under investigation for violating nuclear nonproliferation obligations are currently allowed to serve on the IAEA Board of Governors. . . . No state under investigation for proliferation violations should be allowed to serve on the IAEA Board of Governors—or on the new special committee. . . . Those actively breaking the rules should not be entrusted with enforcing the rules.

As we move forward to address these challenges we will consult with our friends and allies on all these new measures. We will listen to their ideas. Together we will defend the safety of all nations and preserve the peace of the world. . . .The way ahead is not easy, but it is clear. We will proceed as if the lives of our citizens depend on our vigilance, because they do.

Questions to Discuss

1. In Speech 4.1, Bush stresses the need to modernize the U.S. military's weapons and tactics. Does this focus on the future carry the risk of not having the forces needed today?

2. In Speech 4.2, Bush argues for a significant decrease in U.S. troops based abroad. Would such a decrease hurt U.S. alliances or the country's ability to respond to new threats?

3. In Speeches 4.3 and 4.4, Bush argues that the ABM treaty was a product of "a vastly different world." Do modern threats from rogue states and terrorists require moving beyond old treaties and justify building a National Missile Defense?

4. In Speech 4.5, Bush argues that the terms of the Nuclear Nonproliferation Treaty (NPT), which allows states to import peaceful nuclear technology, need to be revisited. Would Bush's policy ideas reestablish the idea that there are different international rules for different countries?

5. In Speech 4.6, Bush argues that other countries should follow Libya's lead in renouncing WMD programs. Is this more likely to occur if the United States and others follow tough policies on proliferation, or use policies of engagement and reward?

Chapter 5

Global Issues

During its first hundred and fifty years of existence, the United States largely followed George Washington's advice to avoid long-term alliances. This choice reflected the reality of U.S. global weakness, but also the sentiments of isolationists, who felt that the country should choose to keep itself separate from the nastiness of international politics. Beginning in the 1940s, U.S. policy began changing dramatically. The country helped form numerous multilateral institutions such as the UN, the World Bank, and the International Monetary Fund. This policy shift was interpreted by some as a permanent rejection of isolationism and a true American embrace of an international society led by cooperative institutions. Others, though, saw it as a largely pragmatic decision by the U.S. leaders to develop institutions for a world in which the United States faced global economic and security challenges and, although a superpower, was not dominant in relation to other major powers. Many of the institutions were heavily shaped by Cold War rivalries, so they did not meet the lofty goals of their founders, but multilateral commitments did become important fixtures of U.S. policy.

The Cold War's end lessened great power conflicts and provided an opportunity to increase focus on nonsecurity oriented global issues. There was also a widespread view in the United States that it was time to shift some of the burdens of world leadership to allies and multilateral institutions. Soon, activity by the UN and other international institutions was at all time highs. This activity reinvigorated the hopes of some who thought that multilateral institutions might play a role in securing global peace and prosperity, but also it raised the fears of others who saw the institutions as increasingly independent actors challenging state sovereignty and U.S. global leadership. By the latter part of the Clinton period, the United States often asserted its own power and interests outside of established international bodies. These actions highlighted that the structures of the UN and many other institutions were designed to acknowledge that some states are more powerful than others, but were not designed to work in a unipolar world. Discussion, therefore, shifted to whether the United States still needed multilateral institutions and whether the institutions could either tame or learn to coexist with the United States.

Despite the increased unilateralism of the later 1990s, George W. Bush criticized President Clinton during the 2000 campaign for still being too focused on multilateral actions. Bush did not reject U.S. participation in international institutions, but was clear that he favored such participation mainly when those institutions followed U.S. desires, gave the United States control over decisions, and did not seek to impose limits on U.S. international or domestic policies. Subsequently, these principles were reflected in the way Bush handled several issues and institutions. His policies on the Kyoto Protocol, the International Criminal Court (ICC), and the UN were particularly crucial and drew either praise or sharp condemnation from observers depending on their underlying views of multilateralism.

Global Warming and the Kyoto Protocol

The idea that human activity is causing global warming began to attract widespread attention in the 1980s when scientists suggested that the increased release of greenhouse gasses was thickening the earth's natural atmospheric blanket, thereby trapping more heat. The main greenhouse gas is CO_2, which is released when fossil fuels are burned. The destruction of forests also increases CO_2 levels since trees absorb and store carbon. Other human activities such as raising cattle, planting rice, and using landfills increase emissions of methane, nitrous oxide, and other greenhouse gasses. Total greenhouse gas emissions are believed to be many times higher than in the preindustrial era. Most scientists agree that global temperatures have increased about 1.1 degrees Fahrenheit over the last century, but there is ongoing debate whether the rise is in fact attributable to human activity and whether temperatures will continue to increase. If temperatures do increase, predictive models suggest that it would have a major impact on weather patterns, sea levels, agricultural production, and disease patterns. Warming drew international attention not only because of the severity of these possible changes, but because it would have truly global impacts.

At the inaugural Earth Summit in 1992, most of the world's major countries, including the United States, signed the United Nations Framework Convention on Climate Change (UNFCC). The agreement acknowledged warming as a global problem demanding coordinated action. Some summit participants sought specific long-term targets for greenhouse gas concentrations and mandatory emissions cutbacks. The United States led by President George H.W. Bush argued that existing scientific knowledge could not establish which gas concentrations were problematic and that emissions cutbacks would limit economic growth, so the countries agreed to only voluntary targets and efforts to reduce emissions.

Five years later, few countries had made progress toward their goals and overall global emissions were higher. There also was increased evidence that warming was already occurring. Consequently, in December 1997, a new meeting concluded with the signing of the Kyoto Protocol. The main idea of the Protocol was that countries pledged to reduce their greenhouse emissions, by the year 2012, to levels of 6 to 8 percent below their respective 1990 levels. At the meeting, the less developed countries (LDCs) refused to agree to mandatory limits, arguing that most historic and current emissions came from the developed countries and that a target based on 1990 levels would permanently cap their economic growth. The issue almost broke apart the meeting, but a strong desire to reach an agreement led to acceptance of only voluntary actions for the LDCs.

The Protocol was set to go into effect if it was ratified by fifty-five countries, including countries that accounted for at least 55 percent of the developed countries' 1990 emissions. These unusual terms were designed to assure that the treaty would have widespread support, but would become binding only if major developed countries committed to reductions. In 1990, the United States was responsible for 36.1 percent of the developed countries' emissions. If the United States did not ratify, the Protocol would need ratification by almost every other major country.

The Clinton administration did sign the Protocol. During the negotiation process, however, the Senate unanimously passed a resolution that stated it would not ratify any treaty which did not include some LDC commitment to reductions or that would seriously harm the U.S. economy. The vote may have overstated true opposition to the final treaty, but made clear that support was far short of the two-thirds constitutionally necessary to ratify a treaty. Therefore, Clinton chose not to submit the Protocol for ratification. The United States could continue to attend meetings at which details of implementing the Protocol were still being established, but would not be bound by the Protocol's terms.

During the 2000 campaign, Bush expressed opposition to the Protocol on grounds that were similar to the Senate's objections. He did promise to set new mandatory limits on power plant emissions of CO_2, but this commitment proved short-lived. On March 13, 2001, Bush, in a letter to four Senators, reversed his CO_2 pledge and stated, "I oppose the Kyoto Protocol because it exempts 80 percent of the world, including major population centers such as China and India, from compliance, and would cause serious harm to the U.S. economy."[1] Because Bush chose to make these major points in a letter rather than a speech, it took some time before

Democrats, environmental groups, and Kyoto supporters in Europe and elsewhere focused on Bush's actions. Subsequently, the criticism was intense, and centered not only on Bush's actions, but on the way that the decision was reached and defended. As a result, Secretary of State Powell and other top officials publicly conceded that the issue "was not handled as well as it should have been."[2] They acknowledged that it was unwise to reject Kyoto without providing a careful explanation of its perceived deficiencies or presenting an alternative plan to address warming.

The administration, therefore, began a cabinet level review of the issue. Bush officials also requested a report from the National Academy of Sciences (NAS) summarizing existing scientific evidence. The much anticipated report concluded that there was increasing evidence that the earth was warming and that human activity was largely responsible. On June 11, 2001, the day before he started his first visit to European allies, Bush gave a speech outlining why he felt the Kyoto Protocol was "fatally flawed" and presenting his alternative plans (Speech 5.1).

In his speech, Bush mentioned the findings of the NAS report, but also stressed continued scientific uncertainties. Bush noted that the earth has gone through previous natural temperature fluctuations from ice ages to warmer periods and the causes and extent of those shifts still are not fully understood. He highlighted the quite varied predictions advanced by the scientific community for the next centuries' temperatures. He, therefore, argued that no major actions should be taken until more knowledge was acquired. Critics of Bush conceded uncertainties, but suggested that Bush was using these points to subtly cast doubt on the now widely accepted basic scientific arguments on warming. Critics also felt that his call for further study was simply a delaying tactic.

Bush's speech again stressed that exempting LDCs from the Protocol's mandatory limits was problematic. Many studies predicted that as China, India, and other countries' economies grew and companies from industrialized countries moved factories to LDCs in search of lower labor costs greenhouse emissions from LDCs would soon surpass those of the developed countries. Therefore, Bush argued that any agreement that did not include all countries would be ineffective in achieving significant global reductions. Also, under Kyoto, companies in developed countries would have to spend significant capital on new technologies and changing production methods, giving companies in LDCs another comparative cost advantage. Many Kyoto supporters agreed that the LDC exemption was unfortunate, but they argued that it was better to move forward with some agreement than to wait for a change in the LDC position. They further argued that countries could be encouraged to adopt mandatory targets once they reached certain levels of industrialization.

In addition to raising scientific questions and concerns about LDCs, Bush's third major argument was that complying with Kyoto "would have a negative economic impact" Under Kyoto, the United States pledged to reduce emissions to 7 percent below 1990 levels. Unfortunately, in the 1990s, U.S. emissions had increased 12 percent, so meeting the target would require closer to a 20 percent reduction from 2001 levels. A reduction of that scale would certainly have an impact on American industry and average citizens, but how severe this economic impact would be was at least as uncertain as predictions of future temperatures. Some studies suggested that implementation of the Protocol would lower U.S. production by $100 to $400 billion by 2010[3] and total U.S. job losses would be 2.4 million.[4] Others, though, argued that long-term savings from increased efficiency would offset many early costs and that efficient U.S. industries might be able to increase their global market share.

After arguing that the Protocol was flawed, Bush presented his plans for the future. The most detailed of those plans were for further domestic and international research on global warming and monitoring of emissions. Bush also suggested a focus on alternative energy sources. He then argued that "market-based incentives" would spur innovation. He did not, though, provide details about these incentives at this time.

Bush's June speech did little to quiet Kyoto supporters domestically or in Europe. European leaders also indicated that they planned to go ahead with the Protocol with or without U.S. support. This position had wide public support internationally. Europeans have generally expressed much more support than Americans for tough environmental policies. Many also saw the issue as a chance to stand up against U.S. unilateralism and power. Others hoped that, if the Protocol went into effect, it would become increasingly difficult for the United States to remain on the outside of such a popular multilateral initiative.

In July 2001, representatives of Kyoto signers met in Bonn, Germany to establish implementation details. The United States sent representatives to Bonn, but did not participate actively in the negotiations. The meeting was crucial for the Protocol's future, since, despite widespread rhetorical support, few countries had actually ratified the Protocol. At Bonn, key new agreements were reached to establish a flexible system for trading emissions credits, so countries such as Russia, who was well below its Kyoto target, could sell credits to countries that were having difficulty. Also, countries were given new credits for protecting forests, which act as "carbon sinks" to absorb CO_2. Ironically, both of these ideas had been important strategies suggested by the Clinton administration to help the United States meet its target, but they were largely rejected by others before 2001. With these agreements in place, the Protocol was soon ratified by more than 100 countries, including most of the developed countries. The two major holdouts were the United States and Russia, which vacillated on its plans to ratify. The Protocol could not go into force until at least one of these countries ratified it.

In February 2002, Bush gave a much anticipated speech further detailing his plans to combat global warming (Speech 5.2). The speech was delivered just before he traveled to Asia and was designed, at least in part, to show allies that he was concerned about the environment. Here, Bush detailed the market forces mentioned in his June 2001 speech. He proposed that industries sign voluntary pledges to cut emissions and encouraged companies to monitor and report their emissions, so they could earn credit for reductions that might someday be mandated. He announced tax credits and other programs to encourage clean energy technologies. He also pledged to help developing countries control their growing emissions.

In the February speech, Bush also proposed a controversial new criterion to measure progress on emissions. He called for an 18 percent reduction over ten years in America's "greenhouse gas intensity," defined as tons of CO_2 emitted for each $1 million in gross domestic product. At first glance, the 18 percent reduction seemed in line with the major reductions called for by the Protocol; in fact, reductions in greenhouse intensity could be achieved even as emission rose. Intensity levels would decrease any time an economy grew quickly. For example, in the 1990s, U.S. emissions rose by 12 percent, but the economy grew by 32 percent so intensity decreased by about 15 percent.[5] Recent increases in emissions have been smaller than growth increases because the U.S. economy is now focused on services and high technology. Bush argued that decreases in intensity would prevent significant future emissions that would have occurred if intensity was constant and that intensity was a measure that would appeal not only to the United States, but to LDCs whose rates would drop with growth. Critics countered that only actual emissions reductions would help the environment and that measuring declines in intensity provided a false sense that countries could make progress without actually taking significant actions.

Disagreements on global warming often rested on very technical disputes over scientific, economic, and environmental measures and projections. They also reflected disagreements on deeper, more philosophical issues. Issues driving the debate included: 1) should one take somewhat disruptive preventative measures in the short term to lessen the chances of a potentially major long-term problem, or should one take only minimal actions in the short term until more evidence develops? 2) should the government use mandatory regulations and other pressures to force businesses to act for the good of the environment, or should government power remain limited and market forces drive decisions? 3) should there be multilateral initiatives and international institutions to establish and enforce global regulations, or should sovereign governments decide their own environmental policies and have flexibility to adjust to local conditions? 4) do great powers have a responsibility to lead global actions and use some of their resources for global initiatives, or should great powers act solely on what is in their national interests? Bush favored waiting for further evidence, a limited government role, domestically-controlled policies, and the promotion of the national interest. Many Europeans disagreed with Bush on each of these four points, so their criticism was very intense. Other international and domestic critics disagreed with Bush on some combination of the points, so their criticism was less intense and also more focused on specific issues.

In the fall of 2004, attention on Kyoto reemerged when Russia announced plans to ratify the Protocol. Apparently, Western European countries suggested they would support Russian entry in the World Trade Organization (WTO), if Russia supported Kyoto. Russian ratification would bring the Protocol into effect and turn it into a case of a major international agreement not supported by the world's major international power, the United States.

International Criminal Court

By signing the UN Universal Declaration of Human Rights of 1948 and several more specific international treaties, most countries in the world committed to respect a long list of individual human rights. In practice, however, countries have not always abided by their pledges. Often, leaders want to maintain personal power, so they choose policies in response to local conditions, even if their policies violate international standards. Another factor leading to continued abuses is that the international community has struggled to find effective ways to punish past actions, and thereby deter future violations. Through both bilateral and multilateral channels, the international community commonly begins by labeling a country as a human rights violator, hoping that the attention will embarrass its leadership into better behavior. The international community sometimes then increases pressure by various means: symbolic measures, including withdrawing diplomats or banning a country from international associations; economic pressure, such as sanctions and trade embargoes; and, in the most extreme cases, military intervention. These tactics, however, have three main deficiencies: 1) they are not applied consistently because economic and security interests often influence decisions of who and how to punish; 2) some tactics hurt the citizenry of both the target and sanctioning country more directly than they hurt the abusing leadership; and 3) international punishments challenge the notion of sovereignty, which holds that a country's government can decide its own policies without outside interference. In the 1990s, human rights advocates began to push for the new tactic of using international courts to punish violators. Advocates hoped that a legal system would be less politicized than other tactics, and would directly punish individuals instead of whole countries. An international court would, however, directly challenge sovereignty.

The idea of such a court was not new. After WWII, the victorious Allies established the Nuremberg tribunals to try Nazi leaders as war criminals. Nuremberg succeeded in punishing some leaders, but was seen by many as a "victor's court," since it did not try any Allied officials. The court idea was revived in 1993 when the International Criminal Tribunal for Yugoslavia was established under UN authority with strong backing from the United States. The next year a similar tribunal was established for Rwanda. The tribunals were not without problems and critics, but their overall success convinced many advocates that the time had come for a permanent international court.

Clinton endorsed the goal of establishing a court in 1995. The U.S. delegation was active in shaping the Rome Statute of 1998, which established the International Criminal Court (ICC). The ICC parallels the tribunals on Yugoslavia and Rwanda in some ways, but from the American perspective there are two important distinctions: first, the ICC operates more independently of the UN, and second, U.S. troops or government officials could face charges at the ICC. During negotiations, the United States pushed hard for UN Security Council control of the court, so that the United States would retain the ability to veto politically-motivated investigations. Other countries argued for an independent court. In the end, the statute included a provision that allowed the Security Council to pass a resolution to suspend an investigation or prosecution for one year, but otherwise the Statute gave the ICC prosecutor much independence. U.S. officials, worrying that U.S. soldiers and officials were at greater risk of prosecution because of America's greater world role, pressed for several other ways to limit the probability that Americans would be brought before the court. Most crucial was the principle of complementarity. The ICC cannot proceed with an investigation or prosecution of a crime that is being, or has been, investigated or prosecuted by a state that has jurisdiction, unless the state is unwilling or unable to carry out a fair investigation. Thus, if a U.S. soldier was accused of a crime and investigated by U.S. military authorities, the case could go to the ICC only if it was found that the U.S. judicial system failed to genuinely investigate the allegation. Clinton officials were pleased by complementarity. They were, however, very critical of the statute's Article 12, which states that the ICC may assert jurisdiction if a crime is committed on the territory of any state that has ratified the Statute. Thus, even if the United States did not ratify the Statute, its soldiers could be brought before the ICC if they committed a crime while in a ratifying country. Overall, the chance of an American being but put on trial was low, but did remain.

The Clinton administration generally favored the court, but concern about the prosecutor's independence and Article 12 led the United States to be one of only seven countries to vote against the draft statute. However, on December 31, 2000, the last day that countries could become party to the treaty without formal ratification, Clinton altered the U.S. position by signing the Statute. As he did so, though, he delineated "significant flaws in the treaty," said he would not submit the treaty for Senate ratification, and pledged to work for evolution of court rules.[6]

In time, it became clear that the Bush administration differed with Clinton in three key ways. Clinton saw the ICC as a generally positive development, with some specific flaws. Bush and some of his key advisers were much less enthusiastic about any international court and felt that the extant ICC was so flawed that it was a danger to U.S. interests. Second, Clinton argued that signing, but not ratifying, the Statute would allow the United States to correct flaws by being part of the ICC's ongoing planning process. Bush felt that the U.S. position should be unambiguous and that any U.S. participation would imply support for all of the provisions. Finally, Clinton worried about the chance of politically motivated charges against Americans, but felt that many safeguards were in place. Bush officials appeared to work under the assumption that unfair charges against Americans were inevitable; thus, they pursued new ways to protect U.S. citizens from ICC investigations and trials.

During Bush's first year in office, the ICC drew little official U.S. comment. Then, in April 2002, the Rome Statute received it sixtieth ratification enabling the ICC to begin operation on July 1. On May 6, 2002, the administration sent a letter to the UN Secretary General declaring that the United States had no plans to be a part of the ICC and was in effect "unsigning" the Statute. It was unprecedented for the United States to take so forceful a position against a human rights institution that was strongly supported by so many American allies.

Interestingly, Bush chose not to make a speech or announcement about the ICC in May. His only formal discussion of the ICC came in a July 2002 speech to U.S. troops. Bush stated:

As we prepare our military for action, we will protect our military from international courts and committees with agendas of their own. You might have heard about a treaty that would place American troops under the jurisdiction of something called the International Criminal Court. The United States cooperates with many other nations to keep the peace, but we will not submit American troops to prosecutors and judges whose jurisdiction we do not accept. Our nation expects and enforces the highest standards of honor and conduct in our military. That's how you were trained. That's what we expect. Every person who serves under the American flag will answer to his or her own superiors and to military law, not to the rulings of an unaccountable international criminal court.[7]

Detailed explanation of Bush's decision was left to advisers such as the U.S. ambassador-at-large for war crimes issues Pierre-Richard Prosper and Under Secretary of State for Arms Control and International Security John R. Bolton, who had been a fierce opponent of the ICC for years. In their comments, they repeated concerns about an ICC prosecutor not controlled by the Security Council and about Article 12. They also argued that the Statute's definitions of international crimes were too vague and not subject to clarifying reservations like most human rights treaties. In addition, administration officials argued the long-standing conservative position that since the U.S. Constitution is the highest law in the land and grants Congress the exclusive power to consider and create all laws, treaty guarantees that go beyond constitutional guarantees or force the United States to change its laws are unconstitutional and violate U.S. sovereignty.

The Bush administration's greatest focus, though, was on the issue of preventing ICC investigations of U.S. citizens. Bolton argued that complementarity is "simply an assertion, unproven and untested."[8] The administration also pointed out that the ultimate decision about whether national courts had been fair was left to the ICC. Bolton, although acknowledging the importance of protecting U.S. soldiers, also said, "Our principal concern is for our country's top civilian and military leaders, those responsible for our defense and foreign policy."[9] He argued that even the threat of investigations might shape U.S. leaders' decisions and might force them to waste resources fending off politically motivated charges.

The Bush administration, therefore, took additional steps. In June 2002, Bush sought permanent immunity from ICC prosecution for UN peacekeeping troops. The United States vetoed a UN resolution reauthorizing the UN peacekeeping mission in Bosnia to demonstrate its determination on the issue. At the time, there were about 600 U.S. soldiers deployed in UN peacekeeping missions globally. European and UN officials sharply criticized the U.S. veto as an attack on both the ICC and the UN. Weeks later, a compromise was struck that prohibited the ICC from investigating peacekeepers from nonratifying countries for one year. A similar UN resolution was passed in 2003.

In the summer of 2002, the United States also began pressing countries to sign bilateral agreements under Article 98 of the Rome Statute. Under the agreements, countries pledged not to surrender U.S. citizens to the ICC without U.S. approval, which would likely never be granted. European Union (EU) officials felt sweeping agreements protecting all U.S. citizens violated the spirit and terms of Article 98. They refused to sign agreements and urged EU candidate countries in Eastern Europe to resist as well. In an August 16, 2002, letter, Secretary of State Powell encouraged the Eastern European countries to sign and suggested that America's role in NATO might change if agreements were not reached.[10] A major break in the alliance was averted when the EU agreed to guidelines that allowed countries to sign agreements as long as the U.S. government guaranteed suspects would be tried in an American court.

In August 2002, Bush signed the American Servicemembers' Protection Act. The legislation authorized the president to use force to release any U.S. citizen held by the ICC. It also prohibited U.S. military assistance to most countries that were party to the ICC, but refused to sign Article 98 agreements; the president could waive the provision for a specific country. In July 2003, the administration suspended over $47 million in military assistance to thirty-five countries. Taking such strong action against the U.S. aid recipients, including important countries such as Colombia and six incoming members of NATO, showed the administration's resolve on the issue. During the next several months, many of the thirty-five countries joined others in signing Article 98 agreements. Bush waived the provision for the future NATO members in November 2003. By the summer of 2004, the United States had concluded over 90 Article 98 agreements, but they were still sharply opposed by many European countries. The agreements were criticized by human rights groups and others who felt that the precedent set by the U.S. efforts to avoid criticism and prosecution will weaken general international efforts on human rights.

The U.S. opposition did not stop development of the ICC. For some, its operation has become a symbol of deeper disputes over the future of the international system. For example, one diplomat explained opposition to the U.S. actions by saying, "The reason this is so hard fought and so emotionally fought—it's not the substance of it. It's the politics of law and order in a one-superpower world and who provides that: the one superpower or international bodies and international consensus."[11] Meanwhile, Bush administration officials said that they were not trying to undermine the court, but would continue to protect U.S. citizens. One sign that international opposition to the U.S. position was mounting was a 2004 dispute over a proposed UN resolution extending protection for the UN peacekeepers. In May 2004, American diplomats were confident that they could obtain a "technical rollover" on the measure.[12] Soon, though, reports of the U.S. mistreatment of Iraqi detainees led some countries to express objections to the resolution. UN Secretary General Kofi Annan took the unusual step of calling on the Security Council to reject the American proposal. Faced with certain defeat, the United States abandoned the resolution, but warned that it would have to reconsider U.S. participation in UN missions. In July, the administration followed through on its threat by deciding to withdraw nine U.S. soldiers serving in UN missions in Kosovo and Ethiopia. The impact of the decision was, however, more symbolic than practical since few U.S. troops were abroad under UN missions.

United Nations

The UN came into existence with strong U.S. backing on October 24, 1945. The UN's core ideas and structures built off the ideas and lessons learned from the League of Nations, which had been established after World War I. The League has generally been viewed as a failure since it did not prevent World War II or other aggressions. Its failure had two root causes. First, the United States decided not to join, primarily because some U.S. Senators felt that the League encroached on U.S. sovereignty. Second, it had only limited power to enforce its resolutions.

The UN's founders succeeded in enticing the United States and other major powers to join by giving them permanent seats and veto power in the crucial Security Council. Some observers felt that the UN structures must become more egalitarian if they were to be respected worldwide; however, superpowers occasionally still feel constrained by the current system. Balancing the need to strengthen the UN's powers of enforcement with respect for sovereignty posed an even greater challenge. The UN is stronger than the League, but it still has important limits. It has no army and is prohibited from interfering in states' domestic politics. Over time, the UN has faced criticism from some who feel it has become too powerful and overstepped its authority, but others lament that the UN is too weak and takes too little action to address global issues.

In looking at U.S. relations with the UN, many people speak as if the UN and its policies are a single, unified entity. Often, though, it is useful to break the discussion into at least three parts: ties with UN institutions, views on the UN's nonsecurity programs and policies, and opinions on its security programs and policies. In addition, while there are some influential UN officials and the UN's unusual voting rules can affect decisions, the UN remains fundamentally a cooperative organization of independent countries. When people praise or criticize the UN, they often are really discussing either the collective will and priorities of the international community, or the very idea of developing multilateral policies and institutions.

The Bush administration's relations with the UN institutions got off to a poor start. Bush's ambassador to the UN did not win Senate approval for several months, so the U.S. delegation was not at full strength. In the spring of 2001, the United States also suffered unprecedented failures in not wining seats on the UN's Human Rights Commission and International Narcotics Board. Over time, though, Bush developed better relations. In 2002, the United States got seats back on the commissions. In addition, Bush pledged renewed U.S. membership in the United Nations Education, Scientific and Cultural Organization (UNESCO). The United States had not been a member of UNESCO since 1984 when President Reagan withdrew citing poor management and anti-American and anti-Israeli bias in its programs. Furthermore, Bush established a generally cordial and mutually respectful relationship with UN Secretary General Kofi Annan, despite some sharp policy disagreements between them.

Bush also helped build relations with the UN by encouraging Congress to pay U.S. dues and accrued debts to the UN. The UN is financed through both assessed and voluntary contributions from member states. Assessments are based primarily on the size of a country's economy, but adjustments to the formula are common. In recent decades, the United States has paid roughly 25 percent of the UN budget. Many Members of Congress, particularly Republicans, came to feel that the UN was expanding programs too greatly, wasting money in its bureaucracy, and expecting the United States to shoulder too much of the burden. Therefore, in the 1990s, Congress often appropriated less than the full U.S. assessment and passed laws saying that the payment of dues and debt was dependent on UN reform and reduction of U.S. obligations. In 1998, the United States was warned that it would soon lose its General Assembly seat if it did not pay the debt. In the 2000 campaign, Bush voiced the general Republican view on the need for reform, but he was not as strident as some in his party. In December 2000, the Clinton administration won UN approval for both reform and a reduction of the main U.S. assessment to 22 percent of the UN budget. The deal satisfied Bush and most Members of Congress. When new issues arose, such as the loss of the Human Rights seat and disputes over the ICC, some members tried to further condition aid, but Bush opposed these efforts and helped pass bills that paid off U.S. debts over three years.

The Bush administration's relations with the UN also have been affected by mixed support for the UN's nonsecurity activities. By rejoining UNESCO, encouraging full payment of dues and praising specific programs, Bush showed support for UN actions. However, if the UN program conflicted with Bush's views, he forcefully denied support. Bush repeatedly denied funds to the United Nations Population Fund on the grounds that the agency cooperated with Chinese activities that promoted abortion. He dismissed those who argued that the denial of funds hurt population control and health programs globally. Bush felt that some UN programs were too costly, slow to be implemented, and lacked oversight. These sentiments, combined with his desire to have control over decisions about condom distribution and drug choice, led Bush to support the UN programs on AIDS, but to channel most of the U.S. money to U.S. programs. When Bush felt UN programs, for example the Kyoto Protocol and the ICC, would hurt U.S. interests, he not only opposed them, but used U.S. power at the UN to shape policy. Many UN officials and U.S. allies opposed Bush's perspectives on a number of these issues and were particularly offended when they felt his actions weakened and politicized UN institutions.

Disputes over security issues caused the greatest tension. Bush did not oppose all UN security activities. He promoted tough inspections of Iranian and North Korean nuclear programs by the International Atomic Energy Agency (IAEA) and favored developing UN sanctions to punish those countries. He supported a number of UN peacekeeping operations, although, in some cases he had to be lobbied hard for his support. Bush praised the UN for its overall support in the war on terrorism and for its role in rebuilding Afghanistan, but military actions in Afghanistan were kept under U.S. control. In general, his support was greatest when the UN followed U.S. goals and did not interfere with U.S. actions.

The traditional U.S. relationship with the UN was most threatened by issues tied to the war in Iraq. Bush's discussions of an Axis of Evil and preemption led many to expect that the United States would act unilaterally in Iraq. Thus, the decision by Bush in August 2000 to take the issue to the UN generated much focus. On September 12, 2002, Bush spoke at the UN General Assembly and made the case for action against Iraq (Speech 3.1). In the speech, Bush challenged the UN to enforce its own resolutions and to take an active role in assuring security or accept the fate of the League. He went on to suggest that the UN faced a defining test of its resolve. "Are Security Council resolutions to be honored and enforced, or cast aside without consequence? Will the United Nations serve the purpose of its founding, or will it be irrelevant?"

Initially, UN supporters felt that Bush had reinforced the institution's importance by not only seeking UN authority to act, but describing the war as an effort to enforce UN resolutions. Thus, work began on what would become Resolution 1441, which set out the terms for Iraq's "final opportunity" to comply. As that resolution was being drafted and implemented, UN supporters found they faced a major dilemma. If it approved a war, the UN risked being seen as just a rubber stamp for U.S. policy. If it opposed a war, the UN could show that it was still independent and could potentially limit U.S. unilateralism. On the other hand, opposition would reinforce the U.S. view that the UN preferred endless talk to real action. Opposition also risked the worst-case scenario of the United States acting despite UN disapproval causing the UN to appear impotent and irrelevant. Some supports felt that the best option was to prolong debate, and hope that Iraq would change policies enough to keep the United States involved in UN actions.

The United States also faced tough choices. Powell and others argued that UN support was important for practical and political reasons. Vice President Cheney, Secretary of Defense Rumsfeld and others countered that independent action would keep decisions on timing, war strategy, and postwar plans in U.S. hands. Both groups agreed that demonstrating a clear U.S. willingness to take action would keep pressure on Iraq, and encourage allies to support UN action in order to preserve unity in multilateral institutions. Therefore, some administration talk of unilateral action might yield multilateral action. If unilateral talk went too far, however, it risked offending those at the UN who did not want it to be seen as a U.S. pawn.

Over time, France, Russia, and other countries made it clear that they would oppose the war. As Bush and his advisers grew increasingly frustrated with the coalition building process, the UN became a target of their frustrations. In February, Bush told a Republican group, "The United Nations gets to decide, shortly, whether or not it is going to be relevant, in terms of keeping the peace, whether or not its words mean anything."[13] "Relevance" was clearly being defined as support for U.S. positions. Bush and his advisers began to openly say that, in the future, they might rely less on the UN and more on "coalitions of the willing." Many observers felt that the UN's future as an important actor was indeed at stake, but could not discern what, if any, action would actually enhance UN power. Some wondered whether the whole crisis proved that multilateral institutions simply cannot coexist with global hegemony.

Even before the Iraqi war began, talk shifted to the role of the UN in postwar Iraq. Rebuilding Iraq's economic and political systems would be a major challenge. Bush was well known for opposing the use of the U.S.

military for nation building. Supporters, therefore, hoped that the UN's importance might be revived. During the war, their optimism was shaken by administration's comments. National Security Adviser Rice and several others suggested that because the U.S.-led coalition had Iraq, it would take the lead role. In April, Bush declared the UN should play a "vital role" in Iraq, but went on to define that as providing food, medicine, and aid, not political control.[14] The UN was guaranteed some voice in debates, because economic sanctions on Iraq remained and the UN had overseen the oil-for-food program designed to help feed Iraqis during the sanctions. On May 21, 2003 three weeks after Bush declared major operations in Iraq to be over, a Security Council resolution lifted the sanctions, set out plans to use the large outstanding balance in the oil-for-food account, and, most importantly, gave the "provisional authorities" in Iraq—namely the United States and England—authority to control Iraq's political, security and economic systems. A UN Special Representative's post was created, but had little real power.

During the next year, UN authority in Iraq gradually increased although not in a linear fashion. At several points, the Bush administration came close to abandoning efforts to get new UN resolutions and it ceded control only grudgingly. A view into the administration's logic for an increased UN role comes from an administration official's August 2003 comments that "The administration is not willing to confront going to the Security Council and saying 'We really need to make Iraq an international operation'. You can make a case that it would be better to do that, but right now the situation in Iraq is not that dire."[15] As violence in Iraq continued, U.S. troops and reserve capabilities were stretched, and the cost of rebuilding rose, the situation seemed more dire. Bush thus, became more willing to allow a greater UN role as a way of encouraging other countries to send troops and resources to Iraq.

On September 23, 2003, Bush returned to the General Assembly and gave a speech very different in tone from the one he had delivered one year earlier (Speech 5.3). Early in the speech, Bush recounted how the Security Council had been rightly alarmed by Iraq, right to demand Iraqi destruction of weapons, and right to vow serious consequences if Iraq did not comply. He then subtly shifted the wording as he spoke about the coalition that enforced those UN views, but quickly returned to praising the UN for its postwar assistance. Later, he described plans for a new Security Council resolution, which would expand the UN's political role in Iraq. The speech continued by describing other important global issues needing action by the UN.

In October 2003, a new resolution was passed that recognized the legitimacy of the Iraqi interim government, authorized a multinational force to take actions necessary to preserve security, and urged countries to contribute military forces and economic aid. It also stated that the UN should increase its role in Iraq through humanitarian aid, economic assistance, and lending its expertise to the process of political transformation. In January 2004, conditions in Iraq worsened further when Iraq's leading Shiite cleric, Grand Ayatollah Ali al-Sistani, objected to the U.S. plans for selecting an interim government. The administration again turned to the UN for assistance. Lakhdar Brahimi, a UN official appointed to guide Iraq's political transition, played a key role in pacifying al-Sistani, developing the structure of Iraq's interim government, and selecting its members.

Throughout 2002 and the first half of 2003, the power to assign the UN a role was in America's hands. By the end of 2003, the situation had reversed, and the UN had the power to decide which role it wanted. Ironically, the UN of the latter period was much less anxious to be involved. This stemmed, in part, from a feeling that those who opposed the war should not be responsible for its aftermath, but also reflected growing security concerns. In August 2003, a bomb at UN headquarters in Iraq killed 22 people, including Sergio Vieira de Mello, a highly regarded UN diplomat and close friend of Annan. After the attack, the UN removed its personnel from Iraq. In subsequent discussions, Annan expressed great concern over the safety of UN officials and was reluctant to increase UN activity on the ground. Even in the summer of 2004, when the UN was preparing for a role in monitoring Iraq's elections, operations remained based out of Jordan.

The evolution of Bush's thinking about the UN's postwar role was dramatic, but he did not change his general views on how the UN should act. In November 2003, he spoke in England about three pillars of peace and security: international organizations, restraining aggression and evil by force, and spreading democracy (Speech 5.4). In his discussion of international organizations, he again reminded the audience of the failure of the League of Nations. He then affirmed America's commitment to the UN, but argued that it could only be effective if it enforced its resolutions. He suggested, America and England had acted "to prevent the United Nations from solemnly choosing its own irrelevance." Both administration critics and supporters noted that Bush had to a large extent appointed the United States as a global enforcer in order to save the international community from its own weak tendencies. Naturally, views on this action depended on observers' underlying views on the importance of international cooperation and institutions.

5.1 Global Climate Change

The White House
Washington, DC
June 11, 2001

I've just met with senior members of my administration who are working to develop an effective and science-based approach to addressing the important issues of global climate change.

This is an issue that I know is very important to the nations of Europe, which I will be visiting for the first time as President. The earth's well-being is also an issue important to America. And it's an issue that should be important to every nation in every part of our world.

The issue of climate change respects no border. Its effects cannot be reined in by an army nor advanced by any ideology. Climate change, with its potential to impact every corner of the world, is an issue that must be addressed by the world.

The Kyoto Protocol was fatally flawed in fundamental ways. But the process used to bring nations together to discuss our joint response to climate change is an important one. That is why I am today committing the United States of America to work within the United Nations framework and elsewhere to develop with our friends and allies and nations throughout the world an effective and science-based response to the issue of global warming.

My Cabinet-level working group has met regularly for the last ten weeks to review the most recent, most accurate, and most comprehensive science. They have heard from scientists offering a wide spectrum of views. They have reviewed the facts, and they have listened to many theories and suppositions. The working group asked the highly-respected National Academy of Sciences to provide us the most up-to-date information about what is known and about what is not known on the science of climate change.

First, we know the surface temperature of the earth is warming. It has risen by .six degrees Celsius over the past 100 years. There was a warming trend from the 1890s to the 1940s. Cooling from the 1940s to the 1970s. And then sharply rising temperatures from the 1970s to today.

There is a natural greenhouse effect that contributes to warming. Greenhouse gases trap heat, and thus warm the earth because they prevent a significant proportion of infrared radiation from escaping into space. Concentration of greenhouse gases, especially CO_2, have increased substantially since the beginning of the industrial revolution. And the National Academy of Sciences indicate that the increase is due in large part to human activity.

Yet, the Academy's report tells us that we do not know how much effect natural fluctuations in climate may have had on warming. We do not know how much our climate could, or will change in the future. We do not know how fast change will occur, or even how some of our actions could impact it.... And, finally, no one can say with any certainty what constitutes a dangerous level of warming, and therefore what level must be avoided.

The policy challenge is to act in a serious and sensible way, given the limits of our knowledge. While scientific uncertainties remain, we can begin now to address the factors that contribute to climate change....

The United States is the world's largest emitter of manmade greenhouse gases. We account for almost 20 percent of the world's man-made greenhouse emissions. We also account for about one-quarter of the world's economic output. We recognize the responsibility to reduce our emissions. We also recognize the other part of the story—that the rest of the world emits 80 percent of all greenhouse gases. And many of those emissions come from developing countries.

This is a challenge that requires a 100 percent effort; ours, and the rest of the world's. The world's second-largest emitter of greenhouse gases is China. Yet, China was entirely exempted from the requirements of the Kyoto Protocol.

India and Germany are among the top emitters. Yet, India was also exempt from Kyoto. These and other developing countries that are experiencing rapid growth face challenges in reducing their emissions without harming their economies. We want to work cooperatively with these countries in their efforts to reduce greenhouse emissions and maintain economic growth....

Kyoto is, in many ways, unrealistic. Many countries cannot meet their Kyoto targets. The targets themselves were arbitrary and not based upon science. For America, complying with those mandates would have a negative economic impact, with layoffs of workers and price increases for consumers. And when you evaluate all these flaws, most reasonable people will understand that it's not sound public policy.

That's why 95 members of the United States Senate expressed a reluctance to endorse such an approach. Yet, America's unwillingness to embrace a flawed treaty should not be read by our friends and allies as any abdication of responsibility. To the contrary, my administration is committed to a leadership role on the issue of climate change.

We recognize our responsibility and will meet it—at home, in our hemisphere, and in the world. My Cabinet-level working group on climate change is recommending a number of initial steps, and will continue to work on additional ideas. The working group proposes the United States help lead the way by advancing the science on climate change, advancing the technology to monitor and reduce greenhouse gases, and creating partnerships within our hemisphere and beyond to monitor and measure and mitigate emissions. . . .

The United States has spent $18 billion on climate research since 1990—three times as much as any other country, and more than Japan and all fifteen nations of the EU combined. Today, I make our investment in science even greater. My administration will establish the U.S. Climate Change Research Initiative to study areas of uncertainty and identify priority areas where investments can make a difference.

I'm directing my Secretary of Commerce, working with other agencies, to set priorities for additional investments in climate change research, review such investments, and to improve coordination amongst federal agencies. We will fully fund high-priority areas for climate change science over the next five years. We'll also provide resources to build climate observation systems in developing countries and encourage other developed nations to match our American commitment.

And we propose a joint venture with the EU, Japan and others to develop state-of-the-art climate modeling that will help us better understand the causes and impacts of climate change. America's the leader in technology and innovation. We all believe technology offers great promise to significantly reduce emissions—especially carbon capture, storage and sequestration technologies.

So we're creating the National Climate Change Technology Initiative to strengthen research at universities and national labs, to enhance partnerships in applied research, to develop improved technology for measuring and monitoring gross and net greenhouse gas emissions, and to fund demonstration projects for cutting-edge technologies, such as bioreactors and fuel cells.

Even with the best science, even with the best technology, we all know the United States cannot solve this global problem alone. We're building partnerships within the Western Hemisphere and with other like-minded countries. . . .

We will work with the Inter-American Institute for Global Change Research and other institutions to better understand regional impacts of climate change. We will establish a partnership to monitor and mitigate emissions. And at home, I call on Congress to work with my administration on the initiatives to enhance conservation and energy efficiency outlined in my energy plan, to implement the increased use of renewables, natural gas and hydropower that are outlined in the plan, and to increase the generation of safe and clean nuclear power.

By increasing conservation and energy efficiency and aggressively using these clean energy technologies, we can reduce our greenhouse gas emissions by significant amounts in the coming years. We can make great progress in reducing emissions, and we will. Yet, even that isn't enough.

I've asked my advisors to consider approaches to reduce greenhouse gas emissions, including those that tap the power of markets, help realize the promise of technology and ensure the widest-possible global participation. As we analyze the possibilities, we will be guided by several basic principles. Our approach must be consistent with the long-term goal of stabilizing greenhouse gas concentrations in the atmosphere. Our actions should be measured as we learn more from science and build on it.

Our approach must be flexible to adjust to new information and take advantage of new technology. We must always act to ensure continued economic growth and prosperity for our citizens and for citizens throughout the world. We should pursue market-based incentives and spur technological innovation.

And, finally, our approach must be based on global participation, including that of developing countries whose net greenhouse gas emissions now exceed those in the developed countries.

I've asked Secretary Powell and Administrator Whitman to ensure they actively work with friends and allies to explore common approaches to climate change consistent with these principles. Each step we take will increase our knowledge. We will act, learn, and act again, adjusting our approaches as science advances and technology evolves.

Our administration will be creative. We're committed to protecting our environment and improving our economy, to acting at home and working in concert with the world. This is an administration that will make commitments we can keep, and keep the commitments that we make.

5.2 Global Climate Initiatives

NOAA
Silver Springs, Maryland
February 14, 2002

Today, I'm announcing a new environmental approach that will clean our skies, bring greater health to our citizens and encourage environmentally responsible development in America and around the world. . . .

America and the world share this common goal: we must foster economic growth in ways that protect our environment. We must encourage growth that will provide a better life for citizens, while protecting the land, the water, and the air that sustain life.

In pursuit of this goal, my government has set two priorities: we must clean our air, and we must address the issue of global climate change. We must also act in a serious and responsible way, given the scientific uncertainties. While these uncertainties remain, we can begin now to address the human factors that contribute to climate change. Wise action now is an insurance policy against future risks.

I have been working with my Cabinet to meet these challenges with forward and creative thinking. I said, if need be, let's challenge the status quo. But let's always remember, let's do what is in the interest of the American people.

Today, I'm confident that the environmental path that I announce will benefit the entire world. This new approach is based on this common-sense idea: that economic growth is key to environmental progress, because it is growth that provides the resources for investment in clean technologies.

This new approach will harness the power of markets, the creativity of entrepreneurs, and draw upon the best scientific research. And it will make possible a new partnership with the developing world to meet our common environmental and economic goals.

We will apply this approach first to the challenge of cleaning the air that Americans breathe. . . .

Now, global climate change presents a different set of challenges and requires a different strategy. The science is more complex, the answers are less certain, and the technology is less developed. So we need a flexible approach that can adjust to new information and new technology.

I reaffirm America's commitment to the United Nations Framework Convention and it's central goal, to stabilize atmospheric greenhouse gas concentrations at a level that will prevent dangerous human interference with the climate. Our immediate goal is to reduce America's greenhouse gas emissions relative to the size of our economy.

My administration is committed to cutting our nation's greenhouse gas intensity—how much we emit per unit of economic activity—by 18 percent over the next ten years. This will set America on a path to slow the growth of our greenhouse gas emissions and, as science justifies, to stop and then reverse the growth of emissions.

This is the common sense way to measure progress. Our nation must have economic growth—growth to create opportunity; growth to create a higher quality of life for our citizens. Growth is also what pays for investments in clean technologies, increased conservation, and energy efficiency. Meeting our commitment to reduce our greenhouse gas intensity by 18 percent by the year 2012 will prevent over 500 million metric tons of greenhouse gases from going into the atmosphere over the course of the decade. And that is the equivalent of taking 70 million cars off the road.

To achieve this goal, our nation must move forward on many fronts, looking at every sector of our economy. We will challenge American businesses to further reduce emissions. Already, agreements with the semiconductor and aluminum industries and others have dramatically cut emissions of some of the most potent greenhouse gases. We will build on these successes with new agreements and greater reductions.

Our government will also move forward immediately to create world-class standards for measuring and registering emission reductions. And we will give transferable credits to companies that can show real emission reductions. We will promote renewable energy production and clean coal technology, as well as nuclear power, which produces no greenhouse gas emissions. And we will work to safely improve fuel economy for our cars and our trucks.

Overall, my budget devotes $4.5 billion to addressing climate change—more than any other nation's commitment in the entire world. This is an increase of more than $700 million over last year's budget. Our nation will continue to lead the world in basic climate and science research to address gaps in our knowledge that are important to decision makers.

When we make decisions, we want to make sure we do so on sound science; not what sounds good, but what is real. And the United States leads the world in providing that kind of research. . . .

My comprehensive energy plan, the first energy plan that any administration has put out in a long period of time, provides $4.6 billion over the next five years in clean energy tax incentives to encourage purchases of hybrid and fuel cell vehicles, to promote residential solar energy, and to reward investments in wind, solar and biomass energy production. And we will look for ways to increase the amount of carbon stored by America's farms and forests through a strong conservation title in the farm bill. I have asked Secretary Veneman to recommend new targeted incentives for landowners to increase carbon storage.

By doing all these things, by giving companies incentives to cut emissions, by diversifying our energy supply to include cleaner fuels, by increasing conservation, by increasing research and development and tax incentives for energy efficiency and clean technologies, and by increasing carbon storage, I am absolutely confident that America will reach the goal that I have set.

If, however, by 2012, our progress is not sufficient and sound science justifies further action, the United States will respond with additional measures that may include broad-based market programs as well as additional incentives and voluntary measures designed to accelerate technology development and deployment.

Addressing global climate change will require a sustained effort over many generations. My approach recognizes that economic growth is the solution, not the problem. Because a nation that grows its economy is a nation that can afford investments and new technologies.

The approach taken under the Kyoto protocol would have required the United States to make deep and immediate cuts in our economy to meet an arbitrary target. It would have cost our economy up to $400 billion and we would have lost 4.9 million jobs.

As President of the United States, charged with safeguarding the welfare of the American people and American workers, I will not commit our nation to an unsound international treaty that will throw millions of our citizens out of work. Yet, we recognize our international responsibilities. So in addition to acting here at home, the United States will actively help developing nations grow along a more efficient, more environmentally responsible path. . . .

It would be unfair—indeed, counterproductive—to condemn developing nations to slow growth or no growth by insisting that they take on impractical and unrealistic greenhouse gas targets. Yet, developing nations such as China and India already account for a majority of the world's greenhouse gas emissions, and it would be irresponsible to absolve them from shouldering some of the shared obligations.

The greenhouse gas intensity approach I put forward today gives developing countries a yardstick for progress on climate change that recognizes their right to economic development. . . .

The United States will not interfere with the plans of any nation that chooses to ratify the Kyoto protocol. But I will intend to work with nations, especially the poor and developing nations, to show the world that there is a better approach, that we can build our future prosperity along a cleaner and better path.

My budget includes over $220 million for the U.S. Agency for International Development and a global environmental facility to help developing countries better measure, reduce emissions, and to help them invest in clean and renewable energy technologies. . . . The new budget also provides $40 million under the Tropical Forest Conservation Act to help countries redirect debt payments towards protecting tropical forests, forests that store millions of tons of carbon. And I've also ordered the Secretary of State to develop a new initiative to help developing countries stop illegal logging, a practice that destroys biodiversity and releases millions of tons of greenhouse gases into the atmosphere.

And, finally, my government is following through on our commitment to provide $25 million for climate observation systems in developing countries that will help scientists understand the dynamics of climate change.

To clean the air, and to address climate change, we need to recognize that economic growth and environmental protection go hand in hand. Affluent societies are the ones that demand, and can therefore afford, the most environmental protection. Prosperity is what allows us to commit more and more resources to environmental protection. . . .

Americans are among the most creative people in our history. . . . We can tap the power of economic growth to further protect our environment for generations that follow.

5.3 The UN's Global Role

The United Nations
New York, New York
September 23, 2003

Twenty-four months ago—and yesterday in the memory of America—the center of New York City became a battlefield, and a graveyard, and the symbol of an unfinished war.... Last month, terrorists brought their war to the United Nations itself. The UN headquarters in Baghdad stood for order and compassion—and for that reason, the terrorists decided it must be destroyed....

By the victims they choose, and by the means they use, the terrorists have clarified the struggle we are in. Those who target relief workers for death have set themselves against all humanity. Those who incite murder and celebrate suicide reveal their contempt for life, itself. They have no place in any religious faith; they have no claim on the world's sympathy; and they should have no friend in this chamber.

Events during the past two years have set before us the clearest of divides: between those who seek order, and those who spread chaos; between those who work for peaceful change, and those who adopt the methods of gangsters; between those who honor the rights of man, and those who deliberately take the lives of men and women and children without mercy or shame.

Between these alternatives there is no neutral ground. All governments that support terror are complicit in a war against civilization. No government should ignore the threat of terror, because to look the other way gives terrorists the chance to regroup and recruit and prepare. And all nations that fight terror, as if the lives of their own people depend on it, will earn the favorable judgment of history.

The former regimes of Afghanistan and Iraq knew these alternatives, and made their choices. The Taliban was a sponsor and servant of terrorism. When confronted, that regime chose defiance, and that regime is no more....

The regime of Saddam Hussein cultivated ties to terror while it built weapons of mass destruction. It used those weapons in acts of mass murder, and refused to account for them when confronted by the world. The Security Council was right to be alarmed. The Security Council was right to demand that Iraq destroy its illegal weapons and prove that it had done so. The Security Council was right to vow serious consequences if Iraq refused to comply. And because there were consequences, because a coalition of nations acted to defend the peace, and the credibility of the United Nations, Iraq is free, and today we are joined by representatives of a liberated country. . . .

Our actions in Afghanistan and Iraq were supported by many governments, and America is grateful to each one. I also recognize that some of the sovereign nations of this assembly disagreed with our actions. Yet there was, and there remains, unity among us on the fundamental principles and objectives of the United Nations. We are dedicated to the defense of our collective security, and to the advance of human rights. These permanent commitments call us to great work in the world, work we must do together. So let us move forward.

First, we must stand with the people of Afghanistan and Iraq as they build free and stable countries. The terrorists and their allies fear and fight this progress above all, because free people embrace hope over resentment, and choose peace over violence.

The United Nations has been a friend of the Afghan people, distributing food and medicine, helping refugees return home, advising on a new constitution, and helping to prepare the way for nationwide elections. . . . In the nation of Iraq, the United Nations is carrying out vital and effective work every day. By the end of 2004, more than 90 percent of Iraqi children under age five will have been immunized against preventable diseases such as polio, tuberculosis and measles, thanks to the hard work and high ideals of UNICEF. Iraq's food distribution system is operational, delivering nearly a half-million tons of food per month, thanks to the skill and expertise of the World Food Program.

Our international coalition in Iraq is meeting it responsibilities. We are conducting precision raids against terrorists and holdouts of the former regime. These killers are at war with the Iraqi people. They have made Iraq the central front in the war on terror, and they will be defeated. . . . And at the same time, our coalition is helping to improve the daily lives of the Iraqi people. . . . Having helped to liberate Iraq, we will honor our pledges to Iraq, and by helping the Iraqi people build a stable and peaceful country, we will make our own countries more secure.

The primary goal of our coalition in Iraq is self-government for the people of Iraq, reached by orderly and democratic process. This process must unfold according to the needs of Iraqis, neither hurried, nor delayed by the wishes of other parties. And the United Nations can contribute greatly to the cause of Iraq self-government. America is working with friends and allies on a new Security Council resolution, which will expand the UN's role in Iraq. As in the aftermath of other conflicts, the United Nations should assist in developing a constitution, in training civil servants, and conducting free and fair elections. . . .

The success of a free Iraq will be watched and noted throughout the region. Millions will see that freedom, equality, and material progress are possible at the heart of the Middle East. Leaders in the region will face the clearest evidence that free institutions and open societies are the only path to long-term national success and dignity. And a transformed Middle East would benefit the entire world, by undermining the ideologies that export violence to other lands. . . .

A second challenge we must confront together is the proliferation of weapons of mass destruction. . . . The deadly combination of outlaw regimes and terror networks and weapons of mass murder is a peril that cannot be ignored or wished away. If such a danger is allowed to fully materialize, all words, all protests, will come too late. Nations of the world must have the wisdom and the will to stop grave threats before they arrive.

One crucial step is to secure the most dangerous materials at their source. For more than a decade, the United States has worked with Russia and other states of the former Soviet Union to dismantle, destroy, or secure weapons and dangerous materials left over from another era. . . .

We're also improving our capability to interdict lethal materials in transit. Through our Proliferation Security Initiative, eleven nations are preparing to search planes and ships, trains and trucks carrying suspect cargo, and to seize weapons or missile shipments that raise proliferation concerns. These nations have agreed on a set of interdiction principles, consistent with current legal authorities. And we're working to expand the Proliferation Security Initiative to other countries. We're determined to keep the world's most destructive weapons away from all our shores, and out of the hands of our common enemies. Because proliferators will use any route or channel that is open to them, we need the broadest possible cooperation to stop them. Today, I ask the UN Security Council to adopt a new anti-proliferation resolution. This resolution should call on all members of the UN to criminalize the proliferation of weapons of mass destruction, to enact strict export controls consistent with international standards, and to secure any and all sensitive materials within their own borders. The United States stands ready to help any nation draft these new laws, and to assist in their enforcement.

A third challenge we share is a challenge to our conscience. We must act decisively to meet the humanitarian crises of our time. The United States has begun to carry out the Emergency Plan for AIDS Relief, aimed at preventing AIDS on a massive scale, and treating millions who have the disease already. We have pledged $15 billion over five years to fight AIDS around the world.

My country is acting to save lives from famine, as well. We're providing more than $1.4 billion in global emergency food aid, and I've asked our United States Congress for $200 million for a new famine fund, so we can act quickly when the first signs of famine appear. Every nation on every continent should generously add their resources to the fight against disease and desperate hunger.

There's another humanitarian crisis spreading, yet hidden from view. Each year, an estimated 800,000 to 900,000 human beings are bought, sold or forced across the world's borders. Among them are hundreds of thousands of teenage girls, and others as young as five, who fall victim to the sex trade. This commerce in human life generates billions of dollars each year—much of which is used to finance organized crime. . . .

The victims of this industry also need help from members of the United Nations. And this begins with clear standards and the certainty of punishment under laws of every country. Today, some nations make it a crime to sexually abuse children abroad. Such conduct should be a crime in all nations. Governments should inform travelers of the harm this industry does, and the severe punishments that will fall on its patrons. . . . The American government is committing $50 million to support the good work of organizations that are rescuing women and children from exploitation, and giving them shelter and medical treatment and the hope of a new life. I urge other governments to do their part. . . .

All the challenges I have spoken of this morning require urgent attention and moral clarity. Helping Afghanistan and Iraq to succeed as free nations in a transformed region, cutting off the avenues of proliferation, abolishing modern forms of slavery—these are the kinds of great tasks for which the United Nations was founded. In each case, careful discussion is needed, and also decisive action. Our good intentions will be credited only if we achieve good outcomes.

As an original signer of the UN Charter, the United States of America is committed to the United Nations. And we show that commitment by working to fulfill the UN's stated purposes, and give meaning to its ideals. The founding documents of the United Nations and the founding documents of America stand in the same tradition. Both assert that human beings should never be reduced to objects of power or commerce, because their dignity is inherent. Both require—both recognize a moral law that stands above men and nations, which must be defended and enforced by men and nations. And both point the way to peace, the peace that comes when all are free. We secure that peace with our courage, and we must show that courage together.

5.4 Three Pillars of Peace and Security

Whitehall Palace
London, England
November 19, 2003

Americans traveling to England always observe more similarities to our country than differences. . . . The people of Great Britain also might see some familiar traits in Americans. . . .

The fellowship of generations is the cause of common beliefs. We believe in open societies ordered by moral conviction. We believe in private markets, humanized by compassionate government. We believe in economies that reward effort, communities that protect the weak, and the duty of nations to respect the dignity and the rights of all. And whether one learns these ideals in County Durham or in West Texas, they instill mutual respect and they inspire common purpose.

More than an alliance of security and commerce, the British and American peoples have an alliance of values. And, today, this old and tested alliance is very strong. . . .

The last President to stay at Buckingham Palace was an idealist, without question. At a dinner hosted by King George V, in 1918, Woodrow Wilson made a pledge; with typical American understatement, he vowed that right and justice would become the predominant and controlling force in the world.

President Wilson had come to Europe with his 14 Points for Peace. Many complimented him on his vision; yet some were dubious. Take, for example, the Prime Minister of France. He complained that God, himself, had only ten commandments. Sounds familiar.

At Wilson's high point of idealism, however, Europe was one short generation from Munich and Auschwitz and the Blitz. Looking back, we see the reasons why. The League of Nations, lacking both credibility and will, collapsed at the first challenge of the dictators. Free nations failed to recognize, much less confront, the aggressive evil in plain sight. And so dictators went about their business, feeding resentments and anti-Semitism, bringing death to innocent people in this city and across the world, and filling the last century with violence and genocide.

Through world war and cold war, we learned that idealism, if it is to do any good in this world, requires common purpose and national strength, moral courage and patience in difficult tasks. And now our generation has need of these qualities. . . .

The peace and security of free nations now rests on three pillars: First, international organizations must be equal to the challenges facing our world, from lifting up failing states to opposing proliferation.

Like eleven Presidents before me, I believe in the international institutions and alliances that America helped to form and helps to lead. The United States and Great Britain have labored hard to help make the United Nations what it is supposed to be—an effective instrument of our collective security. . . . The United Nations has no more compelling advocate than your Prime Minister, who at every turn has championed its ideals and appealed to its authority. He understands, as well, that the credibility of the UN depends on a willingness to keep its word and to act when action is required.

America and Great Britain have done, and will do, all in their power to prevent the United Nations from solemnly choosing its own irrelevance and inviting the fate of the League of Nations. It's not enough to meet the dangers of the world with resolutions; we must meet those dangers with resolve. . . .

Our first choice, and our constant practice, is to work with other responsible governments. We understand, as well, that the success of multilateralism is not measured by adherence to forms alone, the tidiness of the process, but by the results we achieve to keep our nations secure.

The second pillar of peace and security in our world is the willingness of free nations, when the last resort arrives, to retain [sic] aggression and evil by force. There are principled objections to the use of force in every generation, and I credit the good motives behind these views. Those in authority, however, are not judged only by good motivations. The people have given us the duty to defend them. And that duty sometimes requires the violent restraint of violent men. In some cases, the measured use of force is all that protects us from a chaotic world ruled by force. . . .

It's been said that those who live near a police station find it hard to believe in the triumph of violence, in the same way free peoples might be tempted to take for granted the orderly societies we have come to know. Europe's peaceful unity is one of the great achievements of the last half-century. And because European countries now resolve differences through negotiation and consensus, there's sometimes an assumption that the entire world functions in the same way. But let us never forget how Europe's unity was achieved—by allied armies of liberation and NATO armies of defense. And let us never forget, beyond Europe's borders, in a world where oppression and violence are very real, liberation is still a moral goal, and freedom and security still need defenders.

The third pillar of security is our commitment to the global expansion of democracy, and the hope and progress it brings, as the alternative to instability and to hatred and terror. We cannot rely exclusively on military power to assure our long-term security. Lasting peace is gained as justice and democracy advance.

In democratic and successful societies, men and women do not swear allegiance to malcontents and murderers; they turn their hearts and labor to building better lives. And democratic governments do not shelter terrorist camps or attack their peaceful neighbors; they honor the aspirations and dignity of their own people. In our conflict with terror and tyranny, we have an unmatched advantage, a power that cannot be resisted, and that is the appeal of freedom to all mankind. . . .

The movement of history will not come about quickly. Because of our own democratic development—the fact that it was gradual and, at times, turbulent—we must be patient with others. And the Middle East countries have some distance to travel. . . .

The democratic progress we've seen in the Middle East was not imposed from abroad, and neither will the greater progress we hope to see. Freedom, by definition, must be chosen, and defended by those who choose it. Our part, as free nations, is to ally ourselves with reform, wherever it occurs. . . .

As recent history has shown, we cannot turn a blind eye to oppression just because the oppression is not in our own backyard. No longer should we think tyranny is benign because it is temporarily convenient. Tyranny is never benign to its victims, and our great democracies should oppose tyranny wherever it is found. . . .

Ladies and gentlemen, we have great objectives before us that make our Atlantic alliance as vital as it has ever been. We will encourage the strength and effectiveness of international institutions. We will use force when necessary in the defense of freedom. And we will raise up an ideal of democracy in every part of the world. On these three pillars we will build the peace and security of all free nations in a time of danger.

So much good has come from our alliance of conviction and might. So much now depends on the strength of this alliance as we go forward. America has always found strong partners in London, leaders of good judgment and blunt counsel and backbone when times are tough. And I have found all those qualities in your current Prime Minister, who has my respect and my deepest thanks. . . .

The British people are the sort of partners you want when serious work needs doing. The men and women of this Kingdom are kind and steadfast and generous and brave. And America is fortunate to call this country our closest friend in the world.

Questions to Discuss

1. In Speeches 5.1 and 5.2, Bush argues against adopting major new policies until scientific uncertainties on the causes and future prospects of global warming are addressed. Is this prudent caution, or is it better to act early to prevent possible long-term problems?

2. In Speeches 5.1 and 5.2, Bush argues against adopting the Kyoto Protocol. If the Protocol is ratified by others and goes into effect, what impact will that have on U.S. alliances and global leadership?

3. Bush contends that there is major threat that U.S. citizens would be brought before the International Criminal Court (ICC) because of America's global activity and anti-American bias. Is this a real threat and does it justify U.S. opposition to the court?

4. In Speeches 5.3 and 5.4, Bush suggests that the UN must enforce its resolutions or risk becoming "irrelevant." Does that mean "relevance" is defined as support for U.S. policies, and that the United States should act to enforce UN resolutions with or without direct UN authorization?

5. In Speech 5.3, Bush calls on the UN to take an active role in rebuilding Iraq. Is this the proper role for the UN, or should control over key decisions remain with U.S. officials, or be transferred quickly to Iraqi officials?

Chapter 6

Europe and Russia

During the Cold War, there was great consistency in U.S. relations with the European continent. The United States and Western Europe developed one of the closest peacetime alliances in world history based on shared culture, similar economic and political philosophies, and the common enemy of communism. The two regions developed extensive economic ties and committed to mutual defense through the North Atlantic Treaty Organization (NATO). Although partners, both sides generally agreed that U.S. power made it the alliance leader. Meanwhile, U.S. relations with the Soviet Union and its Eastern European allies were the exact opposite. The Soviet bloc was culturally different and the imposition of communism led to sharply different economic and political systems. The Soviets vied with the United States for world leadership, leading to confrontation.

Two major developments shifted these relationships dramatically in the early 1990s. The first was the collapse of the Soviet Union and its empire. Russia was now a country in transition to democracy and capitalism, but one that maintained major military strength and continued to express anti-Western sentiments at times. Eastern Europe was also in transition and hoped to integrate with the West. These changes also raised issues of how the U.S. alliance with Western Europe would operate without its common enemy and whether Cold War era institutions, such as NATO, should be abandoned?

The second major development was the rise of the European Union (EU), which took new steps forward in the early 1990s with the creation of policies of free movement of workers throughout Europe, development of a common currency, and moves to create unified foreign and defense policies. Collective EU economic production was almost equal to that of the United States, and its population, share of world trade, and contributions to international institutions were larger. The one major area in which the EU lagged significantly was military strength. The rise of the EU raised questions of whether Europe would now become a more equal alliance partner, or whether U.S. military superiority and established patterns would keep the United States in a leadership position. In the longer term, the increase in EU power raised the possibility of rivalry between the United States and EU for regional or global influence.

These two changes in Europe, in combination with the concurrent rise of the United States as a global hegemon, led many to expect troubled relations in the 1990s. There were indeed some difficult moments, but changes in NATO's role and membership, new relations with Russia, and collective efforts to stem conflict in the Balkans made Europe more stable, secure, and democratic than ever before. Most observers, though, viewed the 1990s as a decade of transition and felt that the Bush administration would need to establish the pattern for future relations. The new pattern would depend not just on issues directly affecting the two areas, but also on how the United States and Europe chose to exercise their power across the international system.

Bush's Pre–9/11 Relations with Western Europe: Drifting Apart

President Bush inherited some specific policy problems from the Clinton administration. Among those were several trade disputes, debate over U.S. military commitments in the Balkans, and disagreements over how to address global warming. Many analysts argued that these and other specific disputes were in fact symptomatic of a gradual drifting apart of the alliance caused by differences in domestic and foreign policy views. The United States and Europe have cultural and political similarities, but key differences remain on issues such as welfare programs, tax levels, social issues, and the death penalty. Looking at stereotypes, many Americans view Europeans as pompous, wimpy, and living off their past glory, while Europeans often view Americans as arrogant, uncultured cowboys.

With regard to foreign policy, a number of analysts argue that growing tactical differences outweigh similarities. Most famously, Robert Kagan of the Carnegie Endowment for International Peace has suggested, "It is time to stop pretending that Europeans and Americans share a common view of the world, or even that they occupy the same world." He continues, "Americans are from Mars, Europeans are from Venus."[1] There are striking differences between the two regions in their geographic scope of policy focus, issue priorities, and tactics. First, the United States has global interests and devotes resources around the world; whereas, recently, Europeans have focused heavily on European issues. Second, many U.S. officials feel the world is a dangerous, competitive place where security interests still take priority. In contrast, the spread of peace and cooperation in Europe has left many Europeans believing the world is more cooperative and the time has come to devote more resources to nonsecurity issues. Third, the United States often turns to military and economic pressures, and to unilateral actions. On the other hand, Europe's comparative military weakness, and the lessons it learned in forming the EU, make it much more likely to search for solutions through dialogue, engagement, treaties, and multilateral actions.

The divergent views on domestic and foreign policy predated the Bush administration, but Bush's background and personal views reinforced the divide. During his first months in office, major tension appeared to be emerging. Bush stated that he wanted to focus more attention on Latin America and Asia, while Europeans maintained that their issues deserved top attention. Early in his presidency, Bush met with few European leaders and many European officials complained that they were not being consulted. On policies, Bush suggested that U.S. troop levels in the Balkans, and perhaps across Europe, should be reduced. Bush particularly angered Europeans by completely rejecting the Kyoto Protocol on global warming and announcing plans to abrogate the ABM treaty and build a missile defense. On tactics, many European leaders questioned Bush's tough stances on Iraq, Iran, North Korea, and Cuba and began their own efforts at engagement and negotiation. Bush's unilateralist tendencies were also sharply criticized.

Bush's first presidential trip to Europe in June 2001 was greeted by large public protests. His discussions with fellow leaders were unusually tense. Throughout the trip, Bush adopted a somewhat conciliatory tone. In a major address at Warsaw University, he stressed the common heritage and shared goals at the heart of U.S.–European relations and the past successes of alliance cooperation (Speech 6.1). To calm fears that the United States was planning to abandon Europe, Bush employed phrasing used by Secretary of State Powell, "We went into the Balkans together, and we will come out together." To address worries that the United States feared a rising Europe, he stated his belief that the EU was a positive development for peace and stability.

Despite his assurances of strong U.S.–European ties, Bush was not willing to alter his views to please Europeans. In the course of the trip, he called the ABM treaty a "relic of the past" and the Kyoto Protocol "unrealistic."[2] He made no mention of these issues in the Warsaw speech. It was also noteworthy that his first major speech was given in Poland, not Germany, France, or England and that this speech focused heavily on the need to move beyond the Cold War divisions and encourage Eastern European countries into existing institutions. The latter idea was a crucial signal of Bush's views on NATO expansion, as well as an encouragement for the EU to consider Eastern European countries as members. Bush hoped that expanding institutions would spread peace and democracy. In addition, the Eastern European countries were heavily pro-American, so they might serve as a balance to possible anti-American sentiments from the French or others.

9/11 Brings Unity, then Tactical Debate

Throughout the summer of 2001, the U.S.–European tensions continued, but the attacks of September 11 brought the two sides quickly and dramatically back together. The vast majority of Europe's leaders and public expressed revulsion at terrorism and support for a strong response. There was not just sympathy for, but solidarity with, Americans. These feelings were well expressed in the headline of the French newspaper *Le Monde*, "Nous sommes tous des americains" [We are all Americans]. Moving beyond rhetorical support, NATO came together and, for the first time in its history, invoked Article 5 of the North Atlantic Treaty stating that an "attack on one" is considered an "attack on all." In subsequent weeks, European governments were major players investigating suspected al Qaeda operatives based in Europe, sharing intelligence reports, supporting efforts to deny finances to terrorists and, in some cases, pledging military assistance for the U.S. operations.

The renewed cooperation seemed to show that a common enemy and clear security threat serves to minimize differences among allies and push controversies over nonsecurity issues to the backburner. The cooperation also, however, demonstrated that the U.S.–European relationship was still fundamentally sound. Administration officials often described the relationship as a marriage that had gone through rough patches, but ultimately had been held together by underlying shared goals and friendship.

Through the fall of 2001, cooperation continued, but there were some areas of disagreement stemming from underlying differences in capabilities and worldviews. Despite the invocation of Article 5, Bush chose not to conduct the war in Afghanistan as a NATO operation. This decision was based on two perceived lessons from NATO's 1999 war in Kosovo: 1) European militaries were too far behind to add significantly to U.S. power, and 2) NATO operations risked becoming "wars by committee," with too many parties seeking control over operations and goals. Many Europeans acknowledged the validity of the U.S. concerns about European military capability, although it uncomfortably highlighted their own weakness, but felt the second point was further proof that the United States was too quick to abandon multilateral options and unwilling to share world influence with its closest allies.

Some Europeans also felt that the United States was too focused on military action as the prime tool against terrorism. They questioned whether military strikes against Afghanistan might actually increase anti-

Western sentiment leading to future attacks against European targets. Many Europeans also felt military operations only treated expressions of anti-Westernism while ignoring its root causes. They suggested that aid programs and trade assistance would lead to better conditions in developing countries and be a wiser use of resources. They also suggested that the United States should at least acknowledge that policies such as support for Israel and tough actions against Iraq were contributing to anti-American feeling. These points of disagreement with the U.S. actions were expressed repeatedly in large public rallies across Europe and by some European government officials speaking either on or off the record. Formally, though, European governments expressed solidarity with the United States during the first phase of the war on terrorism.

The second phase of the war, signaled by Bush's declaration on the Axis of Evil and doctrine of preemption, drew much more criticism and created splits at higher levels. Many Europeans were surprised that Iran, a country with whom many European countries maintained trade relations and that Europeans argued was gradually reforming, would be placed in the same category as Iraq and North Korea. They also worried that the United States had closed off key policy options of engagement and diplomacy and committed to an eventual war with Iraq. Talk of preemption particularly angered Europeans. Most felt that international law protected countries from outside intervention and that respect for international law was crucial for world stability. Some European criticism was attributable to domestic politics. For example, left-wing politicians in both France and Germany knew that it would be seen as a sign of national assertiveness. Much of the criticism, though, stemmed from renewed frustration over U.S. unilateralism. Christopher Patten, the EU commissioner for foreign policy, expressed this sentiment when he said, "I'm a real friend of America who doesn't happen to confuse friendship with sycophancy," and warned of the dangers of "unilateralist overdrive."[3]

The combination of criticisms of the war on terrorism, continued frustration over lack of U.S. support for international agreements, and new tensions over tariffs that Bush imposed in March 2002 to help U.S. steel makers meant that Bush again faced a hostile reception as he traveled to Europe and Russia in May 2002. The centerpiece of his visit to Western Europe was a speech delivered to the German Bundestag, or parliament (Speech 6.2). The speech included passages on the continued strength of U.S.–European ties, on the impressive moves toward cooperation and peace that Europe had made since WWII, and on new ties with Russia. The speech was notable, though, for how much it centered U.S.–European relations around the war on terrorism. Bush was careful to thank the Germans, and Europeans more broadly, for both their overall support and the role European forces were playing as peacekeepers in Afghanistan. He pleased some observers by speaking of the need for nonmilitary responses to terrorism and of a future NATO role in the war. Bush tried hard to convince Europeans that the war on terrorism, including possible future actions against rogue regimes, was not just a U.S. fight. He stressed, "Those who seek missiles and terrible weapons are also familiar with the map of Europe." To stress the need for action, he argued against appeasement, a reference to European policies that failed to contain Hitler's aggression of the 1930s.

The speech was well received by many German legislators. Still, there were signs of continued tensions. In his introduction of Bush, the Bundestag's president, Wolfgang Thierse, warned, "The pursuit of unilateral interests proves short-sighted more and more frequently."[4] During the speech, four deputies unveiled a banner that read "Stop Your Wars" and then marched out in protest of the U.S. policies.

NATO Expansion and Transformation

In contrast to their often contentious debates about global issues, Bush and European officials were in comparative agreement on the key regional security issue of NATO expansion. NATO was formed in 1949 as an alliance of the United States, Canada and ten western European countries. Its Cold War era purpose was often summarized as keeping the Americans in, the Russians out, and the Germans down. Keeping America formally in an alliance meant it would not revert to isolationist tendencies It also meant cooperation to keep out communist Russia's influence. In addition integrating Germany, whose rise as a major power had been in part responsible for both WWI and WWII, into an alliance would bring peace and stability to Europe.

The end of the Cold War brought great uncertainty to NATO's future. Five key areas that needed to be addressed were: the level of U.S. commitment to NATO, burden sharing within the alliance, possible expansion of its membership, the alliance's relations with Russia, and NATO's mission in this new era. With the Cold War over, there were some isolationists and others who argued that it was time to bring U.S. troops home. These views were rejected by the Clinton administration, which felt that the United States should stay committed to Europe's defense. Even supporters of U.S. involvement, though, believed that it was time for Europeans to take more financial and operational responsibility for their own defense. The issue of expanding membership to include former NATO enemies was addressed with the 1999 admission of Poland, Hungary, and the Czech Republic. The eastward expansion highlighted the question of

NATO's now complicated relations with Russia. Despite some friendly overtures by both sides after the Cold War, many Western and Russian officials remained wary of the other's intentions.

The most crucial issue for NATO was establishing the alliance's mission now that it had succeeded in its security goal of defeating communism. NATO still served its earlier political goals of integrating the United States and Germany into a peaceful European community. Now, supporters argued it could advance a new political goal: spreading democracy and capitalism eastward. NATO could provide potential members necessary security and encourage reform, since a democratic government was a precondition of NATO membership. The real question was whether NATO still had a military purpose. This debate focused on whether NATO should engage in "out-of-area" operations now that Europe was secure and whether it should move from a purely defensive alliance to a force that could be used in the cause of humanitarian intervention. The 1999 NATO policy documents and the Kosovo war partially answered these questions, but they largely remained unsettled as Bush took office.

Over time, the Bush administration and its European allies addressed each of NATO's unsettled issues. Bush stressed the importance of NATO for U.S. defense, but talk of cutting U.S. troop levels in Europe and Bush's later decision not to involve NATO in the attacks on Afghanistan led to some doubts about the U.S. commitment. Bush addressed those doubts at a historic November 2002 NATO summit in Prague. There, he stated, "As for America, we made our choice. We are committed to work toward world peace, and we're committed to a close and permanent partnership with the nations of Europe" (Speech 6.3).

The issue of sharing responsibility for building NATO's military power was harder to resolve. Key European leaders recognized the need to build up their countries' military forces, if they ever wished to act independently of the United States. Then, the technical superiority of U.S. forces in Kosovo and the rejection of European assistance in Afghanistan showed that a buildup was necessary if countries even hoped to act jointly with the United States. Problems existed, though, for those seeking to increase European military power. The European public preferred to spend its tax dollars on social programs, not defense. Also, European defense spending was allocated disproportionately to personnel, not modern weaponry, so closing the technological gap with the United States would be difficult. Furthermore, the goal of establishing a common EU foreign and defense policy necessitated the establishment of joint, rather than national, forces. In 1999, plans were announced to create a 60,000-man European reaction force by 2003. Bush supported the force as long as it complimented, not replaced, NATO forces (Speech 6.1). American officials, therefore, opposed French and German plans to develop a more independent force. These U.S. efforts reinforced the view that the United States really wanted stronger European forces only as long as they remained within a U.S.-led NATO.

In his 2001 Warsaw speech, Bush expressed the idea that every European democracy that could meet its alliance responsibilities should be welcomed into NATO. At Prague, he used nearly identical, inclusive language. Despite this consistency, many observers were surprised when membership was offered to seven countries: Bulgaria, Estonia, Latvia, Lithuania, Romania, Slovakia and Slovenia. Before the 1999 expansion, Russian leaders had expressed strong opposition to NATO expansion. That a mere three years later, NATO could offer membership to three former Soviet republics—Estonia, Latvia, Lithuania—is a testament to changed U.S.–Russian relations. The inclusion of Romania and Bulgaria also showed how times had changed. Both lacked firmly established democratic systems, but had contributed military assistance for the war in Afghanistan. One administration official summed up the logic behind admitting so many countries by saying, "September 11 changed the way we looked at enlargement. . . . We need as many allies as we can get."[5]

The issue of Russian relations had been addressed before Prague. A May 2002 agreement established a NATO-Russia Council. Only the question of NATO's mission was left to resolve. At Prague, the idea of a NATO role in the global war on terrorism was endorsed. This was a major defeat for some Europeans who argued that expanding NATO's area of operation might distract it from its prime job of European security and for those who felt that Europe should not tie itself to U.S. global ambitions. It also was a setback for some U.S. officials who felt that the military gains of NATO assistance rarely outweighed the political hassles of alliance politics. The expanded mission required reorganization of NATO structures and capabilities. Bush ushered in the new era by supporting the creation of a rapid response force designed specifically for action beyond Europe's borders.

War in Iraq Strains the Alliance

During the second half of 2002, the world's attention increasingly focused on the possibility of war in Iraq. Many Europeans remained wary of the U.S. plans. Tensions were eased, however, by the passage of Security Council Resolution 1441 just weeks before the Prague summit. The compromise resolution addressed the concerns of France and other European countries and temporarily seemed to indicate alliance agreement. At Prague, NATO leaders issued a statement of "full support" for the resolution and pledged to "take effective action to assist and support" UN efforts to disarm Iraq.[6] The statement was classic diplomacy as it left it up to individual countries to interpret the strength of action to be taken in support of the UN resolution and it did not delineate any specific NATO actions.

The extent to which the UN resolution and the NATO statement were papering over significant policy disputes soon became apparent. French and German officials increasingly tried to slow moves toward war by calling for extended weapons inspections and further UN debate. France and Germany, along with Belgium, also delayed NATO efforts to supply Turkey with equipment that it might have needed if the war spilled over its borders. They felt such transfers would indicate that a decision to abandon diplomacy had already been made. Bush administration officials grew increasingly frustrated with these delays and criticism from allies. In January, when asked by reporters about recent European efforts, Secretary of Defense Rumsfeld responded, "You're thinking of Europe as Germany and France. I don't. I think that's old Europe."[7] Use of the formulation of "old Europe" versus "new Europe" became widespread, and in many ways guided U.S.–European relations in the months to come.

Some people assumed that "new Europe" referred to the time since a country established its independence or its time as a U.S. ally. In reality, it conveyed that these countries had adopted new ideas about security threats and about the type of multilateral coalitions necessary in the modern world. The leading country in this coalition was England, which for years had enjoyed a "special relationship" with the United States. Despite his ideological differences with Bush on domestic issues, Prime Minister Tony Blair was a strong supporter of Bush policies. England shared intelligence reports with the United States, deployed troops in Afghanistan, and lobbied other countries to align with U.S. positions on terrorism and Iraq. England's populace was, however, far from universally supportive of Bush or Blair's actions. Furthermore, they asked whether Blair's support and personal contact with Bush gave him any significant influence on policies, or whether he was just a junior partner, expected to do some of the political dirty work and quietly accept decisions.

Other members of new Europe included Denmark, Italy, Portugal, Spain, and many eastern European countries, especially Poland. Each country had its own mix of reasons for its position: many countries had experienced terrorism firsthand, others were not far removed from their own domestic authoritarians and saw Saddam as a brutal dictator, some feared that France and Germany might try to dominate European foreign policy making, and many likely assumed that support might some day be repaid on other issues. In a sign of new Europe's view, eighteen countries released a letter in late January expressing solidarity with America's position on Iraq. The letter came just days after a much more restrained EU statement.

The leaders of "old Europe" were Germany and France. German leadership was the first to make a major break with the United States. Chancellor Gerhard Schröder's Social Democrats and their coalition partners were at risk of defeat in September 2002 elections. Schröder needed a new issue that could rally nationalistic sentiment. He had supported the war on terrorism and even taken a major political gamble in gaining support for sending German troops to Afghanistan as peacekeepers—some of the first German troops to go abroad since World War II. Schröder, though, came out strongly against possible war in Iraq. In an interview given just weeks before his reelection, he criticized U.S. tactics, lack of consultation with allies, and, most crucially, the Bush administration's urgency, as he characterized evidence of an increased threat as "highly dubious."[8] He announced Germany would not support an invasion, even if it had UN support. Bush has always valued and expected loyalty among friends, so he took Schröder's actions as a personal affront. Bush refused to congratulate Schröder on his victory, and in coming months kept all their phone and personal contacts brief and businesslike.

The other major old Europe country was France. France did not reject military action outright. Instead, it stressed that action should come only after UN inspectors had been given time and after an explicit UN authorization of force. Some in the Bush administration, particularly Powell, were confident that France would eventually support action. Therefore, France's continued delays, followed by the French foreign minister's surprise January 20 declaration that nothing could justify war left Bush administration officials feeling betrayed. Many also felt France was objecting more to U.S. global power than to its specific actions in Iraq. French President Jacques Chirac repeatedly said that he favored "a multipolar world in which Europe counts and exists."[9] Therefore, he sought to build up EU power and strengthen ties with Germany, Russia and China in hopes that they, along with the UN, might collectively balance U.S. power.

The division between new and old Europe had the potential to greatly reshape international politics. NATO decisions were based on consensus while UN Security Council resolutions could be stopped with a single veto from a major power, such as France. Opposition within NATO or the UN would not stop future U.S. military operations, but forcing the United States to repeatedly conduct operations unilaterally or with ad hoc coalitions would call into question the rationale for these multilateral institutions. Sharp divisions within Europe also threatened future EU cooperation. The division also had major implications for the future of the

U.S.–European relations. For the first time in a decade, there was the chance that the United States might move forward with some European countries, while cooling relations with others.

By May 2003, some of the harshest antiwar criticisms had died down because of the seemingly rapid cessation of hostilities and the discovery of new evidence of Saddam's brutality. Still, public and governmental opposition to Bush remained strong in some countries. Bush, meanwhile, was riding high from events in Iraq and saw no reason to compromise. In a widely used phrase, U.S. policy was to "punish France, isolate Germany, forgive Russia."[10] Russia, despite opposition to Iraq, was seen as a growing friend. Germany and Schröder should feel U.S. displeasure, but were seen as likely to come back to support U.S. positions eventually. France had deeper roots for its policies and, therefore, needed to be forced into more acquiescent behavior. French companies would get no contracts to rebuild Iraq and the United States would consider other ways to lessen French global influence.

The major speech of Bush's 2003 trip to Europe was again given in Poland (Speech 6.4). In the speech Bush, made several references to the need for alliance unity. He made it clear, though, that he expected that unity to come from countries following America's lead. He spoke of the recent "divisive" debate within the alliance, a clear reference to German and French positions. In contrast, he repeatedly praised Poland for its actions in Afghanistan and Iraq. On the second half of his trip, Bush went to a G-8 meeting hosted by France. There, he met quickly with Chirac and expressed support for some of his efforts to provide assistance to the developing world, but Bush also showed his priorities by pushing for a tough group statement on security threats and leaving the conference one day early to visit the Middle East.

Reducing Some Alliance Tension

After sharp disputes in the first half of 2003, tensions eased over the next year for a number of reasons. The U.S. and European leaders recognized that they still had shared interests in fighting terrorism, stabilizing Afghanistan and Iraq, and cooperating on many nonsecurity issues. No country wanted to be seen as the roadblock to real progress. There also was a recognition that many of the leaders could be dealing with each other for several more years, so it was important not to exacerbate personal antagonisms. Ongoing violence in Iraq and the approaching transfer of formal sovereignty to the Iraqis led Bush to be more interested in working through multilateral organizations. Starting in the fall of 2003, Bush encouraged UN activity in Iraq and needed European support for those plans. Lastly, after a WTO ruling against the United States, Bush reversed his position on steel tariffs. Under these new conditions, he had to change his triumphant tone of spring 2003 to a more conciliatory one.

In August 2003, international peacekeeping forces in Afghanistan were placed under NATO command. This decision was a sign of renewed alliance cooperation, and a test of the vision laid out at NATO's Prague summit. At the time, there were about 5,000 peacekeepers who operated separately from the 12,000-man U.S.-led coalition force still pursuing remnants of the Taliban and al Qaeda. In the following year, optimists pointed to some security gains and economic development in Afghanistan. Pessimists, however, pointed out that NATO forces remained largely confined to the capital, while rural Afghanistan became increasingly violent and controlled by regional warlords. In June 2004, NATO agreed to increase troop levels to 10,000 and base troops more widely throughout the country.

Also, in June 2004, NATO agreed to increase its role in Iraq by assisting in the training of Iraqi security forces. Just before the agreement, Bush declared that the "bitter differences" between the United States and Europe were over.[11] The agreement, however, was far from what Bush first sought. France, Germany and others refused repeated administration calls for NATO troop commitments for Iraq. They even argued that training should take place only outside of Iraq. Chirac stated, "Any NATO footprint on Iraqi soil would be unwise."[12]

Thus, U.S.–European tensions remained and continued to be based less on bilateral issues, than on different perspectives on world leadership and global tactics.

The Bush Administration's Early Tensions with Russia

During the course of the Bush administration, the U.S. relationship with some of its Cold War allies in Western Europe became increasingly tense, but its relationship with its Cold War enemy Russia generally progressed in the opposite direction. This progression was surprising considering that the two countries had continued to have disputes even after the fall of communism. Furthermore, Bush signaled during his campaign that he planned to toughen the Clinton era policies towards Russia. Bush's view, as well as National Security Adviser Rice and many other key administration officials, was that Russia's transition toward capitalism and democracy was far from complete and was still in danger of relapse. In the economic arena, they noted that Russia still needed to implement basic reforms in such areas as the tax code and private property laws, and that corruption had become endemic. In the political arena, Russia had not fully committed to protecting rights of free religion and free press, had not developed fully functioning political parties, allowing its politics to be largely controlled by a small group of elite, and had used tough tactics to suppress separatists in Chechnya. Whether President Vladimir Putin, a former intelligence officer known for his desire to centralize power, would continue reforms was uncertain.

During the 1990s, many U.S. analysts and other officials had been optimistic about their ability to lead Russia to reform through aid packages and engagement, but Bush felt that these views were naive and that much of the aid money had been misappropriated. He favored cutting international aid until Russia solidified reforms. He planned to move the relationship from efforts to reform Russia to efforts to deal with bilateral security concerns. Bush also felt that it was time to stop treating Russia as a superpower, since its economic and global political influence had receded.

In his first months in office, Bush began to implement his plans. Russian questions were downgraded in the NSC and State Department hierarchies. Bush rebuffed the suggestion of an early summit with Putin. The United States expelled fifty Russian diplomats on charges of spying. The administration planned a 12 percent cutback of U.S. funds used to help dismantle Russia's aging nuclear weapons and facilities. State Department officials met with the foreign minister of the separatist Chechen leadership. Administration officials expressed worry that a new Russian–Chinese friendship treaty was a sign that Putin planned to turn away from the West. The most contentious bilateral issue, though, was the administration's insistence that it would abrogate the ABM treaty and go ahead with a missile defense. Russian officials repeatedly referred to the treaty as the cornerstone of arms control and warned that the U.S. withdrawal would bring into doubt all arms control agreements and stimulate a new arms race.

In his 2001 Warsaw speech, Bush stated that the United States hoped to build a Europe open to Russia and that "America is no enemy of Russia" (Speech 6.1). At the same time, Bush's statements on expanding NATO and other institutions into Eastern Europe showed that Russia would be given no veto over future expansion. For U.S.–Russian relations, the key event of the trip was Bush's meeting with Putin in Slovenia the next day. Their meeting became the first step away from the preceding months' tensions. Despite differences in their backgrounds, Bush and Putin quickly developed a personal connection. Bush later said, "I looked the man in the eye. I found him to be very straight forward and trustworthy.... I was able to get a sense of his soul."[13] The meeting was also significant because Putin expressed some flexibility on the ABM issue. That flexibility was demonstrated when the two leaders met again the next month and Putin agreed to link the discussion of missile defense with the prospect of large cuts in both countries' offensive nuclear arsenals.

September 11 and New Friendship

The personal ties developed at the meeting in Slovenia and progress on the ABM issue heralded possible changes in the U.S.–Russian relationship, but it was the events of 9/11 that accelerated and cemented those changes. Putin was the first foreign official to call Bush after the attacks. In the subsequent months, Russia provided significant support for the U.S. actions. Russia had fought a long war in Afghanistan beginning in 1979 and, therefore, could provide invaluable intelligence on the area and its Islamic militants. Russia also maintained ties with the Northern Alliance forces fighting the Taliban and soon increased its arms and humanitarian aid shipments. Russia set aside concerns about U.S. encroachment into its sphere of influence and did not object to new U.S. military bases in the former Soviet Republics of Uzbekistan and Tajikistan. In addition, Russia supported UN resolutions on terrorism.

The motives behind Putin's new warmth and cooperation were highly debated in Washington, DC, and elsewhere. Many observers felt Putin recognized that if he settled outstanding security issues, he could concentrate his attention on rebuilding Russia's economy and consolidating his own power. Joining the United States in a partnership against terrorism also was a way for Russia to reinforce its position as a world power. Russia was pleased that the UN was involved, since its veto on the Security Council was one of its remaining signs of power. There is also a view that Putin always has been interested in turning to the west and that 9/11 provided him with the perfect opportunity. For centuries, Russia's elite have been divided between Europhiles, who see Russia as part of Europe and hope to emulate Europe's political, economic, and technological advancements; and Slavophiles, who see Russia as a distinct civilization that should protect both its own culture and great power status. Both groups could agree, though, that Islamic terrorism was such a growing threat that it justified working with the United States and other western countries.

The proper response to Russian overtures was highly debated in the United States. Many Russian experts, both within and outside of the administration, stressed caution. They argued that long-term cooperation between the United States and Russia was unlikely given their cultural and political differences. Others, though, argued that Russia's cooperation was more than just short-term expediency and reflected significant changes that should be rewarded. They also argued that Putin was making progress on economic and political reform. Importantly, Rice came to side with the optimists. In May 2002, when reminded of her earlier criticism of Putin, she argued, "What we knew about him wasn't very encouraging. I think now what we know about him is encouraging."[14]

Although doubts about Russia never completely disappeared, Bush generally adopted the view that Russia had changed and should be rewarded. He announced that aid to Russia would not be cut as planned. A message was sent to separatists in Chechnya demanding that they sever all contacts with terrorists or face isolation. Bush and other officials also expressed sympathy for Putin's characterization of the Chechens as Islamic terrorists. The administration tried to solidify the relationship with new economic initiatives. The Commerce Department declared Russia a "market economy," which changed its status under trade laws. Bush encouraged Congress to repeal the 1974 Jackson-Vanik amendment, which limits trade with nonmarket countries that forbid free emigration. Since the fall of communism, the amendment had little practical impact, but was still seen as a symbol of the Cold War tensions. Bush also supported giving Russia Permanent Normal Trade Relations (PNTR) status, which would reduce tariffs on Russian exports to the United States. Finally, he pledged to support Russian membership in the World Trade Organization (WTO).

Changes in the Security Relationship

The new U.S.–Russian cooperation led to major developments on three long-standing security issues: the ABM treaty, Russia's relations with NATO, and nuclear arms reduction. On the ABM treaty, the major event was really the lack of an event. When Bush announced the U.S. withdrawal from the treaty in December 2001, Putin expressed Russia's displeasure, but said this action was not a threat to Russia's security and would not cause a break in its relationship with the United States. Putin's reaction followed months of negotiations. It became clear, though, that there was no way to claim that U.S. testing plans were allowable under the existing treaty and that the Bush administration had no interest in negotiating new treaty restrictions. Also, it became clear that Russia had little leverage on the issue, since Bush said he planned to go ahead in any case. Putin was more interested in cooperation on other issues than in taking a dramatic stand on the ABM treaty.

One issue where Putin hoped for progress was on Russia's relations with NATO. The issue had been complicated since the end of the Cold War. Although there was occasional talk from both sides that Russia might eventually become a member of NATO as it became a continent-wide security association, there really was little chance that Russia would accept full membership in a U.S.-dominated alliance, or that current members would want to commit to Russia's defense. Therefore, an accord was reached in 1997 that allowed Russia to participate in policy discussions, but only after alliance members reached a common position. Russian officials became dissatisfied with the deal, which they felt implied Russian support of NATO decisions that it had no role in shaping. Discussions under the accord were suspended following the 1999 war in Kosovo, which Russia strongly opposed.

In May 2002, Bush's efforts to reshape Russia's relations with the West led to the creation of a new NATO-Russia Council (Speech 6.2). The council consisted of all NATO members and Russia. The council discussed issues such as nonproliferation, crisis management, missile defense, and counter terrorism. If no consensus could be reached, the issue was decided by the NATO members, without Russia being allowed to veto the actions. Bush hailed the agreement as a final step in ending the Cold War divisions and a way to increase future cooperation.

In May 2002, Bush and Putin also signed a major arms control treaty. The basic terms of the Strategic Offensive Reductions Treaty, commonly referred to as the Moscow treaty, were first agreed to during Putin's visit to Washington in November 2001. At that point, though, Bush signaled that there was no need for a formal treaty. Bush's position was in line with his view that treaties take too long to negotiate and often become unwanted restrictions as circumstances change. Putin, however, pressed for a formal treaty that would bind future presidents. U.S. Senators from both parties also pushed for a treaty arguing that important arms control measures should be submitted to Congress to follow constitutional checks and balances. Bush conceded the point, but, in contrast to the START I treaty that ran 700 pages, the new treaty was only three pages long and its terms were very flexible.

The treaty called for each party to cut the number of its warheads to 1,700–2,200—compared to the roughly 6,000 each then held—by the year 2012. Russia favored deep cuts because maintaining warheads was becoming increasingly expensive. Pentagon officials resisted too big a cut, but accepted that U.S. security could be assured at the high end of the treaty's acceptable range. Also, under the treaty, the warheads could be deactivated and stored in case they were needed in the future, rather than be destroyed. In contrast to previous treaties, there were no limits placed on the composition of each country's arsenal. Each could decide their mix of land, submarine and air basing. Each could also decide whether to use missiles with single or multiple warheads. Bush's desire for flexibility also was seen in clauses that allowed the countries to withdraw from the treaty with just three-months notice and that terminated the treaty in 2012 unless it was extended by mutual agreement.

Bush argued the arms treaty "will liquidate the legacy of the cold war."[15] In his speech to the German Bundestag, he continued that theme by saying, "Many generations have looked at Russia with alarm. Our generation can finally lift this shadow from Europe by embracing the friendship of a new democratic Russia" (Speech 6.2). Bush wanted to end the Cold War relationship, but also lay the foundations for a new era. He and Putin issued a joint declaration on the New Relationship Between the United States and Russia that called for cooperation across security and economic issues going well beyond what seemed possible two years earlier and beyond anything in U.S.–Russian history.

New Tensions, but Continued Friendship

After the high water mark of friendship was seen in the 2002 security deals, the U.S.–Russian relationship became more tense. These tensions stemmed, in part, from economic issues. After Bush put new tariffs on steel imports, Russia, in turn, banned imports of American poultry, citing concerns over *Salmonella* bacteria in American chickens. The dispute was resolved, but lobbying by the poultry industry and by labor unions helped end attempts to quickly give Russia PNTR. Progress on PNTR and repealing Jackson-Vanik was also slowed by the argument that such moves should be tied to Russian entry into the WTO, which was likely years away given the number of reforms Russia would first have to implement. Tensions also arose from security issues. American officials were particularly concerned with Russian exports of nuclear material to Iran. The issue led to sharp exchanges even when relations were warming, but as Bush focused more attention on the Axis of Evil, the issue was given new prominence.

The relationship was also strained by Russia's decision to oppose the Iraqi war. Russia had long-standing interests in Iraq, but was also concerned about the implications of the United States taking actions that bypassed the UN. After the war, however, the Bush administration was quick to "forgive Russia," even as it challenged Germany and France. Bush continued to refer to Putin as a friend. This response stemmed from three factors. First, Russia had not been a long-term U.S. ally and Bush accepted that Russia would still have different interests at times, so Russian opposition was not perceived as a betrayal. Second, while Schröder campaigned against Iraq and Chirac openly spoke about the need to contain U.S. power, Putin was milder in expressing his opposition. Finally, Bush's personal ties to Putin likely influenced his response. Therefore, some critics questioned whether Bush had fallen into the same trap as President Clinton, namely, losing objectivity toward Russia because of personal ties to its leadership.

In late 2003, U.S.–Russian ties became strained once again as Bush administration officials increasingly criticized Russia's lack of political reform. The criticisms took a very public form in January 2004 when Powell published an essay in the Russian newspaper *Izvestia* and spoke publicly about the need for change. On that and other occasions, the U.S. officials expressed concerns about the near monopoly control of power achieved by Putin and his United Russia Party, the arrest of Mikhail Khordorkovsky, a businessman and political rival of Putin, reductions of press freedom, and Russian actions in Chechnya. In turn, Russian officials defended their policies and criticized the United States for meddling in Russia's domestic issues.

Criticism of Russia's domestic politics emerged again in September 2004. Following a brutal terrorist attack at a Russian school, Putin announced further tough policies against Chechen separatists and plans to consolidate his power by ending elections for regional governors and having parliamentary elections based on party slates rather than individuals. Bush criticized Putin for these actions, but the criticism came several days after the actions were announced and was relatively mild. Administration critics, therefore, renewed suggestions that Bush was turning a blind eye to Russia's behavior because of personal friendships and an overblown sense of Russian importance for the war on terrorism. The disagreements showed that the U.S.–Russian relationship remained complicated, but overall was much warmer than it had been in the past.

6.1 Future of Europe

Warsaw University
Warsaw, Poland
June 15, 2001

It's a great honor for me to visit this great city—a city that breathes with confidence, creativity and success of modern Poland. Like all nations, Poland still faces challenges. But I am confident you'll meet them with the same optimistic spirit a visitor feels on Warsaw's streets and sees in the city's fast-changing skyline. . . .

Today, I have come to the center of Europe to speak of the future of Europe. Some still call this "the East"—but Warsaw is closer to Ireland than it is to the Urals. And it is time to put talk of East and West behind us.

Yalta did not ratify a natural divide, it divided a living civilization. The partition of Europe was not a fact of geography, it was an act of violence. And wise leaders for decades have found the hope of European peace in the hope of greater unity. In the same speech that described an "iron curtain," Winston Churchill called for "a new unity in Europe, from which no nation should be permanently outcast."

Consider how far we have come since that speech. Through trenches and shell-fire, through death camps and bombed-out cities, through gulags and food lines men and women have dreamed of what my father called a Europe "whole and free." This free Europe is no longer a dream. It is the Europe that is rising around us. It is the work that you and I are called on to complete.

We can build an open Europe—a Europe without Hitler and Stalin, without Brezhnev and Honecker and Ceausescu and, yes, without Milosevic. Our goal is to erase the false lines that have divided Europe for too long. The future of every European nation must be determined by the progress of internal reform, not the interests of outside powers. Every European nation that struggles toward democracy and free markets and a strong civic culture must be welcomed into Europe's home.

All of Europe's new democracies, from the Baltic to the Black Sea and all that lie between, should have the same chance for security and freedom—and the same chance to join the institutions of Europe—as Europe's old democracies have.

I believe in NATO membership for all of Europe's democracies that seek it and are ready to share the responsibilities that NATO brings. The question of "when" may still be up for debate within NATO; the question of "whether" should not be. As we plan to enlarge NATO, no nation should be used as a pawn in the agendas of others. We will not trade away the fate of free European peoples. . . .

All nations should understand that there is no conflict between membership in NATO and membership in the European Union. My nation welcomes the consolidation of European unity, and the stability it brings. We welcome a greater role for the EU in European security, properly integrated with NATO. We welcome the incentive for reform that the hope of EU membership creates. We welcome a Europe that is truly united, truly democratic, and truly diverse—a collection of peoples and nations bound together in purpose and respect, and faithful to their own roots.

The most basic commitments of NATO and the European Union are similar: democracy, free markets, and common security. And all in Europe and America understand the central lesson of the century past. When Europe and America are divided, history tends to tragedy. When Europe and America are partners, no trouble or tyranny can stand against us.

Our vision of Europe must also include the Balkans. Unlike the people of Poland, many people and leaders in Southeast Europe made the wrong choices in the last decade. There, communism fell, but dictators exploited a murderous nationalism to cling to power and to conquer new land. Twice NATO had to intervene militarily to stop the killing and defend the values that define a new Europe. . . .

Across the region, nations are yearning to be a part of Europe. The burdens—and benefits—of satisfying that yearning will naturally fall most heavily on Europe, itself. That is why I welcome Europe's commitment to play a leading role in the stabilization of Southeastern Europe. Countries other than the United States already provide over 80 percent of the NATO-led forces in the region. But I know that America's role is important, and we will meet our obligations. We went into the Balkans together, and we will come out together. And our goal must be to hasten the arrival of that day. . . .

The Europe we are building must also be open to Russia. We have a stake in Russia's success—and we look for the day when Russia is fully reformed, fully democratic and closely bound to the rest of Europe. Europe's great institutions—NATO and the European Union—can and should build partnerships with Russia and with all the countries that have emerged from the wreckage of the former Soviet Union.

Tomorrow, I will see President Putin, and express my hopes for a Russia that is truly great—a greatness measured by the strength of its democracy, the good treatment of minorities and the achievements of its people. I will express to President Putin that Russia is part of Europe and, therefore, does not need a buffer zone of insecure states separating it from Europe. NATO, even as it grows, is no enemy of Russia. Poland is no enemy of Russia. America is no enemy of Russia. We will seek a constructive relationship with Russia, for the benefit of all our peoples.

I will make the case, as I have to all the European leaders I have met on this trip, that the basis for our mutual security must move beyond Cold War doctrines. Today, we face growing threats from weapons of mass destruction and missiles in the hands of states for whom terror and blackmail are a way of life. So we must have a broad strategy of active non-proliferation; counter-proliferation; and a new concept of deterrence that includes defenses sufficient to protect our people, our forces, and our allies; as well as reduced reliance on nuclear weapons.

And, finally, I'll make clear to President Putin that the path to greater prosperity and greater security lies in greater freedom. The twentieth century has taught us that only freedom gets the highest service from every citizen—citizens who can publish, citizens who can worship, citizens who can organize for themselves—without fear of intimidation, and with the full protection of the law.

This, after all, is the true source of European unity. Ultimately, it's more than the unity of markets. It is more than the unity of interests. It is a unity of values. . . .

All these duties, and all these rights are ultimately traced to a source of law and justice above our wills and beyond our politics—an author of our dignity, who calls us to act worthy of our dignity.

This belief is more than a memory, it is a living faith. And it is the main reason Europe and America will never be separated. We are products of the same history, reaching from Jerusalem and Athens to Warsaw and Washington. We share more than an alliance. We share a civilization. Its values are universal, and they pervade our history and our partnership in a unique way. . . .

This unity of values and aspiration calls us to new tasks. Those who have benefited and prospered most from the commitment to freedom and openness have an obligation to help others that are seeking their way along that path. That is why our trans-Atlantic community must have priorities beyond the consolidation of European peace.

We must bring peace and health to Africa.... We must work toward a world that trades in freedom.... We must confront the shared security threats of regimes that thrive by creating instability, that are ambitious for weapons of mass destruction, and are dangerously unpredictable....

Fifty years ago, all Europe looked to the United States for help. Ten years ago, Poland did, as well. Now, we and others can only go forward together. The question no longer is what others can do for Poland, but what America and Poland and all of Europe can do for the rest of the world....

Today, a new generation makes a new commitment: a Europe and an America bound in a great alliance of liberty—history's greatest united force for peace and progress and human dignity. The bells of victory have rung. The Iron Curtain is no more. Now, we plan and build the house of freedom—whose doors are open to all of Europe's peoples and whose windows look out to global challenges beyond. Our progress is great, our goals are large, and our differences, in comparison, are small. And America, in calm and in crisis, will honor this vision and the values we share.

6.2 German Support Against Terror

The Bundestag
Berlin, Germany
May 23, 2002

I am honored to visit this great city. The history of our time is written in the life of Berlin. . . .

In a single lifetime, the people of this capital and this country endured twelve years of dictatorial rule, suffered forty years of bitter separation, and persevered through this challenging decade of unification. For all these trials, Germany has emerged a responsible, a prosperous and peaceful nation. More than a decade ago . . . my father spoke of Germany and America as partners in leadership—and this has come to pass. A new era has arrived—the strong Germany you have built is good for the world.

On both sides of the Atlantic, the generation of our fathers was called to shape great events—and they built the great transatlantic alliance of democracies. They built the most successful alliance in history. After The Cold War, during the relative quiet of the 1990s, some questioned whether our transatlantic partnership still had a purpose. History has given its answer. Our generation faces new and grave threats to liberty, to the safety of our people, and to civilization, itself. We face an aggressive force that glorifies death, that targets the innocent, and seeks the means to matter—murder on a massive scale.

We face the global tragedy of disease and poverty that take uncounted lives and leave whole nations vulnerable to oppression and terror.

We'll face these challenges together. We must face them together. Those who despise human freedom will attack it on every continent. Those who seek missiles and terrible weapons are also familiar with the map of Europe. Like the threats of another era, this threat cannot be appeased or cannot be ignored. By being patient, relentless, and resolute, we will defeat the enemies of freedom.

By remaining united, we are meeting modern threats with the greatest resources of wealth and will ever assembled by free nations. Together, Europe and the United States have the creative genius, the economic power, the moral heritage, and the democratic vision to protect our liberty and to advance our cause of peace.

Different as we are, we are building and defending the same house of freedom—its doors open to all of Europe's people, its windows looking out to global challenges beyond. We must lay the foundation with a Europe that is whole and free and at peace for the first time in its history. This dream of the centuries is close at hand....

Ours is the first generation in a hundred years that does not expect and does not fear the next European war. And that achievement—your achievement—is one of the greatest in modern times.

When Europe grows in unity, Europe and America grow in security. When you integrate your markets and share a currency in the European Union, you are creating the conditions for security and common purpose. In all these steps, Americans do not see the rise of a rival, we see the end of old hostilities. We see the success of our allies, and we applaud your progress.

The expansion of NATO will also extend the security on this continent, especially for nations that knew little peace or security in the last century. We have moved cautiously in this direction. Now we must act decisively.... America is committed to NATO membership for all of Europe's democracies that are ready to share in the responsibilities that NATO brings....

Another mission we share is to encourage the Russian people to find their future in Europe, and with America. Russia has its best chance since 1917 to become a part of Europe's family. Russia's transformation is not finished; the outcome is not yet determined. But for all the problems and challenges, Russia is moving toward freedom—more freedom in its politics and its markets; freedom that will help Russia to act as a great and a just power. A Russia at peace with its neighbors, respecting the legitimate rights of minorities, is welcome in Europe.

A new Russian-American partnership is being forged. Russia is lending crucial support in the war on global terror. A Russian colonel now works on the staff of U.S. Army General Tommy Franks, commander of the war in Afghanistan. And in Afghanistan, itself, Russia is helping to build hospitals and a better future for the Afghan people.

America and Europe must throw off old suspicions and realize our common interests with Russia.... The United States and Russia are ridding ourselves of the last vestiges of Cold War confrontation. We have moved beyond an ABM treaty that prevented us from defending our people and our friends. Some warned that moving beyond the ABM treaty would cause an arms race. Instead, President Putin and I are about to sign the most dramatic nuclear arms reduction in history. Both the United States and Russia will reduce our nuclear arsenals by about two-thirds—to the lowest levels in decades.

Old arms agreements sought to manage hostility and maintain a balance of terror. This new agreement recognizes that Russia and the West are no longer enemies.

The entire transatlantic alliance is forming a new relationship with Russia. Next week in Rome, Chancellor Schroeder, NATO allies, and I will meet as equal partners with President Putin at the creation of the NATO-Russia Council. The Council gives us an opportunity to build common security against common threats. We will start with projects on nonproliferation, counterterrorism, and search-and-rescue operations. Over time, we will expand this cooperation, even as we preserve the core mission of NATO. Many generations have looked at Russia with alarm. Our generation can finally lift this shadow from Europe by embracing the friendship of a new democratic Russia.

As we expand our alliance, as we reach out to Russia, we must also look beyond Europe to gathering dangers and important responsibilities. As we build the house of freedom, we must meet the challenges of a larger world. And we must meet them together. . . .

Given this threat, NATO's defining purpose—our collective defense—is as urgent as ever. America and Europe need each other to fight and win the war against global terror. My nation is so grateful for the sympathy of the German people, and for the strong support of Germany and all of Europe.

Troops from more than a dozen European countries have deployed in and around Afghanistan, including thousands from this country—the first deployment of German forces outside of Europe since 1945. German soldiers have died in this war, and we mourn their loss as we do our own. German authorities are on the trail of terrorist cells and finances. And German police are helping Afghans build their own police force. And we're so grateful for the support. . . .

The evil that has formed against us has been termed the "new totalitarian threat." The authors of terror are seeking nuclear, chemical and biological weapons. Regimes that sponsor terror are developing these weapons and the missiles to deliver them. If these regimes and their terrorist allies were to perfect these capabilities, no inner voice of reason, no hint of conscience would prevent their use.

Wishful thinking might bring comfort, but not security. Call this a strategic challenge; call it, as I do, axis of evil; call it by any name you choose, but let us speak the truth. If we ignore this threat, we invite certain blackmail, and place millions of our citizens in grave danger.

Our response will be reasoned, and focused, and deliberate. We will use more than our military might. We will cut off terrorist finances, apply diplomatic pressure, and continue to share intelligence. America will consult closely with our friends and allies at every stage. But make no mistake about it, we will and we must confront this conspiracy against our liberty and against our lives.

As it faces new threats, NATO needs a new strategy and new capabilities. Dangers originating far from Europe can now strike at Europe's heart—so NATO must be able and willing to act whenever threats emerge. This will require all the assets of modern defense—mobile and deployable forces, sophisticated special operations, the ability to fight under the threat of chemical and biological weapons. Each nation must focus on the military strengths it can bring to this alliance, with the hard choices and financial commitment that requires. We do not know where the next threat might come from, we really don't know what form it might take. But we must be ready, as full military partners, to confront threats to our common security. . . .

Trans-Atlantic nations must resolve the small, disputed portion of our vast trading relationship within the rules and settlement mechanisms of the World Trade Organization—whether those disputes concern tax law, steel, agricultural or biotechnology. . . .

The pledges of the Magna Carta, the learning of Athens, the creativity of Paris, the unbending conscience of Luther, the gentle faith of St. Francis—all of these are part of the American soul. The New World has succeeded by holding to the values of the Old.

Our histories have diverged, yet we seek to live by the same ideals. We believe in free markets, tempered by compassion. We believe in open societies that reflect unchanging truths. We believe in the value and dignity of every life.

These convictions bind our civilization together and set our enemies against us. These convictions are universally true and right. And they define our nations and our partnership in a unique way. And these beliefs lead us to fight tyranny and evil, as others have done before us.

6.3 Historic NATO Summit

Hilton Prague
Prague, Czech Republic
November 20, 2002

This NATO summit that convenes tomorrow will be the first ever held at the capital of a Warsaw Pact [country]. The days of the Warsaw Pact seem distant . . . tomorrow, we will invite new members into our alliance. It's a bold decision—to guarantee the freedom of millions of people.

At the summit, we'll make the most significant reforms in NATO since 1949—reforms which will allow our Alliance to effectively confront new dangers. And in the years to come, all of the nations of Europe will determine their place in world events. They will take up global responsibilities, or choose to live in isolation from the challenges of our time.

As for America, we made our choice. We are committed to work toward world peace, and we're committed to a close and permanent partnership with the nations of Europe. The Atlantic Alliance is America's most important global relationship. We're tied to Europe by history; we are tied to Europe by the wars of liberty we have fought and won together. We're joined by broad ties of trade. And America is bound to Europe by the deepest convictions of our common culture—our belief in the dignity of every life, and our belief in the power of conscience to move history. . . .

America believes that a strong, confident Europe is good for the world. . . . Because America supports a more united Europe, we strongly support the enlargement of NATO, now and in the future. Every European democracy that seeks NATO membership and is ready to share in NATO's responsibilities should be welcome in our Alliance. The enlargement of NATO is good for all who join us. The standards for membership are high, and they encourage the hard work of political and economic and military reform.

And nations in the family of NATO, old or new, know this: Anyone who would choose you for an enemy also chooses us for an enemy. Never again in the face of aggression will you stand alone.

A larger NATO is good for Russia, as well. Later this week I will visit St. Petersburg. I will tell my friend, Vladimir Putin, and the Russian people that they, too, will gain from the security and stability of nations to

Russia's west. Russia does not require a buffer zone of protection; it needs peaceful and prosperous neighbors who are also friends. We need a strong and democratic Russia as our friend and partner to face the next century's new challenges. Through the NATO-Russia Council we must increase our cooperation with Russia for the security of all of us.

Expansion of NATO also brings many advantages to the Alliance, itself. Every new member contributes military capabilities that add to our common security. We see this already in Afghanistan—for forces from Romania, Bulgaria, Estonia, Lithuania, Slovakia and others have joined with sixteen NATO allies to help defeat global terror.

And every new member of our Alliance makes a contribution of character. Tomorrow, NATO grows larger. Tomorrow, the soul of Europe grows stronger. Members recently added to NATO and those invited to join bring greater clarity to purposes of our Alliance, because they understand the lessons of the last century. Those with fresh memories of tyranny know the value of freedom. Those who have lived through a struggle of good against evil are never neutral between them.... In Central and Eastern Europe the courage and moral vision of prisoners and exiles and priests and playwrights caused tyrants to fall. The spirit now sustains these nations through difficult reforms. And this spirit is needed in the councils of a new Europe.

Our NATO Alliance faces dangers very different from those it was formed to confront. Yet, never has our need for collective defense been more urgent.... We're threatened by terrorism, bred within failed states, it's present within our own cities. We're threatened by the spread of chemical and biological and nuclear weapons which are produced by outlaw regimes and could be delivered either by missile or terrorist cell.... We're making progress on this, the first war of the twenty-first century. Today more than ninety nations are joined in a global coalition to defeat terror.... Today the world is also uniting to answer the unique and urgent threat posed by Iraq....

To meet all of this century's emerging threats from terror camps in remote regions to hidden laboratories of outlaw regimes, NATO must develop new military capabilities. NATO forces must become better able to fight side by side. Those forces must be more mobile and more swiftly deployed. The allies need more special operations forces, better precision strike capabilities, and more modern command structures.

Few NATO members will have state-of-the-art capabilities in all of these areas; I recognize that. But every nation should develop some. Ours is a military alliance, and every member must make a military contribution to that alliance. For some allies, this will require higher defense spending. For all of us, it will require more effective defense spending, with each nation adding the tools and technologies to fight and win a new kind of war.

And because many threats to the NATO members come from outside of Europe, NATO forces must be organized to operate outside of Europe. When forces were needed quickly in Afghanistan, NATO's options were limited. We must build new capabilities and we must strengthen our will to use those capabilities.

The United States proposes the creation of a NATO response force that will bring together well-equipped, highly ready air, ground and sea forces from NATO allies—old and new. This force will be prepared to deploy on short notice wherever it is needed. A NATO response force will take time to create and we should begin that effort here in Prague. . . .

International stability must be actively defended, and all nations that benefit from that stability have a duty to help. In this noble work, America and the strong democracies of Europe need each other, each playing our full and responsible role. The good we can do together is far greater than the good we can do apart. . . .

The hopes of all mankind depend on the courage and the unity of great democracies. In this hour of challenge, NATO will do what it has done before: We will stand firm against the enemies of freedom, and we'll prevail.

The transatlantic ties of Europe and America have met every test of history, and we intend to again. U-boats could not divide us. The threats and stand-offs of the Cold War did not make us weary. The commitment of my nation to Europe is found in the carefully tended graves of young Americans who died for this continent's freedom. That commitment is shown by the thousands in uniforms still serving here, from the Balkans to Bavaria, still willing to make the ultimate sacrifice for this continent's future.

For a hundred years place names of Europe have often stood for conflict and tragedy and loss. Single words evoke sad and bitter experience— Verdun, Munich, Stalingrad, Dresden, Nuremberg and Yalta. We have no power to rewrite history. We do have the power to write a different story for our time.

When future generations look back at this moment and speak of Prague and what we did here, that name will stand for hope. In Prague, young democracies will gain new security; a grand Alliance will gather a strength and find new purpose. And America and Europe will renew the historic friendship that still keeps the peace of the world.

6.4 Remarks to the People of Poland

Warsaw Royal Castle
Krakow, Poland
May 31, 2003

In Warsaw two years ago, I affirmed the commitment of my country to a united Europe, bound to America by close ties of history, of commerce and of friendship. I said that Europe must finally overturn the bitter legacy of Yalta and remove the false boundaries and spheres of influence that divided this continent for too long.

We have acted on this commitment. Poland, the United States and our allies have agreed to extend NATO eastward and southward, bringing the peace and security of our alliance to the young democracies of Europe. And as the Atlantic alliance has expanded, it has also been tested. America and European countries have been called to confront the threat of global terror. Each nation has faced difficult decisions about the use of military force to keep the peace. We have seen unity and common purpose. We have also seen debate—some of it healthy, some of it divisive.

I have come to Krakow to state the intentions of my country. The United States is committed to a strong Atlantic alliance, to ensure our security, to advance human freedom and to keep peace in the world.

Poland struggled for decades to gain freedom and to fully participate in life in Europe. And soon you will be a member of the European Union. You also struggled to become a full member of the Atlantic alliance, yet you have not come all this way. . . . only to be told that you must now choose between Europe and America. Poland is a good citizen of Europe and Poland is a close friend of America—and there is no conflict between the two.

America owes our moral heritage of democracy and tolerance and freedom to Europe. We have sacrificed for those ideals together, in the great struggles of the past. . . . And today our alliance of freedom faces a new enemy. . . . This is a time for all of us to unite in the defense of liberty and to step up to the shared duties of free nations. This is no time to stir up divisions in a great alliance. . . .

For my country, the events of September the 11th were as decisive as the attack on Pearl Harbor and the treachery of another September in 1939.

And the lesson of all those events is the same: aggression and evil intent must not be ignored or appeased; they must be opposed early and decisively....

One of the main fronts in this war is right here in Europe, where al Qaeda used the cities as staging areas for their attacks. Europe's capable police forces and intelligence services are playing essential roles in hunting the terrorists. And Poland has led the effort to increase anti-terror cooperation amongst central and eastern European nations. And America is grateful.

Some challenges of terrorism, however, cannot be met with law enforcement alone. They must be met with direct military action.... In the battles of Afghanistan and Iraq, Polish forces served with skill and honor. America will not forget that Poland rose to the moment. Again you have lived out the words of the Polish motto: for your freedom and ours.

In order to win the war on terror, our alliances must be strong.... NATO must show resolve and foresight to act beyond Europe, and it has begun to do so. NATO has agreed to lead security forces in Afghanistan and to support our Polish allies in Iraq. A strong NATO alliance, with a broad vision of its role, will serve our security and the cause of peace.

The greatest threat to peace is the spread of nuclear, chemical and biological weapons. And we must work together to stop proliferation.... When weapons of mass destruction or their components are in transit, we must have the means and authority to seize them. So today I announce a new effort to fight proliferation called the Proliferation Security Initiative. The United States and a number of our close allies, including Poland, have begun working on new agreements to search planes and ships carrying suspect cargo and to seize illegal weapons or missile technologies. Over time, we will extend this partnership as broadly as possible to keep the world's most destructive weapons away from our shores and out of the hands of our common enemies....

To meet these goals of security and peace ... we welcome, we need the help, the advice and the wisdom of our European friends and allies. New theories of rivalry should not be permitted to undermine the great principles and obligations that we share. The enemies of freedom have always preferred a divided alliance—because when Europe and America are united, no problem and no enemy can stand against us....

Europe and America will always be joined by more than our interests. Ours is a union of ideals and convictions. We believe in human rights, and justice under law, and self-government, and economic freedom tempered by compassion. We do not own these beliefs, but we have carried them through the centuries. We will advance them further and we will defend them together.

Questions to Discuss

1. In several speeches, Bush stresses the historic and cultural ties between the United States and Europe. Does this make them natural allies, or do the relationships depend more on the extent of current overlapping national interests?

2. In Speeches 6.1, 6.2, 6.3 and 6. 4, Bush speaks of America's need to work with allies in addressing terrorism and other issues, but also frequently notes recent disagreements within the alliance. Are these disagreements a result of U.S. unilateralism, of tactical differences between the U.S. and Europe, or of other factors?

3. In Speech 6.3, Bush argues for an active role for NATO in the future. Can NATO successfully expand to include new members and new missions, or has it outlived its original purpose and usefulness?

4. In Speech 6.2, Bush argues that Russia is developing important ties with the United States. Can the two countries establish a long-term alliance or will disputes over culture, political systems, and security interests reignite tensions?

5. In several speeches and comments, Bush has praised the leadership of Russian President Vladimir Putin. Has the personal relationship between President Bush and President Putin affected U.S.-Russian relations?

Chapter 7

Relations with Asian Powers

In 1949, Mao Zedong and his communist forces won a civil war and established control of China. The defeated Kuomintang fled to the island of Taiwan. In line with its global anticommunist policies, the United States chose to diplomatically recognize the Taiwanese leadership as China's one, true government. For decades, the United States had no official diplomatic, trade, or other ties with mainland China. During the Korean War, the United States and China fought on opposite sides and, subsequently, tensions between the two potential regional powers remained high. In the early 1970s, President Richard Nixon argued that emerging tensions between China and the Soviet Union provided the United States with a new strategic opportunity. He began secret diplomatic overtures to China. Ties between the two countries were enhanced as Deng Xiaoping introduced a series of economic reforms in China. These reforms moved the country away from a pure communist economy and encouraged foreign trade and investment. Gradually, the United States reversed its policies and developed more ties with mainland China. In 1979, the United States gave formal diplomatic recognition to the communist government.

In 1989, the growing relationship suffered a major setback when the Chinese government used force to end student led protests at Tiananmen Square. For several years afterward, many Democrats, conservative Republicans, human rights groups, and others sought to punish China for its actions at Tiananmen and its broader human rights policies. In contrast, President George H.W. Bush and others argued that Tiananmen, although a tragedy, should not poison the whole U.S.–China relationship and that continued diplomatic and economic engagement would better promote reform. In 1993, President Clinton set human rights goals for China to achieve by the following year in order to keep its Most Favored Nation (MFN) trade status with the United States. In 1994, despite China's failure to meet the goals, Clinton chose to "de-link" the human rights and trade issues. This shift was the beginning of closer ties between the Clinton administration and China. In time, Clinton came to speak of China as a "strategic partner" and strengthened security and economic ties.

Ongoing Sources of U.S.–China Tension

Over time, China's internal reforms, the end of the Cold War, and the growth of bilateral ties have lessened focus on overall ideological disputes between the countries. Instead, attention has shifted to four particular areas of concern, which rise and fall in importance depending on recent events and the priorities of particular leaders.

The status of Taiwan is the most consistent and, arguably, most potentially explosive point of contention. As the U.S. position on recognition shifted, the United States and communist China agreed to three joint communiqués. Collectively, the communiqués stated that Taiwan is part of one China, that the United States would maintain only unofficial ties with Taiwan, and that Taiwan's final status should be resolved peacefully. In 1979, though, the Taiwan Relations Act (TRA) became U.S. law. It committed the United States to sell arms to Taiwan for its defense and to treat with "grave concern" any nonpeaceful attempts to alter Taiwan's status. The communiqués and the TRA, although somewhat contradictory in tone and ambiguous in detail, formed the basis for subsequent discussions of the issue. Over time, the Taiwanese government largely dropped claims to govern all China, but new tensions emerged when some Taiwanese officials suggested that it should move to become an independent country.

China's human rights policies are the second point of contention. Focus on this issue peaked with Tiananmen Square, but remained important subsequently. The annual State Department human rights report has consistently been sharply critical and the United States frequently has advanced resolutions criticizing China at the UN Commission on Human Rights. Presidential comments on human rights are part of almost every bilateral summit. U.S. statements have included criticisms of China's lack of democracy, limitations on freedom of speech, politically influenced legal system, unfair labor practices, and lack of religious freedom. U.S. officials remain divided on how central to make the human rights issue in the bilateral relationship, and whether to pursue change through punishment or engagement.

A third issue that has led to tensions is China's export of technology that can be used to produce weapons of mass destruction. China has not joined several multilateral export control groups and has used the export of nuclear, missile, and other technology as a way of building relations with countries such as Pakistan, Iran, and Libya. In November 2000, China committed not to export nuclear-capable missile-related technology and to strengthen other export controls, and the United States agreed to waive sanctions for past missile exports and to resume licensing Chinese companies to launch U.S. commercial satellites. Details of the new rules and their implementation remained to be worked out as George W. Bush took office.

A fourth area of concern has been the U.S.–China economic relationship. For centuries, Westerners have looked at China's huge population as a large potential market and cheap labor force. Into the late 1970s, though, China's economy remained largely isolated from trade; its technology levels relatively low; and its people poor. Then, under the leadership of Deng Xiaoping, China began to reform its communist economy. Over the last two decades, China's economy has grown phenomenally, and it has become a major player in world trade. This rapid growth has brought new issues and tensions with the United States. Chinese exports often underprice U.S. goods, which has led to a mounting U.S. trade deficit with China and the loss of U.S. jobs in companies that compete with China. Also, the Chinese government continues to control and heavily regulate the economy, so U.S. companies in China are often frustrated by delays, corruption, and low profits. At times, the United States has criticized China's economic policies, but it has not wanted to antagonize the Chinese to the point of risking market access. In 2000, President Clinton, and candidate Bush, supported the idea that further reform would come as China engaged in trade and joined international institutions. They promoted a new law that gave China permanent normal trade relations (PNTR, the renamed MFN status) and supported China's efforts to join the World Trade Organization (WTO).

China's rapid economic rise highlighted the questions of whether China is the world's next superpower and whether the United States would cooperate or conflict with a stronger China. China's economic growth gave it new regional and global influence, and helped support an increase in its military power. Over the last decade, Chinese military spending has risen exponentially with a new focus on high technology coupled with maintaining the world's largest standing army. China also has sought other routes to increase its international power and prestige, such as building ties to regional organizations and seeking to host the Olympics. Some Americans argue that China's rising overall power and conflicting views make a clash with the United States almost inevitable; therefore, the United States should begin to take a firm stance against China now. Others hope that shared economic and security interests will allow the countries to develop a cooperative partnership; they fear that tough policies might actually promote mutual animosity. Other views fall between these two extremes.

Bush's Early Tough Stance

During the 2000 campaign and his first months in office, Bush made it clear that he favored a tougher stance on China than Clinton (Speech 1.2). This was somewhat ironic given that Clinton had strongly criticized the senior Bush for being too soft on China. The younger Bush was not as convinced as some of his advisers that conflict with China was inevitable, but he did directly reject Clinton's view of possible partnership and favored firm stances on some security issues. He still hoped, though, to enhance economic ties to help the U.S. economy and to promote reform in China. The Bush administration's overall views were nicely summed up by the comment of Secretary of State Powell that "a strategic partner China is not, but neither is China our inevitable and implacable foe. China is a competitor, potential regional rival, but also a trading partner willing to cooperate in areas where our strategic interests overlap."[1]

Bush had plans for how he would show America's new tougher attitude, but events interceded. On April 1, 2001, two F-8 Chinese fighter jets intercepted a U.S. EP-3 surveillance plane on a routine mission to collect signals from telecommunications sources in China. One of the F-8s collided with the EP-3. The damaged U.S. plane made an emergency landing at a Chinese base. China held the crew, began stripping the plane's technology, and demanded that the United States apologize for the incident and cease aerial reconnaissance missions. Bush forcefully rejected these demands and suggested that Chinese actions risked undermining the overall relationship. Over eleven days of negotiations, both sides toned down their rhetoric and a compromise was reached. The U.S. ambassador expressed "sincere regret" over the death of the Chinese pilot and said the United States was "very sorry" for the unauthorized landing, but there was no admission of responsibility for the accident or promise to end future flights.[2] Some experts feared that Bush's tough stance would antagonize the Chinese, but others argued that it would gain their respect. All agreed it would be noted by China. Also to be noted was that, while Bush was involved behind the scenes in negotiations, he never spoke to the Chinese leaders directly. This level of attention sent the subtle signal that tensions with China would not automatically be considered a top-level crisis.

Later in April, Bush took his planned steps to show tougher security policies. He approved the largest package of arms for Taiwan since his father's time in office. The $5 billion package included advanced destroyers, antisubmarine aircraft, diesel submarines, antiship missiles, and minesweeping helicopters. Chinese officials strongly criticized the sale and suggested it violated the communiqués. Days later, when asked by an interviewer on *Good Morning, America* if he would use the U.S. military to defend Taiwan, Bush said the United States would do "whatever it took."[3] This statement confirmed what many people already suspected would be U.S. policy. Still, the statement was important since it cleared up the ambiguity of the TRA's pledge to consider action, and it put Bush's position on record. In August, Bush kept up pressure by revealing evidence that China had exported missile components to Pakistan in violation of the 2000 agreement. The United States imposed sanctions on both the Chinese and Pakistani companies and maintained the ban on licenses for satellite launches.

After 9/11: A New Beginning

September 11 led to a major shift in U.S.–China relations. China's President Jiang Zemin quickly sent a telegram to Bush expressing condolences and reiterating China's opposition to terrorism. Chinese and U.S. interests overlapped on the issue because pro-independence Islamic groups were active in Tibet and Xinjiang. Also, China, as a great power, had an interest in maintaining global stability and global norms of warfare. The full impact of 9/11, though, was more complicated. As explained by a leading Chinese strategist, the attacks "changed the world for the United States, but for China, it is the U.S. response that has changed the world."[4]

There were at least two major shifts in U.S. thinking that affected the U.S.–China relationship. First, 9/11 answered the question of who was America's next great global enemy. As the United States placed its focus on the immediate threat from terrorists, worries that China might someday pose a threat seemed of lesser importance. Second, Bush defined the battle lines of the post–9/11 world to be drawn between terrorists and their supporters versus the civilized states of the world. China had exported technology to anti-American states, but had no history or natural alliance with terrorists groups. Therefore, the United States could easily move China into the coalition of civilized friends.

U.S. statements and actions also greatly shaped China's options. The United States quickly demonstrated strong determination to take military action. The Chinese could, and did, warn against unilateral action or excessive force, but active opposition to U.S. action would have made China appear weak. Opposition also would have left China isolated. Prior to 9/11, China had made efforts to build ties with other countries that questioned the merits of U.S. hegemony; now, France was supporting the United States and Russia was building new ties. Furthermore, there were perceived advantages to supporting U.S. actions. China hoped that the United States would remember and reward its help when issues more central to China's interests were at stake. Also, a period of reduced confrontation would allow the Chinese to focus time and energy on their planned transition of leadership in 2002–2003.[5]

The new priorities and tone in the U.S.–China relationship were fully apparent when the White House titled remarks given by Bush after his first meeting with Jiang, "U.S., China Stand Against Terrorism" (Speech 7.1). The meeting was held in October 2001, while Bush was in Shanghai attending an Asia-Pacific Economic Cooperation (APEC) summit. In his remarks, Bush noted how dramatically China had changed since 1975, when he had visited his father, who at the time was the top U.S. diplomat in China. In a short paragraph, he referenced human rights issues by saying that anti-terrorism should "never be an excuse to persecute minorities," Taiwan policy, and missile exports, but made no direct criticisms of China. Bush focused most of his comments on recent cooperation against terrorism. He then provided what would be the slogan for coming years stating, "We seek a relationship that is candid, constructive, and cooperative." The word "candid" was designed to signal that the United States would continue to openly express concerns about Chinese policy, but the overall rhetoric was far different from the earlier description of China as a "competitor."

The dynamics of the new relationship were apparent again in the Chinese response to Bush's December 2001 announcement of U.S. withdrawal from the ABM Treaty. For years, Chinese officials had sharply criticized any discussion of a U.S. missile defense and suggested that China might increase its missile arsenal to overwhelm any defense. Now, though, Bush's announcement drew only mild criticism, and the two countries agreed to hold security discussions in the future.

Expanding the Cooperative Relationship

In 2002, the leaders of both countries sought to further enhance and solidify cooperation. Bush traveled to China again in February 2002. After meeting with top officials, he gave a speech at Tsinghua University (Speech 7.2). The speech was broadcast live on Chinese television, but, in an important sign of Chinese policy, transcripts of the speech released later were highly edited. Bush began the speech by trying to dispel the notion that the United States feared a strong China. He then took the opportunity to educate the Chinese public about life in the United States. He put major focus on the role of religion in America and in his own life. These comments illustrated that under Bush religious freedom had risen to be a major priority of U.S. human rights concerns. He also expressed his firm view that economic reform would "inevitably" bring future legal, political, and social change. The speech, however, contained few specific comments on current or future Chinese policies. In fact, throughout the visit, Bush sidestepped strong positions on contentious issues such as Taiwan, proliferation, and trade imbalances.

Over the next months, U.S. and Chinese officials made progress on joint antiterrorism efforts, trade expansion, and other issues. There were, however, reminders that underlying tensions remained. U.S. sales of weapons to Taiwan and decisions to grant visas to Taiwanese officials so that they could travel through or attend meetings in the United States drew sharp Chinese criticism. The CIA reported ongoing Chinese missile technology exports and sanctions were imposed against several more Chinese companies. The Pentagon's focus on China as a military threat was shown in leaked documents that identified China as a country against which the United States might need to use nuclear weapons and in an assessment of China's military strength that argued China's rapid increase in defense spending and new military technology could pose a threat to Japan, the Philippines, and Taiwan in the future. Some observers felt that these reports showed a split within the administration between Pentagon hawks and other departments seeking cooperation. Thus, the possibility emerged that the administration's policy would be a bad compromise between the "China threat" view and the engagement strategy, with the problems of both, and the strengths of neither.

In October 2002, the pro-cooperation groups seemed to rise as Jiang visited Bush at his Texas ranch, an honor granted to few foreign leaders. Both sides had taken action in the months before to help smooth discussions. The United States announced that it now considered one group in China's Xinjiang region to be an international terrorist organization and thus subject to international sanctions. For its part, China finally implemented new laws to control its missile exports, which brought it closer to following through on its pledges of 2000. At the summit, the leaders discussed the usual range of issues, but also the mounting crises in Iraq and North Korea. Plans to restart exchanges on military issues and human rights, both of which had been suspended during earlier periods of tension, were announced. The relationship now appeared cordial and strong.

Cooperation and Friendly Disagreements

In 2003, much of the world's attention was focused on events in Iraq and North Korea. On these two issues, the United States and China did not completely agree, but were able to mute many of their differences. China opposed the war in Iraq, but was much less vehement than might have been expected. In the past, China had forcefully opposed any interventions that could increase U.S. global influence. It also had opposed interventions that challenged state sovereignty because it did not want a precedent set that might promote international action in support of Taiwan or dissidents within China. On Iraq, China reiterated these views, but let France and Germany take the public lead in opposing U.S. action.

With regard to North Korea, the United States and China had shared interests in a nuclear-free Korean Peninsula and maintaining regional stability. China, however, was less convinced that North Korea's program posed a major threat to the region, felt North Korea's desires for security guarantees were reasonable, and opposed employing tough economic sanctions or military strikes because they feared the implications of a collapsing country on their border. Despite these differences, China agreed to host multilateral talks and actively encouraged North Korean attendance. In the talks, China pressed the United States to make concessions, but also pressured the North Koreans.

Because of these cooperative efforts and positive negotiations on trade and human rights, Powell argued in a September 2003 speech, "U.S. relations with China are the best they have been since President Nixon's first visit" in 1972.[6] China's new President Hu Jintao made similar comments. The close ties were reaffirmed when China's number two official, Premier Wen Jiaboa, visited the White House in December 2003. Bush used the occasion to praise China's actions in fighting terrorism, dealing with North Korea, and building global trade (Speech 7.3). In language quite similar to Clinton's, he declared China "partners in diplomacy."

Very importantly, Bush used a post-meeting photo opportunity to comment on Taiwanese President Chen Shui-bian's provocative campaign remarks about possible Taiwanese independence and plans to hold a referendum that would condemn China's missile build-up across from the island. Bush carefully stated:

> The United States government's policy is one China, based upon the three communiqués and the Taiwan Relations Act. We oppose any unilateral decision by either China or Taiwan to change the status quo. And the comments and actions made by the leader of Taiwan indicate that he may be willing to make decisions unilaterally to change the status quo, which we oppose.[7]

The comments greatly pleased the Chinese who had often pressed Bush to more forcefully oppose Taiwan's independence. Some in Bush's conservative base, though, criticized the comments as another sign of his drifting away from his initial strong support of Taiwan.

Despite the new U.S.–Chinese friendship, tensions remained on the four long-term unsettled issues. First, Taiwan remained a point of contention. In 2004, Chinese officials criticized the United States for not exerting more influence over Chen to further rein in his comments. Second, human rights disputes continued. In 2003, the United States did not submit a UN resolution on China's practices because China had promised in bilateral talks to move forward in four specific areas. China's actions in these areas were minimal, however, so the United States returned to its previous strategy and submitted a tough resolution in 2004. Third, despite the 2000 missile agreement and its 2002 laws, China continued to export some missile technology and the United States continued to impose sanctions. Fourth, trade ties grew, but were increasingly one-sided with U.S. imports from China now five times larger than U.S. exports. Chinese officials suggested this gap could be closed with more U.S. technology exports, but some in the United States argued the gap resulted from unfair Chinese labor practices and government efforts to keep China's currency undervalued. Interestingly, Democratic presidential candidates criticized Bush for being too lenient on China's economic policies. These criticisms represented the third time in twelve years that a sitting president had been accused of being too soft on China.

U.S.–Japanese Relations Over Time

During the first decades of the twentieth century, U.S. and Japanese interests clashed repeatedly. In World War II, the countries fought a brutal war and many officials in both countries demonized their opponents. After the war, the combination of Japanese rejection of prewar policies and leaders, and the U.S. occupation of Japan until 1952 completely altered the relationship. The two countries established a firm and long-lasting alliance, although it was clear that Japan was the junior partner.

Japan adopted a largely U.S. drafted constitution that included Article 9 rejecting war as a policy tool and prohibiting a Japanese army. Over time, the pacifist constitution was reinterpreted to allow for a Japanese "self-defense force" and some participation in international operations. In 1951, the countries signed a Mutual Security Assistance Pact that guaranteed U.S. defense of Japan and long-term U.S. military bases in Japan. Providing protection gave the United States leverage to pressure Japan on other issues. However, as memories of World War II faded and Japanese economic power grew, some Americans felt Japan should assume more of the burden of international leadership and regional defense. Change was slow, since Article 9 remained popular in Japan. Most Japanese also remained in favor of U.S. basing rights, but this support was strained by repeated cases of U.S. servicemen assaulting Japanese women and slow U.S. military cooperation in the investigations of those incidents.

Changes in the U.S.–Japanese economic relationship have been more dramatic as a result of Japan's sharply increasing economic strength. Right after the war, the United States provided Japan with economic aid. Over time, Japan rebuilt, and then took advantage of cheap wages, government policies that supported particular industries and promoted exports, and innovative business practices to develop the world's second largest economy. At first, the United States welcomed Japan's growth, since it strengthened a key ally. By the 1980s, Japanese growth rates were far in excess of U.S. rates and many Americans began to worry. U.S. businessmen and politicians became increasingly critical of Japanese policies that aided industry and kept out foreign competition. They demanded Japanese trade concessions. In the 1990s, Japan's economic fortunes reversed and the country suffered several recessions. The very government and corporate policies praised as the wave of the future in the 1980s were now criticized as impediments to future growth. U.S. policy during the 1990s was a mix of tough trade policies and criticism born from Japan's economic strength, and lectures about failed policies and demands for structural reform born from Japan's weakness.

Bush Administration Plans and Early Frustrations

Bush came to office with plans for three major changes to Clinton's Japan policies. First, he felt that Clinton had not appreciated the importance of the alliance, and, therefore, had made Japan of secondary importance to China. Bush promised to restore Japan's role as America's top Asian focus. Second, Bush and his advisers wanted to encourage Japan to take a more active role on security issues. Enhanced Japanese activity would lower U.S. burdens and decrease China's ability to expand its regional influence. Finally, Bush planned to decrease U.S. criticism of Japan's economic reform efforts and to promote the idea that economic growth was primarily dependent on strong private businesses, not government intervention.

Once in office, Bush found the first change the easiest to accomplish. The administration's focus on Japan was established by a series of symbolic moves. Bush met with Japanese Prime Minister Mori Yoshiro in March, and made a point of postponing any meetings with Chinese officials until after the visit. Powell began his first trip to Asia with a stop in Japan. Deputy Secretary of State Richard Armitage declared that ties with Japan already were America's "most important alliance in Asia" and could grow to be similar to U.S. ties with England.[8]

Efforts to reshape the security relationship were setback by new cases of U.S. personnel arrested for assault and by a February 2001 accident in which a U.S. submarine collided with a Japanese fisheries training ship, killing nine students and instructors. Problems in the economic arena were even harder to address as Japan's economy weakened further. Bush administration officials feared a new Japanese downturn for several reasons. First, the United States and Japan together accounted for about 40 percent of world production. It appeared that they were entering recessions at the same time, which would send ripple effects throughout the global economy and further complicate each country's recovery. Second, the declining economy was weakening Mori's government, making it less likely that he would have the resources or political will to expand Japan's security role. Finally, Bush officials worried that Japan might attempt to postpone difficult economic reforms by increasing its exports. In 1991 and 1992, Japan's efforts to export its way out of recession had hurt the U.S. economy, and been a factor in the defeat of Bush's father. U.S. officials, therefore, hoped that Japan was ready to implement major reforms, but were disappointed when Mori appeared to have no new ideas and appeared unwilling to challenge powerful domestic groups.

Events Reshape the Relationship

After spinning in place for several months, U.S.–Japanese ties were reinvigorated by Koizumi Junichiro's April 2001 election as prime minister and Japan's response to the September 11 attacks. Koizumi was seen as a maverick within the Liberal Democratic Party, which has dominated Japanese politics since the 1950s. He called for major economic reforms, including efforts to address an ongoing banking crisis and curb government spending. He also suggested that Japan should move toward a more "normal" role in international affairs.[9] Koizumi enjoyed unusually strong public support, but the major uncertainty was whether he could use his election momentum to force change on Japan's older leaders and conservative political system.

Bush was very pleased with Koizumi's rise and invited him for a June 30 visit to the presidential retreat at Camp David, Maryland. The event was quite casual. The leaders played catch with a baseball and then told reporters how quickly they had established a good personal relationship. Bush also told reporters, "I believe he's the leader that Japan needs for this moment in her history" and "I have no reservations about the economic reform agenda that the Prime Minister is addressing" (Speech 7.4).

Koizumi's efforts to change Japanese security policies were greatly reinforced by the war on terrorism. Like many world leaders, he quickly expressed sympathy for the victims of September 11 and support for U.S. actions. Soon, he announced a seven-point legislative package on terrorism. The package was approved by late-October, which surprised many observers who had watched Japan cautiously debate its world role for years. The legislation enabled the Japanese Self-Defense Force to provide noncombatant support to the U.S. coalition in Afghanistan and to defend U.S. facilities in Japan so that U.S. resources could be employed elsewhere. Japan also took a lead role in organizing international reconstruction conferences and supplying funds for Afghanistan. Total Japanese funding was well below the billions it contributed to help finance the Gulf War in 1991, but now Japan had moved beyond "checkbook diplomacy," and taken real action.

Bush expressed his support for Japan's new policies on a number of occasions, including in a February 2002 speech to the Japanese Diet, or parliament (Speech 7.5). The speech also included a long discussion of how Japan could play a major international role through means such as foreign aid and work in international organizations. In addition, the speech served as something of a pep talk for Japan and Koizumi, since Japan's economy had continued to weaken and Koizumi's public support had declined significantly. Bush suggested, "The twenty-first century will be the Pacific century," with the United States joining Asians in peace and prosperity. Bush also took the occasion to effusively praise Koizumi. In private, Bush and other officials pressed the need for further economic reform, but in public, the message was all upbeat and supportive. This tone was important because of a growing sense in the world's financial sector that Koizumi was strong on talk, but short on real action. The extent of worry was manifested when the Japanese yen dipped in currency markets after Bush misspoke during a press conference, saying that the leaders had discussed currency "devaluation" when he meant to say "deflation."[10]

Developing Closer Ties

Having been reinvigorated by shared national interests and close personal ties between leaders, the U.S.–Japan alliance grew stronger between 2002 and 2004. Coordinated action was particularly notable on security issues. Japanese leaders provided vocal support for the Iraq war, and encouraged other Asian nations to support U.S. plans. For the war, Japan provided logistical support, such as refueling coalition naval ships and using AWACS surveillance planes to monitor air and sea activity. Then, it made multibillion-dollar commitments to help rebuild Iraq. Later, as instability in Iraq continued and the United States sought international support, Japan authorized the deployment of noncombatant troops in Iraq. The deployment was the first use of Japanese troops overseas without UN authorization since World War II.

The two countries also worked closely together in responding to North Korea. Historic tensions and proximity meant that Japan was interested in containing North Korean power. However, Japan had long feared that international pressure might lead North Korea to respond aggressively. Japan, therefore, had been more willing than the United States to negotiate with North Korea. Koizumi visited the country in the fall of 2002 and spoke of possibly normalizing relations. However, when new evidence of North Korean nuclear activity surfaced, Japan began to follow Bush's harder line. Japanese views also were shaped by North Korea's confirmation that it had kidnapped twelve Japanese citizens during the 1970s and 1980s to provide documents and linguistic training for North Korean spies. The Bush administration pressed hard for Japan to be included in multilateral talks with North Korea, and for the kidnapping issue to be put on the agenda of those meetings.

Japanese support for U.S. positions on Iraq and North Korea led U.S. Ambassador to Japan Howard Baker to declare, "Japan's staunch support for the U.S. position . . . is perhaps a high point in the Japan–U.S. relationship in the last fifty years. . . . With the possible exception of the United Kingdom, we have no better friend in the world."[11] The only major problem in the security relationship was that the Japanese public did not strongly support Japan's expanded foreign role. Many felt that the United States was strong-arming Japan into new commitments. If the operations in Iraq or elsewhere went badly, it could shake the relationship.

Meanwhile, economic relations between the countries continued to be shaped by Japan's economic weakness. Bush, though, continued to avoid criticizing Japan's lack of reform. That long-term Bush policy was reinforced by views that it would seem ungrateful to speak against Japan after all its security aid and that Koizumi would be unable to advance foreign policy changes if proposed economic reforms angered key Japanese special interests and old guard politicians. In 2003, Japan's economy finally returned to significant growth. One reason for the growth was the government's efforts to keep the yen undervalued by buying U.S. dollars. An undervalued yen made Japanese exports cheaper abroad and made imports more expensive for Japanese consumers, encouraging them to buy domestically produced goods. Bush and his advisers spoke in general about the problem of government interference in currency markets, but chose not to make it a major issue with either Japan or China, the two key offenders. There were also economic tensions over U.S. tariffs on Japanese steel and limits on U.S. beef exports after mad cow disease was found in American cattle. These disputes were relatively minor and, in part, reflected election year politics in both Japan and the United States.

7.1 U.S., China Stand Against Terrorism

Western Suburb Guest House
Shanghai, People's Republic of China
October 19, 2001

I've come to Shanghai because China and other Asia Pacific nations are important partners in the global coalition against terror. I've also come because the economic future of my nation and this region are inseparable. The nations of APEC share the same threat, and we share the same hope for greater trade and prosperity.

Thank you so much for hosting this meeting. You [Jiang Zemin] and the city of Shanghai have done an outstanding job. Mr. President, I visited this city a little over twenty-five years ago. Then I could not have imagined the dynamic and impressive Shanghai of 2001. It's an impressive place, and I know you're proud. It's a tribute to the leadership of the current officials of Shanghai, as well as to your leadership as a former mayor, Mr. President.

We have a common understanding of the magnitude of the threat posed by international terrorism. All civilized nations must join together to defeat this threat. And I believe that the United States and China can accomplish a lot when we work together to fight terrorism.

The President and the government of China responded immediately to the attacks of September 11th. There was no hesitation, there was no doubt that they would stand with the United States and our people during this terrible time. There is a firm commitment by this government to cooperate in intelligence matters, to help interdict financing of terrorist organizations. President Jiang and the government stand side by side with the American people as we fight this evil force.

China is a great power. And America wants a constructive relationship with China. We welcome a China that is a full member of world community, that is at peace with its neighbors. We welcome and support China's accession into the World Trade Organization. We believe it's a very important development that will benefit our two peoples and the world.

In the long run, the advance of Chinese prosperity depends on China's full integration into the rules and norms of international institutions. And in the long run, economic freedom and political freedom will go hand in hand.

We've had a very broad discussion, including the fact that the war on terrorism must never be an excuse to persecute minorities. I explained my views on Taiwan and preserving regional stability in East Asia. I stressed the need to combat the proliferation of weapons of mass destruction and missile technology.

Today's meetings convinced me that we can build on our common interests. Two great nations will rarely agree on everything; I understand that. But I assured the President that we'll always deal with our differences in a spirit of mutual respect. We seek a relationship that is candid, constructive and cooperative.

I leave my country at a very difficult time. But this meeting is important because of the campaign against terror, because of the ties between two great nations, because the opportunity and hope that trade provides for both our people.

7.2 Bush Speaks at Tsinghua University

Tsinghua University
Beijing, People's Republic of China
February 22, 2002

My visit to China comes on an important anniversary.... Thirty years ago this week, an American President arrived in China on a trip designed to end decades of estrangement and confront centuries of suspicion. President Richard Nixon showed the world that two vastly different governments could meet on the grounds of common interest, in the spirit of mutual respect. As they left the airport that day, Premier Zhou Enlai said this to President Nixon: "Your handshake came over the vastest ocean in the world—twenty-five years of no communication."

During the 30 years since, America and China have exchanged many handshakes of friendship and commerce. And as we have had more contact with each other, the citizens of both countries have gradually learned more about each other. And that's important. Once America knew China only by its history as a great and enduring civilization. Today, we see a China that is still defined by noble traditions of family, scholarship, and honor. And we see a China that is becoming one of the most dynamic and creative societies in the world—as demonstrated by the knowledge and potential right here in this room. China is on a rising path, and America welcomes the emergence of a strong and peaceful and prosperous China.

As America learns more about China, I am concerned that the Chinese people do not always see a clear picture of my country. This happens for many reasons, and some of them of our own making. Our movies and television shows often do not portray the values of the real America I know. Our successful businesses show a strength of American commerce, but our spirit, community spirit, and contributions to each other are not always visible as monetary success. Some of the erroneous pictures of America are painted by others. My friend, the Ambassador to China, tells me some Chinese textbooks talk of Americans of "bullying the weak and repressing the poor." Another Chinese textbook, published just last year, teaches that special agents of the FBI are used to "repress the working people." Now, neither of these is true—and while the words may be leftovers from a previous era, they are misleading and they're harmful.

In fact, Americans feel a special responsibility for the weak and the poor. Our government spends billions of dollars to provide health care and food and housing for those who cannot help themselves—and even more important, many of our citizens contribute their own money and time to help those in need. . . .

My country certainly has its share of problems, no question about that. And we have our faults. Like most nations we're on a long journey toward achieving our own ideals of equality and justice. Yet there's a reason our nation shines as a beacon of hope and opportunity, a reason many throughout the world dream of coming to America. It's because we're a free nation, where men and women have the opportunity to achieve their dreams. . . .

Those who fear freedom sometimes argue it could lead to chaos, but it does not, because freedom means more than every man for himself. Liberty gives our citizens many rights, yet expects them to exercise important responsibilities. Our liberty is given direction and purpose by moral character, shaped in strong families, strong communities, and strong religious institutions, and overseen by a strong and fair legal system. . . .

Many of the values that guide our life in America are first shaped in our families, just as they are in your country. American moms and dads love their children and work hard and sacrifice for them, because we believe life can always be better for the next generation. . . . And many Americans voluntarily devote part of their lives to serving other people. An amazing number—nearly half of all adults in America—volunteer time every week to make their communities better. . . .

America is a nation guided by faith. Someone once called us "a nation with the soul of a church." This may interest you—95 percent of Americans say they believe in God, and I'm one of them.

When I met President Jiang Zemin in Shanghai a few months ago, I had the honor of sharing with him how faith changed my life and how faith contributes to the life of my country. Faith points to a moral law beyond man's law, and calls us to duties higher than material gain. Freedom of religion is not something to be feared, it's to be welcomed, because faith gives us a moral core and teaches us to hold ourselves to high standards, to love and to serve others, and to live responsible lives.

If you travel across America—and I hope you do some day if you haven't been there—you will find people of many different ethic backgrounds and many different faiths. We're a varied nation. We're home to 2.3 million Americans of Chinese ancestry. . . .

Life in America shows that liberty, paired with law is not to be feared. In a free society, diversity is not disorder. Debate is not strife. And dissent is not revolution. A free society trusts its citizens to seek greatness in themselves and their country.

It was my honor to visit China in 1975—some of you weren't even born then. It shows how old I am. And a lot has changed in your country since then. China has made amazing progress—in openness and enterprise and economic freedom. And this progress previews China's great potential.

China has joined the World Trade Organization, and as you live up to its obligations, they inevitably will bring changes to China's legal system. A modern China will have a consistent rule of law to govern commerce and secure the rights of its people. The new China your generation is building will need the profound wisdom of your traditions. The lure of materialism challenges society in our country, and in many successful countries. Your ancient ethic of personal and family responsibility will serve you well.

Behind China's economic success today are talented, brilliant and energetic people. In the near future, those same men and women will play a full and active role in your government. This university is not simply turning out specialists, it is preparing citizens. And citizens are not spectators in the affairs of their country. They are participants in its future.

Change is coming. China is already having secret ballot and competitive elections at the local level. Nearly twenty years ago, a great Chinese leader, Deng Xiaoping, said this—I want you to hear his words. He said that China would eventually expand democratic elections all the way to the national level. I look forward to that day.

Tens of millions of Chinese today are relearning Buddhist, Taoist, and local religious traditions, or practicing Christianity, Islam, and other faiths. Regardless of where or how these believers worship, they're no threat to public order; in fact, they make good citizens. For centuries, this country has had a tradition of religious tolerance. My prayer is that all persecution will end, so that all in China are free to gather and worship as they wish.

All these changes will lead to a stronger, more confident China—a China that can astonish and enrich the world, a China that your generation will help create. This is one of the most exciting times in the history of your country, a time when even the grandest hopes seem within your reach.

My nation offers you our respect and our friendship. Six years from now, athletes from America and around the world will come to your country for the Olympic games. And I'm confident they will find a China that is becoming a *da guo,* a leading nation, at peace with its people and at peace with the world.

7.3 Welcoming Premier Wen of China

The White House
Washington, DC
December 9, 2003

Mr. Premier [Wen Jiabao], members of the delegation, it is my honor to welcome you to the White House. Your visit reflects the increasing ties of cooperation and commerce between our two nations.

America and China share many common interests. We are working together in the war on terror. We are fighting to defeat a ruthless enemy of order and civilization. We are partners in diplomacy working to meet the dangers of the 21st century. We are full members of a world trading system that rewards enterprise and lifts nations.

Our two nations seek a Korean Peninsula that is stable and at peace. The elimination of North Korea's nuclear programs is essential to this outcome. Realizing this vision will require the strong cooperation of all North Korea's neighbors. I am grateful for China's leadership in hosting the six-party talks which are bringing us closer to a peaceful resolution of this issue. And my government will continue to work with China as it plays a constructive role in Asia and in the world.

The rapid rise of China's economy is one of the great achievements of our time. China's increasing prosperity has brought great benefits to the Chinese people and to China's trading partners around the world. We recognize that if prosperity's power is to reach in every corner of China, the Chinese government must fully integrate into the rules and norms of the international trading and finance system.

China has discovered that economic freedom leads to national wealth. The growth of economic freedom in China provides reason to hope that social, political and religious freedoms will grow there, as well. In the long run, these freedoms are indivisible and essential to national greatness and national dignity.

As our two nations work constructively across areas of common interest, we are candid about our disagreements. The growing strength and maturity of our relationship allows us to discuss our differences, whether over economic issues, Taiwan, Tibet, or human rights and religious freedom, in a spirit of mutual understanding and respect.

China is a great civilization, a great power, and a great nation. Premier Wen, when my country looks forward to—my country looks forward to working with you as China increasingly takes its place among the leading nations of the world.

The United States and China have made great progress in building a relationship that can address the challenges of our time, encourage global prosperity and advance the cause of peace. It is my hope that your visit will further that progress.

7.4 Welcoming Koizumi of Japan

Presidential Retreat
Camp David, Maryland
June 30, 2001

It is my honor to welcome the Prime Minister [Junichiro Koizumi] . . . of our close friend and ally. We had a two-hour meeting, very frank and open discussion. There's no question we will work together. There's no question in my mind our relationship will never be stronger than under our leadership.

We talked about security matters. We talked about economics, and I want to praise the Prime Minister for his vision for reform of the Japanese economy. He's willing to make difficult choices. And that's what a leader does. We talked about the environment. We talked about baseball. And we talked about the need to make sure that we work for a more peaceful world. And I'm confident we'll be able to do so. . . .

The Prime Minister recognizes that there needs to be deep and meaningful reform. I talked to him about our experiences in Texas in the '80s, where we acted—or the marketplace acted, we acted to remedy a situation in which we had bad loans, nonperforming assets, and there was some pain. But as a result of making the very difficult decisions, our economy was restructured and came back stronger than before.

I support the Prime Minister—strongly support the Prime Minister's reform agenda for the economy. He reminded me that in the course of winning his election he had to appeal to the people of Japan, and made a very strong, direct appeal in laying out this aggressive agenda. And we support him strongly.

I believe . . . it's in our nation's best interests that the Japanese economy flourish, that it's strong and vibrant. And we had a very meaningful discussion, ranging from economic restructuring and reform to trade, the new global round of WTO, as well. And I believe he's the leader that Japan needs for this moment in her history. . . .

I have no reservations about the economic reform agenda that the Prime Minister is advancing. He talks about tackling some difficult issues that some leaders in the past refused to address.

I came—I knew the Prime Minister was dynamic; I've heard that, I've read it. But you don't really realize how dynamic he is until you have a chance to witness his conversation. He's got a great sense of humor. He loves to laugh. But he's a courageous leader, as well. And I admire a person who recognizes that his duty is not to avoid, but to lead. His duty is to speak plainly to the people of his country. And I believe strongly that we will have a good relationship, not only to foster what's in the best interests of our country—countries—and in the region, but we'll have a good personal relationship, as well. After all, he's the only world leader I've ever played catch with, with a baseball.

7.5 Unity Between the U.S. and Japan

The Diet
Tokyo, Japan
February 18, 2002

A century ago, our two countries were beginning to learn from, and about, one another after a long period of suspicion and mistrust. The great Japanese scholar and statesman, Inazo Nitobe—a man who understood both our peoples, envisioned a future of friendship as he wrote, "I want to become a bridge across the Pacific." That bridge has been built—not by one man, but by millions of Americans and Japanese.

My trip to Asia begins here in Japan for an important reason. It begins here because for a century and a half [half a century] now, America and Japan have formed one of the great and enduring alliances of modern times. From that alliance has come an era of peace in the Pacific. And in that peace, the world has witnessed the broad advance of prosperity and democracy throughout East Asia.

From its very birth, our alliance has been based on common interests, common responsibilities and common values. The bonds of friendship and trust between our two people were never more evident than in the days and months after September the 11th. We were grateful, so very grateful, for the condolences and compassion of the Japanese people and the Japanese government. . . .

Last fall in Shanghai, the Prime Minister gave me a special gift—a samurai arrow in a box in which the Prime Minister had written, "The arrow to defeat the evil and bring peace to the Earth." He also said, "This is a fight we have to win to ensure the survival of freedom."

I assured him then, and I assure you today, freedom will prevail. Civilization and terrorism cannot coexist. By defeating terror, we will defend the peace of the world.

Japan and America are working to find and disrupt terrorist cells. Your diplomats helped build a worldwide coalition to defend freedom. Your Self Defense forces are providing important logistical support. And your generosity is helping to rebuild a liberated Afghanistan.

Your response to the terrorist threat has demonstrated the strength of our alliance, and the indispensable role of Japan that is global, and that begins in Asia. The success of this region is essential to the entire world, and I'm convinced the twenty-first century will be the Pacific century.

Japan and America share a vision for the future of the Asia Pacific region as a fellowship of free Pacific nations. We seek a peaceful region where no power, or coalition of powers, endangers the security or freedom of other nations; where military force is not used to resolve political disputes. We seek a peaceful region where the proliferation of missiles and weapons of mass destruction do not threaten humanity.

We seek a region with strong institutions of economic and political cooperation that is open to trade and investment on a global scale. A region in which people and capital and information can move freely, breaking down barriers and creating bonds of progress, ties of culture and momentum toward democracy. We seek a region in which demilitarized zones and missile batteries no longer separate people with a common heritage, and a common future.

Realizing this vision—a fellowship of free Pacific nations—will require Japan and America to work more closely together than ever. Our responsibilities are clear. Fortunately, our alliance has never been stronger.

America, like Japan, is a Pacific nation, drawn by trade and values and history to be a part of Asia's future. We stand more committed than ever to a forward presence in this region. We will continue to show American power and purpose in support of the Philippines, Australia and Thailand. We will deter aggression against the Republic of Korea. Together, Japan and the United States will strengthen our ties of security. America will remember our commitments to the people on Taiwan. And to help protect the people of this region, and our friends and allies in every region, we will press on with an effective program of missile defenses. . . .

America and Japan have joined to oppose danger and aggression. We have also joined to bring aid and hope to those who struggle throughout the developing world. We are the world's two largest economies, and the two most generous contributors of economic and humanitarian aid. Japan's commitment to development is known and honored throughout the world. So is Japan's leading role in great international institutions—the United Nations, the World Bank and the G-8, among others. . . .

Our two countries have unique strengths, and a unique opportunity to combine them for the benefit of the world. . . .

Japan is making these great contributions even in a time of economic uncertainty and transition that has caused some to question whether your nation can maintain these commitments and your leadership in the world. I have no such questions, and I'm confident that Japan's greatest era lies ahead.

Japan has some of the most competitive corporations, and some of the most educated and motivated workers in the world. And Japan, thanks to my friend, the Prime Minister, is on the path to reform. I value my relationship with the Prime Minister. He is a leader who embodies the energy and determination of his country. He and I have had very good visits. I trust him. I enjoy his sense of humor. I consider him a close friend. He reminds me of a new American star, Ichiro. The Prime Minister can hit anything you throw at him.

Over the years we Americans have seen our share of economic challenges. In the late '70s and early '80s, our competitiveness was weak, our banks were in trouble, high taxes and needless regulation discouraged risk-taking and strangled innovation. America overcame these difficulties by reducing taxes and by reducing regulations. We moved non-performing loans to market, making way for new investment. As we made reforms, foreign investors regained faith in us, especially investors from Japan.

We learned that in times of crisis and stagnation, it is better to move forward boldly with reform and restructuring than to wait, hoping that old practices will somehow work again. Through bold action, we emerged a better and stronger economy—and so will you.

Over the past few years, Americans have increased our investments in Japan, further binding our nations and showing confidence in your future. Japan has a proud history of moving forward—not through revolutions, but through restorations. . . .

More than a century ago, competition helped propel Japanese economy into the modern era. A half-century ago, it accelerated the Japanese postwar economic miracle admired by the world. Now Japan has embarked on a new restoration. A restoration of prosperity and economic growth through fundamental reform and the full embrace of competition

In all the work that lies ahead, in the defense of freedom, in the advance of development, in the work of reform, you'll have a firm ally in the American government. And you'll have a constant friend in the American people.

Questions to Discuss

1. Is Bush correct in his suggestion in Speech 7.2 that China's economic development and membership in international institutions will "inevitably" lead to further reform?

2. In Speeches 7.1, 7.2, and 7.3, Bush welcomes China's rise as a major power. Is China's power a threat to, or a positive development for, the United States?

3. In Speech 7.2, what does it reveal about Bush's personal views and policy priorities that he chooses to focus on the role of religion in America and his own life?

4. In Speech 7.5, Bush encourages Japan to take an active role in international politics. Is it in America's interest for Japan to develop its military capabilities?

5. In Speeches 7.4 and 7.5, Bush gives high personal praise to Japan's Prime Minister Koizumi Junichiro. Is it wise for a U.S. president to associate himself so closely with a foreign leader?

Chapter 8

Middle East Peace and Reform

Historically, the United States has pursued three main goals in the Middle East. First, it has sought to preserve Israel as a strong and independent state. Current U.S. support for Israel stems from the desire to have a reliable ally in a key strategic area, cultural and historic ties between the countries, and activity by U.S. domestic groups including Jewish Americans and conservative Christians. Second, the United States has tried to build ties to moderate Arab governments. These ties expand U.S. regional influence, encourage stable oil exports, assure U.S. basing privileges in the area, and limit the chance that strongly anti-American nationalist or Islamic fundamentalist movements will come to power. Third, the United States has tried to prevent regional powers, or outside powers such as the Soviet Union, from dominating the area.

Because of the region's political realities, the three U.S. goals have often been incompatible forcing the United States to balance competing objectives, or temporarily give priority to one goal above the others. The one policy that has promised long-term progress on all three goals is negotiating peace between Israel and its Arab neighbors. The peace process, therefore, has been a major focus of U.S. diplomacy under most recent presidents. George W. Bush, however, made it clear as he campaigned that the goal of preventing the rise of regional powers would be the particular focus of his administration, and it seemed this objective might overshadow other policies. Over time, though, Bush became convinced that achieving long-term success in Iraq and meeting America's other regional goals required renewed U.S. involvement in the peace process. Later, he also enhanced focus on the spread of democracy in the region.

The Peace Process Inherited by Bush

Tensions and violence between Jews and Arabs go back centuries. Hostilities intensified significantly in the twentieth century after Jewish emigration to Palestine increased and the dissolution of the Ottoman Empire led to the creation of several new independent states in the region, while leaving Palestine under British control. Both Jews and Arab Palestinians felt they had historic and practical claims to Palestine. In 1947, the UN attempted to settle the dispute by partitioning the territory. The partition never took full effect and conflict between the two sides erupted. After Israel's formal declaration of statehood in May 1948, the neighboring Arab countries of Egypt, Syria, Lebanon, and Jordan joined Palestinian efforts to destroy the nascent state. The Israelis defeated their enemies on all fronts. Israel won significantly more territory than was allocated under the partition plan. The Palestinians were left stateless with many living in refugee camps. Over the next three decades, the Arab states and the Palestinians attempted to redraw the region's borders through a series of wars, uprisings, and terrorist actions. In this period, Israel not only defended its existing territory, but won important new territory including the Golan Heights, Gaza Strip, West Bank, and East Jerusalem in 1967 and the Sinai in 1973. After the 1967 war, the UN passed Security Council Resolution 242, which set forth the basis for a just and lasting peace based on Israeli withdrawal from territories occupied in the war and recognition of every area state's right to live in peace with secure borders. In 1973, UN Resolution 338 called for the full implementation of 242.

In 1977, Egyptian President Anwar el-Sadat triggered a new phase in regional history by calling for Israel to return the Sinai in exchange for peace between the countries. President Jimmy Carter played a major role in the ensuing negotiations that led to the Camp David Accords. These negotiations helped establish the formula of trading "land for peace" and the idea that the United States could play the role of mediator. The land for peace formula was not easily implemented with other Arab countries, but the possibility of future negotiated settlements, coupled with Israel's continued military strength, greatly lessened the prospect of major wars between Israel and the Arab states.

Beginning in the 1970s, Palestinian issues rose to new prominence when Yasir Arafat came to lead the Palestine Liberation Organization (PLO). Many outside observers judged the PLO to be a terrorist organization and considered negotiations impossible unless it changed tactics and its stated goal of destroying Israel. In 1982, Israel destroyed many PLO bases during its invasion of Lebanon; however, the United States helped Arafat and other top leaders withdraw their forces to Tunis. Beginning in 1987, tensions in the West Bank and Gaza further escalated when an uprising or *intifada*, developed. Many Palestinians, including young adults and children, began to harass and throw stones at Israeli soldiers. Israel responded with tough military actions. They not only failed to stop the uprising, but led many critics to portray Israel as a brutal occupier using disproportionate force.

In 1991, acting in the wake of the Gulf War, the United States played a role in establishing the first direct talks between Israel and the PLO. Such talks served Arafat's interests because they repositioned him as the accepted Palestinian leader. Under the historic Oslo Accords of 1993, Israel withdrew military forces from much of Gaza and several population centers on the West Bank and transferred sovereignty of some of them. Arafat returned from exile and formed the Palestinian Authority (PA) to administer the areas now under Palestinian control. The final status of the occupied territories and other key issues were to be negotiated over a five year period. The following years, though, saw little further progress. Opposition from hardliners on both sides made compromise. Israeli officials increasingly complained that the PA was not doing enough to control extremists, especially suicide bombers, so they began to impose tough new restrictions in the territories.

In his final years in office, President Clinton repeatedly organized and mediated talks and continued to advance detailed proposals, known as the "Clinton Parameters," until almost his last day in office. For a time, a settlement appeared possible, but Arafat felt the concessions made by Israeli Prime Minister Ehud Barak did not go far enough and rejected what many observers thought was the best deal he would ever get. Pessimists, therefore, declared the Oslo process, and negotiations in general, dead. More optimistic observers pointed out that, over the preceding decade, important advances had been made in persuading both sides to pursue negotiations, convincing most moderates on both sides to agree in principle to a two state solution, and establishing the PA as a forerunner to a Palestinian state government.

Several crucial issues remained unsettled. First, would Israel withdraw from all of the land it had occupied since 1967? This idea was rejected by many Israelis who felt that the pre-1967 borders put Israeli security at risk and that withdrawal would reward terrorism. Full withdrawal was further complicated by two other issues. Since 1967, the Israeli government had encouraged Jewish settlement of the territories. By 2000, there were over 175,000 Jews living in close to 200 settlements in the West Bank and Gaza. Many of these settlers considered the land indisputably part of Israel and demanded government commitments to protect their new homes. Possible withdrawal from Jerusalem raised even more complicated issues since it was home to an additional 175,000 Jews, contained the Temple Mount, Judaism's holiest sight, and was considered by both Israelis and Palestinians to be their capital. Another long-standing issue was whether Palestinians displaced in the 1947–48 period should be allowed a "right of return" to reclaim property now in Israel. Israelis argued that this was impractical since it would mean uprooting Israelis who had lived there for

238 *Middle East Peace and Reform*

two generations and because a full right of return for the roughly 3.7 million displaced Palestinians would create a massive demographic shift in a country with less than five million Jews. Acknowledging a right of return would also mean taking on a burden of guilt about the founding of their state. Many of these issues had been disputed for years. Thus, observers dissected even the slightest shifts in strategy or word choice from Israeli, Palestinian, and U.S. officials for clues on whether and how the issues might ever be resolved.

Bush Slowly Becomes Involved in the Peace Process

During Clinton's many efforts to reinvigorate the peace process, Bush was careful not to limit future options by commenting on specific proposals. He did, though, repeatedly make clear that he planned to be less personally involved in negotiations than recent presidents, and that his administration generally would not be focused on the peace process. These positions reflected a number of factors. Bush's top Middle East priority was refocusing international attention on Iraq. It also was politically risky for a president to invest large amounts of his and the country's reputation in an area where progress was often slow and beyond his control. In addition, Bush felt Clinton had gone beyond mediation and tried to impose American "plans and timetables" for peace.[1] Bush believed true progress would come only when the two parties involved were ready for compromise and recent events seemed to show that they were in fact moving in the opposite direction. In September 2000, a new, more violent *intifada* began. Soon after, Arafat rejected Barak's final peace proposals. Then, in February 2001, Barak was resoundingly defeated by hardliner Ariel Sharon, who promised no negotiations would begin until violence ended.

The first months of 2001 saw a sharp reduction in U.S. diplomatic activity. As the only area in the world with both prominent U.S. strategic interests and political instability the Middle East always drew some attention—for example Secretary of State Powell's visited the region, Bush met with Sharon in March, and lower level officials continued to meet with both Israeli and Palestinian representatives—but there was no consistent, high-level involvement. By May 2001, the administration was forced to increase its efforts. This shift reflected the reality that Arab leaders vowed not to support either U.S. policies in Iraq or broader regional goals unless the U.S. increased pressure on Israel and made progress on Palestinian issues. In addition, violence in the region was escalating. Therefore, the focus shifted away from reaching a comprehensive peace settlement toward the need for short-term efforts to reduce bloodshed.

Further pressure on the administration came when an international panel led by former Senator George Mitchell released a report on May 21, 2001. The report focused on the causes and actions of the new *intifada,* but also proposed a sequence of events to restart the peace process: a cessation of violence, followed by confidence building measures, a cooling-off period, and finally resumption of negotiations. Secretary of State Colin Powell, speaking for the administration, strongly endorsed the sequence, although the Bush team modified some of the specific proposed actions. In subsequent weeks, several high level State Department officials visited the region to push the Mitchell plan. In June, Director of Central Intelligence George Tenet visited and worked out a tentative ceasefire. The ceasefire did not hold, but the Mitchell and Tenet plans became the focus of administration activities. By the first week of September, Bush was considering even bolder actions. It was decided that Powell would detail a major new initiative including explicit U.S. support for the creation of a Palestinian state. Plans were also made for Bush to have his first meeting with Arafat. These initiatives would have brought Bush's statements and actions much closer to those of Clinton.

The terrorist attacks of September 11 came before the new initiatives were announced, and altered the dynamics of U.S. policy. Some Israelis and their supporters hoped that the attacks would show Americans the dangers that Israelis had lived with for years and lead the United States to support tough action against Palestinian groups as part of the global war on terrorism. On the other hand, Arab state cooperation in investigating terrorist networks, arresting suspects, cutting off terrorist financing, and supporting military actions was vital for the war on terrorism's success. In addition, building a coalition that included Arab states would help the U.S. claim to be fighting a war against a small group of dangerous extremists, not against all Muslims.

In the fall of 2001, the Bush administration increased its role in the peace process with the appointment of retired Marine General Anthony C. Zinni as Middle East envoy. Zinni and other officials pleased Israel with continued criticism of specific Palestinian attacks. However, they also criticized Israeli responses to those attacks, enhanced relations with some previously criticized countries such as Syria and Yemen, and chose not to put anti-Israeli organizations Hamas and Hezbollah on the list of terrorist groups whose financial assets would be seized. In November, Bush further pleased Arabs by announcing American support for a Palestinian state (Speech 2.2). Although the announcement had been planned before 9/11, it was now interpreted by some as part of a pro-Arab tilt in U.S. policy. Sharon, for example, was so frustrated by the U.S. actions and advanced rumors of Bush's announcement that he warned the United States not to "appease the Arabs at our expense."[2] This comment drew very pointed rebukes from U.S. officials, illustrating the unusual tension in U.S.–Israeli relations.

Developing New U.S. Initiatives in the Peace Process

The U.S.–Israeli tensions and any emerging pro-Arab tilt greatly diminished after a series of terrorist attacks began in Israel in December 2001. The attacks triggered even tougher Israeli retaliatory responses than earlier incidents, but the responses appeared to get a green light from U.S. officials who spoke of the right of Israel to defend itself and the need for all countries to aggressively combat terrorism. By March 2002, though, concern grew that Israel's forceful tactics, including reestablishing Israeli army control of several Palestinian towns and holding Arafat in virtual house arrest, were escalating to dangerous levels. On March 13, Bush commented that recent Israeli actions were "not helpful" and went beyond self-defense.[3] However, when new suicide bombings occurred, Bush renewed calls for Arafat and other leaders to crack down on terrorists and accepted Israeli retaliation without further comment. These incidents led top administration officials to concur with the view of some critics that U.S. policy was becoming too reactive to specific events. The U.S. position appeared to vacillate depending on who had attacked most recently and did not provide clear guidelines for the long-term.

On April 4, 2002, Bush sought to end uncertainty over U.S. policy by delivering his first major speech on the peace process (Speech 8.1). Bush reiterated his view that a just settlement with "two states, Israel and Palestine, living side by side, in peace and security" was possible, but only if all parties took new action. Bush specifically criticized Arafat for not consistently opposing terrorism, and suggested that he was largely responsible for inducing Israel's retaliatory actions. Bush continued to treat Arafat as a key player and gave him what many perceived as a final opportunity to show positive leadership. This was in notable contrast to Israel's attempts to isolate Arafat in the hope that more moderate leadership would emerge.

After putting much of the responsibility on Arafat, Bush suggested that Israel also needed to take positive steps, such as halting incursions into Palestinian-controlled territory and beginning to withdraw from recently reoccupied cities. In the speech no specific timetable was suggested for these Israeli actions. Furthermore, Bush suggested them only after stressing "Israel's right to defend itself from terror." Bush also called for longer term Israeli actions. On broader regional issues, he called on Arab states, particularly Iraq, Iran, and Syria, to stop all support for terrorists. Perhaps the most significant aspect of the entire speech was Bush's announcement that he was sending Powell to the region to help promote a sequence of steps toward peace. This action signaled a new U.S. commitment to mediation, and showed that the previous year's violence had convinced Bush that the United States could not afford to stay out of the peace process.

Bush's speech was designed to bring clarity to U.S. policy, but that goal was complicated by other international efforts to address the violence. On his way to the Middle East, Powell went to Madrid for a meeting of four parties seeking to create a unified international position on the peace process. The "Quartet" of the United States, the United Nations, the European Union, and the Russian Federation had begun to coordinate efforts in the fall of 2001, and were now ready to issue a joint communiqué outlining their position. Traditionally, the United States had been hesitant to involve others in the Middle East peace-making process because it broad involvement might lessen U.S. negotiating flexibility and policy influence, and because many European countries and the UN often had been sharply critical of Israel and more supportive of Palestinian positions. Observers have speculated that in this case the administration favored multilateral efforts to please Arabs by including their supporters, to spread the blame should negotiation fail, or to counter the perception of frequent Bush unilateralism.[4]

The Quartet's communiqué was released on April 10, and differed significantly from Bush's April 4 speech.[5] Whereas Bush was sharply critical of Arafat, the Quartet focused on his role as the Palestinians' recognized leader. Bush suggested implementation of a ceasefire before withdrawal of Israeli troops, but the Quartet put the focus on ending Israeli operations as a first step. The Quartet demanded less of Arab states by not emphasizing their need to end support for terrorists. Whether Bush's speech or the Quartet's statement represented true U.S. policy generated much debate. Many experts believed that the State Department favored the Quartet's view, while the Pentagon and other administration hardliners on terrorism favored the more anti-Arafat presidential speech.

Any internal administration disputes about Arafat's future role disappeared during the next few months. Continued violence and new evidence of Arafat's personal connections to terrorists frustrated Bush and convinced him that Arafat either could not, or would not, end terrorist attacks. On June 24, 2002, Bush declared, "Peace requires a new and different Palestinian leadership" (Speech 8.2). He then called for significant Palestinian reforms, including a new constitution, new authority for a legislative body, and multiparty elections as part of establishing a democracy and free market economic system. If steps toward political reform and stopping terrorism were taken, the United States would support not only the long-term goal of establishing two states, but the shorter-term solution of creating a provisional Palestinian state until a final peace settlement. Bush did call for future Israeli actions, but they all were contingent on "progress towards security."

Not surprisingly, Bush's speech received a mixed reaction. Critics argued that putting such intense focus on Arafat distracted attention from the conflict's long-term unsettled issues. They also argued that, even if Arafat was a barrier to peace, having Bush and Israel's government call for his removal would make other Palestinians unlikely to challenge him and that the United States could ever be considered an impartial mediator after calling for leadership change In addition, since Arafat was an elected leader, demanding his removal made U.S. calls for democracy seem less sincere. Finally, critics suggested there were few moderate voices emerging within Palestinian politics. In fact, the groups that were growing in popular support and might assume the mantle of leadership after Arafat were more militant. On the other hand, supporters of Bush's noted that Arafat had proven unwilling to negotiate in good faith, stop terrorism, or develop a strong, corruption free PA. Therefore, they argued he was neither the right man to lead peace negotiations, nor the right man to lead state building efforts. Thus, it was better the Palestinians find new leadership now while there was still chance to move forward. Supporters also felt that the United States had followed the middle road for too long, trying to please all concerned parties. Generally, the middle road failed to encourage progress toward a final settlement and had pleased no one in the end.

The "Roadmap" for Peace

Soon after Bush's June speech calling for new Palestinian leadership, top administration officials turned their attention to planning for war in Iraq. Therefore, Quartet meetings and plans became the main focus of peace initiatives. By September 2002, the Quartet had developed a tentative three-phase roadmap to peace. The plan was given to Palestinian and Israeli leaders, with the understanding that suggestions for revisions would be considered. Details of the roadmap quickly became public, so other countries' officials, private experts, journalists, and others contributed their critiques at the draft stage. The details of each phase shifted over the following months, but the broad outline was consistent. In Phase One, both sides would issue statements acknowledging the other's right to a state. Palestinians would reject all terrorism, rebuild PA security institutions, and reform their political system. Israel would improve humanitarian conditions in the territories, freeze settlement activity, and, as security increased, withdraw from territory that had been occupied since the second *intifada*'s inception in September 2000. In Phase Two, an independent Palestinian state with provisional borders would be established. In Phase Three, a comprehensive permanent status agreement would resolve border issues, settlement questions, the status of Jerusalem, and the refugee issue. The plan included target dates for each phase. The whole process was expected to take only three years. Diplomats, though, stressed that movement from one phase to the next would be based on performance measures, not preset timetables. Bush portrayed the roadmap as an outgrowth of his June 24, 2002 speech. Some observers, though, noted that discrepancies between Bush's statements and Quartet plans had never been fully reconciled; the roadmap did not call for Arafat's removal, modified Bush's idea of a "provisional state" to a "state with provisional borders," and moved some Israeli actions forward in the sequence.

Several events delayed the formal release of the roadmap until late April 2003. These events included planning for the war in Iraq, January 2003 elections in Israel that reinforced Sharon's coalition, and, most significantly, reforms within the Palestinian political system. In March 2003, Mahmoud Abbas was appointed to the newly created post of prime minister. He assumed responsibility for day-to-day governance, including security and public order, in PA-controlled areas of the West Bank and Gaza. Arafat remained president holding power to select the prime minister and maintaining significant control over foreign policy, security issues, and negotiations with Israel. Abbas was considered a moderate and had vocally criticized the ongoing *intifada*. Some saw his appointment as an important step toward the reform; others felt time would reveal that Arafat had skillfully conceded just enough formal power to reduce international calls for his removal, while actually maintaining true control.

Soon after its formal release, the PA accepted the roadmap. Initially, Sharon withheld full support, apparently hoping to modify terms on ending settlements and the refugee issue. After Bush rebuffed his efforts to modify the plan at that point, Sharon accepted the outlines of the plan and pushed it through his cabinet in late May—but with fourteen distinct "reservations" to his acceptance. In June, Bush attempted to keep progress moving. He left a G-8 meeting in France early, so that he could meet with Arab leaders and then personally lead discussions between Sharon and Abbas in Jordan. The administration was so determined to capture an image of Bush playing an active role that a footbridge was rebuilt so that all of the leaders could make a dramatic entrance together. No major breakthroughs occurred at the meeting, but its tone was positive. The very fact that leaders from Israel, Palestine, and the United States came together for direct talks showed that each of the parties had modified their positions significantly since 2000.

Over the summer, talks continued and, after a wave of violence failed to disrupt progress, a ceasefire supported by key militant groups emerged. Progress came to an abrupt end with an August 2003 suicide bombing that killed twenty people on a Jerusalem bus. Israel retaliated with a helicopter attack that killed a senior Hamas leader. Within a month, several more rounds of bombings and retaliations had occurred. Israeli officials began speaking of the need to deport or otherwise eliminate Arafat. Abbas resigned in frustration at not being able to assert control and end the violence. The road map was in tatters. All parties shared some responsibility for this latest failure at peace: Palestinian militants refused to end attacks; Arafat never gave Abbas the political or material support necessary to crackdown on extremists; Arab countries did not press the militants or Arafat for change; Israel took few serious steps to end settlement expansion or begin withdrawal; and the United States never forced Israel to take quicker action. The shared failures and renewed violence convinced many that a negotiated settlement would not come anytime soon.

Unilateral Disengagement

Because the prospect of a negotiated settlement was becoming increasingly dim and terrorist attacks were continuing, Israel decided to follow a new plan of unilateral disengagement. The first component of this plan was to build a security fence in the West Bank to cordon off the settlements and Israel proper from would-be Palestinian suicide bombers. The fence, modeled after a similar fence already built in Gaza, was originally supported by Israeli liberals, but Sharon came to support the plan. Construction began in early 2003. The fence was very popular with an Israeli public in search of some sense of security, but it drew criticism from others. Some argued it signaled a lack of confidence in Palestinian leadership just at a time when Israel was pursuing negotiations. Many felt that the complex of walls, trenches, and electronic fences would become the permanent border and thus Israel was unilaterally determining an issue that should have been resolved in a permanent status agreement. Contributing to the controversy, the fence was not following the pre-1967 borders. Instead, it enclosed many Jewish settlements and East Jerusalem. The fence also separated some Palestinians from their farms on the Israeli side, and put some Palestinian towns in a no-man's land since residents could neither legally enter Israel, nor pass easily through the fence to reach the West Bank. In July 2003, Bush commented, "I think the wall is a problem, and I discussed this with Ariel Sharon."[6] At that point, focus was on the roadmap, so real U.S. pressure was minimal. Once terrorist attacks in Israel renewed in the fall of 2003, the United States became more supportive of Israel's actions to protect itself.

The second component of the disengagement plan was the evacuation of all Jewish settlements from Gaza and some from the West Bank. Sharon argued this would give Israel more defensible borders, address the demographic reality that Jews would soon be a minority if Israel maintained control of all Gaza and West Bank territory, and force the Palestinians and Arab countries that might assist them to develop a true government. Sharon had been an early architect of settlement policies, so the move was a sharp change. Some skeptics felt it might be a tactical move to allow Israel to further consolidate its hold on the remaining West Bank areas or to let Sharon divert attention from a corruption scandal that was weakening his government. Disengagement was sharply opposed by most settlers, many members of Sharon's Likud party, and by several small parties that were part of his governing coalition. They argued that the territory belonged to Israel and withdrawal triggered by fear would encourage more terrorism. Sharon attempted to mollify some of these critics by continuing other tough policies, including ordering strikes that killed two key Hamas leaders.

On April 14, 2004, Sharon traveled to Washington. Through an exchange of letters and comments at a joint news conference, Bush endorsed Sharon's planned Gaza and West Bank withdrawals (Speech 8.3). Bush portrayed the actions as consistent with his June 2002 speech and the goals of the roadmap. He commented that the fence should be temporary, not prejudice final status discussions, and take into account Palestinian interests, but he accepted its continued existence. Having endorsed or accepted both parts of Sharon's plan, Bush further supported Israel's positions by opposing a full right of return and supporting Israeli control of some of the land conquered in 1967. Bush's points were phrased as observations, not firm policy commitments, but certainly would influence any future negotiations. Furthermore, they showed how far Bush had come from the days in which he criticized Clinton for being too personally involved in the peace process and for trying too hard to shape ultimate agreements.

Promoting Democracy in the Middle East

By 2003, Bush had addressed two of America's long-term goals in the Middle East. He had tried to assure Israel's survival by advancing the roadmap and supporting Israel's right to defend itself, and he had attempted to prevent the rise of a dominant regional power by confronting Iraq and to a lesser degree Iran. Therefore, he shifted more attention to relations with Arab states, with the goal of promoting democratic reform within the region. Promoting Middle East democracy was not a new idea. For years, human rights advocates and others had suggested that, for humanitarian and philosophical reasons, the United States should help spread freedom. They also held that such a policy might aid U.S. strategic interests by not tying the United States to repressive governments that could be overthrown by strongly anti-American groups, as happened in Iran in 1979. Calls for active democracy promotion had been countered by those who argued that, in the strategically important and oil rich Middle East, the paramount need for stability justified ties with nondemocratic governments. Some also feared that moves toward democracy might give more power to anti-American nationalists or fundamentalist Islamic groups.

The September 11 attacks shifted the debate by suggesting the assumed trade-off between spreading democracy and assuring security interests might be a false one. In fact, lack of political reform appeared to exacerbate security risks. Many of the 9/11 terrorists came from Saudi Arabia. Analysts suggested that its lack of free expression may have promoted the development of more extremist views, which then went unchecked. Furthermore, the lack of political opportunities may have promoted a turn to violence. American support for the Saudi regime made it a natural target in the intellectual civil war for the future of Saudi Arabia. Reforms might lessen the conditions breeding terrorism. On the other hand, the administration's priorities of fighting terrorism, confronting Iraq, and advancing the Middle East peace process all depended in part on support from the very Arab states that would have been pressured by an active U.S. democracy program. Therefore, few major efforts were made shortly after 9/11. For example, in June 2002, even as Bush detailed necessary democratic reforms for the PA, he did not call for similar changes across the region (Speech 8.2). The farthest the administration went in its first two years was the establishment of the Middle East Partnership Initiative in December 2002. The initiative was designed to promote economic reform, strengthen civil society organizations, and spread education. In announcing the program, Powell did not call directly for democracy, but only for "a stronger political voice" for the "peoples of the Middle East."[7]

The lack of strong democracy promotion was driven primarily by competing priorities and the desire not to offend regional allies. It may also have been affected by widespread debate in academic and policy circles over whether Arab states were unprepared to adopt democracy. These discussions were triggered by the fact that as waves of democracy had swept across Asia, Eastern Europe, Latin America and Africa in recent decades, the Arab region had seen few significant reforms. Of the twenty-two members of the League of Arab States, only tiny Djibouti was rated as fully "free" in the widely regarded Freedom House surveys. Some scholars suggested that these facts reflected that Arab culture had no tradition of equality, dissent, or representative decision making. Others made similar arguments, but put the focus on Islam. They argued that the lack of separation of church and state stifled free debate and that fundamentalists especially asserted a religious basis for repression of women and non-Muslims. The much discussed *Arab Human Development Report 2002* produced by UN and Arab development experts put much of the blame on social and economic conditions, such as low literacy rates, lack of access to modern communication technology, and poverty. Still others focused more on historical factors. They argued that under the Ottoman Empire and colonialism strong central authority dominated. After independence, many Arab countries had weak state institutions and little national unity, so they tended to rally around new authoritarian leaders.

The war in Iraq brought new attention to democracy promotion. Although the war was fought primarily for security reasons, the United States hoped to establish an Iraqi political system that could show others in the region the possibilities and merits of democracy. Bush developed this theme in a key speech on democracy promotion in November 2003 (Speech 8.4). Bush discussed factors that had promoted the spread of democracy in the twentieth century, including U.S. democracy promotion efforts. He then addressed the arguments that the Middle East's culture, socioeconomic conditions, and history precluded democratic development. He noted recent reforms implemented by area governments. Notably, though, many of the countries Bush cited as great successes were small and relatively weak. Key states, such as Saudi Arabia and Egypt, were largely just encouraged to implement future reform. Bush pleased Arab listeners and others by saying "modernization is not the same as Westernization" and that all countries were not expected to adopt a U.S. political model or act at the same speed. Near the end of the speech, Bush came close to apologizing for decades of past U.S. policy saying, "Sixty years of Western nations excusing and accommodating the lack of freedom in the Middle East did nothing to make us safe—because in the long run, stability cannot be purchased at the expense of liberty."

The months ahead showed just how difficult it could be to move from sweeping rhetoric to successful policy outcomes. In February 2004, U.S. officials began to circulate a draft proposal called the "Greater Middle East Initiative," which called on the world's wealthiest countries to support economic, political, and cultural programs in the Middle East. It was to be adopted at the June G-8 meeting hosted by Bush in Georgia. The draft was leaked and published before it had been discussed with Arab governments. Several key Arab leaders reacted angrily to what they perceived as an American attempt to ignore local concerns, and impose reform. This reaction renewed the fears of some reformers that the U.S. democracy promotion might actually slow reform if governments made it a matter of national pride to reject foreign-supported reform. The U.S. plan also worried some European diplomats who were working on similar ideas, but did not want their plans to be seen as derivative of the U.S. initiatives. Meanwhile, continued violence in Iraq and reports of U.S. soldiers abusing Iraqi soldiers tarnished America's image, and weakened the claim that Iraqi democracy would soon be successful. Bush was determined to focus the G-8 meetings on Middle East democracy, so the draft proposal was modified, not abandoned. The new proposal reduced calls for reform, endorsed reforms already being taken, and called for renewed efforts to settle the Israeli-Palestinian conflict as part of regional reform efforts. Even the name of the initiative was altered to take out the word "Greater," since some German officials felt it had overtones of imperialism. Even with all the changes, the leaders of Saudi Arabia, Kuwait, Morocco, Egypt, and Pakistan turned down invitations to attend the G-8 meetings. Informed diplomats attributed these actions to the countries being uncomfortable with planned declaration language on certain specific reforms, viewing the United States as trying to dictate reforms, and not being anxious to be closely associated with Bush. There appeared to be little enthusiasm for significant democratic reforms, but the United States maintained its focus and significantly increased funds for democracy promotion in the region.

8.1 Sending Powell to the Middle East

The White House
Washington, DC
April 4, 2002

During the course of one week, the situation in the Middle East has deteriorated dramatically. Last Wednesday, my Special Envoy, Anthony Zinni, reported to me that we were on the verge of a cease-fire agreement that would have spared Palestinian and Israeli lives. That hope fell away when a terrorist attacked a group of innocent people in a Netanya hotel, killing many men and women in what is a mounting toll of terror.

In the days since, the world has watched with growing concern the horror of bombings and burials and the stark picture of tanks in the street. Across the world, people are grieving for Israelis and Palestinians who have lost their lives.... We mourn the dead, and we mourn the damage done to the hope of peace, the hope of Israel's and the Israelis' desire for a Jewish state at peace with its neighbors; the hope of the Palestinian people to build their own independent state....

This could be a hopeful moment in the Middle East.... The United States is on record supporting the legitimate aspirations of the Palestinian people for a Palestinian state. Israel has recognized the goal of a Palestinian state. The outlines of a just settlement are clear: two states, Israel and Palestine, living side by side, in peace and security.

This can be a time for hope. But it calls for leadership, not for terror.... The Chairman of the Palestinian Authority has not consistently opposed or confronted terrorists. At Oslo and elsewhere, Chairman Arafat renounced terror as an instrument of his cause, and he agreed to control it. He's not done so.

The situation in which he finds himself today is largely of his own making. He's missed his opportunities, and thereby betrayed the hopes of the people he's supposed to lead. Given his failure, the Israeli government feels it must strike at terrorist networks that are killing its citizens.

Yet, Israel must understand that its response to these recent attacks is only a temporary measure. All parties have their own responsibilities. And all parties owe it to their own people to act.

We all know today's situation runs the risk of aggravating long-term bitterness and undermining relationships that are critical to any hope of peace. I call on the Palestinian people, the Palestinian Authority and our friends in the Arab world to join us in delivering a clear message to terrorists: blowing yourself up does not help the Palestinian cause. To the contrary, suicide bombing missions could well blow up the best and only hope for a Palestinian state.

All states must keep their promise, made in a vote in the United Nations to actively oppose terror in all its forms. No nation can pick and choose its terrorist friends. I call on the Palestinian Authority and all governments in the region to do everything in their power to stop terrorist activities, to disrupt terrorist financing, and to stop inciting violence by glorifying terror in state-owned media, or telling suicide bombers they are martyrs. They're not martyrs. They're murderers. And they undermine the cause of the Palestinian people.

Those governments, like Iraq, that reward parents for the sacrifice of their children are guilty of soliciting murder of the worst kind. All who care about the Palestinian people should join in condemning and acting against groups like Al-Aqsa, Hezbollah, Hamas, Islamic Jihad, and all groups which opposed the peace process and seek the destruction of Israel.

Arab states must rise to this occasion and accept Israel as a nation and as a neighbor. Peace with Israel is the only avenue to prosperity and success for a new Palestinian state. The Palestinian people deserve peace and an opportunity to better their lives. They need their closest neighbor, Israel, to be an economic partner, not a mortal enemy. They deserve a government that respects human rights and a government that focuses on their needs—education and health care—rather than feeding their resentments.

It is not enough for Arab nations to defend the Palestinian cause. They must truly help the Palestinian people by seeking peace and fighting terror and promoting development.

Israel faces hard choices of its own. Its government has supported the creation of a Palestinian state that is not a haven for terrorism. Yet, Israel also must recognize that such a state needs to be politically and economically viable. Consistent with the Mitchell plan, Israeli settlement activity in occupied territories must stop. And the occupation must end through withdrawal to secure and recognize boundaries consistent with United Nations Resolutions 242 and 338. Ultimately, this approach should be the basis of agreements between Israel and Syria and Israel and Lebanon.

Israel should also show a respect for and concern about the dignity of the Palestinian people who are and will be their neighbors. It is crucial to distinguish between the terrorists and ordinary Palestinians seeking to provide for their own families. The Israeli government should be compassionate at checkpoints and border crossings, sparing innocent Palestinians daily humiliation. Israel should take immediate action to ease closures and allow peaceful people to go back to work.

Israel is facing a terrible and serious challenge. For seven days, it has acted to root out terrorist nests. America recognizes Israel's right to defend itself from terror. Yet, to lay the foundations of future peace, I ask Israel to halt incursions into Palestinian-controlled areas and begin the withdrawal from those cities it has recently occupied.

I speak as a committed friend of Israel. I speak out of a concern for its long-term security, a security that will come with a genuine peace. . . .

The world expects an immediate cease-fire, immediate resumption of security cooperation with Israel against terrorism. An immediate order to crack down on terrorist networks. I expect better leadership, and I expect results. . . .

And to those who would try to use the current crisis as an opportunity to widen the conflict, stay out. Iran's arms shipments and support for terror fuel the fire of conflict in the Middle East. And it must stop. Syria has spoken out against al Qaeda. We expect it to act against Hamas and Hezbollah, as well. It's time for Iran to focus on meeting its own people's aspirations for freedom and for Syria to decide which side of the war against terror it is on.

The world finds itself at a critical moment. This is a conflict that can widen or an opportunity we can seize. And so I've decided to send Secretary of State Powell to the region next week to seek broad international support for the vision I've outlined today. As a step in this process, he will work to implement an immediate and meaningful cease-fire, an end to terror and violence and incitement; withdrawal of Israeli troops from Palestinian cities, including Ramallah; implementation of the already agreed upon Tenet and Mitchell plans, which will lead to a political settlement.

I have no illusions. We have no illusions about the difficulty of the issues that lie ahead. Yet, our nation's resolve is strong. America is committed to ending this conflict and beginning an era of peace. . . . The violence and grief that troubled the Holy Land have been among the great tragedies of our time. The Middle East has often been left behind in the political and economic advancement of the world. That is the history of the region. But it need not and must not be its fate.

The Middle East could write a new story of trade and development and democracy. And we stand ready to help. Yet, this progress can only come in an atmosphere of peace. And the United States will work for all the children of Abraham to know the benefits of peace.

8.2 New Palestinian Leadership

The White House
Washington, DC
June 24, 2002

For too long, the citizens of the Middle East have lived in the midst of death and fear. The hatred of a few holds the hopes of many hostage. The forces of extremism and terror are attempting to kill progress and peace by killing the innocent. And this casts a dark shadow over an entire region. For the sake of all humanity, things must change in the Middle East.

It is untenable for Israeli citizens to live in terror. It is untenable for Palestinians to live in squalor and occupation. And the current situation offers no prospect that life will improve. Israeli citizens will continue to be victimized by terrorists, and so Israel will continue to defend herself.

In the situation the Palestinian people will grow more and more miserable. My vision is two states, living side by side in peace and security. There is simply no way to achieve that peace until all parties fight terror. Yet, at this critical moment, if all parties will break with the past and set out on a new path, we can overcome the darkness with the light of hope. Peace requires a new and different Palestinian leadership, so that a Palestinian state can be born.

I call on the Palestinian people to elect new leaders, leaders not compromised by terror. I call upon them to build a practicing democracy, based on tolerance and liberty. If the Palestinian people actively pursue these goals, America and the world will actively support their efforts. If the Palestinian people meet these goals, they will be able to reach agreement with Israel and Egypt and Jordan on security and other arrangements for independence.

And when the Palestinian people have new leaders, new institutions and new security arrangements with their neighbors, the United States of America will support the creation of a Palestinian state whose borders and certain aspects of its sovereignty will be provisional until resolved as part of a final settlement in the Middle East. . . .

A Palestinian state will never be created by terror—it will be built through reform. And reform must be more than cosmetic change, or veiled attempt to preserve the status quo. True reform will require entirely new political and economic institutions, based on democracy, market economics and action against terrorism.

Today, the elected Palestinian legislature has no authority, and power is concentrated in the hands of an unaccountable few. A Palestinian state can only serve its citizens with a new constitution which separates the powers of government. The Palestinian parliament should have the full authority of a legislative body. Local officials and government ministers need authority of their own and the independence to govern effectively.

The United States, along with the European Union and Arab states, will work with Palestinian leaders to create a new constitutional framework, and a working democracy for the Palestinian people. And the United States, along with others in the international community will help the Palestinians organize and monitor fair, multi-party local elections by the end of the year, with national elections to follow.

Today, the Palestinian people live in economic stagnation, made worse by official corruption. A Palestinian state will require a vibrant economy, where honest enterprise is encouraged by honest government. The United States, the international donor community and the World Bank stand ready to work with Palestinians on a major project of economic reform and development. The United States, the EU, the World Bank, the International Monetary Fund are willing to oversee reforms in Palestinian finances, encouraging transparency and independent auditing.

And the United States, along with our partners in the developed world, will increase our humanitarian assistance to relieve Palestinian suffering. Today, the Palestinian people lack effective courts of law and have no means to defend and vindicate their rights. A Palestinian state will require a system of reliable justice to punish those who prey on the innocent. The United States and members of the international community stand ready to work with Palestinian leaders to establish finance—establish finance and monitor a truly independent judiciary.

Today, Palestinian authorities are encouraging, not opposing, terrorism. This is unacceptable. And the United States will not support the establishment of a Palestinian state until its leaders engage in a sustained fight against the terrorists and dismantle their infrastructure. This will require an externally supervised effort to rebuild and reform the Palestinian security services. The security system must have clear lines of authority and accountability and a unified chain of command.

America is pursuing this reform along with key regional states. The world is prepared to help, yet ultimately these steps toward statehood depend on the Palestinian people and their leaders. If they energetically take the path of reform, the rewards can come quickly. If Palestinians embrace democracy, confront corruption and firmly reject terror, they can count on American support for the creation of a provisional state of Palestine.

With a dedicated effort, this state could rise rapidly, as it comes to terms with Israel, Egypt and Jordan on practical issues, such as security. The final borders, the capital and other aspects of this state's sovereignty will be negotiated between the parties, as part of a final settlement. Arab states have offered their help in this process, and their help is needed. . . .

Leaders who want to be included in the peace process must show by their deeds an undivided support for peace. And as we move toward a peaceful solution, Arab states will be expected to build closer ties of diplomacy and commerce with Israel, leading to full normalization of relations between Israel and the entire Arab world.

Israel also has a large stake in the success of a democratic Palestine. Permanent occupation threatens Israel's identity and democracy. A stable, peaceful Palestinian state is necessary to achieve the security that Israel longs for. So I challenge Israel to take concrete steps to support the emergence of a viable, credible Palestinian state.

As we make progress towards security, Israel forces need to withdraw fully to positions they held prior to September 28, 2000. And consistent with the recommendations of the Mitchell Committee, Israeli settlement activity in the occupied territories must stop.

The Palestinian economy must be allowed to develop. As violence subsides, freedom of movement should be restored, permitting innocent Palestinians to resume work and normal life. Palestinian legislators and officials, humanitarian and international workers, must be allowed to go about the business of building a better future. And Israel should release frozen Palestinian revenues into honest, accountable hands.

I've asked Secretary Powell to work intensively with Middle Eastern and international leaders to realize the vision of a Palestinian state, focusing them on a comprehensive plan to support Palestinian reform and institution-building.

Ultimately, Israelis and Palestinians must address the core issues that divide them if there is to be a real peace, resolving all claims and ending the conflict between them. This means that the Israeli occupation that began in 1967 will be ended through a settlement negotiated between the parties, based on UN Resolutions 242 and 338, with Israeli withdrawal to secure and recognize[d] borders.

We must also resolve questions concerning Jerusalem, the plight and future of Palestinian refugees, and a final peace between Israel and Lebanon, and Israel and a Syria that supports peace and fights terror.

All who are familiar with the history of the Middle East realize that there may be setbacks in this process. Trained and determined killers, as we have seen, want to stop it. Yet the Egyptian and Jordanian peace treaties with Israel remind us that with determined and responsible leadership progress can come quickly.

As new Palestinian institutions and new leaders emerge, demonstrating real performance on security and reform, I expect Israel to respond and work toward a final status agreement. With intensive effort by all, this agreement could be reached within three years from now. And I and my country will actively lead toward that goal.

I can understand the deep anger and anguish of the Israeli people. You've lived too long with fear and funerals, having to avoid markets and public transportation, and forced to put armed guards in kindergarten classrooms. The Palestinian Authority has rejected your offer at hand, and trafficked with terrorists. You have a right to a normal life; you have a right to security; and I deeply believe that you need a reformed, responsible Palestinian partner to achieve that security.

I can understand the deep anger and despair of the Palestinian people. For decades you've been treated as pawns in the Middle East conflict. Your interests have been held hostage to a comprehensive peace agreement that never seems to come, as your lives get worse year by year. You deserve democracy and the rule of law. You deserve an open society and a thriving economy. You deserve a life of hope for your children. An end to occupation and a peaceful democratic Palestinian state may seem distant, but America and our partners throughout the world stand ready to help, help you make them possible as soon as possible.

If liberty can blossom in the rocky soil of the West Bank and Gaza, it will inspire millions of men and women around the globe who are equally weary of poverty and oppression, equally entitled to the benefits of democratic government.

I have a hope for the people of Muslim countries. Your commitments to morality, and learning, and tolerance led to great historical achievements. And those values are alive in the Islamic world today. You have a rich culture, and you share the aspirations of men and women in every culture. Prosperity and freedom and dignity are not just American hopes, or Western hopes. They are universal, human hopes. And even in the violence and turmoil of the Middle East, America believes those hopes have the power to transform lives and nations.

This moment is both an opportunity and a test for all parties in the Middle East: an opportunity to lay the foundations for future peace; a test to show who is serious about peace and who is not. The choice here is stark and simple. The Bible says, "I have set before you life and death; therefore, choose life." The time has arrived for everyone in this conflict to choose peace, and hope, and life.

8.3 Bush Commends Sharon's Plan

The White House
Washington, DC
April 14, 2004

I'm pleased to welcome Prime Minister Sharon back to the White House. For more than fifty years, Israel has been a vital ally and a true friend of America. I've been proud to call the Prime Minister my friend. I really appreciate our discussions today. The policy of the United States is to help bring peace to the Middle East and to hope—bring hope to the people of that region.

On June 24, 2002, I laid out a vision to make this goal a reality. We then drafted the road map as the route to get us there. The heart of this vision is the responsibility of all parties—of Israel, of the Palestinian people, of the Arab states—to fight terror, to embrace democracy and reform, and to take the necessary steps for peace.

Today, the Prime Minister told me of his decision to take such a step. Israel plans to remove certain military installations and all settlements from Gaza, and certain military installations and settlements from the West Bank. These are historic and courageous actions. If all parties choose to embrace this moment they can open the door to progress and put an end to one of the world's longest running conflicts.

Success will require the active efforts of many nations. . . . We're consulting closely with other key leaders in the region, in Europe, and with our Quartet partners—the EU, Russia, and the United Nations. These steps can open the door to progress toward a peaceful, democratic, viable Palestinian state. Working together, we can help build democratic Palestinian institutions, as well as strong capabilities dedicated to fighting terror so that the Palestinian people can meet their obligations under the road map on the path to peace.

This opportunity holds great promise for the Palestinian people to build a modern economy that will lift millions out of poverty, create the institutions and habits of liberty, and renounce the terror and violence that impede their aspirations and take a terrible toll on innocent life.

The Palestinian people must insist on change and on a leadership that is committed to reform and progress and peace. We will help. But the most difficult work is theirs. The United States is strongly committed, and I am strongly committed, to the security of Israel as a vibrant Jewish state. I reiterate our steadfast commitment to Israel's security and to preserving and strengthening Israel's self-defense capability, including its right to defend itself against terror.

The barrier being erected by Israel as a part of that security effort should, as your government has stated, be a security, rather than political, barrier. It should be temporary rather than permanent, and, therefore, not prejudice any final status issues, including final borders. And its route should take into account, consistent with security needs, its impact on Palestinians not engaged in terrorist activities.

In an exchange of letters today and in a statement I will release later today, I'm repeating to the Prime Minister my commitment to Israel's security. The United States will not prejudice the outcome of final status negotiations. That matter is for the parties. But the realities on the ground and in the region have changed greatly over the last several decades, and any final settlement must take into account those realities and be agreeable to the parties.

The goal of two independent states has repeatedly been recognized in international resolutions and agreements, and it remains the key to resolving this conflict. The United States is strongly committed to Israel's security and well being as a Jewish state. It seems clear that an agreed, just, fair and realistic framework for a solution to the Palestinian refugee issue, as part of any final status agreement, will need to be found through the establishment of a Palestinian state and the settling of Palestinian refugees there, rather than Israel.

As part of a final peace settlement, Israel must have secure and recognized borders which should emerge from negotiations between the parties, in accordance with UN Security Council Resolutions 242 and 338. In light of new realities on the ground, including already existing major Israeli population centers, it is unrealistic to expect that the outcome of final status negotiations will be a full and complete return to the armistice lines of 1949. And all previous efforts to negotiate a two-state solution have reached the same conclusion. It is realistic to expect that any final status agreement will only be achieved on the basis of mutually agreed changes that reflect these realities.

I commend Prime Minister Sharon for his bold and courageous decision to withdraw from Gaza and parts of the West Bank. I call on the Palestinians and their Arab neighbors to match that boldness and that courage. All of us must show the wisdom and the will to bring lasting peace to that region.

8.4 Freedom in Iraq and the Middle East

United States Chamber of Commerce
Washington, DC
November 6, 2003

Thanks for inviting me to join you in this 20th anniversary of the National Endowment for Democracy. . . . The roots of our democracy can be traced to England, and to its Parliament—and so can the roots of this organization. In June of 1982, President Ronald Reagan spoke at Westminster Palace and declared, the turning point had arrived in history. He argued that Soviet communism had failed, precisely because it did not respect its own people—their creativity, their genius and their rights.

President Reagan said that the day of Soviet tyranny was passing, that freedom had a momentum which would not be halted. He gave this organization its mandate: to add to the momentum of freedom across the world. . . .

A number of critics were dismissive of that speech by the President. According to one editorial of the time, "It seems hard to be a sophisticated European and also an admirer of Ronald Reagan." Some observers on both sides of the Atlantic pronounced the speech simplistic and naive, and even dangerous. In fact, Ronald Reagan's words were courageous and optimistic and entirely correct.

The great democratic movement President Reagan described was already well underway. In the early 1970s, there were about 40 democracies in the world. By the middle of that decade, Portugal and Spain and Greece held free elections. Soon there were new democracies in Latin America, and free institutions were spreading in Korea, in Taiwan, and in East Asia. This very week in 1989, there were protests in East Berlin and in Leipzig. By the end of that year, every communist dictatorship in Central [Europe] had collapsed. Within another year, the South African government released Nelson Mandela. Four years later, he was elected president of his country—ascending, like Walesa and Havel, from prisoner of state to head of state.

As the 20th century ended, there were around 120 democracies in the world—and I can assure you more are on the way. Ronald Reagan would be pleased, and he would not be surprised.

We've witnessed, in little over a generation, the swiftest advance of freedom in the 2,500 year story of democracy. Historians in the future will offer their own explanations for why this happened. Yet we already know some of the reasons they will cite. It is no accident that the rise of so many democracies took place in a time when the world's most influential nation was itself a democracy. The United States made military and moral commitments in Europe and Asia, which protected free nations from aggression, and created the conditions in which new democracies could flourish. As we provided security for whole nations, we also provided inspiration for oppressed peoples. . . .

Historians will note that in many nations, the advance of markets and free enterprise helped to create a middle class that was confident enough to demand their own rights. They will point to the role of technology in frustrating censorship and central control—and marvel at the power of instant communications to spread the truth, the news, and courage across borders.

Historians in the future will reflect on an extraordinary, undeniable fact: Over time, free nations grow stronger and dictatorships grow weaker. . . . Liberty is both the plan of Heaven for humanity, and the best hope for progress here on Earth.

The progress of liberty is a powerful trend. Yet, we also know that liberty, if not defended, can be lost. The success of freedom is not determined by some dialectic of history. By definition, the success of freedom rests upon the choices and the courage of free peoples, and upon their willingness to sacrifice. . . .

The sacrifices of Americans have not always been recognized or appreciated, yet they have been worthwhile. . . . Every nation has learned, or should have learned, an important lesson: Freedom is worth fighting for, dying for, and standing for—and the advance of freedom leads to peace.

And now we must apply that lesson in our own time. We've reached another great turning point—and the resolve we show will shape the next stage of the world democratic movement.

Our commitment to democracy is tested in countries like Cuba and Burma and North Korea and Zimbabwe—outposts of oppression in our world. . . . Our commitment to democracy is tested in China. . . .

Our commitment to democracy is also tested in the Middle East, which is my focus today, and must be a focus of American policy for decades to come. In many nations of the Middle East—countries of great strategic importance—democracy has not yet taken root. And the questions arise: Are the peoples of the Middle East somehow beyond the reach of liberty? Are millions of men and women and children condemned by history or culture to live in despotism? Are they alone never to know freedom, and never even to have a choice in the matter? I, for one, do not believe it. I believe every person has the ability and the right to be free.

Some skeptics of democracy assert that the traditions of Islam are inhospitable to the representative government. This "cultural condescension," as Ronald Reagan termed it, has a long history. After the Japanese surrender in 1945, a so-called Japan expert asserted that democracy in that former empire would "never work." Another observer declared the prospects for democracy in post-Hitler Germany are, and I quote, "most uncertain at best"—he made that claim in 1957. . . .

Time after time, observers have questioned whether this country, or that people, or this group, are "ready" for democracy—as if freedom were a prize you win for meeting our own Western standards of progress. In fact, the daily work of democracy itself is the path of progress. It teaches cooperation, the free exchange of ideas, and the peaceful resolution of differences. As men and women are showing, from Bangladesh to Botswana, to Mongolia, it is the practice of democracy that makes a nation ready for democracy, and every nation can start on this path.

It should be clear to all that Islam—the faith of one-fifth of humanity—is consistent with democratic rule. Democratic progress is found in many predominantly Muslim countries—in Turkey and Indonesia, and Senegal and Albania, Niger and Sierra Leone. Muslim men and women are good citizens of India and South Africa, of the nations of Western Europe, and of the United States of America.

More than half of all the Muslims in the world live in freedom under democratically constituted governments. They succeed in democratic societies, not in spite of their faith, but because of it. A religion that demands individual moral accountability, and encourages the encounter of the individual with God, is fully compatible with the rights and responsibilities of self-government.

Yet there's a great challenge today in the Middle East. In the words of a recent report by Arab scholars, the global wave of democracy has—and I quote—"barely reached the Arab states." They continue: "This freedom deficit undermines human development and is one of the most painful manifestations of lagging political development." The freedom deficit they describe has terrible consequences, of the people of the Middle East and for the world. In many Middle Eastern countries, poverty is deep and it is spreading, women lack rights and are denied schooling. Whole societies remain stagnant while the world moves ahead. These are not the failures of a culture or a religion. These are the failures of political and economic doctrines.

As the colonial era passed away, the Middle East saw the establishment of many military dictatorships. Some rulers adopted the dogmas of socialism, seized total control of political parties and the media and universities. They allied themselves with the Soviet bloc and with international terrorism. Dictators in Iraq and Syria promised the restoration of national honor, a return to ancient glories. They've left instead a legacy of torture, oppression, misery, and ruin.

Other men, and groups of men, have gained influence in the Middle East and beyond through an ideology of theocratic terror. Behind their language of religion is the ambition for absolute political power. . . .

Many Middle Eastern governments now understand that military dictatorship and theocratic rule are a straight, smooth highway to nowhere. But some governments still cling to the old habits of central control. There are governments that still fear and repress independent thought and creativity, and private enterprise—the human qualities that make for a—strong and successful societies. Even when these nations have vast natural resources, they do not respect or develop their greatest resources—the talent and energy of men and women working and living in freedom.

Instead of dwelling on past wrongs and blaming others, governments in the Middle East need to confront real problems, and serve the true interests of their nations. The good and capable people of the Middle East all deserve responsible leadership. For too long, many people in that region have been victims and subjects—they deserve to be active citizens.

Governments across the Middle East and North Africa are beginning to see the need for change. Morocco has a diverse new parliament; King Mohammed has urged it to extend the rights to women. . . . The future of Muslim nations will be better for all with the full participation of women.

In Bahrain last year, citizens elected their own parliament for the first time in nearly three decades. Oman has extended the vote to all adult citizens; Qatar has a new constitution; Yemen has a multiparty political system; Kuwait has a directly elected national assembly; and Jordan held historic elections this summer. Recent surveys in Arab nations reveal broad support for political pluralism, the rule of law, and free speech. These are the stirrings of Middle Eastern democracy, and they carry the promise of greater change to come.

As changes come to the Middle Eastern region, those with power should ask themselves: Will they be remembered for resisting reform, or for leading it? In Iran, the demand for democracy is strong and broad, as we saw last month when thousands gathered to welcome home Shirin Ebadi, the winner of the Nobel Peace Prize. The regime in Teheran must heed the democratic demands of the Iranian people, or lose its last claim to legitimacy.

For the Palestinian people, the only path to independence and dignity and progress is the path of democracy. And the Palestinian leaders who block and undermine democratic reform, and feed hatred and encourage violence are not leaders at all. They're the main obstacles to peace, and to the success of the Palestinian people.

The Saudi government is taking first steps toward reform, including a plan for gradual introduction of elections. By giving the Saudi people a greater role in their own society, the Saudi government can demonstrate true leadership in the region.

The great and proud nation of Egypt has shown the way toward peace in the Middle East, and now should show the way toward democracy in the Middle East. Champions of democracy in the region understand that democracy is not perfect, it is not the path to utopia, but it's the only path to national success and dignity.

As we watch and encourage reforms in the region, we are mindful that modernization is not the same as Westernization. Representative governments in the Middle East will reflect their own cultures. They will not, and should not, look like us. Democratic nations may be constitutional monarchies, federal republics, or parliamentary systems. And working democracies always need time to develop—as did our own. We've taken a 200-year journey toward inclusion and justice—and this makes us patient and understanding as other nations are at different stages of this journey.

There are, however, essential principles common to every successful society, in every culture. Successful societies limit the power of the state and the power of the military—so that governments respond to the will of the people, and not the will of an elite. Successful societies protect freedom with the consistent and impartial rule of law, instead of selecting applying—selectively applying the law to punish political opponents. Successful societies allow room for healthy civic institutions—for political parties and labor unions and independent newspapers and broadcast media. Successful societies guarantee religious liberty—the right to serve and honor God without fear of persecution. Successful societies privatize their economies, and secure the rights of property. They prohibit and punish official corruption, and invest in the health and education of their people. They recognize the rights of women. And instead of directing hatred and resentment against others, successful societies appeal to the hopes of their own people.

These vital principles are being applied in the nations of Afghanistan and Iraq. With the steady leadership of President Karzai, the people of Afghanistan are building a modern and peaceful government. . . . In Iraq, the Coalition Provisional Authority and the Iraqi Governing Council are also working together to build a democracy—and after three decades of tyranny, this work is not easy. . . .

This is a massive and difficult undertaking—it is worth our effort, it is worth our sacrifice, because we know the stakes. The failure of Iraqi democracy would embolden terrorists around the world, increase dangers to the American people, and extinguish the hopes of millions in the region. Iraqi democracy will succeed—and that success will send forth the news, from Damascus to Teheran—that freedom can be the future of every nation. The establishment of a free Iraq at the heart of the Middle East will be a watershed event in the global democratic revolution.

Sixty years of Western nations excusing and accommodating the lack of freedom in the Middle East did nothing to make us safe—because in the long run, stability cannot be purchased at the expense of liberty. As long as the Middle East remains a place where freedom does not flourish, it will remain a place of stagnation, resentment, and violence ready for export. And with the spread of weapons that can bring catastrophic harm to our country and to our friends, it would be reckless to accept the status quo.

Therefore, the United States has adopted a new policy, a forward strategy of freedom in the Middle East. This strategy requires the same persistence and energy and idealism we have shown before. And it will yield the same results. As in Europe, as in Asia, as in every region of the world, the advance of freedom leads to peace.

The advance of freedom is the calling of our time; it is the calling of our country. . . . We believe that liberty is the design of nature; we believe that liberty is the direction of history. We believe that human fulfillment and excellence come in the responsible exercise of liberty. And we believe that freedom—the freedom we prize—is not for us alone, it is the right and the capacity of all mankind.

Working for the spread of freedom can be hard. Yet, America has accomplished hard tasks before. Our nation is strong; we're strong of heart. And we're not alone. Freedom is finding allies in every country; freedom finds allies in every culture. And as we meet the terror and violence of the world, we can be certain the author of freedom is not indifferent to the fate of freedom.

With all the tests and all the challenges of our age, this is, above all, the age of liberty.

Questions to Discuss

1. In Speeches 8.1 and 8.2, Bush suggests that Palestinian leaders must stop terrorism and that Israel has a right to defend itself from terrorists. Is the Israeli-Palestinian dispute properly seen as part of the global war on terrorism, or is it better seen as a nationalist insurgency?

2. In Speech 8.2, Bush calls for new Palestinian leaders and political reform. Is this an interference in local politics? Will it make it impossible for the United States to be seen as a fair mediator in the future?

3. In a number of speeches, Bush closes his comments with Biblical references. What does this reveal about the way that his religious views may shape his policy in the Middle East?

4. Are arguments that Middle Eastern countries are not ready for democracy indicative of "cultural condescension," as Bush argues in Speech 8.5, or of accurate assessments of local cultural, economic, and political factors?

5. In Speech 8.4, Bush states, "modernization is not the same as Westernization." Is it possible to adopt democracy without adopting Western values on other political and social issues?

Chapter 9

Latin America and Africa

The United States has long considered Latin America within its natural sphere of influence. The Monroe Doctrine, numerous U.S. military interventions, and the use of U.S. economic leverage all indicated that the United States felt the need to protect and guide its neighbors. The relationship also has been shaped by geographic proximity; Latin American issues such as immigration, drug flow, and the spread of leftist ideologies could directly affect the United States. On the other hand, no Latin American countries rose to great economic or military power in the twentieth century. So they were not perceived to be either crucial allies or threatening powers. Also, significant differences exist between the regions including language, religion, economic policies, and political structure. The net effect of these factors has been U.S. policies based on three underlying patterns. First, the relationship has been unequal, with the United States exerting dominant influence and expecting Latin American countries to support its policies unconditionally. Second, the policy agenda has often been driven by the desire to limit the impact of negative developments, rather than to enhance positive contacts. Third, the United States has increased focus only when it viewed regional developments as part of global phenomena, such as the end of colonialism or the Cold War. Overall, U.S. policy has varied between benign neglect and short, intense periods of activity.

Beginning in the 1980s, the underlying dynamics of the relationship appeared to be changing. Democracy spread throughout Latin America. Also, through both local decisions and international pressure, many countries adopted free market economic policies. These policies focused on cutting excessive government spending, privatizing industry, lowering trade restrictions, and encouraging foreign investment. The countries' policies were now more in line with U.S. patterns and desires and new policies could stimulate economic growth to make Latin America a more important U.S. trade partner. In addition, the end of the Cold War gave the United States a new opportunity to view Latin America on its own terms, rather than through an anticommunist lens. The end of superpower funding forced regional groups to sign peace treaties ending several civil wars.

Warmer hemispheric relations were seen in a more active and unified Organization of American States (OAS), which adopted an important pro-democracy resolution at Santiago in 1991, in passage of NAFTA to open trade with Mexico, and in a 1994 Summit of the Americas where leaders pledged to strive for a regional free trade area and more equality in relations among states.

Early Focus on Latin America

During his campaign, George W. Bush pledged to make Latin American policy a priority of his administration and to help make the next years the "Century of the Americas" (Speech 1.4). In his first months in office, Bush showed his personal commitment by meeting with seven of the region's heads of state. His first major foreign trip was to the third Summit of the Americas held in Quebec in April 2001. The leaders of all thirty-four democracies in the hemisphere attended the summit. Fidel Castro, from nondemocratic Cuba, was not invited. Speaking to his fellow leaders, Bush outlined his vision for the region (Speech 9.1). He stressed the region had entered a new era with the spread of democracy. The other key to success was economic growth stimulated by trade. Bush pledged to move forward on numerous trade deals, including a Free Trade Area of the Americas (FTAA) by 2005. Such an area would include 800 million people, with a combined production of over $10 trillion. Many countries' economies would be helped and the region would be able to compete with the European Union and others in world trade. Bush also noted the continued importance of dealing with drug exports, health issues, the environment, and education. On many of these issues, Bush acknowledged that the United States bore partial responsibility for some of the region's problems and pledged to cooperate with others in addressing them.

The country that Bush focused the most early attention on was Mexico. Coming from Texas, Bush had long-standing interests in and experiences with Mexico. He was particularly close to the country's newly elected president, Vicente Fox. Bush traveled to Fox's ranch in February 2001. The two laid out a bold agenda on trade, drug enforcement, energy, and immigration issues. In the following months, the countries made progress on a number of these issues and seemed ready to announce major new policies on immigration and the status of Mexican workers in the United States. In early September 2001, Fox made a state visit to Washington and was treated as a major international figure. At the meetings,

Bush proclaimed, "Mexico is an incredibly important part of the United States' foreign policy. It is our most important relationship."[1]

Politics as Usual after September 11

The September 11 terrorist attacks and subsequent U.S. policies had a profound effect on U.S. relations with Latin America. No Latin American country was prepared to make major military or economic contributions to the war on terrorism. Therefore, the United States quickly turned to stronger allies in Europe and Asia. England, not Mexico, suddenly became America's most important partner. Also, since none of the Latin American countries were home to terrorists, at least not al Qaeda terrorists, they did not warrant the same attention as countries in the Middle East, Asia, and northern Africa. Overall, Latin American countries seemed less important than on September 10. In addition, some Latin American issues such as poverty and the environment now took a backseat to security issues, such as antiterrorism and weapons proliferation. Other issues, such as immigration, were now cast in a new light as the United States sought ways to protect the homeland.

U.S. responses to the attacks, particularly subsequent action against Iraq, raised some tensions. Given the long history of U.S. interventions in Latin America, many countries were extremely wary of the United States preparing to act militarily throughout the world, acting unilaterally when necessary, and stretching international law by launching preemptive attacks against sovereign countries. Many also felt that Bush was paying too much attention to short-term threats while ignoring the underlying economic and social conditions that led people in other countries to adopt anti-American ideologies. The United States was perceived to be following the Cold War patterns of seeing the world in black and white terms and viewing local problems as part of global patterns. Most Latin American countries still expressed early support for the war on terrorism, but, as war in Iraq neared, leftist leaders in Brazil, Venezuela, and Cuba became increasingly vocal critics. More notably, key U.S. allies Mexico and Chile refused to support a U.S.-proposed UN Security Council resolution authorizing war against Iraq in spring 2003.

New tensions also entered U.S.–Latin American relations because of a decline in Latin America's economic performance. The decline stemmed from decreases in global commodity prices, a series of natural disasters that cut agricultural production, slowdowns in the regionally crucial economies of Brazil and Argentina, and a global recession that decreased markets for Latin American exports and reduced capital inflows. These problems led to a 4 percent decrease in regional trade in 2001 and a 2.6

percent decrease in per capita production in 2002. These were not huge declines, but were enough to shift attitudes. A Latin America in decline made new trade agreements less attractive to the United States. At the same time, Latin American countries became more determined to get trade concessions from the United States, such as cutbacks in U.S. farm subsidies and reductions in particular U.S. tariffs. The decline also led many Latin American citizens to question the merits of free market and democratic policies. In their eyes, those reforms had increased corruption, allowed more foreign and elite control of the economy, and decreased social programs for the poor. If reforms were not producing growth as a tradeoff for these hardships, there was little reason to continue them. Polls in 2003 showed that 52 percent of Latin Americans were willing to accept nondemocratic governments if they could solve economic problems. Finally, the economic decline led some Latin Americans to look to the United States for new assistance, but they became disillusioned when little significant help was forthcoming. Reflecting tensions over the war on Iraq and the economy, a 2003 survey of opinion leaders in six Latin American countries showed that 87 percent of the respondents had a negative opinion of Bush.

With Latin America seeming less important, unsupportive on key policies, and less appealing as a trade partner, Bush turned attention elsewhere. The region was "once again an Atlantis, a lost continent."[2] Even U.S. relations with Mexico suffered. Fox commented in May 2002 that U.S.–Mexican relations had "stalled."[3] Later in the year, he complained after a regional trade meeting that the United States was not ready to treat Mexico as a "partner."[4]

U.S. policy returned to the pattern of neglect punctuated by episodes of crisis management, but even the crises drew limited responses. When the Argentinean economy began to collapse in 2001, Treasury Secretary Paul O'Neill made comments suggesting that the problems were largely self-created and that significant foreign assistance risked creating the problem of "moral hazard," in which debtors come to expect bailouts and postpone needed policy reform. Eventually, the administration did support some new loans, but let the International Monetary Fund (IMF) take the lead. Similarly, Bush was slow to criticize an April 2002 attempted coup in Venezuela, leading many people to question the administration's focus and its commitment to democracy when a leftist was in power.

The pattern of seeing issues as part of global battles also returned. For decades, the Colombian government had been fighting against the leftist Revolutionary Forces of Colombia (FARC). The United States favored the government, but worried about becoming enmeshed in the battle. Colombia became the third largest recipient of U.S. military aid in the world, but aid was restricted solely to counternarcotics efforts. The line between counternarcotics and counterinsurgency was blurry because FARC increasingly funded its activities through drug trade. Bush added the overlapping concern of counterterrorism. FARC had been added to the U.S. list of terrorist organizations in 1998 because of a number of kidnappings for ransom. In 2002, language to lift the previous aid restrictions and allow funding of Colombia's "unified campaign against narcotics trafficking, terrorist activities, and other threats to national security" was included in the White House request for emergency antiterrorism aid.[5] Many countries in the region hoped for an end to violence in Colombia, but were wary of steps that increased further militarized Colombia's policies.

Bush tried to downplay tensions in the region by pointing to movement on trade agreements. In 2002, the United States signed a free trade agreement with Chile. There were, though, also setbacks on trade. Bush was unable to win Senate renewal of the Andean Trade Preference Act, which encouraged alternative exports to discourage drugs trafficking. He angered Latin Americans by supporting new subsidies for U.S. farmers and imposing tariffs on foreign steel imports. Most important, little progress was made on the FTAA. Ongoing disputes between the United States and Brazil and others made Bush's 2005 target date for an agreement appear unrealistic.

U.S.–African Relations Over Time

For many decades the United States paid little attention to Africa. As in U.S. relations with Latin America, U.S. attention was limited by the lack of a major local power and by differences to the United States. In addition, with Africa, there was no geographic proximity, so it was easier for the United States to ignore the continent. Also, the United States did not view Africa as part of its natural sphere of influence, so allowed others—first Africa's former colonial powers in Europe and later international institutions—to take the lead on Africa policy. When the United States did focus attention on Africa, it was mainly in the context of non-African issues, such as supporting European allies or stopping the spread of Soviet influence. During the Cold War, the United States gave military and economic aid to some of the continent's most brutal and corrupt leaders, because those leaders opposed Soviet-supported factions. Direct U.S. attention on African problems came only at times of crisis—famines, civil wars, and so on—and lasted only long enough to treat the crisis, not address its underlying roots.

In Africa, like in Latin America, the end of the Cold War and the concurrent spread of democracy and market reforms seemed to bring new possibilities for enhanced U.S. action. Somalia served as an early test of that possibility. In December 1992, President George H.W. Bush authorized a joint U.S. and UN mission to bring stability to the war-torn country and feed its people. Initially, the mission was considered a success, but Somali opposition to subsequent nation building efforts led to an attack that killed eighteen U.S. soldiers. The Clinton administration rapidly pulled out U.S. troops, and the country returned to civil war and famine. The "lessons of Somalia" deeply affected U.S. views on Africa. Two years later, the United States did not intervene in Rwanda despite the deaths of over one million people in ethnic fighting. More generally, pessimistic views on Africa's prospects dominated Washington policy discussions.

In the late 1990s, the rise of African leaders who supported reform led to new talk of an "African Renaissance." The Clinton administration responded to these developments by devoting new attention to Africa. In 1998, President Clinton made a historic twelve-day visit to the continent and he returned two years later. In 2000, he signed the African Growth and Opportunity Act (AGOA), which established economic and political criteria for countries to meet and rewarded successes by allowing over 90 percent of their exports to enter the United States duty free. While troubling signs of political instability and economic difficulties still existed across the continent, there was considerable optimism about both Africa's prospects and U.S.–African relations.

Bush's Early Policy Towards Africa

During the 2000 campaign, Bush rarely spoke directly about African issues, although his opposition to nation building, the Kyoto Accord on global warming, and population control programs that included abortion all had implications for the continent. He repeatedly left Africa off the list of areas that would be top priorities of his administration. In February 2000, Bush famously declared, Africa "doesn't fit into the national strategic interests, as far as I can see them."[6]

Once in office, though, the administration seemed determined to make a conscious effort to repair the damage done by Bush's earlier comments. At a six month review of policy, Bush's top State Department and NSC officials for Africa stressed his personal commitment to Africa, citing as evidence that he had met with many African leaders and that Secretary of State Powell had made an early trip to the continent.[7] Powell and National Security Adviser Rice, were known to be interested in developing Africa policy. As African-Americans, they gave the administration a significantly different look than past Republican administrations. Several Members of Congress from both parties also were known for their interest. A key congressional player and close Bush ally was Senator Bill Frist, a heart surgeon who had gone on medical missions to Africa. There were also domestic groups pushing Bush to focus attention on Africa. These groups included human rights and African-American groups, neither of which had historically strong ties to Republicans, but also evangelical Christian groups that were increasingly focused on African poverty and AIDS.

Bush's first major speech on Africa policy was delayed by the events of September 11. Bush began his October 29, 2001 address by thanking African countries for their sympathy and political support in the war on terrorism (Speech 9.2). He continued that, while terrorists seek to destroy, others seek to move forward by adopting "a model of successful development, a market economy trading with the world that respects human rights and the rule of law." African countries that adopted the model would be supported by the United States opening markets through AGOA, increasing trade through a new Trade for African Development and Enterprise Program, and encouraging investment through U.S. government guarantees for private investors. More important, Bush's focus was all on trade programs, not on increasing U.S. foreign aid.

Interest in AIDS

Bush did acknowledge in his October 2001 speech that, beyond wise economic polices, "Nations need citizens that are educated and are healthy" (Speech 9.2). The reference to health was primarily a reference to the impact of AIDS. Although AIDS had spread globally, the numbers that reflected Africa's AIDS problem were truly staggering. By 2001, it was believed that over 17 million Africans had died from AIDS-related illnesses and between 25 and 30 million were actively infected. Seven African states had infection rates of 20 percent or higher among people 15 to 49. Life expectancies had plunged below 50 years in many countries. The causes behind these numbers are complex, but include social and economic factors that have fueled much higher heterosexual and mother-to-child transmission rates than those that occur in Western countries. The situation is compounded by the lack of government funds for adequate healthcare. AIDS commonly affects people in their prime, who would normally be working, supporting their family, and serving in the military. Thus, for Africa, AIDS is not just a health crisis, but an economic, social, and political crisis as well.

The magnitude of the AIDS crisis started to become apparent to government officials outside Africa in the 1990s. In 1996, a UN program was created to coordinate global efforts, but funding was minimal. In time, Clinton administration officials came to speak of AIDS as a national security issue and gave it increased prominence. Funding of U.S. programs to combat the disease was gradually increased. However, some of the largest programs gave loans, instead of direct aid, and were criticized for adding to Africa's debt burden. In 1999, Clinton took a subtle, but important, step. He announced that the United States would no longer seek sanctions against countries that bought cheaper generic versions of AIDS drugs, even if foreign companies had broken U.S. patent laws to produce those drugs.

Bush's first action on AIDS was his February 2001 decision not to alter Clinton's policy on enforcing patent rights. This decision was controversial among Bush supporters. Some were suspicious about anything Clinton had done, but also U.S. pharmaceutical companies were aggressively lobbying for a firmer stand. His decision had implications both for AIDS programs, since only approximately 1 percent of Africans could afford the $10,000-a-year price of name-brand drugs, and for broader trade matters, since intellectual property rights were looming as a major issue to be addressed in global trade talks.

In the spring of 2001, UN Secretary General Kofi Annan put new pressure on world governments by announcing a Global Fund to Fight AIDS, Tuberculosis, and Malaria. UN experts suggested the fund would need $7–8 billion annually to have a significant impact. This figure was many times higher than previous world commitments. After some debate, Bush, who generally was wary of UN initiatives and bureaucracy, decided AIDS was one African policy issue on which his administration would take new multilateral actions. On May 27, 2001, Bush announced that the United States would make a founding contribution of $200 million to the global fund and pledged to add more once programs proved to be effective. This money was in addition to the over $700 million Bush had already committed to U.S.-funded AIDS programs. Critics suggested that U.S. contributions were still small in proportion to the need and in light of U.S. wealth, but total U.S. spending was more than twice that of any other country.

Increased Attention to Africa

Bush's first year actions focused primarily on trade and AIDS. Critics suggested he had no comprehensive plan to bring stability and development to Africa. After 9/11, there were also worries that the war on terrorism would lead to further U.S. disengagement and future funding cuts. There were, however, a number of factors that pushed Africa higher on Bush's priority list in 2002. First, prominent African leaders, including Thabo Mbeki of South Africa, Addoulaye Wade of Senegal, and Olesegun

Obasanjo of Nigeria, developed the New Partnership for African Development (NEPAD). NEPAD sought to increase investment and trade by committing African countries to good governance, democracy, peace, and free markets. These African-initiated policies were important. For years, U.S. officials and others had blamed many African problems on poor governance and suggested that no aid or trade packages would ever have significant impact until African leaders took responsibility for reform.

Second, some African countries also got more attention as the war on terrorism progressed. Although home to millions of Muslims, Africa was not a major breeding ground for Islamic terrorists. However, the lack of security technology and weak police forces in many African countries made them appealing targets for international terrorists. Al Qaeda's 1998 bombings of U.S. embassies in Kenya and Tanzania dramatically demonstrated this vulnerability and there were rumors of future strikes. In addition, weak states could become havens for terrorist training grounds. Thus, ongoing turmoil in Somalia and elsewhere was seen as a potential threat to U.S. interests. Finally, some African countries could play a role in the war by providing key bases for U.S. power projection.

Another factor driving attention was that Africa's oil supplies looked increasingly attractive in light of possible instability in the Middle East. While African states already provided about 15 percent of U.S. crude oil imports, that number was projected to rise to 25 percent as new sources were developed. Most African oil lies on the West African coast, so transport to the United States is relatively simple. Also, since African states, with the exception Nigeria, do not belong to the Organization of the Petroleum Exporting Countries (OPEC), production and pricing levels are not set by the cartel. Bush administration officials did not publicly talk extensively about African oil possibilities to avoid offending Middle Eastern allies or looking as if they were interested in stripping Africa's resources, but the administration did increase diplomatic and economic contacts with oil producing countries such as Angola, Gabon, and Equatorial Guinea.

Finally, focus on Africa's health and development challenges was good politics. Internationally, some anti-Americanism stems from a perception of the United States as a stingy, security-focused world power. Assistance for the developing world could help to negate that stigma. Domestically, particular types of aid played well with certain constituencies. The administration hoped to increase Bush's share of the African-American vote. Bush's conservative Christian constituency and some moderate swing voters also wanted evidence of Bush's "compassionate conservatism."

The combined effect of these factors, along with continued support from key advisers and Bush's personal views, led to significant policy changes in 2002. In March, prior to a UN development conference, Bush proposed a 50 percent increase in U.S. foreign aid over three years. This new $5 billion per year would be distributed, through the Millennium Challenge Account (MCA), to countries that were "ruling justly, investing in their people, and encouraging economic freedom" (Speech 9.3). Bush hoped that conditioning aid would promote further reform and avoid sending money to corrupt regimes. Traditionally, foreign aid increases had been opposed by many Republicans, who felt that aid programs were often wasteful and could be cut to reduce the U.S. government budget. Bush's plan to encourage reform and increase accountability pleased some in his party, but many remained unconvinced. Supporters of foreign aid were pleased by the significant new monetary commitment, but they worried that the program's criteria might be politicized. They further noted that many of the world's poorest countries would not qualify for the new aid. The number of qualifying African states was not immediately clear, but total future aid was expected to far exceed the roughly $1 billion per year that previously had been going to sub-Saharan Africa. Thus, aid would join trade as a force to drive development.

In a June 20, 2002 speech, Bush announced several other new initiatives and announced his plan to visit Africa in 2003 (Speech 9.4). The proposed trip would be the first time a sitting Republican President had ever made an extended visit to sub-Saharan Africa. Bush then described a vision of a successful continent based on democracy and economic growth built by Africans with U.S. assistance in addressing obstacles. He described four specific obstacles and the U.S. policies designed to address them. To confront AIDS, Bush pledged $500 million to prevent mother-to-child transmission of HIV, which complemented the nearly $1.5 billion already committed to various AIDS efforts. Mother-to-child policies were politically popular and side stepped more controversial prevention issues such as condom distribution. To address Africa's education deficits, he announced specific plans to provide $630 million over five years to train teachers, buy textbooks, and provide scholarships for African girls. To reduce trade barriers, Bush spoke of enhancing AGOA and exploring a free trade agreement with the Southern African Customs Union. Such an agreement would enable those countries to increase exports to the United States, but also allow the United States better access to South Africa's regionally dominant market. Finally, Bush spoke of the need for Africans to be safe and secure. He pledged an additional $55 million to help fight terrorism and mentioned U.S. activity attempting to negotiate an end to Sudan's civil war. The week after his speech, Bush attended a G-8 summit in Canada. There, leaders of NEPAD presented their plans and the G-8 leaders committed to an Africa Action Plan that closely paralleled Bush's initiatives.

Bush's new initiatives were generally well received. Many analysts, though, recognized that it was one thing for a president to propose new spending figures and quite a different thing to get full congressional appropriations. There were also complaints from some Africans and Westerners that Bush was still suggesting only minimal changes on two key issues: debt relief and agricultural subsidies. African countries owed more than $350 billion in foreign debt. Much of the debt was accrued by corrupt leaders during the 1970 and 1980s, but high interest rates made full repayment difficult. Many countries were spending significantly more on debt payments than on health or education programs. Much of the capital gained through foreign trade or international aid returned abroad in payments. Under Clinton, a global program of debt relief was developed to help Heavily Indebted Poor Countries (HIPC). Bush supported the HIPC program, but resisted calls for further relief with the ideas that further debt relief would encourage reckless borrowing behavior, and go to countries that had not implemented economic reforms.

Agricultural subsidies were widespread and politically popular in both Europe and the United States. Since richer countries already had advantages in such areas as access to fertilizer, use of machinery, and transport costs, the added benefits of subsidies meant that Western farmers could dominate markets. Bush agreed to address the subsidy issue, but felt it should be handled through global trade talks. In 2002, he further disappointed many Africans by signing a farm bill that included over $100 million in direct subsidies for U.S. farmers.

Increased Funding for AIDS Programs

In his 2003 State of the Union speech, Bush surprised most observers by announcing a plan to commit $15 billion over five years to AIDS programs in 12 African countries, plus Haiti and Guyana. Three days later, he provided further details in a speech devoted to AIDS policy (Speech 9.5). Bush began with a clear sign of his religious convictions. He argued, "America believes deeply that everybody has worth, everybody matters, everybody was created by the Almighty, and we're going to act on that belief and we'll act on that passion." He also suggested that his AIDS proposal was part of a long tradition of American support for human dignity. Bush outlined a three-prong approach of prevention, treatment and care. The new money would prevent 7 million new infections, treat at least 2 million people, and care for orphans and others affected by the disease.

Insiders reported that Bush had been interested in massive new funding since the previous summer, but wanted to wait until existing programs had proven their worth and the cost of treatment had been reduced. Others cynically noted that the AIDS plan had been included in a speech largely devoted to preparing the country for war with Iraq, so wondered if it was a real commitment or just an effort to soften America's world image.

As the administration moved forward on the plan in 2003 and 2004, issues arose concerning which programs to fund, what prevention methods to use, and what drugs to provide. The first issue centered on the division of funds between the Global Fund and U.S. programs. Many Democrats and some AIDS activists tended to favor global funding that would go to more countries and reduce program duplication. Bush remained wary of the UN bureaucracy and preferred direct U.S. control. He earmarked only $1 billion over five years for the global fund.

The second issue was what preventive methods to promote. Bush's proposed programs were modeled on Uganda's "ABC approach." People were encouraged to Abstain from sex, or at least to Be faithful to one partner, and to use a Condom. Aggressive government support had helped Uganda significantly lower infection rates. In response to Bush's plan, Christian and other conservatives revived arguments used in domestic debates that distribution of condoms would increase teenage sexual activity, so programs should focus on abstinence. They also feared that the program would violate the Mexico City policy—developed by Ronald Reagan and brought back into force by Bush—which bars foreign aid to family planning organizations that promote abortion. The administration defended the ABC approach, but eventually made several concessions to win support: 1) thirty percent of prevention money would go to abstinence programs; 2) only organizations that kept their AIDS and family planning programs separate would receive money; 3) aid could be delivered through faith-based programs.

A final dispute revolved around which drugs would be purchased with U.S. funds. The underlying clash between protecting patent rights and providing cheap drugs to the poor had become increasingly contentious and been a major factor in the collapse of global trade talks. Thus, there was widespread global opposition to the Bush administration's March 2004 announcement that U.S. funds would not be spent on foreign generic drugs until the safety and efficacy of those drugs had been further studied by the U.S. Food and Drug Administration (FDA). Critics suggested the policy was a thinly veiled effort to support American pharmaceutical companies. They also felt further testing was unnecessary since the drugs had been reviewed by the World Health Organization and already were being distributed through UN programs. In May 2004, the administration significantly modified its policy. Foreign generics would still need FDA approval, but the usual processing fees would be waived and existing data could be used to demonstrate safety. Most important, the approval process would be expedited reducing the typical six month wait period to two to six weeks. The program also would buy drugs that combined the usual "cocktail" of drugs into a single pill, which reduced costs and increased patient compliance. At the time, only foreign companies were producing such a pill. These changes lessened foreign anger, but there still was no immediate rush to attain FDA approval.

Overall, some optimism existed as the first dollars of Bush's plan were spent in the spring of 2004. Significant problems, particularly the lack of healthcare infrastructure and encouraging foreign governments to meet their funding pledges, still had to be overcome.

Moving Forward on Other African Issues

Bush's planned January 2003 trip to Africa was postponed because of mounting tensions with Iraq. Bush, therefore, announced the intended centerpiece of his trip—his support for extending AGOA beyond its original sunset date of 2008—in Washington. With AGOA, U.S. imports from Africa had increased from $14 billion in 1999 to $21 billion in 2001, but subsequent growth had been limited by America's recession. These trade numbers were small compared to the $10 trillion U.S. economy, but represented important growth for some African countries. A major problem was that most of the surge came from only a handful of countries. The administration thus hoped to broaden trade by making African businesses more aware of the rules and opportunities. Broader trade still, though, was held back by U.S. agricultural subsidies and restrictions on certain products such as textiles.

Bush's trip to Africa was rescheduled for July 2003. The itinerary for the original trip included a visit Kenya, but al Qaeda attacks against Israeli tourists in Kenya prompted the State Department to recommend that Americans not travel there, and Kenya was not included in Bush's trip. Instead, Bush visited five countries that were all considered success stories—Senegal, Botswana, South Africa, Uganda, and Nigeria. Bush spoke several times during the course of the trip, but the speech that most significantly outlined his agenda, came before he left Washington (Speech 9.6). In that speech, Bush spoke optimistically about African prospects. He touched on many past themes, including the need to build democracy, increase counter-terrorism efforts, fight AIDS, provide aid to reformers, and promote trade.

What was novel about Bush's June 2003 speech was his focus on the problems of specific countries. He first discussed new efforts to end the complicated civil and international war in Congo. He chose not to mention that his administration had resisted UN calls to increase the number of peacekeepers in the country. The United States relented on that issue in July.

Next, Bush spoke of Liberia and clearly stated his view that "President Taylor needs to step down so that his country can be spared further bloodshed." Liberia is the one African country with deep historic ties to the United States. Its name reflects the fact that, beginning in the 1820s, it became a home for freed American slaves. The United States subsequently maintained close ties. In 1990, dictator Samuel Doe was overthrown, tortured, and killed, triggering an intermittent civil war that lasted for thirteen years. Charles Taylor came to power in 1997, but soon antagonized many of his countrymen with his brutal tactics and angered his regional neighbors by supporting rebellions in Sierra Leone, Guinea, and the Ivory Coast. A UN tribunal indicted him as a war criminal. By 2003, he had lost most international support and was facing attacks from two rebel groups. Many people in Liberia and elsewhere felt that the United States should take responsibility and intervene to bring stability. Bush's opposition to nation building and the extent to which Afghanistan and Iraq had already stretched U.S. forces made a massive intervention problematic. While in Africa, Bush spoke harshly about Taylor, but did not promise U.S. troops. In August, after Taylor had agreed to exile in Nigeria and an African peacekeeping force was ready, the United States deployed 200 Marines.

The third country specifically mentioned in Bush's June 2003 speech was Sudan. For over twenty years, Sudan's northern Muslim government had been fighting southern Christian and animist rebels who wanted more autonomy and a larger share of Sudan's oil revenue. Many American Christians and African-Americans became intensely interested in the war and advocated for humanitarian efforts in the south. More broadly, U.S. officials accused Sudan's government of numerous human rights violations and of supporting international terrorism. Efforts to pressure Sudan were somewhat complicated by the government's cooperation after 9/11; however, Bush signed legislation in 2002 that called for sanctions if the government did not take part in peace talks. Bush appointed former Senator John Danforth as Special Envoy for Peace in Sudan. Danforth and Powell were active in peace talks. At one point, peace seemed imminent and held the promise of being a major success for the Bush administration. Instead, government support for Arab militia groups terrorizing black Muslims in the region of Darfur near the Chad border complicated the talks and forced the international community to apply new pressure. As in Liberia, Bush chose to let African troops take the lead in peacekeeping efforts for Darfur.

Later in his speech, Bush mentioned one other country that had drawn particular administration focus. He urged "all nations, including the nations of Africa, to encourage a return to democracy in Zimbabwe." Robert Mugabe had ruled Zimbabwe since its creation in 1980, after years of white rule as the country of Rhodesia. Over time, Zimbabwe became increasingly less politically free with frequent intimidation of Mugabe's political opponents and members of the press. Mugabe also became increasingly strident in his criticism of Western pressure, which he described as an effort to recolonize the country. Many African states opposed Mugabe's political crackdowns and his plan to redistribute white-owned farms to blacks, but were hesitant to openly criticize him since they feared regional instability if he weakened and the appearance of siding with outsiders against a black leader. The Bush administration tried to encourage reform with promises of future aid increases. After violence and intimidation helped ensure Mugabe's 2002 reelection, Bush imposed travel and economic sanctions against Mugabe and his top supporters. Bush, Powell, and others encouraged South Africa and NEPAD states to take a harder stance against Zimbabwe. Despite these efforts, Mugabe remained in power and defiant.

Thus, the United States has not achieved all of its objectives in any of the four countries singled out by Bush. In something of a surprise, the failures stemmed not from Bush's lack of involvement, but rather from intransigent local realities.

Celebrating Africa's Success

In July 2004, Bush fulfilled his pledge on AGOA by signing legislation that extended its main provisions to 2015. At the signing ceremony, Bush noted the legislation's bipartisan support, mentioned the rapid increase in U.S.–African trade and lauded the progress of many African countries in implementing reforms. Four years earlier, only a few optimists would have predicted any of these positive developments. Before its passage in 2000, AGOA endured several legislative defeats and had to overcome intense lobbying by some textile and labor groups, and a widespread congressional view that Africa represented only problems and poverty. By 2004, promoting U.S. ties with Africa had become popular with both political parties and several interest groups, so the legislation extending AGOA moved quickly and easily through Congress. In 2003, African exports covered by the program totaled roughly $14 billion, a 55 percent increase over the previous year, and U.S. exports to Africa totaled almost $7 billion, a 15 percent increase. Trade growth came from reforms within Africa led by NEPAD countries increased business familiarity with AGOA rules, and greater stability in Africa that increased foreign investment in manufacturing. Although Bush did not state it directly, it was clear that Africa, not Latin America, was being touted as the administration's policy success story in the developing world.

9.1 Summit of the Americas

The Hilton Hotel
Quebec City, Canada
April 21, 2001

Amigo y amigos, it's an honor to be here.... My fellow Presidents and Prime Ministers and leaders of our hemisphere's thirty-four democracies, it is a great honor to be here.

We have a great vision before us, a fully democratic hemisphere bound together by goodwill and free trade. That's a tall order. It is a chance of a lifetime. It is a responsibility we all share....

[O]ur hemisphere, united by geography, has too often been separated by history of rivalry and resentment. But we have entered a new era. The interests of my nation, of all our nations, are served by strong, healthy democratic neighbors, and are served best by lasting friendships in our own neighborhood.

My country, more than ever, feels the ties of kinship, commerce and culture that unite us. And I'm proud to have the privilege so early in my administration to meet with all the leaders of this hemisphere's democratic countries.

Our task is to take the vital principles shaped at Miami and Santiago and translate them into actions that directly benefit the people we answer to. I'm here to offer my own ideas. I'm here to learn, and to listen from voices—to those inside this hall, and to those outside this hall who want to join us in constructive dialogue.

The single most important thing we will do here is to reaffirm that this summit is a gathering of, by, and for democracies, and only democracies. Today, freedom embraces the entire hemisphere, except for one country. And we look forward to the day when all this hemisphere's peoples will know the benefits and dignity of freedom. Jose Marti said it best: La libertad no es nogociable.

We also understand that democracy is a journey, not a destination. Each nation here, including the United States, must work to make freedom succeed. Elections are the foundation of democracy, but nations need to build on this foundation with other building blocks, such as a strong judiciary, freedom to speak and write as you wish, efficient banking and social services, quality schools, secure ownership of land, the ability to start and own a business. We must strengthen this architecture of democracy for the benefit of all our people.

This is the spirit behind the American Fellows exchange program that I announce here today. This program will sponsor one-year exchanges of outstanding civil servants among nations throughout the Americas. We'll also provide resources to help reform and modernize judicial institutions, protect basic human rights, root out corruption and other threats to the institutions that sustain freedom.

Our hemisphere support for democracy and freedom is principled, but it is also pragmatic. Freedom is not only a right, it is also our best weapon against tyranny and poverty. Some complain that despite our democratic gains, there is still too much poverty in equality. Some even say that things are getting worse, not better. For too many, this may be true. But the solution does not lie in statism or protectionism; the solution lies in more freedom.

And that is why we seek freedom not only for people living within our borders, but also for commerce moving across our borders. Free and open trade creates new jobs and new income. It lifts the lives of all our people, applying the power of markets to the needs of the poor. It spurs the process of economic and legal reform. And open trade reinforces the habit of liberty that sustains democracy over the long haul.

The United States will work for open trade at every opportunity. We will seek bilateral free trade agreements with friends and partners, such as the one we aim to complete this year with Chile. We will work for open trade globally through negotiations in the World Trade Organization. And here in the Americas, we will work hard to build an entire hemisphere that trades in freedom. . . .

Our commitment to open trade must be matched by a strong commitment to protecting our environment and improving labor standards. Yet, these concerns must not be an excuse for self-defeating protectionism. . . .

The time has come to extend the benefits of free trade to all our peoples and to achieve a free trade agreement for the entire hemisphere. Our challenge is to energize our negotiations on a free trade area for the Americas, so that they can be completed no later than the year 2005. . . .

Partnership in trade is fundamental to the hemisphere's well-being. But we know it is not, by itself, sufficient to guarantee the quality of life we seek for ourselves and for our children. Too many people in our hemisphere grow, sell and use illegal drugs. I want to make this clear: The United States is responsible to fight demand for drugs within our own borders. We have a serious obligation to do so. And we will expand our efforts, with meaningful resources, to work with producer and transit countries to fortify their democratic institutions, to promote sustainable development, and to fight the supply of drugs at the source.

This is a message I carried yesterday to the leaders of the Andean countries. The United States so appreciates the difficult challenge they face in fighting drugs, and stands ready to be a consistent and true partner. We're also committed to deepening our cooperation throughout the hemisphere in fighting the spread of HIV/AIDS, responding to natural disasters, and making sure the benefits of globalization are felt in even the smallest of economies. . . .

We're committed to protecting the hemisphere's natural resources. That's why I'm committed to using the Tropical Forest Conservation Act to help countries redirect debt repayments toward local projects that will protect biodiversity and tropical forests. . . .

We're committed to making education a centerpiece of our economic agenda, because learning and literacy are the foundations for development and democracy. The United States will sponsor the creation of hemispheric centers for teacher excellence. These centers will provide teacher training for improving literacy and basic education, both in person and over the Internet.

And finally, we will sponsor the creation of the new Latin E-business Fellowship program. This will give young professionals from throughout the Americans the opportunity to learn about information technology by spending time with United States companies. It will empower them with the skills and background to bring the benefits of these technologies to their own societies.

On the day I became President, I talked of liberty as a seed upon the wind, taking root in many nations. For over two decades, our hemisphere has been fertile ground for freedom. . . .Together, let us go forward to build an age of prosperity in a hemisphere of liberty. Together, let us use this Summit of the Americas to launch the century of the Americas.

9.2 U.S. Economic Ties with Africa

Department of State
Washington, DC
October 29, 2001

This conference was delayed by the events of September the 11th, but our common goal will not be delayed or denied. We have a unique opportunity to build ties of trade and trust that will improve the lives on both our continents. And we will seize this opportunity. . . .

Let me begin by thanking the nations of Africa for their support following September the 11th. America will never forget the many messages of sympathy and solidarity sent by African heads of state. . . .

Over eighty countries, including Ethiopia and Egypt, Ghana and Gambia, Kenya, Nigeria, South Africa, Togo and Zimbabwe, lost citizens along with the Americans on September the 11th. The United States is deeply grateful to all countries and all African countries that have now joined in a great coalition against terror.

We are grateful for the political support offered by the Organization of African Unity and by many African regional organizations. We appreciate the basing and overflight rights offered by African countries and the growing number of African nations that have committed to cracking down on terrorist financing. . . .

In an era of global trade and global terror, the futures of the developed world and the developing world are closely linked. We benefit from each other's success. We're not immune from each other's troubles. We share the same threats; and we share the same goal—to forge a future of more openness, trade and freedom.

Recent events have provided the world with a clear and dramatic choice. Our enemies, the terrorists and their supporters, offer a narrow and backward vision. They feed resentment, envy and hatred. They fear human creativity, choice and diversity. Powerless to build a better world, they seek to destroy a world that is passing them by. And they will not succeed.

We offer a better way. When nations respect the creativity and enterprise of their people, they find social and economic progress. When nations open their markets to the world, their people find new ways to create wealth. When nations accept the rules of the modern world, they discover the benefits of the modern world.

This vision of progress is not owned by any nation or any culture, it belongs to humanity—every African, every Muslim, every man or woman who wants to make it real. Good governments, of course, will look different from place to place. Cultures must preserve their unique values. Yet, everywhere—East and West, North and South—there is a model of successful development, a market economy trading with the world that respects human rights and the rule of law. Every nation that adopts this vision will find in America a trading partner, an investor, and a friend.

And it's for this reason that America welcomes and supports the new African initiative, put forward by visionary African leaders. To fulfill this vision of progress we must return to the steady, patient work of building a world that trades in freedom.

No nation in our time has entered the fast track of development without first opening up its economy to world markets. The African Growth and Opportunity Act is a road map for how the United States and Africa can tap the power of markets to improve the lives of our citizens.

This law is just over a year [old], but it is already showing its tremendous power. During the first half of this year, the total trade with sub-Sahara Africa rose nearly 17 percent, compared to last year. U.S. imports from the region now exceed $11.5 billion. Some individual countries have shown staggering increases in trade. Four countries—Senegal, Seychelles, Eritrea and Madagascar—saw their exports to the United States grow by over 100 percent.

Behind these numbers are investments in projects that are making a real impact on people's lives. In Kenya, the government projects that AGOA will create 150,000 new jobs over the next several years; propose new projects, in Lesotho, textiles sectors alone are expected to inject $122 million of investment into that country's economy—four times the amount of all official development assistance the country received in 1999.

We need to build on these successes. Across the continent, African governments are reforming their economies and their governments in order to take advantage of AGOA. These nations are working hard to fight corruption, improve labor standards and reform their customs regimes. The United States will work in partnership with African nations to help—to help them build the institutions and expertise they need to benefit from trade.

Today, I'm pleased to announce the creation of $200 million Overseas Private Investment Corporation support facility that will give American firms access to loans, guarantees and political risk insurance for investment projects in sub-Sahara Africa.

I've asked our trade and development agency to establish a regional office in Johannesburg, to provide guidance to governments and companies which seek to liberalize their trade laws, improve the investment environment and take advantage of the Free Trade Act between our two continents.

I'm also announcing today the launch of the Trade for African Development and Enterprise Program. With $15 million in initial funding, the trade program will establish regional hubs for global competitiveness that will help African businesses take advantage of AGOA, to sell more of their products on the global markets. . . .

Trade and sound economic policies are essential to growth and development, but they are not, themselves, sufficient to seize the hopeful opportunities of markets and trade. Nations need citizens that are educated and are healthy.

My government will continue its strong support for responsible debt relief, so that nations can devote more resources to education and health. We will continue to press multilateral development banks to provide more assistance in the form of grants, instead of loans. We are moving forward on an initiative I announced in July to improve basic education and teacher training in Africa. And the United States is ready to commit more resources to the new global fund to combat HIV-AIDS and other infectious diseases, once the fund demonstrates success.

And, finally, as AGOA makes clear, economic freedom and political freedom must go hand in hand. People who trade in freedom want to live in freedom. From Nigeria to South Africa, African nations have made great strides—great strides—toward democracy. The democratic transitions of the last decade mean that a majority of Africans now live in democratic states. That is progress we will praise, and progress we must work hard to continue. . . .

Out of the sorrow of September 11th, I see opportunity, a chance for nations to strengthen and rethink and reinvigorate their relationships. We share more than a common enemy; we share a common goal: to expand our ties of commerce and culture, to renew our commitment to development and democracy. And, together, we will meet that goal.

9.3 Millennium Challenge Accounts

Inter-American Development Bank
Washington, DC
March 14, 2002

I'm honored to be at the Inter-American Development Bank, which has done a lot of good in our hemisphere over the last forty years. . . .

I'm here today to announce a major new commitment by the United States to bring hope and opportunity to the world's poorest people. Along with significant new resources to fight world poverty, we will insist on the reforms necessary to make this a fight we can win. . . .

As you all know and we all know, America is engaged in a global struggle, a mighty struggle against the forces of terror. Yet, even as we fight to defeat terror, we must also fight for the values that make life worth living: for education, and health, and economic opportunity. This is both the history of our country and it is the calling of our times. . . .

The advances of free markets and trade and democracy and rule of law have brought prosperity to an ever-widening circle of people in this world. . . . Yet in many nations, in many regions, poverty is broad and seemingly inescapable, leaving a dark shadow across a world that is increasingly illuminated by opportunity. Half the world's people still live on less than $2 a day. For billions, especially in Africa and the Islamic world, poverty is spreading, and per capita income is falling. . . .

This growing divide between wealth and poverty, between opportunity and misery, is both a challenge to our compassion and a source of instability. We must confront it. We must include every African, every Asian, every Latin American, every Muslim, in an expanding circle of development.

The advance of development is a central commitment of American foreign policy. As a nation founded on the dignity and value of every life, America's heart breaks because of the suffering and senseless death we see in our world. We work for prosperity and opportunity because they're right. It's the right thing to do. We also work for prosperity and opportunity because they help defeat terror.

Poverty doesn't cause terrorism. Being poor doesn't make you a murderer. Most of the plotters of September 11th were raised in comfort. Yet persistent poverty and oppression can lead to hopelessness and despair.

And when governments fail to meet the most basic needs of their people, these failed states can become havens for terror.

In Afghanistan, persistent poverty and war and chaos created conditions that allowed a terrorist regime to seize power. And in many other states around the world, poverty prevents governments from controlling their borders, policing their territory, and enforcing their laws. Development provides the resources to build hope and prosperity, and security.

Development is not always easy, but the conditions required for sound development are clear. The foundation of development is security, because there can be no development in an atmosphere of chaos and violence. Today, the United States is leading a broad and vast coalition defending global security by defeating global terror. Meeting this commitment is expensive, but securing peace and freedom is never too expensive.

Development also depends upon financing. Contrary to the popular belief, most funds for development do not come from international aid—they come from domestic capital, from foreign investment, and especially from trade. America buys and imports over $450 billion in products from the developing world every year—$450 billion of purchases every single year. That is more than eight times the amount developing countries receive in aid from all sources. Trade is the engine of development. And by promoting it, we will help meet the needs of the world's poor.

Successful development also requires citizens who are literate, who are healthy, and prepared and able to work. Development assistance can help poor nations meet these education and health care needs. That's why the United States provides more than $10 billion a year for development assistance for food and for humanitarian aid. That is also why my administration has committed $500 million to the global fund to fight aids and other infectious diseases. . . .

Yet many of the old models of economic development assistance are outdated. Money that is not accompanied by legal and economic reform are oftentimes wasted. In many poor nations, corruption runs deep. Private property is unprotected. Markets are closed. Monetary and fiscal policies are unsustainable. Private contracts are unenforceable.

When nations refuse to enact sound policies, progress against poverty is nearly impossible. In these situations, more aid money can actually be counterproductive, because it subsidizes bad policies, delays reform, and crowds out private investment.

The needs of the developing world demand a new approach. . . . To make progress, we must encourage nations and leaders to walk the hard road of political, legal and economic reform, so all their people can benefit.

Today, I call for a new compact for global development, defined by new accountability for both rich and poor nations alike. Greater contributions from developed nations must be linked to greater responsibility from developing nations. The United States will lead by example. We will increase our development assistance by $5 billion over the next three budget cycles. This new money is above and beyond existing aid requests in the current budget I submitted to the Congress.

These funds will go into a new Millennium Challenge Account. Under this account, among other efforts, we will expand our fight against AIDS; we will bring computer instruction to young professionals in developing nations; we will assist African businesses and their people to sell goods abroad; we will provide textbooks and training to students in Islamic and African countries; we will apply the power of science and technology to increase harvests where hunger is greatest.

These are some of the examples of what we intend to do. The goal is to provide people in developing nations the tools they need to seize the opportunities of the global economy. In return for this additional commitment, we expect nations to adopt the reforms and policies that make development effective and lasting.

The world's help must encourage developing countries to make the right choices for their own people, and these choices are plain. Good government is an essential condition of development. So the Millennium Challenge Account will reward nations that root out corruption, respect human rights, and adhere to the rule of law. Healthy and educated citizens are the agents of development, so we will reward nations that invest in better health care, better schools and broader immunization.

Sound economic policies unleash the enterprise and creativity necessary for development. So we will reward nations that have more open markets and sustainable budget policies, nations where people can start and operate a small business without running the gauntlets of bureaucracy and bribery.

I've directed Secretary Powell and Secretary O'Neill to reach out to the world community, to develop a set of clear and concrete and objective criteria for measuring progress. And under the Millennium Challenge Account, we will apply these criteria rigorously and fairly.

Countries that live by these three broad standards—ruling justly, investing in their people, and encouraging economic freedom—will receive more aid from America. And, more importantly, over time, they will really no longer need it, because nations with sound laws and policies will attract more foreign investment. They will earn more trade revenues. And they will find that all these sources of capital will be invested more effectively and productively to create more jobs for their people.

The evidence shows that where nations adopt sound policies, a dollar of foreign aid attracts $2 of private investment. And when development aid rewards reform and responsibility, it lifts almost four times as many people out of poverty, compared to the old approach of writing checks without regard to results. . . .

The new compact I propose would multiply this progress. I challenge other nations, and the development banks, to adopt this approach as well. America's support for the World Bank will increase by almost 20 percent over the next three years. We expect the World Bank to insist on reform and results, measured in improvements in people's lives. All the development banks should adopt a growth agenda, increasing their support for private sector enterprises and focusing more on education, as the Inter-American Development Bank has done.

And I challenge the development banks to provide up to half of the funds devoted to poor nations in the form of grants, rather than loans. Grants instead of loans that may never be repaid. Many have rallied to the idea of dropping the debt. I say let's rally to the idea of stopping the debt.

This new compact for development can produce dramatic gains against poverty and suffering in the world. I have an ambitious goal for the developed world, that we ought to double the size of the world's poorest economies within a decade. I know some may say that's too high a hurdle to cross—I don't believe so, not with the right reforms and the right policy. This will require tripling of current growth rates, but that's not unprecedented. After all, look at the dramatic growth that occurred in Asia in the 1990s.

With the world's help and the right policies, I know—I know—that the developing world can reform their own countries. I know it can happen. And, therefore, better their own lives. . . .

I carry this commitment in my soul. And I'll carry it with me to Monterrey next week. As the civilized world mobilizes against the forces of terror, we must also embrace the forces of good. By offering hope where there is none, by relieving suffering and hunger where there is too much, we will make the world not only safer, but better.

9.4 A Vision of Africa

Marriott Wardman Park Hotel
Washington, DC
June 20, 2002

The free people of America have a duty to advance the cause of freedom in Africa. American interests and American morality lead in the same direction: We will work in partnership with African nations and leaders for an African continent that lives in liberty and grows in prosperity. . . .

I'm really grateful, though, that the Secretary of State and Treasury are here. See, it was last May that Secretary Powell became the first member of my Cabinet to travel to Africa. And this May, Secretary O'Neill was the latest member of my Cabinet to travel to Africa. He and Bono were quickly dubbed "The Odd Couple." But they soon found out that the rock star could hold his own in debates on real growth rates and that the Secretary of Treasury is second to none in compassion. I knew that the trip had had an effect on our Secretary when he showed up in the Oval Office wearing blue sunglasses.

Here's what we believe. Africa is a continent where promise and progress are important. And we recognize they sit alongside disease, war and desperate poverty—sometimes even in the same village. Africa is a place where a few nations are havens for terrorism, and where many more—many more—are reaching to claim their democratic future. Africa is a place of great beauty and resources, and a place of great opportunity. So tonight I announce that in order to continue to build America's partnership with Africa, I'll be going to the continent next year. . . .

I look forward to the trip, I really do. It's going to be a great trip. And I look forward to focusing on the challenges that we must face together. Everyone in this room is joined by a common vision of an Africa where people are healthy and people are literate. A vision that builds prosperity through trade and markets. A vision free from the horrors of war and terror. America will not build this new Africa, Africans will. But we will stand with the African countries that are putting in place the policies for success through important new efforts such as the Millennium Challenge Fund. And we will take Africa's side in confronting the obstacles to hope and development on the African continent.

One of the greatest obstacles to Africa's development is HIV/AIDS, which clouds the future of entire nations. The world must do more to fight the spread of this disease, and must do more to treat and care for those it afflicts. And this country will lead the effort.

My administration plans to dedicate an additional $500 million to prevent mother-to-child transmission of HIV. And as we do so, we will work to improve health care delivery in Africa and in the Caribbean. This will allow us to treat one million women annually and to reduce the mother-to-child transmission by 40 percent within five years or less in the countries we target: . . .

We will pursue proven and effective medical strategies that we know will make a difference. . . . We will make a major commitment to improve health care delivery systems in these countries. . . . And as we see what works, as we're confident that our money will be well spent and results will matter, we will make more funding available. . . .

It's important for you to know that this funding will complement the nearly $1 billion we already contribute to international efforts to combat HIV/AIDS; the money will complement the $2.5 billion we plan to spend on research and development of new drugs and treatments; and it will complement the $500 million we've committed to the Global Fund to fight AIDS and other infectious disease.

Lack of education is the second great barrier to progress in Africa. Tonight I announce that my administration plans to double—to $200 million over five years—the funding devoted to an initiative I put forward last year to improve basic education and teacher training in Africa.

Here's what we believe we can achieve. With that money we will train more than 420,000 teachers; provide more than 250,000 scholarships for African girls; and partner with historically black colleges and universities in America to provide 4.5 million more textbooks for children in Africa. As we do so, we'll make sure the school system is more open and more transparent, so African moms and dads can demand needed reform.

Education is the foundation of development and democracy—in every culture, on every continent. And we'll work to give Africa's children the advantages of literacy and learning so they can build Africa's future.

The third great obstacle to Africa's development is the trade barriers in rich nations—and in Africa, itself—that impede the sale of Africa's products.

The African Growth and Opportunity Act is a tremendous success. My administration strongly supports efforts in Congress to enhance AGOA. And to encourage more U.S. companies to see Africa's opportunities firsthand. . . . We will continue to explore a regional free trade agreement with the Southern African Customs Union.

Africa also stands to gain even greater benefits from trade if and when we lower trade barriers worldwide.... Expanding global trade in products and technologies and ideals is a defining characteristic of our age—capable of lifting whole nations out of the cycle of dependency and want. In this country we will work to ensure that all Africa—all of Africa is fully part of the world trading system and fully part of the progress of our times. It is important for my fellow citizens to know we will build trade with Africa because it is good for America's prosperity; trade is good for building prosperity in Africa, and it is good for building the momentum of economic and political liberty across that important continent.

And, finally, for Africans to realize their dream of a more hopeful and prosperous future, Africa must be free from war and free from terror. Many African nations are making real contributions to the global war on terror.... I've asked Congress this year to provide an additional $55 million in funds to help African nations on the front lines of our mutual war to defend freedom.

The United States is committed to helping African nations put an end to regional wars that take tens of thousands of lives each week. We will help African nations organize and develop their ability to respond to crises in places such as Burundi. We'll work closely with responsible leaders and our allies in Europe to support regional peace initiatives in places such as the Congo. And we will also continue our search for peace in Sudan. My policy towards Sudan seeks to end Sudan's sponsorship of terror and to promote human rights and the foundations of a just peace within Sudan itself. My envoy for peace in Sudan, former Senator John Danforth, has made progress toward a cease-fire and improved delivery of humanitarian aid to such places as the Nuba Mountain region of Sudan.

Since September the 11th, there's no question the government of Sudan has made some useful contributions in cracking down on terror. But Sudan can and must do more. And Sudan's government must understand that ending its sponsorship of terror outside Sudan is no substitute for efforts to stop war inside Sudan. Sudan's government cannot continue to talk peace but make war, must not continue to block and manipulate UN food deliveries, and must not allow slavery to persist.

America stands united with responsible African governments across the continent—and we will not permit the forces of aggression and chaos to take away our common future. We jointly fight for our liberty; we chase down cold-blooded killers one at a time, and we do so for the common good of all people.

9.5 Fighting Global HIV/AIDS

The Eisenhower Executive Office Building
Washington, DC
January 31, 2003

This is an historic year for America. It's a year of great consequence. It's a year in which we have an opportunity to work with others to shape the future of our globe. We have a chance to achieve peace. We have a chance to achieve a more compassionate world for every citizen. America believes deeply that everybody has worth, everybody matters, everybody was created by the Almighty, and we're going to act on that belief and we'll act on that passion. . . .

As I said in my State of the Union, freedom is not America's gift to the world, freedom is God's gift to humanity. Freedom means freedom from a lot of things. And today, on Africa, in the continent of Africa, freedom means freedom from the fear of a deadly pandemic. That's what we think in America. And we're going to act on that belief. The founding belief in human dignity should be how we conduct ourselves around the world—and will be how we conduct ourselves around the world.

I want you all to remember, and our fellow citizens to remember, that this is nothing new for our country. Human dignity has been a part of our history for a long time. We fed the hungry after World War I. This country carried out the Marshall Plan and the Berlin Airlift. Today we provide 60 percent—over 60 percent of all the international food aid. We're acting on our compassion. It's nothing new for our country.

But there's a pandemic which we must address now, before it is too late. And that's why I took this message to our fellow citizens, that now is the time for this country to step up our efforts to save lives. After all, on the continent of Africa, 30 million people have the AIDS virus—30 million people. Three million children under the age of 15 have the AIDS virus. More than 4 million people require immediate drug treatment. Yet, just about 1 percent of people receive drug treatment. It is a significant world problem that the United States of America can do something about. We can be involved. . . .

So many people are dying. But the graves are unmarked. The pandemic is creating such havoc that there are mass burials, that there are wards of children that are dying because of AIDS. Not a ward, not some wards, but wards after wards full of dying children because of AIDS. That there are millions of orphans, lonely children, because their mom or dad has died—children left, in some cases, to fend for themselves.

Because the AIDS diagnosis is considered a death sentence, many folks don't seek treatment, and that's a reality. It's as if the AIDS pandemic just continues to feed upon itself over and over and over again, because of hopelessness. This country needs to provide some hope—because this disease can be prevented and it can be treated, that's important for our fellow citizens to know. Anti-retroviral drugs are now dramatically more affordable in many nations, and these drugs are used to extend the lives of those with HIV. In other words, these drugs are really affordable. . . . And when the treatment has come to Africa, it is also important for our citizens to understand the effect of that treatment. It's called the Lazarus effect. When one patient is rescued by medicine, as if back from the dead, many others with AIDS seek testing and treatment, because it is the first sign of hope they have ever seen.

We have the opportunity to bring that hope to millions. It's an opportunity for this nation to affect millions and millions of lives. So that's why I've laid out the Emergency Plan for AIDS Relief. I called it in my State of the Union a work of mercy, and that's what I believe it is.

With the approval of Congress, we will devote $15 billion to the fight AIDS abroad over the next five years, beginning with $2 billion in the year 2004. I've been asked whether or not we're committed to the Global AIDS Fund. Well, first of all, I wouldn't put [Secretary of Health and Human Services] Tommy [Thompson] as the head of it if we weren't. And more importantly, he wouldn't have joined if we weren't.

And so we're still committed to the Global AIDS Fund to fight disease. This program in no way diminishes our commitment to the fund. We will continue bilateral AIDS programs in more than 50 countries. . . .

But this plan that I've laid out in front of the Congress and will work with members of the Senate and the House on will dramatically focus our efforts. You notice I didn't say, "focus our efforts," I said, "dramatically focus our efforts." And that's important for the American people to understand, because we want to bring a comprehensive system. It's more than money that we bring, we bring expertise and compassion and love and the desire to develop a comprehensive system, work with people in Africa to do so, for diagnosis and treatment and prevention.

We are determined to turn the tide against AIDS. And we're going to start in fourteen African and Caribbean countries, where the disease is most heavily concentrated. We whip it in those fifteen—or fourteen—we will show what is possible in other countries. . . .

The model has been applied with great success in Uganda. Anybody who knows the issue of AIDS on the African continent appreciates the efforts of Uganda. And we feel like that it can be duplicated. And that's the mission, the goal. Even though we're on fourteen countries initially with this major focus, we understand there's suffering elsewhere, and we want to expand beyond. We want to encourage others to join us, as well.

The funding will initially go toward expanding existing hospitals, and of course, drawing on the knowledge and the expertise of local physicians. That makes sense. You've got a doc in place; we want to encourage that doc to be able to continue his or her healing. We'll build satellite facilities that can serve more people. Of course, we'll provide antiretroviral drugs, and as well, work with folks on the ground for education and care.

It's important for our citizens to know that the infrastructure is—it's hard for many Americans to imagine the lack of infrastructure that we're working with on the continent of Africa. So we use motorcycles, trucks, bicycles. We use nurses and local healers to go to the farthest villages and farms to test for the disease and to deliver medications that will save lives. It doesn't matter how the medications get there; what matters is they do get there.

The facilities across Africa and the Caribbean will have now the medicine.... We're going to work with other governments, of course, private groups, there's all kinds of faith-based programs involved on the continent of Africa, and we welcome that, of course. And we encourage that. And we thank you for that....

And here's what the experts believe that will be accomplished, the Emergency Plan for AIDS Relief. In this decade, we will prevent 7 million new infections. They will treat at least 2 million people with life-extending drugs. We'll provide humane care, of course, for those who suffer and, as importantly, for the orphans.

To me, that's just the beginning. But it's a pretty good start. Most important thing is we're providing hope, which is immeasurable.... This project is urgent, and as we move forward on this program we will continue to call upon other nations to join. The United States doesn't mind leading and we believe others have a responsibility as well, that we're not the only blessed nation. There are many blessed nations. And we hope they join us....

I'm a person who believes that there's no obstacle put in our path that we can't overcome, I truly believe that. I love what our country stands for. I love the strength of America. The strength of America really is the—lies in the hearts and souls of our fellow citizens.... Today's initiative is one—it's a step toward showing the world the great compassion of a great country.

9.6 Agenda for U.S.–African Relations

Washington Hilton Hotel
Washington, DC
June 26, 2003

All of us here today share some basic beliefs. We believe that growth and prosperity in Africa will contribute to the growth and prosperity of the world. We believe that human suffering in Africa creates moral responsibilities for people everywhere. We believe that this can be a decade of unprecedented advancement for freedom and hope and healing and peace across the African continent. That's what we believe.

In eleven days I leave for Africa, and I will carry a message. And I will carry this message: The United States believes in the great potential of Africa. We also understand the problems of Africa. And this nation is fully engaged in a broad, concerted effort to help Africans find peace, to fight disease, to build prosperity, and to improve their own lives. . . .

Botswana is a stable democracy; was one of the strongest economies of all of Africa. And I look forward to my trip. I'll go to Senegal and see West Africa's longest-standing democracy. A country with a vibrant civil society and a growing independent media. I look forward to going to South Africa, where I'll meet with elected leaders who are firmly committed to economic reforms in a nation that has become a major force for regional peace and stability. I'm looking forward to my trip to Uganda—where the government's visionary policies have brought about the most dramatic decline in the rate of HIV infection of any country in the world. And finally, I'll be going to Nigeria—a multiethnic society that is consolidating civilian rule, is developing its vast resources, and is helping its African neighbors keep the peace.

My trip should signal that I am optimistic about the future of the continent of Africa. After all, there's a generation of leaders who now understand the power of economic liberty and the necessity for global commerce. I also understand that freedom and prosperity are not achieved overnight. Yet the forty-eight nations of Sub-Saharan Africa have an historic opportunity to grow in trade, and to grow in freedom and stability, and most importantly, to grow in hope.

On the path to freedom, and with the friendship of the United States and other nations, Africa will rise, and Africa will prosper.

This is a long-term commitment. And I know there are serious obstacles to overcome. Introducing democracy is hard in any society. It's much harder in a society torn by war, or held back by corruption. The promise of free markets means little when millions are illiterate and hungry, or dying from a preventable disease. It is Africans who will overcome these problems. Yet the United States of America and other nations will stand beside them. We will work as partners in advancing the security and the health and the prosperity of the African peoples.

The first great goal in our partnership with Africa is to help establish peace and security across the continent. Many thousands of African men and women and children are killed every year in regional wars. These wars are often encouraged by regimes that give weapons and refuge to rebel groups fighting in neighboring countries. The cycle of attack and escalation is reckless, it is destructive, and it must be ended.

In Congo, nine countries took part in a five-year war that brought death to millions. Now the parties to the conflict are moving to form a government of national unity, holding out the real possibility of peace. President Mbeki of South Africa deserves credit for his efforts to broker a peace agreement. All the Congo's neighbors have officially withdrawn their forces. Now I urge these governments to actively support the creation of an integrated national army and the establishment by June 30th of a transitional government. The United States is working with the Congo and its neighbors to ensure the security and integrity of their borders. To encourage progress across all of Africa, we must build peace at the heart of Africa.

In Liberia, the United States strongly supports the cease-fire signed earlier this month. President Taylor needs to step down—so that his country can be spared further bloodshed. All the parties in Liberia must pursue a comprehensive peace agreement. And the United States is working with regional governments to support those negotiations and to map out a secure transition to elections. We are determined to help the people of Liberia find the path to peace.

The United States is also pressing forward to help end Africa's longest-running civil war in Sudan, which has claimed an estimated 2 million lives over twenty years. Progress over this past year, aided by the leadership of Kenya, has brought us to the edge of peace. Now the north and south must finalize a just and comprehensive peace agreement, and the world must support it. I've asked my Special Envoy for Peace in Sudan, former Senator John Danforth, to return to the region in two weeks. He will make clear that the only option on the table is peace. Both sides must now make their final commitment to peace and human rights, and end the suffering of Sudan.

The United States supports efforts by African governments to build effective peacekeeping forces. America is providing resources and logistical support to African Union peacekeeping forces in Burundi, and ECOWAS forces in the Ivory Coast. During my visit to South Africa, U.S. military forces will participate in a joint humanitarian and disaster relief training exercise with South African defense forces. Skilled and well-equipped peacekeeping forces are essential, because in the long run, Africans will keep the peace in Africa.

The United States is also working with African nations to fight terrorists wherever they are found. . . . Today I announced that the United States will devote $100 million over the next fifteen months to help countries in the region increase their own counter-terror efforts. . . . Many African governments have the will to fight the war on terror, and we are thankful for that will. We will give them the tool and the resources to win the war on terror.

The second great goal of our partnership with Africa is to make the advantages of health and literacy widely available across the continent. And that work begins with the struggle against AIDS, which already affects nearly 30 million Africans. . . .

The health of Africa also depends on the defeat of hunger. Forty million Africans are now at risk of starvation. They face severe food shortages, or lack of clean drinking water. This year the United States will provide more than $800 million to address food emergencies in Africa. I've also asked Congress to provide $200 million new dollars for a Famine Fund, so that when the first signs of famine appear we can move quickly and save lives.

Yet the problem of hunger requires more than emergency measures. To help Africa become more self-sufficient in the production of food, I have proposed the initiative to end hunger in Africa. This initiative will help African countries to use new high-yield bio-tech crops and unleash the power of markets to dramatically increase agricultural productivity. But there's a problem. At present, some governments [in Europe] are blocking the import of crops grown with biotechnology, which discourages African countries from producing and exporting these crops. The ban of these countries is unfounded; it is unscientific; it is undermining the agricultural future of Africa. And I urge them to stop this ban. . . .

Africa's progress also depends on the education of Africa's children. Forty-two million boys and girls across Sub-Sahara Africa are not even enrolled in schools. If Africa is to meet its full potential, these children must have the chance to study and learn. . . .

The third great goal of our partnership with Africa is to help African nations develop vibrant, free economies through aid and trade. Wealthy nations have a responsibility to provide foreign aid. We have an equal duty to make sure that aid is effective, by rewarding countries that embrace reform and freedom.... Corrupt regimes that give nothing to their people deserve nothing from us. Governments that serve their people deserve our help, and we will provide that help.

Many African leaders are currently pledged to the path of political and economic reform. That shared commitment is expressed in the standards of NEPAD, the New Partnership for Africa's Development. Yet those standards are mocked by some on the continent, such as the leader of Zimbabwe, where the freedom and dignity of the nation is under assault. I urge all nations, including the nations of Africa, to encourage a return to democracy in Zimbabwe.

We can add to the prosperity of Africa through development assistance that encourages your reform. Yet aid alone is not enough.... The powerful combination of trade and open markets is history's proven method to defeat poverty on a large scale, to vastly improve health and education, to build a modern infrastructure while safeguarding the environment, and to spread the habits of liberty and enterprise that lead to self government.

Trade is the great engine of economic progress, the great engine of human progress. Yet Sub-Sahara Africa, with 11 percent of world's population, has less than 2 percent of the world's trade. The peoples of Africa have been left out long enough. The United States is committed to making the transforming power of trade available to all Africans....

We must build on AGOA's success. Today, I call on the United States Congress to extend AGOA beyond 2008. We must extend AGOA beyond 2008 to give businesses the confidence to make long-term investments in Africa. At America's urging, the World Bank will provide more than $200 million over the next three years to support loans to small businesses in ten African countries. These loans will give African entrepreneurs the capital they need to achieve their dreams.

Here's what we believe in America—and it's true elsewhere: Ownership and independence are the hopes of men and women in every land.

To expand commerce between America and Africa, we're working towards a free trade agreement with the Southern African Customs Union. And in the global trade negotiations, we are pushing to open agricultural markets, reduce farm subsidies in wealthy nations, and to create new opportunities for African farmers.

I also urge African nations to lower their own trade barriers against each other's products. Just as America can do more to open its markets, so can the nations of Africa. Together we can ensure that all our citizens have access to the opportunities of markets around the globe.

The measures I've outlined today—actions on security, and health, education, hunger, foreign aid, and global trade—constitute a major focus of American foreign policy. America is committed to the success of Africa because we recognize a moral duty to bring hope where there is despair, and relief where there's suffering. America is committed to the success of Africa because we understand failed states spread instability and terror that threatens us all. America is committed to the success of Africa because the peoples of Africa have every right to live in freedom and dignity, and to share in the progress of our times.

The responsibilities we have accepted in Africa are consistent with the ideals that have always guided America and the world. Our nation has more than a set of interests; I believe we have a calling. For a century, America has acted to defend the peace, to liberate the oppressed, and to offer all mankind the promise of freedom in a better life. And today, as America fights the latest enemies of freedom, we will strive to expand the realm of freedom for the benefit of all nations.

Questions to Discuss

1. In Speech 9.1, Bush suggests that countries in the Western hemisphere should listen to each other's concerns and cooperate on trade and other issues to benefit everyone. Is it possible for the United States to develop such egalitarian and cooperative relations with countries that are so much weaker in economic and military strength?

2. In Speech 9.3, Bush argues that, in the future, U.S. aid should go to countries that are "ruling justly, investing in their people, and encouraging economic freedom." Do such conditions risk leaving the world's poorest countries behind and widening the gap between the world's richest and poorest nations?

3. In Speech 9.4, Bush argues that the United States should take the lead in assisting African countries struggling with the AIDS epidemic. Is such assistance in the U.S. national interests? Should some humanitarian action be taken even if there are no direct benefits to the United States?

4. In a number of speeches, Bush argues that countries that adopt democracy and free trade policies are making the choice to succeed and join the "modern world." Does this imply that there is only one path to development? How much must countries pattern their policies on those of the United States to succeed?

5. Bush argues that, while aid is important, only trade will lead to long-term economic development. Is the United States hypocritical in promoting trade, while maintaining policies that protect American farmers, textile workers, and so on?

Notes

Notes to Chapter One

1. James Traub, "The Bush Years; W's World," *New York Times Magazine*, January 14, 2001.
2. These and many other quotations are available at http:// politicalhumor.about.comlibrary/blbushisms.htm.
3. Quoted in Elaine Sciolino, "Bush's Foreign Policy Tutor: An Academic in the Public Eye," *New York Times*, June 16, 2000.
4. Quoted in Eric Schmitt, "A Cadre of Familiar Foreign Policy Experts Is Putting Its Imprint on Bush," *New York Times*, December 23, 1999.
5. George W. Bush, *A Charge to Keep* (New York: William Morrow, 1999); Donald F. Kettl, *Team Bush* (New York: McGraw-Hill, 2003); and David Frum, *The Right Man: The Surprise Presidency of George W. Bush* (New York: Random House, 2003).
6. Richard Brookhiser, "The Mind of George W. Bush," *Atlantic Monthly* 291, no. 3 (April 2003): 55–66.
7. Quoted in Bob Woodward, *Bush at War* (New York: Simon & Schuster, 2002), 137.
8. Quoted in Eric Schmitt, "Bush Opposes G.O.P. Bill on Kosovo," *New York Times*, May 17, 2000.
9. Quoted in Frank Bruni and Eric Schmitt, "Bush Rehearsing for a World Stage," *New York Times*, November 19, 1999.
10. Quoted in William Safire, "Bush's Foreign Policy," *New York Times*, April 19, 1999.
11. Ivo H. Daalder and James M. Lindsay, *America Unbound: The Bush Revolution in Foreign Policy* (Washington, DC: Brookings Institution Press, 2003), 15.
12. Quoted in Katharine Q. Seelye, "Gore Faults Bush on Foreign Policy," *New York Times*, April 30, 2000.
13. Condoleezza Rice, "Promoting the National Interest," *Foreign Affairs* 79 (Jan/Feb 2000): 47.
14. Ibid, 48.
15. Quoted in Steven Mufson, "A World View of His Own; On Foreign Policy, Bush Parts Ways with Father," *Washington Post*, August 11, 2000.
16. "Interview with George W. Bush," *ABC's This Week*, January 23, 2000.

17. Quoted in John Lancaster, "In Saddam's Future, A Harder U.S. Line; Bush, Gore Depart from Clinton Policy," *Washington Post*, June 3, 2000.
18. Quoted in "2nd Presidential Debate Between Gov. Bush and Vice President Gore," *New York Times*, October 12, 2000.
19. Quoted in Eric Schmitt, "When 'I'm No. 2' Becomes Something to Cheer About," *New York Times*, December 31, 2000.
20. Quoted in Alison Mitchell, "Powell to Head State Dept. as Bush's First Cabinet Pick," *New York Times*, December 17, 2000.
21. Quoted in Elaine Sciolino, "Bush's Foreign Policy Tutor."
22. Paul Wolfowitz, "Remembering the Future," *National Interest*, no. 59 (Spring 2000): 39.

Notes to Chapter Two

1. Quoted in Woodward, *Bush at War*, 15.
2. "Statement by the President in His Address to the Nation," September 11, 2001, available at www.whitehouse.gov/news/releases/2001/09/20010911-16.html.
3. Quoted in Bernard Lewis, "License to Kill: Usama bin Ladin's Declaration of Jihad," *Foreign Affairs*, 77 (Nov/Dec 1998): 15.
4. Quoted in Bill Scammon, *Fighting Back: The War on Terrorism From Inside the White House* (Washington, DC: Regnery Press, 2002), 107.
5. Quoted in Todd S. Purdum, "Bush Warns of Wrathful, Shadowy and Inventive War," *New York Times*, September 17, 2001.
6. Scammon, *Fighting Back*, 335.
7. Woodward, *Bush at War*, 81.
8. Ibid., 281.

Notes to Chapter Three

1. Quoted in Woodward, *Bush at War*, 99.
2. Woodward, *Bush at War*, 83–5.
3. Quoted in Glenn Kessler, "U.S. Decision on Iraq Has Puzzling Past," *Washington Post*, January 12, 2003.
4. Woodward, *Plan of Attack* (New York: Simon & Schuster, 2004), 52–66.
5. Quoted in Woodward, *Plan of Attack*, 150
6. Richard Cheney, "Vice President Speaks at VFW 103rd National Convention," August 26, 2002, available at www.whitehouse.gov/news/releases/ 2002/08/print/20020826.html.
7. George W. Bush, "Remarks at John Cornyn for Senate Reception," September 26, 2002, available at www.whitehouse.gov/news/releases/2002/09/ 20020926-17.html

8. Michael T. Klare, "For Oil and Empire? Rethinking the War with Iraq," *Current History*, (March 2003): 132–35.
9. Cheney, "Vice President Speaks at VFW."
10. George W. Bush, "State of the Union," January 28, 2003, available at www.whitehouse.gov/news/releases/2003/01/20030128-19.html.
11. Quoted in Daalder and Lindsay, *America Unbound*, 164.
12. Ibid, 151.
13. Quoted in Scott Wilson, "Bremer Adopts Firmer Tone for U.S. Occupation of Iraq," *Washington Post*, May 26, 2003.
14. "President Bush Names Randall Tobias to be Global AIDS Coordinator," July 3, 2003, available at www.whitehouse.gov/news/releases/2003/07/20030702-3.html.
15. Zogby International and Gallup Polls discussed in Patrick Clawson; "How Iraqis View U.S. Role Is Key to Evaluating Progress in Iraq," *Policywatch*, no. 787, September 29, 2003.
16. Quoted in Daalder and Lindsay, *America Unbound* 162.
17. Quoted in Woodward, *Plan of Attack*, 249
18. Quoted in Philip Shenon and Christopher Marquis, "Panel Finds No Qaeda-Iraq Tie; Describes a Wider Plot for 9/11," *New York Times*, June 17, 2004.
19. Quoted in David E. Sanger and Robin Toner, "Bush and Cheney Talk Strongly of Qaeda Links with Hussein," *New York Times*, June 18, 2004.
20. Quoted in Glenn Kessler, "Rice: Iraqi Nuclear Plans Unclear," *Washington Post*, October 4, 2004.
21. Quoted in David E. Sanger, "A Doctrine Under Pressure: Pre-emption Is Redefined," *New York Times*, October 11, 2004.
22. Quoted in Woodward, *Plan of Attack*, 424.

Notes to Chapter Four

1. Eliot Cohen, "A Tale of Two Secretaries," *Foreign Affairs*, 81 (May/June 2002), 33.
2. *National Security Strategy of the United States of America*, available at www.whitehouse.gov/nsc/nssall.html.
3. James Dao, "Plan to Stop Missile Threat Could Cost $238 Billion," *New York Times*, February 1, 2002.
4. Quoted in Ted Plafker, "China, Joins Russia in Warning U.S. on Shield; Missile Defense Plan Assailed at Meeting," *Washington Post*, July 19, 2000.
5. Quoted in Amy Goldstein and Alan Sipress, "ABM Withdrawal Likely, but Not Set, Bush Says," *Washington Post*, August 24, 2001.
6. *National Security Strategy of the United States of America*.
7. "Fact Sheet: Proliferation Security Initiative," available at www.whitehouse.gov/news/releases/2003/09/print/20030904-11.html.
8. Quoted in Woodward, *Bush at War*, 340.

9. Quoted in Christopher Marquis, "Absent From the Korea Talks: Bush's Hard-Liner," *New York Times*, September 2, 2003.
10. Quoted in David E. Sanger, "Bush Warns Iran on Building Nuclear Arms," *New York Times*, June 19, 2003.
11. Quoted in Glenn Kessler and Robin Wright, "U.S., Allies Agree on Iran Move; Nuclear Steps Deplored; U.N. Could Get Involved," *Washington Post*, November 25, 2003.
12. Flynt Leverett, "Why Libya Gave Up on the Bomb," *New York Times*, January 23, 2004.

Notes to Chapter Five

1. "Text of a Letter from the President to Senators Hagel, Helms, Craig, and Roberts," March 13, 2001, available at www.whitehouse.gov/news/releases/2001/03/20010314.html.
2. Quoted in David E. Sanger, "Leaving for Europe, Bush Draws on Hard Lessons of Diplomacy," *New York Times*, May 22, 2002.
3. Margo Thorning, *A U.S. Perspective on the Economic Impact of Climate Change Policy*, American Council for Capital Formation's Center for Policy Research Special Report, December 2000.
4. Global Climate Coalition, "The Impacts of the Kyoto Protocol," available at www.globalclimate.org/kyotoimpacts.pdf.
5. Clive Crook, "Bush Broke His Promise on Global Warming," *National Journal*, March 2, 2002.
6. Bill Clinton, "The Right Action," *New York Times*, January 1, 2001.
7. George W. Bush, "President Salutes Troops of the 10th Mountain Division," July19, 2002, available at www.whitehouse.gov/news/releases/2002/07/20020719.html.
8. John R. Bolton, "The United State and the International Criminal Court," remarks to the Federalist Society, November 14, 2002, available at www.state.gov/t/us/rm/15158.htm.
9. Ibid.
10. Letter quoted and discussed in Elizabeth Becker, "U.S. Issues Warning to Europeans in Dispute Over New Court," *New York Times*, August 26, 2002.
11. Quoted in Felicity Barringer, "U.S. Resolution on World Court Revives Hostility," *New York Times*, June 11, 2003.
12. Quoted in Warren Hoge, "U.S. Drops Plan to Exempt G.I.'s from U.N. Court," *New York Times*, June 24, 2004.
13. Quoted in "Remarks by the President at the 2003 'Congress of Tomorrow' Republican Retreat Reception," February 9, 2003, available at www.whitehouse.gov/news/releases/2003/02/print/20030209-1.html.
14. Quoted in Richard W. Stevenson, "Bush Sees Aid Role of U.N. as Limited in Rebuilding Iraq," *New York Times*, April 9, 2003.

15. Quoted in Steven R. Weisman and Felicity Barringer, "U.S. Abandons Idea of Bigger U.N. Role in Iraq Occupation," *New York Times*, August 14, 2003.

Notes to Chapter Six

1. Robert Kagan, "Power and Weakness," *Policy Review*, 113 (Jun/Jul 2002), 3.
2. Quoted in Frank Bruni, "Pushing His Missile Plan in Spain, Bush Calls Arms Treaty a 'Relic'," *New York Times*, June 13, 2001.
3. Quoted in Steven Erlanger, "Europe Seethes as the U.S. Flies Solo in World Affairs," *New York Times*, February 23, 2002.
4. Quoted in David E. Sanger, "In Reichstag, Bush Condemns Terror as New Despotism," *New York Times*, May 24, 2002.
5. Quoted in Robert G. Kaiser, "NATO Ready to Admit 7 Eastern Bloc Countries; Three Ex-Soviet States Part of Historic Move," *Washington Post*, September 26, 2002.
6. Quoted in Karen DeYoung and Keith B. Richburg, "NATO Approves New Direction; Enlarged Alliance to Reorganize Forces; Leaders Endorse Statement on Iraq," *Washington Post*, November 22, 2002.
7. Quoted in Steven R Weisman, "U.S. Set to Demand that Allies Agree Iraq Is Defying U.N.," *New York Times*, January 23, 2003.
8. Quoted in Steven Erlanger, "German Leader's Warning: War Plan Is a Huge Mistake," *New York Times*, September 5, 2002.
9. Quoted in "Against America? Moi?" *Economist*, March 15, 2003, 47.
10. Quoted in "Memo to Bush: Europe Is Listening," *Washington Post*, May 28, 2003.
11. Quoted in Elisabeth Bumiller, "Amid Protests, Bush Sees Thaw in Europe Over Iraq," *New York Times*, June 27, 2004.
12. Quoted in Eric Schmitt and Susan Sachs, "NATO Agrees to Help Train Iraqi Forces," *New York Times*, June 29, 2004.
13. Quoted in Jane Perlez, "Cordial Rivals: How Bush and Putin Became Friends," *New York Times*, June 18, 2001.
14. Quoted in David E. Sanger, "Leaving for Europe, Bush Draws on Hard Lessons of Diplomacy," *New York Times*, May 22, 2002.
15. Quoted in Patrick E. Tyler, "Pulling Russia Closer," *New York Times*, May 14, 2002.

Notes to Chapter Seven

1. Quoted in Bonnie S. Glaser, "First Contact; Qian Qichen Engages in Wide-ranging, Constructive Talks with President Bush and Senior U.S. Officials," *Comparative Connections*, 1st Quarter 2001: U.S.-China Relations, available at www.csis.org/pacfor/cc/0101qus_china.html.

308   *Notes to pages 212 to 244*

2. Quoted in David E. Sanger and Steven Lee Myers, "Delicate Diplomatic Dance Ends Bush's First Crisis," *New York Times*, April 12, 2001.
3. Quoted in David E. Sanger, "U.S. Would Defend Taiwan, Bush Says," *New York Times*, April 26, 2001.
4. Quoted in Bonnie S. Glaser, "Face to Face in Shanghai: New Amity amid Perennial Differences," *Comparative Connections*, 4th Quarter 2001: U.S.-China Relations, available at www.csis.org/pacfor/cc/0104qus_china.html.
5. Robert Sutter, "Bush Administration Policy Toward Beijing and Taipei," *Journal of Contemporary China*, 12 (August 2003): 491.
6. Quoted in Bonnie S. Glaser, "The Best Since 1972 or the Best Ever?" *Comparative Connections*, 3rd Quarter 2003: U.S.-China Relations, available at www.csis.org/pacfor/cc/0303qus_china.html.
7. "President Bush and Premier Wen Jiabao Remarks to the Press," December 9, 2003, available at www.whitehouse.gov/news/releases/2003/12/20031209-2.html.
8. Quoted in Howard W. French, "Top Bush Aide Urges Japan to Form In-Depth Ties With U.S.," *New York Times*, May 9, 2001.
9. Quoted in Brad Glosserman, "Koizumi Steals the Spotlight," *Comparative Connections*, 2nd Quarter 2001: U.S. Japan Relations, available at www.csis.org/ pacfor/cc/0102qus_japan.html.
10. Elisabeth Bumiller, "On Asian Trip, a Few Stumbles," *New York Times*, February 25, 2002.
11. Quoted in Brad Glosserman, "How High is Up?" *Comparative Connections*, 1st Quarter 2003: U.S. Japan Relations, available at www.csis.org/pacfor/cc/0301qus_japan.html

Notes to Chapter Eight

1. Quoted in Alison Mitchell, "Bush Says Clinton Misstepped in Israel," *New York Times*, May 23, 2000.
2. Quoted in Jane Perlez and Katherine Q. Seelye, "U.S. Strongly Rebukes Sharon for Criticism of Bush, Calling it 'Unacceptable'," *New York Times*, October 6, 2001.
3. Quoted in David E. Sanger, "Israeli Offensive Is 'Not Helpful,' President Warns," *New York Times*, March 14, 2002.
4. Robert Satloff, "Subtle Backtracking: Assessing the Quartet's New York Statement," *Policywatch*, no. 636, July 17, 2002.
5. Robert Satloff, "The Bush Speech Vs. The Powell Mission: Assessing Washington's Twin and Competing Middle East Policies," *Policywatch*, no. 616, April 15, 2002.
6. Quoted in "President Bush Welcomes Prime Minister Abbas to White House," July 25, 2003, available at www.whitehouse.gov/news/releases/2003/07/ 20030725-6.html.

7. Quoted in Robert Satloff, "Powell on Democracy in the Muslim World: Assessing the Latest Exposition of U.S. Policy," *Policywatch*, no. 692, December 17, 2002.

Notes to Chapter 9

1. "Presidents Bush, Fox Discuss State Visit," September 6, 2001, available at www.whitehouse.gov/news/releases/2001/09/20010906-6.html.
2. Jorge G. Castaneda, "The Forgotten Relationship," *Foreign Affairs*, 82 (May/June 2003): 70.
3. Quoted in Christopher Marquis, "U.S. Hasn't Kept Promise to Latin America, Critics Say," *New York Times*, May 19, 2002.
4. Quoted in "End of an Affair?" *Economist*, November 9, 2002, 38.
5. "HR 4775: 2002 Supplemental Appropriations Act for Further Recovery From and Response to Terrorist Attacks on the United States."
6. "Newsmaker: George W. Bush," February 16, 2000, available at www.pbs.org/newshour/bb/election/jan-june00/bush_2-16.html.
7. Walter Kansteiner and Jendayi Frazer, "Bush Administration Africa Policy: The First Six Months and Looking Ahead," July 3, 2001, available at http://fpc.state.gov/fpc/7506.htm.

Index

Abbas, Mahmoud, 243–244
Abu Ghraib prison, 105
Achille Lauro, 91
Additional Protocol, 142
Afghanistan, 3, 70, 85, 180
    bin Laden and, 71
    Northern Alliance, 45–46, 123, 190
    post-war rebuilding, 94, 96, 170, 288
    Soviet invasion of, 20, 190
    Taliban and war on terrorism, 39, 43–46, 51, 56, 59, 98, 110
Africa
    African Renaissance, 270
    AIDS crisis, 271–272, 275–277
    anti-terrorism efforts, 299
    Bush and, 270–275
    debt relief and agricultural subsidies, 285
    hunger and starvation crisis, 299
    other issues, 277–279
    successes of, 278–280
    U.S.-African relations, 269–270
Africa Action Plan, 275
African Growth and Opportunity Act (AGOA), 270–271, 274, 277, 279, 285–286, 292, 300
AIDS crisis, 271–272, 274–277, 283, 286, 292
    Global AIDS Fund, 295
    relief efforts, 15, 157, 171
    Uganda's ABC approach, 276, 296
Airport security, 62
Al-Aqsa, 250
Al Qaeda, 39–41, 51, 70, 74, 180, 251, 273
    financial networks of, 44
    Iraq and, 80, 83–84, 91–92, 102
    nuclear weapons, 118, 129
    War on terrorism and, 44–47, 94, 96–98
Al-Sistani, Grand Ayatollah Ali, 81, 160
Allawi, Iyad, 82
Alliances, 15, 17, 144

American Fellows program, 35
American ideals, 22, 26
American internationalism, 9, 11, 27–28
American Servicemembers' Protection Act, 154
Andean Trade Preference Act, 269
Angola, 273
Annan, Kofi, 81, 155–156, 160, 272
Anthrax, 70, 91, 129
Anti-Ballistic Missile System (ABM) Treaty, 24, 32, 112–115, 119, 130, 133–137, 179, 189, 191, 200, 214
Anticommunism, 13
Arab Human Development Report 2002, 247
Arafat, Yasir, 236–242, 244, 249
Argentina, 36, 267
Armitage, Richard, 218
Arms control; *see* Weapons of mass destruction (WMD)
Asia-Pacific Economic Cooperation (APEC) summit, 214, 222
Asian powers; *see* China; Japan
Atlantic Alliance, 203
Australia, 29, 95, 232
Axis of Evil, 46–48, 70, 117, 120–125, 157, 181, 193
Ayatollah Khomeini, 123

Baath Party, 67, 78
Bahrain, 261
Baker, Howard, 221
Baker, James, 105
Balkans, 19, 178–179, 196
Ballistic missile technology, 63; *see also* Anti-Ballistic Missile System (ABM) Treaty
Barak, Ehud, 237–238
Belgium, 185
Bin Laden, Osama, 39–40, 46–47, 51, 71, 83; *see also* Al Qaeda
Bioterrorism, 62
Blair, Tony, 72, 185

311

Index

Bolivia, 36
Bolton, John R., 122, 153
Border security, 62
Bosnia, 23, 60, 153
Botswana, 277
Brahimi, Lakhdar, 103, 160
Brazil, 36, 267, 269
Bremer, L. Paul, 78, 81
Buchanan, Patrick, 11
Bulgaria, 184, 204
Burma, 259
Bush, George H. W., 5–8, 13, 18–21, 67, 74, 112, 145, 209
Bush, George W.
   2000 presidential campaign, 4–6
   decision-making style of, 6–8
   foreign policy issue, 4–6
   foreign policy priorities, 8–10
   principled provincialism of, 4
   African policy, 270–271, 274, 278–289
   assertive nationalism of, 11, 14–17
   challenging enemies, 16–17
   harbor resources, 15–16
   tools of American power, 14–15
   unilateral action, 17
   China and, 212–213
   European relations, 179
   evangelical faith of, 7, 41
   foreign policy team of, 18–21
   Japan and, 218–219
   Kyoto Protocol, 146, 148
   Latin America and, 266–267
   leadership style of, 8
   Middle East and, 235–240, 256–257
   military strategy and, 110
   nuclear counterproliferation strategy, 118–120
   personal feelings on terrorism, 41
   personality of, 6–7
   post-September 11th foreign policy, 3
   presidential authority of, 7
   Russia and, 188–190, 193–194
   security issues and, 108–124, 113
   style of, 7–8
   unilateral actions of, 145
   United Nations and, 156–157
   world view compared, 14–18

Bush Doctrine of global antiterrorism, 42

Camp David Accords, 236
Canada, 34
Car bombings, 22
Caribbean, 36
Carnegie Endowment for International Peace, 178
Carter, Jimmy, 20, 236
Castro, Fidel, 266
Central America; see Latin America
Central Intelligence Agency (CIA), 40, 46, 71, 82–83
Chalabi, Ahmed, 68
Chechnya, 10, 16, 189, 191, 194
Chemical and biological weapons, 24–25, 59, 64, 68, 73, 87, 91, 204
Chen Shui-bian, 216
Cheney, Richard, 18, 20, 38, 41, 67, 70, 72–74
Chile, 34, 36, 65, 269, 282
China, 9–10, 12, 14–15, 22, 62, 114, 135, 167
   Bush and, 212–213
   as competitor, 28–29
   cooperative relationship, 214–217
   economic relationship with, 211
   human rights abuses, 209–210
   ongoing tensions with, 210–212
   post-September 11th, 43, 213–214
   Taiwan and, 210
   and terrorism, 222–223
   as threat, 16–17
   U.S.-China relationship, 210–217
Chirac, Jacques, 186, 188, 193
Churchill, Winston, 195
Clarke, Richard A., 69
Clinton, Bill, 7–9, 12–15, 19, 41, 93, 109, 112–114, 121
Clinton administration, 19, 21
   Africa and, 270
   AIDS crisis, 271–272
   China and, 209, 211
   European relations, 178
   international criminal court, 151–152
   Iran and, 123
   Japan and, 218

Clinton administration *(continued)*
    Kyoto Protocol, 145–146
    Latin America and, 34
    nuclear arms policy, 32, 118
Clinton Parameters, 237–238
Cold War era, 8, 10, 138, 197
    doctrines of deterrence, 3, 10, 48, 64
    European relations during, 177
    NATO and, 182
    post-era peace dividend, 15, 108
    two war strategy, 108
Colombia, 10, 36, 154, 268–269
Colonialism, 265
Communist threat, 42, 48
Compassionate conservatism, 273
Complementarity principle, 151
Comprehensive Test Ban Treaty, 11, 30, 119
Congo, 278, 298
Containment, 3, 10, 48, 64
Cooperative Threat Reduction (CTR) program, 117, 119, 141
Cuba, 10, 35, 259, 266–267
Cultural condescension, 260
Cyber terrorism, 22
Czech Republic, 182

Danforth, John, 278, 293, 298
De Mello, Sergio Viera, 160
"Declaration of the World Islamic Front for Jihad against the Jews and the Crusaders" (bin Laden), 39
Defense Counterproliferation Initiative, 118
Defense Department, 111
    Office of Reconstruction and Humanitarian Assistance, 78
Defense spending, 9, 14, 23, 109–111, 114, 131
Democracy, 14
    global expansion of, 175, 260
    in Iraq, 102–106
    in Latin America, 35, 265, 281–282
    in Middle East, 245–248
Deng Xiaoping, 209, 211, 226
Denmark, 185
Department of Energy, 83

Deterrence, 3, 10, 48, 64, 112, 134
Development assistance, 288
Dictatorships, 260–261
Dirty bomb, 70
Doctrines, 42
Doe, Samuel, 278
Drug cartels/trade, 22, 36, 39

Earth Summit, 145
Ebadi, Shirin, 261
Economic sanctions, 150
Egypt, 52, 236, 247, 254, 262
Emergency response, 62
Emissions credits, 148
Energy resources, 164, 166
Environmental issues, 15; *see also* Global warming; Kyoto Protocol
Eritrea, 285
Estonia, 184, 204
Ethnic cleansing, 16
Europe, 177–188
    Iraqi war and, 184–188
    NATO expansion/transformation, 182–184
    old vs. new Europe, 185–186
    pre-September 11th relations, 178–180
    September 11th attacks and, 180–182
European Union (EU), 36, 154, 163, 177–178, 196
Evil empire, 22, 26; *see also* Axis of evil
Executive Order 13224, 44

Federal Bureau of Investigation (FBI), 53, 64
Financial networks, 44
Ford administration, 18, 20–21
Foreign policy, 27
    assertive nationalism, 11–12
    isolationism, 9, 11–12
    liberal internationalists, 11–12
    neoconservative (necon) movement, 12–14
    traditional internationalism, 12–13
    world views compared, 12
Fox, Vicente, 266
France, 68, 75–77, 158, 184–187, 213

Franks, Tommy, 70, 95, 200
Free trade, 11, 29
Free Trade Act, 286
Free Trade Area of the Americas (FTAA), 34, 266
Freedom, 22, 26, 52–53, 95–96, 259, 282
Freedom House, 247
Frist, Bill, 271

Gabon, 273
Garner, Jay M., 78
Genocide, 16
Germany, 127, 185–87
Gerson, Michael, 46
Ghadafi, Colonel, 125, 140
Global Fund to Fight AIDS, Tuberculosis, and Malaria, 272, 295
Global Hawk, 130
Global issues, 144–160
    global warming and Kyoto Protocol, 145–150
    international criminal court, 150–155
    United Nations, 155–160
Global poverty, 15, 275, 299
Global warming, 145–150, 178, 270
    issues of, 149–150
Gore, Al, 4–6, 9–12, 14–15
Great Britain, 34, 50, 77–78, 95, 100, 105, 173–174
"Greater Middle East Initiative," 247
Greece, 258
Greenhouse gas emissions, 16, 145, 149, 161–163, 166
Guantanamo Bay detention center, 59
Guinea, 273, 278
Gulf War, 13, 18–19, 21, 28, 31, 39, 47, 67–68, 74, 77, 86–88, 90, 112, 128
Guyana, 275

Haiti, 16, 275
Hamas, 60, 239, 244–245, 250–251
Hamilton, Alexander, 27
Havel, Vaclav, 26, 258
Heavily Indebted Poor Countries (HIPC), 275
Hezbollah, 60, 239, 250–251

Homeland defense, 24, 64, 114
Homeland Security, 44, 53, 62, 129
Hu Jintao, 216
Human dignity, 22, 26, 62
Human rights, 150, 170, 209–210, 214
Human rights violations, 11–12, 86
Humanitarian crises, 12, 172
Humanitarian missions, 16, 45, 108, 288, 294
Hungary, 182

Inazo Nitobe, 231
India, 62, 117, 127, 167
Individual dignity, 22, 26, 62
Indonesia, 260
Intelligence, 62, 130
Intelligence agencies, 24, 40–41, 44, 53, 64
Inter-American Development Bank, 290
Inter-American Institute for Global Change Research, 163
International Atomic Energy Association (IAEA), 117, 120, 123–124, 139–140, 142, 157
International coalition, 71
    War on terrorism, 43–44
International criminal court (ICC), 145, 150–155
    Bush administration and, 152–155
    Clinton administration and, 151–152
    complementarity principle, 151
International Criminal Tribunal for Yugoslavia, 151
International Monetary Fund (IMF), 31, 105, 144, 268
Internationalism, 9, 11, 27–28
Intifada, 236, 238–239, 243
Iran, 21, 24, 46–47, 60, 70, 78, 113, 157, 210
    as security issue, 117, 123–124
    weapons of mass destruction and, 139
Iraq, 3, 8, 16, 19, 21–22, 24, 40, 45–47, 60, 67–84
    case for war, 71–75
    challenges and shifting plans, 79–82

Iraq *(continued)*
   European response to war, 184–188
   final steps to war, 75–77
   Gulf War, 21, 31, 39, 67–68, 74, 77, 86
   impact of September 11th, 69–71
   insurgent violence, 79–81, 99
   interim Iraqi government, 81
   justifications for war, 82–84
   national elections, 81–82, 101, 106
   oil as motive, 74–75
   postwar assumptions, 78
   as security issue, 117
   strategy objectives, 100, 170
   UN weapons inspections, 68, 138
   U.S. relations with, 67
   war and aftermath, 77–79
Iraqi National Congress, 68
Iron curtain, 195
Islamic fundamentalism, 39, 51, 79
Islamic Jihad, 51, 60, 250
Islamic Movement of Uzbekistan, 51
Isolationism, 9, 11, 31, 144
Israel, 15, 28, 40, 48, 52, 58, 117, 235–236, 240, 250–251, 254, 257
Italy, 185
Ivory Coast, 278

Jackson-Vanik amendment, 191, 193
Jaish-i-Mohammed, 60
Japan, 15, 29, 65, 127, 163
   anti-terrorism efforts, 219–220, 231
   Bush administration and, 218–219
   Clinton administration, 218
   closer ties to, 220–221
   post-September 11th, 219–220
   U.S.-Japan relations, 217–221
Jiang Zemin, 213–215, 222, 225
Jihad, 40
Jordan, 52, 236, 254, 261

Kagan, Robert, 178
Karzai, President, 262
Kenya embassy bombing (1998), 39, 41, 51, 273
Kerry, John, 74
Khan, A. Q., 119–120, 125, 139–140

Khatami, Mohammad, 123
Khordorkovsky, Mikhail, 194
Kim Dae Jung, 121
Kim Il Sung, 120
Kim Jon II, 121
Koizumi Junichiro, 219–221, 229
Korean War, 209
Kosovo, 14, 23, 180, 183, 192
Kuomintang, 209
Kurds, 68, 79
Kuwait, 19, 67, 86–87, 134, 261
Kyoto Protocol, 11, 16, 145–150, 157, 161–162, 167–168, 179, 270

Latin America, 10, 15, 265–269
   Bush and, 34–36, 266–267
   post-September 11th, 267–269
   as trading partner, 268
Latin E-business Fellowship program, 283
Latvia, 184
League of Arab States, 247
League of Nations, 155, 160, 173–174
Lebanon, 236, 250
Lee Teng-hui, 5
Less developed countries (LDCs), Kyoto Protocol and, 146–147
Liberal internationalism, 11, 16
Liberia, 278, 298
Libya, 117, 119, 139–140, 210
   as security issue, 124–125
Lithuania, 184
Lugar, Richard, 30

McCain, John, 14
Madagascar, 285
Madrid train bombing, 81
Mandela, Nelson, 26, 258
Mao Zedong, 209
Marshall Plan, 126, 294
Marti, Jose, 281
Mbeki, Thabo, 272, 298
Mercosur, 36
Mexico, 10, 34–35, 266–267
Middle East, 28, 58, 175
   Bush and peace process, 235–240
   new U.S. initiatives, 240–242
   peace and reform, 235–248

Middle East *(continued)*
    post-September 11th attacks, 239
    promoting democracy, 245–248
    "Quartet" communiqué, 241, 243, 256
    roadmap for peace, 242–244
    unilateral disengagement, 244–245
    U.S. goals in, 235
Middle East Partnership Initiative, 246
Military, 22–23, 26
    defense spending, 9, 14, 23, 109–111, 114, 131
    defining missions, 23–23
    foreign-based troops, 111
    national missile defense, 112–116
    precision-guided munitions, 128
    Predator drones, 110, 128
    preparing for 21st century, 108–111
    Quadrennial Defense Review (QDR), 109–110
    transformational goals of, 110
    use of, 16
Missile defense systems, 9, 16, 22, 30, 32, 64, 179, 189; *see also* National missile defense (NMD)
Mitchell, George, 239
Mitchell Plan, 239, 250–251, 254
Modernization, 262
Monroe Doctrine, 265
Moral hazard problem, 268
Mori Yoshiro, 218–219
Most Favored Nation (MFN) trade status, 209
Mugabe, Robert, 279
Multilateral institutions, 17, 144–145; *see also* United Nations
Multilateralism, 12, 17, 187
Mushaaraf, Pervez, 43, 60, 140
Mutual Assured Destruction (MAD), 112, 114
Mutual Security Assistance Pact, 217

NAFTA, 34, 36, 266
Nation building, 13, 16, 159
National Academy of Sciences (NAS), 147, 161–162
National Climate Change Technology Initiative, 163
National Endowment for Democracy, 258
National Intelligence Estimate (NIE), 73
National interest, 28
National missile defense (NMD), 112–116
    Bush's speech on, 133–137
    critics of, 114
National security, 3–4, 29, 62; *see also* Security issues
    nuclear deterrence and, 32
NATO, 15–16, 20, 31, 34, 45, 53, 65, 115, 126, 154, 174, 177, 180, 188, 196
    expansion and transformation, 179, 182–184, 200–202
    Historic NATO Summit, 203–205
    Russia and, 191–192
Neoconservative (necon) movement, 13–14, 16, 21
New Partnership for African Development (NEPAD), 273, 275, 300
Nigeria, 273, 277
Nixon, Richard, 18, 20, 209, 224
No-fly zones, 68
North Atlantic Treaty Organization (NATO); *see* NATO
North Korea, 22, 24, 78, 111, 259
    Axis of Evil, 46–47, 70
    Japan and, 221
    nuclear program of, 60, 112, 118, 157, 227
    as security issue, 16, 21, 117, 120–122, 139, 216
Northern Alliance, 45–46, 123, 190
Nuclear arms, Bush's policy, 32–33
Nuclear Non-Proliferation Treaty (NPT), 117, 121–122, 124, 141
Nuclear Suppliers Group, 142
Nuclear terrorism, 24
Nuclear weapons, 10, 16, 29–30, 47, 64; *see also* Weapons of mass destruction (WMD)
    Iran and, 123–124
    Moscow Treaty, 192
    North Korea and, 121–122

Nuclear weapons *(continued)*
    nuclear proliferation, 116–120, 129, 134, 141
    Russia and, 191–192
Nunn, Sam, 30
Nunn-Lugar program (Cooperative Threat Reduction), 30, 117, 119, 141
Nuremberg tribunals, 151

Obasanjo, Olesegun, 272
Oil exports, 235, 273
Oil-for-food program, 68, 159
Oil industry, 75
Oman, 261
O'Neill, Paul, 44, 268, 289, 291
Organization of American States (OAS), 35, 266
Organization of the Petroleum Exporting Countries (OPEC), 273
Organization for the Prohibition of Chemical Weapons, 140
Oslo Accords (1993), 237
Overseas Private Investment Corporation, 285

Pakistan, 43, 46, 60, 117, 119, 127, 139–140, 210
Palestine Liberation Organization (PLO), 236; *see also* Arafat Yasir
Palestinian Authority (PA), 237, 249–250, 255; *see also* Middle East
Pan Am flight 103 bombing, 125
Pastrana, Andres, 36
Patriot Act, 44
Patriot defense system, 112
Patten, Christopher, 181
Peace dividend, 15, 108
Peacekeeping operations, 108, 153, 157
Pearl Harbor attack, 3, 126, 206
Perle, Richard, 8, 14
Permanent normal trade relations (PNTR), 191, 193, 211
Persian Gulf War, 13, 18–19, 21, 28, 31, 39, 47, 67–68, 74, 77, 86–88, 90, 112, 128
Peru, 36
Philippines, 15, 29, 60, 232

Poland, 95, 100, 182, 185, 187, 206–207
Policy drift, 9
Political freedom, 26
Population control programs, 270
Portugal, 185, 258
Powell, Colin, 19, 121, 147, 154, 158, 164, 179, 186, 270, 278–279, 289, 291
    on China, 212, 216
    European diplomacy, 179, 186
    International Criminal Court (ICC), 154
    Iraqi war, 67–68, 71–72, 75–76, 100–101, 158
    Korea diplomacy, 121
    Kyoto protocol, 147, 164
    Middle East peace process, 238–239. 241, 246
    war on terrorism, 38, 43
Powell Doctrine, 19
Pre-September 11th speeches, 22–36
    Century of the Americas, 34–36
    Distinctly American Internationalism, A, 26–31
    Future Nuclear Arms Policy, 32–33
    Period of Consequences, A, 22–26
Predator drones, 110, 128
Preemption strategy, 48–49, 74, 82, 118, 181
Presidential authority, 7
Presidential campaign (2000), foreign policy and, 4–6
Proliferation Security Initiative (PSI), 119–120, 125, 140–141, 171, 207
Prosper, Pierre-Richard, 153
Putin, Vladimir, 43, 115–116, 123, 136–137, 189–192, 194, 197, 203; *see also* Russia

Qatar, 261
Quadrennial Defense Review (QDR), 109–110

Reagan, Ronald, 6–9, 13, 18, 26–27, 29, 112–113, 131, 156, 258, 260, 276
Revolutionary Forces of Colombia (FARC), 268–269
Reza Shah Pahlevi (Shah of Iran), 123

Rice, Condoleezza, 5–6, 12–13, 16, 20, 83–84, 159, 188, 191, 270
Rogue nations, 10, 16–17, 29–30, 32, 97, 116
Romania, 184, 204
Rome Statute of 1998, 151, 154
Roosevelt, Franklin, 22
Rumsfeld, Donald, 20–21, 38, 45, 68, 70, 77, 95, 108–112, 134, 158, 185
Rumsfeld Commission, 21
Russia, 9–10, 20, 22, 28, 158, 213
    Bush administration and, 188–190
    current relationship with, 127, 193–194
    Europe and, 196
    foreign policy, 29–31
    Kyoto Protocol, 148, 150
    missile defense, 24, 115–116, 135–136
    NATO and, 191–192
    nuclear weapons, 32–33, 117, 120, 129, 133
    security relationship changes, 191–193
    September 11th attacks and, 62, 76, 190–191
    as threat, 16
Russian school attack, 194
Rwanda, 151

Sadat, Anwar, 236
Saddam Hussein, 17, 21, 47, 67–69, 71–76, 79–80, 83–84, 86–88, 90–92, 94, 99, 102, 134, 169
Saleem, Izzedin, 102
Saudi Arabia, 39–40, 52, 246–247, 262
Saudi Arabia military barracks bombing (1996), 39
Schröder, Gerhard, 186–187, 193, 201
Security issues, 108–125
    ABM Treaty, 136–137
    axis of evil, 120–125
    Iran, 123–124
    Libya, 124–125
    military of 21st century, 108–111
    National Missile Defense, 112–116, 133–135
    North Korea, 120–122
    nuclear proliferation, 116–120
    Russia and, 191–193

Security threats, 14
Senegal, 272, 277, 285
September 11th terrorist attacks;
    see also War on terrorism
    Bush's response to, 38, 42, 50–55
    China and, 213–214
    as defining event, 3, 61
    European relations and, 180–182
    foreign policy and, 3
    Iraq policy and, 69–71, 96
    Japan and, 219–220
    Latin America and, 267–269
    military strategy and, 109
    missile defense debate and, 115, 136
    Russia and, 190–191
Sex trade, 172
Seychelles, 285
Sharon, Ariel, 238, 243–245
Shi'a Islam, 47
Shiites, 68, 79, 82
Sierra Leone, 278
Slovakia, 184, 203
Slovenia, 184
Somalia, 13, 60, 270
South Africa, 272, 277, 298
South Korea, 15, 29, 65, 258
Soviet Union, 108, 136, 177
Spain, 81, 119, 185, 258
Special Operations Forces, 24
START I/ START II, 30, 32, 192
State sovereignty, 73–74, 151
State sponsored terrorism, 46, 127, 129
Strategic Defense Initiative ("Star Wars"), 112, 114
Strategic Offensive Reductions Treaty (Moscow Treaty), 192
Sudan, 41, 44, 278, 293, 298–299
Sunni Arabs, 79
Sunni Islam, 47
Sununu, John, 7
Syria, 44, 46, 78, 236, 239, 250–51

Taiwan, 16–17, 114, 209–210, 213–217, 258

Taiwan Relations Act (TRA), 210
Taliban, 39, 43, 45–47, 51–52, 56–57, 94, 96, 128, 190; *see also* Afghanistan
Tanzania embassy bombing (1998), 39, 41, 51, 273
Taylor, Charles, 278, 298
Team B, 21
Technology
    terrorism and, 24, 64
    war technology, 25
Tenet, George, 40, 83, 239, 251
Terrorism, 9, 16, 26, 222
    defined, 38
    Iraq's links to, 73, 77, 91
    Madrid bombing, 81
    technology and, 24, 64
Terrorist cells, 45, 92
Terrorist groups, 10, 32, 60, 79, 215
Terrorist training camps, 51–52, 59–60
Texas Air National Guard, 4
Thailand, 29, 232
Thierse, Wolfgang, 182
Thompson, Tommy, 295
Tiananmen Square tragedy, 209
Trade for African Development and Enterprise Program, 271, 286
Trade embargoes, 150
Traditional internationalism, 13, 19
Tropical Forest Conservation Act, 168
Truman, Harry S., 27, 42
Truman Doctrine, 42
Turkey, 40, 185, 260

Uganda, 276–277, 296
UNICEF, 170
Unilateral action, 17, 71, 75, 144, 158, 179, 181
Unilateral disengagement, 244–245
United Nations, 13, 17, 45, 85, 144
    Bush administration and, 156–160
    Bush's General Assembly speech, 43, 55–58, 85–89
    Commission on Human Rights, 86, 210
    economic sanctions, 68–69
    Education, Scientific and Cultural Organization (UNESCO), 156–157
    Framework Convention on Climate Change (UNFCC), 145, 166
    global issues of, 155–160
    Human Rights Commission, 156
    humanitarian missions of, 57
    Iraq and UN resolutions, 72
    multilateral forces, 80
    peacekeeping missions, 108, 153, 157
    Population Fund, 157
    role of, 31, 157–58, 160
    Security Council Resolutions
    Resolution 242, 236, 250, 257
    Resolution 338, 236, 250, 257
    Resolution 687, 68, 86
    Resolution 688, 86
    Resolution 1373, 44, 57, 86
    Resolution 1441, 75–76, 158
    Universal Declaration of Human Rights of 1948, 150
    weapons inspections, 47, 61, 68, 75–76, 93
U.S. Agency for International Development, 168
U.S. Climate Change Research Initiative, 163
USS Abraham Lincoln, 77, 95
USS Cole bombing (2000), 39, 43, 51

Venezuela, 267
Vulcans, 6–7, 18, 21

Wade, Addoulaye, 272
Walesa, Lech, 26, 258
War on terrorism, 3, 38–49
    Axis of Evil, 46–47
    Bush Doctrine of global antiterrorism, 42
    Bush's personal feelings, 41
    challenging al Qaeda, 44–46
    costs of, 61–62
    historical perspective on, 38–42
    international coalition, 43–44
    Iraq policy and, 70, 96–97
    key ideas of, 39
    new strategy for new war, 48–49
    preemption strategy, 48–49
    rallying the country, 41–42
Warsaw Pact, 203
Washington, George, 27, 144

Weapons of mass destruction (WMD), 8, 10, 17, 22, 28, 32
  Iraq and, 70, 72–74, 76, 80, 82–84, 91, 93
  Libya disarmament and, 124–125
  missile defense, 113
  nuclear proliferation, 116–120, 129, 136, 141
  UN inspections, 47, 61, 68, 75–76, 83, 87–88
  War on terrorism and, 46–48, 61
Wen Jiaboa, 216, 227–228
Westernization, 262
Wilson, Woodrow, 173
Wolfowitz, Paul, 5, 14, 21, 45, 68–69
World Bank, 31, 105, 144, 232, 253, 290, 300
World Food Program, 170
World Health Organization (WHO), 276
World Trade Center 1993 bombing, 39, 41
World Trade Organization (WTO), 29, 105, 150, 188, 191, 202, 211, 222, 226, 282

Yemen, 43, 118, 239, 261

Zhou Enlai, 224
Zimbabwe, 259, 279
Zinni, Anthony C., 239, 249

About the Author

John W. Dietrich is Assistant Professor at Bryant University in Rhode Island. He earned a B.A. from the University of Pennsylvania and a Ph.D. from Johns Hopkins University. His research has focused on U.S. foreign policy-making, security issues, and U.S. human rights policy.